NIGHTCAP
AT
DAWN

Skyhorse Publishing books may be purchased in bulk at special discounts for sales promotion, corporate gifts, fund-raising, or educational purposes. Special editions can also be created to specifications. For details, contact the Special Sales Department, Skyhorse Publishing, 307 West 36th Street, 11th Floor, New York, NY 10018 or info@skyhorsepublishing.com.

Skyhorse® and Skyhorse Publishing® are registered trademarks of Skyhorse Publishing, Inc.®, a Delaware corporation.

Visit our website at www.skyhorsepublishing.com

10 9 8 7 6 5 4 3 2

Library of Congress Cataloging-in-Publication Data is available on file.

ISBN: 978-1-61608-617-6

Printed in the United States of America

NIGHTCAP
AT
DAWN

AMERICAN SOLDIERS' COUNTERINSURGENCY
IN IRAQ

These experiences, impressions, imaginations, and hallucinations
were compiled by a group of enlisted Airborne Infantrymen, with the help
of many friends and colleagues. The opinions, assessments, and conclusions
are our own and do not represent the views of our chain of command or
of the United States Army.

J. B. WALKER

SKYHORSE PUBLISHING

All authors' proceeds of publication
will go to charities that serve military families.

CONTENTS

Contents

PROLOGUE:
SCATTERED CRUMBS[1]

I t was an air assault mission into an insurgent enclave in the summer of 2006. Some soldiers were monitoring an insurgent safe house from behind a dirt mound next to a canal. One of them slipped down into the canal, filled with a viscous brown goo instead of water, and everyone, of course, started laughing. It was the second day—still two more to go—and the team leader suggested, "Well, you can sit here smelling like a shit rat, or you can grab a couple of guys and go jump in the other canal; it just might clean you up." More laughter, but he did go and jump in the other canal. Later, nearly freezing, he continued watching the house all night, wrapped in a poncho liner and snuggling his buddies to stay warm, all the while mumbling a string of profanities. "I'm telling you man, the next idiot that tells me Iraq is a desert, I'm gonna punch in the face. Yeah, everyone talks about the desert, nobody talks about the goddamn canals!" For the rest of that mission he was an endless source of humor.

Soldiers joked that *somebody should write this stuff down,* the simple charms of soldiering.

A week later, the same soldiers were walking the streets of another insurgent enclave. On the third day of the mission, eight hours before pick-up, some of them walked to a little house in an orchard where, they had learned, there were some surviving victims of insurgent violence. The family—a prematurely aged mother, two adolescent kids,

---

[1] *Scattered Crumbs*, a novel by Iraqi author Mushin al-Ramli (translated by Yasmeen S. Hanoosh).

1

and a disabled father—told the same story of violence, displacement, destitution, and constant fear that soldiers had heard repeatedly in theocratic enclaves. Soldiers have seen entire villages emptied, every house booby-trapped, sometimes bodies of villagers piled inside—it just depended on the rabidity of the particular insurgent group that ran the show. This man had resisted leaving his house, and they shot him through the knee. The wound is not properly healed; some kind of fluid was still seeping out.

What could anyone possibly say at this moment?

Because "sorry" does not quite capture it; in fact it feels like it would be an insult. Blank stares and grinding teeth, that's all. A soldier asked, "Is this all the children you have?"

"No." Of course not, that's why he asked.

They had a teenage daughter, but she is missing—because the Salafist virtue enforcers had taken her. Blank stares all around, what can one possibly say? There are many times when soldiers are constrained in their ability to act. Then they would resort to the only thing left: they collected some money and pathetically handed it to the family.

Standing around and having a smoke before walking to the patrol base, one of them casually commented, "Ya know, why don't people write about this shit, about these fucking lunatics that they deal with?"

What started off as a casual attempt to recount the soldiers' personal story, in the summer of 2006 in an insurgent enclave, quickly changed into something else when we entered into a different neighborhood—controlled by an identical bunch.

It was a deliberate decision to write about this reality, that of Iraqis living through an insurgency as we understood it.

Soldiers would get glimpses of TV news stories, accounts that captured little of the reality of life in the Iraqi streets. The human essence was always stripped from the images. Iraqis remained a grand abstraction with no names, voices or faces.

Some soldiers and their leaders were increasingly obsessed with idea: Let's write about counterinsurgency the way it really is— putting people center stage, weaving together the many stories of the Iraqi people we met, how we understood what was going on, and what some guys did. So other soldiers could use it, take what is valid from it, and try to improve upon it. It eventually became a simple promise among some friends . . .

INTRODUCTION

> When in doubt, tell the truth. That maxim I did
> invent, but never expected it to be applied to *me*.
> I did say, "When you are in doubt," but when
> I am in doubt myself I use more sagacity.
>
> —Mark Twain, "When in Doubt, Tell the Truth"
> (speech, March 8, 1906)

This is an impressionistic account of our counterinsurgency in Iraq. We hope it will bring to life the stories and voices of the many Iraqi people in neighborhoods where we walked.

Given the nature of our job and the requirements of military security and the safety of the people concerned, this is written in the form of "creative non-fiction." This account is truthful in the most important sense of the word, but it is also part hallucination. We have deliberately obscured time and fictionalized names and places, but we have remained true to reality in the illustrations of experiences, impressions, sentiments, imagining, and even our hallucinations.

In these pages, we re-create the war that we were part of, and as we understood its historical, political, and cultural context—through the stories of people: ourselves and our friends, and the many Iraqis we encountered. The stories make up a larger whole: our counterinsurgency in Iraq.

These impressions capture the way we fought and how we learned on the job. But we also capture an intellectual journey: how we came to understand a particular group of people—Iraqis—and how we learned from them about their world, their struggles and aspirations.

This is mainly the story of enlisted men and enlisted leaders on the ground, along with a few young officers—friends—who shared their observations and insights. It relates how we came to terms with the (at times absurd) reality of counterinsurgency, and how we navigated in a culturally prohibitive atmosphere as American soldiers.

These impressions were compiled with the hope that they would help young leaders better understand the gritty realities that soldiers face on the ground in a counterinsurgency. We hope it is filled with common sense, because counterinsurgency will always predominantly be basic common sense. War (and counterinsurgency is a form of warfare) is as much about life as it is about death—only in war they exist much closer together. An elemental part of combat will always remain how soldiers and leaders come to terms with this demanding reality and how well they follow through at the point of decision with a sense of responsibility.

The impressions recorded here are drawn from many friends from myriad branches of the army, but the narrative centers on a group of very fortunate soldiers—fortunate in having had the experience of several dimensions of this conflict. A soldier's experience in combat is usually limited by his or her occupational specialty, the particular mission-set, and the area in which the unit is deployed. We felt very fortunate to conduct three very different mission-sets in succession and to work side by side with a unique group of colleagues from other branches.

We had the good fortune to conduct air assault missions into Jihadist theocratic enclaves in far-flung areas of Iraq during 2006 at the height of the Sunni insurgency, when Iraq was considered a lost cause. (Some of our friends continued this mission until 2008.) Some of us were then switched to fighting an entrenched Shia insurgency in an urban setting in the following year. Others were conducting Time Sensitive Target Acquisition (TST) missions, trying to capture insurgent leaders during 2006 and 2007. Some of us had the rare fortune to do all three mission-sets back-to-back. These disparate mission-sets provided a unique learning experience, a challenge that rarely comes around.

A brief guide to what follows:

> *Part I* tries to capture the initial bewilderment of navigating a "battle space" that consists of *people*—with a different, even alien, culture.
>
> *Part II* introduces the reader to some of the remarkable people we encountered in Iraq, and even got to know a bit; no one could be more surprised than we were to find that many of these people were women.
>
> *Part III* takes us into the labyrinth of insurgency on the ground: How we began to understand the nature of insurgent control and the many insurgencies in Iraq.
>
> In *Part IV* we dive into the Sunni insurgency—itself a complex assortment of actors and motives—and we visit the Kurdish "non-insurgency insurgency," with horrors of its own.
>
> *Part V* is an extended encounter with the Shia insurgency, well-entrenched—even well-established—in its urban setting.
>
> Finally, *Part VI* provides our reflections on soldiering in a counterinsurgency, followed by an Epilogue.

We have written primarily for an interested military audience, but a nonmilitary audience may also appreciate these stories and reflections on counterinsurgency. Soldiers slogging through mud, canals and dirt piles, in unimaginable humidity and heat, are only part of the story. How soldiers keep their wits about them, capture the simple charms, maintain a strong sense of responsibility, and keep taking the next step with that deep sense of responsibility—this is the story we hope to communicate. The reader will find in these pages an intimate and honest ghost story that provides a glimpse into our world, our experiences, our imaginations, and, yes, even our hallucinations.

PART I

ENCOUNTERS

The peculiar reality of a counterinsurgency dawned on some of us in the very first mission. The enemy—the insurgent—does not wear uniforms, and he can be anywhere and nowhere all at once.

But soldiers need to be able to distinguish the enemy from the innocent—the children, women, and men—the people all of a sudden become integral to the way soldiers and leaders view the field of battle and make combat decisions.

But American soldiers are not in Texas, they are in Iraq. And Iraqis are Muslim, speak Arabic, and tend to look askance at our presence, while the local, regional media and insurgent propaganda denounces us as an occupying force. We quickly learned that Iraq is a culturally prohibitive atmosphere that we somehow had to navigate.

1

THE BEGINNING, OR THE END

In Counter-insurgency, the side that learns faster and adapts more rapidly—the better learning organization—usually wins.

—Counterinsurgency Field Manual
(USA FM3:24)

Waiting and waiting. It is an elemental part of a soldier's life. But today everyone is waiting with a purpose, in that strangely agitated way that soldiers wait just before a mission. Picking at the final details, going over the mission one more time, each time as if it's the first and the last time. Everyone is sprawled across the makeshift helipad next to the tents, swapping jokes that range from the familiar to the obscenely perverted. Everyone is chewing too much tobacco. Very soon, after the Black Hawks and Chinooks drop them off, soldiers will be on their own for about four days.

Despite the thick of night, the heat index is over 130 degrees. Even the little breeze that sweeps across the helipad feels moist and heavy. One thought clouds the mind: The walk to the objective, humping too much gear and stumbling through muddy fields in the green haze of night vision, will be painful. But the simple achievements at the end of the combat mission make everything bearable.

Movement to the Objective

On the ground once again, you encounter a thick wall of solid musty air that has to be chewed into pieces and swallowed in chunks—the only way to breach it—all the while mumbling the same phrase: "Goddamn, this can't be real."

In the movement to the objective—the distance, terrain, the geographic reference grids—everything is etched in the brain. The weight of the rucksack sinks its way through the spine straight to the aching heart. Every soldier walking counterbalances the physical burden of the gear on their backs with the inspiration they get from one another and from the proud lineage of better men who dared far more and fared far worse. Yes, we do think of them. Our grandfathers before us who froze and starved and exploded in the Ardennes; who sweated, delirious with disease, at Guadalcanal; those who braved the incomprehensible quietly in the mountains of Korea, in that forgotten war; and fathers who dealt with the unimaginable in the Mekong Delta. No, none of us can complain in Iraq, and we know it: We have it far too easy.

The thought eases the weight somewhat. Everyone steps off towards the objective bearing the weight of lineage, tradition, and gear—along with any number of ideas, instilled practices, and ingrained maxims of how one is supposed to fight in a war.

Everyone is walking through the fields, orchards, and backyards in that dizzying green haze known as "night vision": strange, alien, suffocating, disorienting, too damn hot and humid. The brain goes numb. Salty rivulets of sweat pour down through the optical device, hopelessly fogging it and increasing the disorientation. The physical senses overwhelmed, logic becomes subservient. But it's the moment that matters, so soldiers keep looking, their heads always on swivel.

They look with a purpose. Peering into dark crevices, through garbage and piles of dirt, at decrepit buildings, and through barely transparent windows; looking at civilians (maybe, who the hell ever really knows?) and their vehicles. Soldiers try to sift through all of this visual information in an instant, sifting through it for any incongruities. You seek the obvious, but you look for the *not-so-obvious*.

A vehicle is parked slightly aslant from the rest; a van seems to be weighted down; a house has a half-open window on the second floor that doesn't look quite right; a random guy looks like anyone else, but his strange gait catches attention; in an alleyway, the way shadows fall becomes etched in the mind. With every step, soldiers instinctively evaluate any possible signs of danger. Soldiers call it pulling security—trying to anticipate and see from the point of view of the enemy. It becomes second nature.

A single thought focuses all our minds, keeps our heads swiveling, our eyes watchful, our hands on our weapons: The enemy is determined and formidable.

He is elusive and hides among the innocent. He does not move in formation, clicking his heels and saluting. A scared-looking guy who scurries by with a sheepish grin could be the one who takes a shot at you later, or who attempts to sidle up to you in the market wearing a suicide vest. This elusive enemy is comfortable in his strengths, aware of his weaknesses, and has the ability to sneer at soldiers at a time and place of his choosing.

The insurgents can be anywhere and nowhere all at once.

The weight of the rucksack straps has by now dug creases into the collarbones. A glance at the guy next to you shows you a mirror image of yourself. He trudges along, seemingly nonchalant, muttering random curses, but always with that focused sense of purpose. His weapon is at the low ready. Behind the night vision goggles, his eyes scan calmly in all directions. He has the same painfully contorted expression on his face, and it is not from the heat or fatigue: He is busy trying to take it all in and figure it out somehow. You look at one another, slightly shake your head, and whisper the inevitable: "Shiiiiiiit man"—with the inevitable reply, "Yeah, shit is right!"

Nothing more needs to be said. No one is alone, everyone feels exactly the same way. The weight on our backs seems a little less burdensome. The staggered column, the green vision of brothers scattered across the field is eerie yet intimate. Another wad of chewing tobacco wedges in the lip: inspiration in a can. We take the next step with more equanimity, moving closer to the objective—an elusive enemy that hides amid the innocent.

How do we adjudicate between the enemy and the innocent on the ground?

To assume innocence is to get blindsided. Sooner or later, the enemy will use that assumption to his advantage. To assume guilt is to alienate the innocent, to give more credibility to the enemy and his cause. Damned if you do and damned if you don't. The clearly defined logic and clarity soldiers always covet, seeing the world in terms of grid-squares and flanking elements and visibly fortified bunkers, these methods and ideas don't always work in a counterinsurgency. Nothing is what it seems.

The Point of Decision

After a few such missions, you and your buddies are trying to come to grips with this utterly unfamiliar reality, sitting on the ground, hiding from superiors and savoring long swigs of illicit booze while commiserating. The booze calms the raging soul and the commiseration warms the heart. It begins to sink in: Fighting a counterinsurgency on the ground means grasping all the imperfect information, internalizing all the moving elements, and making the best possible trade-off *at the point of decision*. Counterinsurgency is all about trade-offs—the good, the bad, and the ugly. It is like trying to find the alcoholic's "delicate balance between the shakes of too little and the abyss of too much." It's an unreal reality, and we sure as hell ain't in Kansas anymore.

An American infantryman, a leader in the field, or a Commander in charge of an Area of Operation (AO)—all of them enter into a labyrinthine and nuanced environment. The enemy is waging an insurgency centered on the population.[2] It is a struggle for power against the elected government and also against the American presence

---

[2] The reality is that we fight *multiple* insurgencies in Iraq: the numerous Sunni and Shia groups, as well as multiple civil wars and wars of attrition involving many actors. For now we use the term "insurgents" broadly, reserving details for later chapters.

that supports the elected government. Insurgents fight using every exploitable advantage: military, social, economic, cultural, and religious.[3] Soldiers trying to counter the insurgency have to constantly innovate, improvise, reassess.

Of the many factors we consider on the ground, the singular challenge that alters the assumptions of soldiers is the role of the people: children, women, and men. *People are center stage.* Fighting effectively in a counterinsurgency, with all the trade-offs and the constant delicate balance, has its startling epiphany the moment soldiers recognize the population as "the battle space."[4] This recognition alters the weight of the many variables soldiers instinctively consider; it fundamentally changes the way soldiers operate.

Counterinsurgency and People

At the outset, things seem simple. Soldiers are supposed to defeat the enemy, however elusive, and to gain control and win the support of the Iraqi people. *Roger that.*

The difficulty is that this population that we are supposed to secure from insurgents (and at times from our own actions) will feign indifference, or possibly resent us, as the enemy hides among them. The notion of *the people* ceases to be an abstract concept and becomes entirely too concrete. Soldiers get to *see* the people—talk to them, listen to their stories, stare at their eyes, and remember their voices.

Conventionally, "the people" are viewed as prominent but (paradoxically) also peripheral, considered mainly in terms of the collateral damage that needs to be minimized. That logic still applies, of course.

---

[3] "Joint doctrine defines an *insurgency* as an organized movement aimed at the overthrow of a constituted government through the use of subversion and armed conflict" (JP 1-02). "*Counterinsurgency* is those political, economic, military, paramilitary, psychological, and civic actions taken by a government to defeat an insurgency" (JP 1-02).

[4] Battle space: The total awareness of the area of operation necessary in order to apply combat power effectively.

But in a counterinsurgency, the ultimate outcome in fact *depends on the people* and the way they react to the actions of soldiers—not just on the actions of soldiers. Soldiers' actions affect the way people make their decisions, just as the people's decisions affect the way soldiers act and react, each reinforcing the other in a circle that may be virtuous or vicious. This feedback loop saps the clarity we seek in the field of battle. Coming to terms with ambiguity is the hardest part of being a soldier on the ground in a counterinsurgency.

Soldiers encounter an outlandish reality when *people* become central to our decisions, when we contend with an elusive enemy roaming freely among the very population we are trying to win the support of. In military jargon, the people become an integral part of the *battle space*; the people and their culture become the *terrain* that you navigate.

The people are part of the battle space because the decisions of the soldiers and the people are inextricably linked, each influencing the other. The people are the terrain of the fight because, as a foreign intervention force, we are navigating an unfamiliar culture as we search for insurgents, gather intelligence, and try to safeguard the population.

The Population as Part of the Battle Space

People become part of the battle space in two ways. First, people's actions affect the way we make decisions and the way we apply combat power. Secondly, people are, almost by definition, part of the battle space since our mission is to secure the population from insurgents.

In a conventional battle space, a commander makes decisions based on understanding and anticipating enemy movements so as to outwit the enemy in the field. There is clarity, coherence, and an enviable sense of logic. In that conceptualization, even though people figure prominently, their presence does not determine how decisions are made; decisions are based on enemy movements (and anticipated enemy movements). People are normally a significant but peripheral consideration.[5]

The same underlying logic of decision making applies in counterinsurgency, except that the people cease to be peripheral. The people become integral to the soldiers' and leaders' grasp of the battle space. The people are central to the way both *insurgents* and *counterinsurgents* make decisions in applying combat power—though sometimes in opposite ways.

Insurgents, counterinsurgents, and the population become one extremely awkward threesome. Soldiers don't walk around thinking in those terms, but we are faced with this elemental reality at the most unexpected moments when we are compelled to use combat power.

End of the Night: Sunrise at a Girls' School

❖ The people become part of the battle space

Some places evoke an instinctive wariness that cuts through soldiers' fatigue. This is one of the worst parts of town, an area right next to a girls' school. After a long night of firefights (finally rounding up an insurgent leader and his cache of toys that go boom), soldiers arrive there at sunrise. The insurgent leader they captured happens to live right next to the school.

You stand there keeping watch as the young girls line up, chirping incessantly, entering the school by dozens in their crisp white-and-navy-blue uniforms. They are distinguishable only by their unique facial features and their colorful headscarves and plastic bangles.

---

[5] This is based on the military strategist Colonel John R. Boyd's hypotheses on tactical decision making. We continually create and destroy mental patterns of meaning, and the ones who do it best, in the shortest possible time span, emerge victorious in battle. The construction of meaning involves a process he terms the OODA loop: **O**bservation (collecting data); **O**rientation (analyzing and synthesizing data); **D**ecision (determined course of action); **A**ction. (Colonel John R Boyd, "Destruction and Creation," September 1976.)

Younger girls would come near the soldiers and talk to them in broken English. The older girls would walk by bashfully, making sly comments at soldiers and to each other. Infantrymen try out their hapless Arabic and are rewarded with hearty giggles and some attempts at conversation. A few soldiers seize the moment to try to befriend some female teachers (who spoke perfect English) and get their email addresses: no one knows the neighborhoods better than the women.[6]

❖ Actions of insurgents and people as part of the battle space

It was a sudden sharp, ringing, snapping sound. A soldier instantly dropped. Some soldiers scattered to secure the area and set up a cordon, while others aided the possibly wounded soldier. In the next instant, an incredible amount of lead was directed in the direction of the sniper fire. But soldiers, paradoxically going against all soldiering instincts, did not fire a single round.

The best of insurgents are well aware of their own and their enemy's strengths and weaknesses. They make judicious tactical decisions to further their positions, trying to outsmart the Americans at every turn. The insurgent sniper used his combat power effectively, hiding in a densely populated area and targeting soldiers near a school, at the precise moment when hundreds of children were lining up to go to class. The deliberate insurgent timing made the population part of the battle space. Turning people into part of the battle space, by applying combat power without compunction, is one of the greatest, and most perverse, strengths of the insurgent. Tactically speaking, it is genius. It minimizes the asymmetry in power in insurgents favor.

Any action by counterinsurgents can be portrayed in a negative light as part of the insurgent narrative that presents their own actions as better than the American response. Insurgents can make tremendously

---

[6] One soldier deserves mention for his ability to get email addresses. He once actually managed to get a woman's email address *during a firefight,* announcing with a big grin: "Well, that's one check box done—getting an email address when rounds were pinging off." Now, *there's* a combat leader on the ground who, despite the stress of the moment, always had his priorities straight.

effective use of any overwhelming response or, especially, the death of civilians: One dead school girl in her bloodied uniform would be the insurgents' ultimate wet dream. This is a driving objective in their tactical decisions, as in this case. The insurgent used his comparatively limited combat power (in relation to the soldiers') very effectively by turning the population into part of the battle space.

❖ Actions of soldiers and people as part of the battle space

Every soldier knew the direction, distance, and the general description of the area of the sniper fire. The impulse was overwhelming, with so much firepower and destructive capacity at their fingertips. Yet, despite the fatigue, not a single soldier or leader on the ground even thought of using their heavy weapons or flattening the city block. Instead, they cordoned, cleared, and questioned the people. And they returned (as always seems to be the case) empty-handed.

Returning, they learned that the soldier, an officer, had been very fortunate. It was his first day in Iraq, and he evidently had the knack of making a grand entrance. Procedural cherry that he was, he actually wore *all* the prescribed body armor, and it saved his life. The soldiers had called him a retard[7] for wearing all of it—in that endearing way grunts have when they like their officers. Later on they told him, amid general laughter, "Well, sir, good to have you in the fight." What a hell of a lucky first day—and after that experience, the teasing would go in the other direction.

The civilian considerations, the presence of all those school girls, the densely populated neighborhood—these were not a peripheral

---

[7] The words "retard" and "retarded" are used as either a supreme compliment or the worst epithet and are very much part of the enlisted Airborne Infantry vernacular. Calling a soldier "retarded" (as the epithet) means that his actions were inexcusable, and he is about to be in a lot of pain. A cognitively challenged person can always be excused—by definition—but not a trained soldier who acts as if he were cognitively challenged. "Retard" as a compliment means that a soldier has done something that defies all reason and logic, has gone above and beyond, and has miraculously lived to tell the tale.

concern. They had to be integral and instinctive to the way soldiers and leaders on the ground made their tactical decisions. No one considered using the overwhelming force of machineguns laying hell in unison (the clanking empty shell casings so reassuring in combat). To be shot at and to have all that firepower at your disposal *and not use it* goes against every human instinct. Yet that is the defining way in which Americans fight the insurgency; it is the rule, not the exception. It is what differentiates us from those we fight and gives us the tactically essential moral upper hand.

Soldiers instead resorted to a more arduous, painstaking method: cordon and walk around and question people—without success. Returning empty handed, angry, and filled with the "shakes of too little," soldiers endured more sarcasm than hookers at a cheap whorehouse. Yes, flattening the city block might (or might not) have caused the death of the sniper, but the Americans erred on the side of saving the civilians. For both insurgents and counterinsurgents, the presence of the people became integral to the way they made tactical decisions and the way they used combat power.

❖ Act IV: People caught in the middle of the "awkward threesome"

At the moment of the sharp snapping noise of that sniper round, the difference between civilians and soldiers became instantly apparent. Soldiers reacted instinctively, moving toward the direction of fire, swiftly, cautiously, and with a purpose. The civilians find themselves running away, or perhaps frozen in place. In the first few seconds of a firefight, people find themselves trapped, their fate hanging in the balance with no means of control, frantically asking themselves, "Am I going to live, am I going to die, what could I possibly do?" The soldiers sprint instinctively away from the girls. The world of the chirping little girls was frozen in time for that fleeting moment, looks of apprehension and fear contorting their young faces. They took a few tiny steps in trepidation and then hurried away.

But afterwards, an amazing thing: Slowly the chirps, the giggles, and the sly comments were back. A short while later, the little girls, teachers, and some parents were moving about, laughing and joking. And so were the soldiers, of course keeping a constant watchful eye to catch a glimpse of the sniper. That day the schoolgirls remained schoolgirls and not collateral damage. The sniper walked away to eat his goddamn falafel for another day—we would find him or his brother one of these days, we pledged ourselves—and the officer stayed on to fight and fight well, to have other close calls but still return home. For this rare instance, the stars were aligned.

When tactical decisions are made and combat power is applied, the stars play no role. Insurgents, counterinsurgents, and guns decide, and someone ends up dying. Americans try their damnedest to make sure it's the insurgents. Insurgents try their best to make sure it's the Americans—*and their own people*: If not at their own hands, then at the hands of the Americans. And in the meantime, the people have to navigate the contesting claims of control and the multiple forms of violence.

When people become integral to one's decision making, clearly understood as an inherent part of the battle space, the necessary trade-off between "the shakes of too little and the abyss of too much" finally ceases to be a metaphor: it becomes the cold, hard bitch of everyday life.

People as Part of the Battle Space in the Area of Control

Getting rid of the bad guys is the offense of counterinsurgency; preventing them from coming back is the defense. But even if one miraculously succeeds at offense and defense, soldiering does not stop at that point—it merely enters a new phase. The ongoing challenge is still to get people to make favorable decisions: to obtain their support and complicity and prevent their active opposition. This adds a painful new dimension to the conventional idea of the battle space. This third task, dealing directly with people, at first resembles a bad dream, and soldiers begin to rigorously debate the meaning and sanity of their enlistment contract. Now they need to learn some diplomacy. It's part of the new job—and it causes a roiling stomachache.

The reaction is not unique to the grunts; in some ways it pervades the entire chain of command. A leader on the ground is engaged in a tenuous high-wire act in a new dimension—but to complain is to get screwed from both above and below, so he buries his head, muttering to himself, and stepping on his own foot. A commander in charge of the area of operation finds himself faced with a new challenge, so he puts on his best Commander Face, fighting his own contorted expression and trying for a stoic appearance. "Of course, sir, oh, absolutely," is his only response, though he may later mumble his true opinions in his sleep. Dealing with people: It is what it is, it's part of the new job description, everyone's in it.

Soldiers, leaders on the ground, and commanders in charge of an area of operation now need to acquire a nuanced understanding of the social dynamics of the population. Dealing with people is taxing on the soul, but it is imperative for controlling the population and for intelligence gathering. It forces soldiers to question the obvious, to take nothing for granted, and to find meaning in the incongruities they see every day.

The elemental question for soldiers is just this: How do the insurgents retain their offensive and defensive capabilities? As you go after them, other questions erupt: How do new insurgents emerge, who in the hell are they, how are the leaders replaced, where were these guys before, how do they deepen control through the use of violence, how do they sustain themselves, where is the money goddammit—and how do the people react to the actions of insurgents?

You have to pay attention to the changing power relations on the ground, the crisscrossing loyalties to personalities, insurgent groups, political parties, clans, and sects. A voodoo queen or the village prostitute, whoever it turns out to be—if someone has intelligence value, you have to find a way to get at it. You pay attention to the machinations of local big-wigs (sometimes entertaining, sometimes not). Knowing the personal affiliations of the locally important personalities helps illuminate how the local agenda is manipulated within the city councils responsible for delivering basic services (the Neighborhood Advisory Councils and District Advisory Councils). These organizations proved to be pork-barrel politics on steroids, and some of the members were affiliated with the very insurgents we fought on the ground. These people get your special attention. And despite the risks, what started as a royal pain in the ass begins to develop its peculiar charms. Soldiers drinking obscene amounts of tea and listening to people's stories and hanging out on the army's dime: That's never too bad.

Part of the new job requires listening, listening until the brain goes numb. Talking as little as possible and hanging out with Iraqis from all walks of life and doing it systematically. That adds a new dimension. It's a new mission set for which we are woefully unprepared. When you wake up from the long bad dream with a tremendous gut ache, you do what you always do when in doubt. You look to your left and right, at the brothers around you, and find your solace in seeing that everyone shares the same sentiment: "Are you serious?" Masked, of course, with the usual sarcastic nonchalant grin. And that's always a good sign, at least we will have a laugh.

People and Culture as Part of the Terrain in the Battle Space

Navigating the people and their culture *as terrain* is more than simply understanding the neighborhood and the people. This is, in fact, a tactical military concern in a counterinsurgency. Insurgents, being at a disadvantage in military and technical capability, use their local knowledge to minimize the asymmetry of power. And at that point the terrain—that is, the people and the culture—becomes a tactical concern.

While Americans try desperately to navigate the people and their culture, the insurgents swim in it, and do so in style. Insurgents have an instinctive and intuitive understanding of their own people and neighborhoods. That is their greatest strength, and they know it. By exploiting the differences between Americans and the local people, insurgents minimize the asymmetry of power, both tactically and as a matter of control. Their deep understanding of their own people (fears, prejudices, loyalties, and beliefs) assists in the attempt to control them. They know well how to exploit the differences between Americans and locals, how to posit a narrative that appears better than the reality the counterinsurgents represent.

Not only are insurgents aware of the changing social dynamics, power relations, and loyalties of the people, they are sometimes very much a part of the dynamic. They show up, things stop happening; they make a phone call, things start happening. They know how to manipulate the agenda at the neighborhood advisory council meetings, skillfully securing contracts to reward helpful local bigwigs. With a nod of the head, someone can change the agenda of a meeting, gaining the support of the few and the complicity of the rest, and running circles around Americans all the while.[8]

The insurgents' advantage is control attained through subversion by changing events on the ground. They have the ability even to anticipate future points of friction and eliminate them without leaving fingerprints. For counterinsurgents, minimizing this subversive advantage of insurgents is absolutely critical.

It was a quick-dawning realization. Insurgents can hide amid the innocent *because of* their subversive advantage. To blow them out of their subversive advantage, we need to be able to distinguish the enemy from the innocent, and that requires the help of the people.

Subversion is a prominent tool of any successful insurgency. An insurgent engaging in subversion skillfully straddles two realities at once, maintaining the convincing pretense of working for the government and being a believer in its project. The deception has to be more convincing than the truth. The insurgent engaging in subversion has to be surefooted, constantly on his toes and steady on his feet—and he has to know when to fold 'em. Successful subversion is not about doing it as long as possible. Subversion requires focusing on a single-minded objective, picking fights carefully, and recognizing that sooner or later things come to a head and everyone will get

---

[8] A painful, demoralizing moment: You sit in the relatively modest house of a politically well-connected Iraqi who hobnobs with high-ranking Americans—fully aware of all he is capable of, what he has accomplished, and the American blood he has on his hands (circumstantial evidence, of course; he is always clean).

burned. Not all insurgents are that astute, but some are very, very good indeed. Their success in subversion comes from the intuitive contextual knowledge they have at their fingertips: the neighborhood, the people, the culture—the feeling and pulse of the people they can feel creeping along their flesh in a way Americans can't. Without that contextual grasp, subversion is damn near impossible. But facing an adversary that is a foreign intervention force makes subversion infinitely easier.

Insurgents can be in plain sight and yet still be indistinguishable to the intervention force. That simple reality vastly diminishes the asymmetry in capabilities between insurgents and counterinsurgents; it is why the enemy can be everywhere and nowhere all at once.

It adds an extra layer of complexity and burden to the Americans' task on the ground. People may intuitively see what is happening; Americans have to look purposefully in order to see. Americans as an intervention force have a daunting learning curve to overcome and no time for gradual enlightenment: Subversion is an immediate tactical concern.

Distinguishing the enemy hiding among the innocent is, therefore, the elemental concern in counterinsurgency. It becomes possible only if counterinsurgents develop formidable intelligence capabilities in their area of operation. Understanding how insurgents use their contextual knowledge requires deepened intelligence gathering, centered on the population you seek to control. And now we have come full circle. It's about people, once again, but now it is also about their culture and how you navigate it with a purpose.

It's a very different fight from the one the soldiers imagined, the first time they got on a bird flying into some far-flung area of Iraq. But soldiers got the hang of it. One soldier summed it up, walking out of the house of an Iraqi gentleman they knew quite well: "Goddamn, man, you know, these Iraqis, they will smile, laugh, even kiss you if you let them, but it's like a goddamn rabbit hole—you just don't know how deep it goes."

He was right on the mark. Fighting a counterinsurgency as a foreign intervention force *is* a rabbit hole. One must make a conscious choice to see the unfamiliar reality, come to terms with the nature of the peculiar fight, slide into the rabbit hole to grasp the unfamiliar and the unknown. It is a choice we make. A beginning if we get the hang of it, and an end if we don't.

We do not know how the rabbit hole ends, but we do know how the rabbit hole begins. It begins with a concussion.

2

ENCOUNTERING THE OTHER: NAVIGATING WITH A CONCUSSION

> People thus had three choices when they encountered
> the other: they could choose war, they could build
> a wall around themselves, or they could enter into
> dialogue.
>
> —Ryszard Kapuscinski, *Encountering the Other*

A good concussion: You lose your bearings; you stumble around, disoriented. "Man, you guys did the crab walk, looked like Cheech and Chong," a soldier commented sagely, a few hours after the Improvised Explosive Device (IED) cratered their Humvee.[9]

It is humorous only in retrospect. At the moment of the concussion, the "Oh shit" moment, the graceful internal balance between the senses, the brain, and the body is momentarily disrupted. The brain

---

[9] The soldiers survived that particular incident with relatively minor injuries. Their buddy's comment was right on the mark: The explosion filled the HMMWV with smoke, and as the doors opened, the smoke, the coughs, the profanities, and the crab walk of five disoriented soldiers made it vintage Cheech and Chong.

tells you to maintain "situational awareness": Be aware of the sur-roundings, anticipate further dangers. The senses try to keep up. Trained instincts guide you to find a tactical disposition,[10] but the body has lost its bearing and carries you sideways—the crab walk. After a few seconds that feel like an eternity, you recover that delicate internal balance, despite some residual ringing and the momentary brain blips.

A New Terrain: Culture

The first encounter with a culture and people so profoundly different has the same effect, strangely enough: you momentarily do the crab walk inside your head, trying desperately to figure it out, mumbling all the while, "Are you serious?" Walking through the bustling market among people's stares, sheepish grins, and hastened steps, one feels like an alien, utterly lost in the colorful collage. Soldiers recognize the absurdity of their situation (made worse by presenting such a great target for a suicide bomber[11]) and they joke, "Man, where is the clown music?" The soldiers' laughter merely evokes more perturbed and quizzical looks from the puzzled Iraqis.

American soldiers in the midst of hundreds of Iraqis: different lan-guage, different culture, different people—but physically next to each other in this moment in time, so close that everyone can smell each other's sweat, mingled with the smells of raw sewage and garbage that hang over the market. There is no confluence, no common points of reference of the two parallel worlds: two groups of people, as close and as far apart as humanly possible. But backtrack now to the start-ing point. Yes, differences—that is what counts. If one can navigate

---

[10] Good Tactical Disposition: A good place to take a shot and not get shot at.
[11] Eventually the place did go up in flames, killing about sixty people instantly and wounding over one-hundred. All the dead and wounded were Iraqi chil-dren, women, and men. The entire shopping strip was completely obliterated by the car bomb.

the differences, taking people as they are, you quickly get around the disorienting feeling of a concussion.

Then you pause for a moment, startled by the simple, glaring realization that amid the sheepish grins, scared faces, and occasional enthusiastic greeting hides the enemy.

The culture of the Iraqi people, the web of meaning behind the Iraqi way of doing things—language, religion, manners, beliefs, and whatever else one can think of to throw into the mix—it all gets seared in your head.[12] Not as an abstraction, "culture," but as the dramatic differences between two groups of people: Iraqis and American soldiers. The reality of culture will always be important because navigating those differences is critical for a soldier in a counterinsurgency.

Soldiers do it, strange to say, just the way you get around in any inhospitable terrain, by playing GI Joe in the woods. It's only that this time, it involves *people*. People become the waypoints and the terrain features. This is land navigation with a built-in concussion.

In land navigation, some prominent features of roads, rivers, and creeks are the "waypoints" (the predetermined coordinates). They are the hand-rails—the wider parameters—and the backstops (predetermined points we pass, so we know we are headed in the right direction). They define the limits of navigation. Prominent terrain features—saddles, hills, depressions, etc.—help us navigate to the end. Navigating in Iraq, *people* are the waypoints and backstops: Their questions, concerns, issues, bitches, moans, and gripes are the terrain features that help us travel within the culture, or at least get around it instead of getting hung up on it.

---

[12] FM 3–24: 89–90. Culture, as the manual posits, is "a web of meaning shared by members of a particular society or group within a society" with "repeating patterns" that are changeable through interaction between people and groups.

Navigating the Terrain: Us vs. Them[13]

Americans take pride in wearing their hearts on their sleeve and place a premium on being frank and forthright. In Iraq, you encounters a very different mindset, a culture that is completely opaque. At first one concludes that this society has mastered prevarication as a veritable art form. Yet you quickly realize that this may have less to do with culture than with trying to survive. The intimidating idea of cultural differences slowly diminishes as you begin to see people as just people.

❖ First few concussions

The difficulties are obvious: Soldiers are bunch of sunburned, sweaty men with guns. Americans in America are uncomfortable or aggravated at being stopped by their neighborhood police officer. How many would invite armed police officers into their homes to drink coffee? An average Iraqi is faced with armed foreigners. And the propaganda of insurgents, abetted by the regional media, promotes the worst perception of American soldiers.

When an American soldier and an Iraqi face each other, they are not simply two people. So much ignorance, prejudice, suspicion, history, and bad blood is captured in that moment. At first, they lack any common ground or shared points of reference. That becomes the job of soldiers on their patrols: finding that common ground. *The burden is with us,* the counterinsurgents; it is the nature of the fight. Finding this common ground needs to be a priority, whatever our personal preferences might be. Over time, this simple idea paid great dividends.

Another concussion: There is the simple human paradox that an encounter between a soldier and an Iraqi cannot be normal because it never takes place on an equal footing. The advantage of being a

---

[13] This section pertains only to "hearts and minds" patrols, intelligence gathering, and essentially trying to get on the good side of people that naturally look askance at soldiers' presence. But soldiers are soldiers, and there are plenty of moments for saying, the hell with culture, let's get the job done.

soldier becomes a distinct *disadvantage* in a counterinsurgency. Overcoming this disadvantage becomes imperative.

Soldiers can choose who they talk to, when, where, and how; they have the power to enforce a meeting. Iraqis have no way of denying that request—a distinct disadvantage. Every time an Iraqi is stopped, or Americans go to a house or talk to an Iraqi in a restaurant, no matter how humble or polite the soldiers may be, there is the reminder that Iraqis have no capacity to object to these armed foreigners. Technically, of course, they could object with impunity—but how many people would decide to simply brush off a bunch of armed men?

It is not the best way to start a meeting. As there is no way of avoiding it, we simply recognize that behind each and every encounter is an asymmetry of power in our favor.

For the meeting to be meaningful, the burden has to be deliberately borne by the soldiers. Soldiers do this by simply being polite (as most American soldiers are) or, better, by minimizing the asymmetry of power by being *humble.* The best case is the soldiers who attempt to speak Arabic. These are soldiers who have chosen to learn Arabic on their own, using self-study Arabic materials with the help of interpreters.

The advantage of having some rudimentary language skills cannot be underestimated. When soldiers take off their dark shades and brain bucket (the Advanced Combat Helmet, ACH) and try out their pathetic Arabic, they find themselves stumbling and smiling at their own amateurish phrases. The interaction for a moment takes on an equal footing. The asymmetry of power disappears as the soldier becomes someone asking for help, needing forbearance and assistance. It gives the Iraqi the edge in the conversation. Iraqis appreciate the effort. They may laugh at the soldier's antics, but he has established an important point, and he has almost achieved a genuine human interaction. On many occasions Iraqis—patriarchs, matriarchs, girls, or boys—would simply stare at the soldiers, laugh, and correct them. Or they would simply shake their head and brush off the soldier's effort with a wave of the hand and start speaking in crisp English. At that point, the cultural task is accomplished.

Not all encounters are so heartwarming in a war zone. The primary concern of grunts is anticipating dangers; nothing can be taken for granted. To do so would be to risk the life of those around you. Any encounter with an Iraqi evokes one single, immediate thought: Is this guy up to no good? Is he insurgent, militia? If so, what would he try? You hold the pistol grip a little tighter.

If it is a woman, the encounter holds another element of danger—that has nothing, and everything, to do with the way she looks.

The first thought is always about her *shape*. "Checking a woman out" takes on new meaning in a counterinsurgency, as soldiers have to be mindful of suicide bombers. Well, this woman is a bit on the plump side, a suicide vest might fit perfectly around her gut. You cannot strip search or frisk a woman—let alone at random—so you have to trust your instincts, your deductive capacities, and your humor. If it's a Sunni woman dressed by the book—covered head to toe with a tiny slit for the eyes—you look at the eyes and you look for the quick waddling step. Sometimes the woman is not covered head to toe, especially if she is Shia, and you try to gauge her body in proportion to everything else. Look at the fingers, are they chubby or nimble? Is the gut or the back flabby? Does the body look in proportion to her apparently nimble hands and fingers? If she looks in proportion, she must be the real deal, just another woman trying to make it through the day, trying to live. As long as nothing goes boom when she waddles by, good job, soldier.

❖ **Getting around**

The ability to successfully navigate a terrain does not mean the soldier is an expert. It means he has the basic ability to get to where he wants to be. He has the skills to follow the terrain, be a part of it, take the short cuts. Follow the saddles, avoid the hills, and exploit the inherent strengths and weaknesses in the terrain to make it to the end.

Slogging it out in a cultural terrain is no different. Soldiers will not be culture experts at the end of their tour. Nor do soldiers need to be anthropologists, trying to define the deeper meanings and myriad nuances in order to complete the mission. Culture only means the differences between people—and at the bottom, everyone seems to have the same issues.

While no soldier on the ground will ever be a culture expert, it soon becomes possible to get around and have meaningful encounters and even build lasting acquaintances—while always being mindful of the first rule. No matter what, *never give anyone the benefit of the doubt*. That would be to invite an ambush. After all, this is Iraq, and someone is always prepared to take a shot.

The singular challenge in navigating among the people as soldiers is to evoke a human interaction, to convey the sense that, behind the shades and the weapons, there is a man—a rather ignorant one—who does not mean harm unless he is forced.

Soldiers have to start by avoiding the obvious. Avoid asking about the insurgents because the answer is predictable: "Oh this area, it is very safe." Avoid preaching our own magnanimity: They have lived the results of our actions and empty promises long enough. Instead, we talk about the general politics of the country or the mountains of Irbil, and, above all, we listen to their concerns. The respectful conversation means that we will be welcome in the house the next time.

People who are sick of the insurgents will simply start sounding off. But they will usually only talk to American soldiers alone, without interpreters. This is when even a rudimentary level of Arabic is a great boon. At first, people's stories seem convoluted. A story that starts in Baghdad might end up in Basra by way of Nasiriya, with a hiatus in Kirkuk. You are left wondering, "Wait a minute, so how did the guy in the gutter end up in Basra?"

The Iraqi patriarch laughs and wags his finger, "Oh no, no." He proceeds to clarify by telling another story, highlighting what the soldiers had missed, and this becomes a story all by itself: another cultural concussion.

But then you get a peculiar handle on how, in some stories, the sense of time collapses, events signify some sort of time and place instead of a precise date. The moment of concussion becomes simply, "what the hell," and you get hooked on the story and begin to go down-down-down the rabbit hole.

The many gains that American soldiers and leaders on the ground have made in Iraq show that getting hung up on culture is not the key to this counterinsurgency. Culture will always matter, but for soldiers, the practical "operational concept" on the ground is how you navigate the differences. Those differences represent a singular enemy advantage that insurgents exploit to hide among the civilian population. Navigating the differences is the way to minimize that advantage to be able to distinguish the enemy from the innocent. The effort needs to be serious and systematic and done right; it has the effect of bringing the neighborhood to life.

Rabbit Holes and Stories: Intelligence Gathering

Good intelligence gathering and its astute exploitation, will determine how effective soldiers can be on the ground in a counterinsurgency. Intelligence, when stripped of its mind-numbing jargon, always means, in essence, a series of great stories.

Nearly every kill-capture and Time-Sensitive Target acquisition mission has its seed—usually, a story told by some pissed off Iraqi that, in the hands of competent soldiers and leaders, turned into actionable intelligence yielding results on the ground. Those stories, of course, are just supplements to all the high-tech and low-tech wizardry the armed forces use, the stuff that puts a grin on the faces of soldiers on the ground.

If soldiers walk the streets every day, meeting people from all walks of life, they have more chances of discovering useful rabbit holes. Listening to stories, however ordinary, eventually helps develop the best sources of intelligence. But it has to be done systematically, following a special kind of common sense.

Navigating the population is all about seeing behind the surface, seeing everything that helps sustain that particular reality. We begin to see a hidden reality, the subversive world of insurgents. Making systematic attempts to listen to stories can help us develop this capacity to instantly recognize multiple realities. The obvious is always tempting, but critical to resist. Seeing only the obvious instills a dangerous consistency in thinking. On the ground, a belief in consistency means predictability—and we walk into an ambush sooner or later.

Finding credible actionable intelligence and credible sources is very similar to locating illicit drugs in a neighborhood. Anyone can buy drugs on certain street corners, but that is never the good stuff. Parents in the suburbs wisely tell their kids to stay out of that part of town—but neighborhoods are not the whole story. In so many cities, you can have the shit delivered to your house, hell, they will throw in an ounce of the latest and the greatest "on the house" for a good customer. The guy's neighbors have no clue: he is good guy; he's a doctor, the neighborhood kids even play in his swimming pool.

Stumbling around like a jackass without a clue gets you nowhere. The idea is to locate some *sources*. Locating a reliable source with quality goods is ninety percent of the battle. So you look around, keep your eyes and ears open, get a feel for what is out there in the streets, locate people that might have some idea, who just might be near the source, perhaps even find some possible sources. One cannot hurry it, you try to get into the flow of things. Eventually you get to one of the sources with potentially good stuff, and a strange thing happens: You develop the ability to distinguish the obvious and the not-so-obvious that exist side by side.

As you begin to get a general idea for the drug scene in the town, it dawns on you that many people have been aware of it all along; after all, it is their neighborhood. Surprise: More people than you imagined are actually smoking some good stuff. It's a different reality, underneath and next to the obvious. "How in the hell could I have missed this?" But better late than never. So, the next time you walk down the street, you nod at the doctor—not as neighbors anymore, but a knowing nod. And you nod at the perceptive neighbors who also see both realities simultaneously.

In Iraq, we are looking for insurgents, not drugs, and we have to find the people, the observers and neighbors, who can lead us to the source. We must pass many credibility tests, many charades, before people will actually say anything. (Not always, however; some people will immediately inform us, depending on how much they hate the insurgents and how credible the soldiers have been in their actions.) Eventually we get to the source, some insurgent nut-job, and you find that everyone has been aware of him all along. "Oh, mister, yes, he was always ferry, ferry bad."

The Rabbit-Hole Matrix

Walking into a neighborhood for the fiftieth time, it is easy to indulge in the mistaken belief that we know it intimately just because we've walked it long enough. One senior enlisted leader with multiple deployments always kept repeating this phrase: "You've got to feel it *on your skin* as you walk in." Even so, intuition and gut are never enough to make decisions, when lives depend on those decisions. The trick is to apply rigorous logic along with the intuition. Soldiers heard it repeatedly after their first few missions and follow-on operations: *Follow some goddamn common sense.*

The Rabbit Hole Matrix (RHM)[14] is a commonsense template that simply adds some logic to that feeling in the skin. We recognize the obvious, we find inconsistencies within it, and then you try to make sense of the insurgents and their affiliations. It is strangely exciting; it can bring the neighborhood to life through the stories of people.

---

[14] An NCO provided the inspirational impetus for this RHM exercise when he commented on the difficulty of navigating a rabbit hole—with its twists and connecting tunnels. Colleagues in other areas used similar approaches, sometimes dictated from higher, sometimes developed on the fly, just like the RHM.

The Rabbit-Hole Matrix is a simple template of making profiles of people we meet based on a set of criteria. We begin to see them in relation to one another and to the neighborhood, in shifting alliances. A simple database made it possible to collate the many stories and gauge their credibility. It helped us cross-reference people and their affiliations, adding location grids and sometimes photos, email addresses, or phone numbers. It is an imperfect picture, of course. But the steady accretion of marginal information eventually adds up to something greater than the sum of its parts.[15]

With this semblance of a logical system in hand, it becomes possible to see the affiliations, sectarian identities, and political and clan loyalties behind the stories—knowledge that exposes their inherent biases. It made our lives easier and our work that much better, and we even had a good time along the way.

The essential criterion for inclusion in the Rabbit-Hole Matrix was simple: Is the house worth visiting another time, and is there a possibility of actionable intelligence? In more concrete terms: Does he have great stories? Do the stories have any relevance and does he have a good grasp of the events that surround him? If "yes," do a quick profile of the person or family.

Soldiers try to include a family's ethnic, sectarian, professional, educational, economic, and familial background. After one gets familiar with the neighborhood and its sectarian and ethnic composition, basic situational awareness does the rest. Is he affiliated in any form or manner with the current or the former regime? Soldiers then add their own impressions: Is he a lying sack of shit? Does he look at us favorably, or can you feel the hatred and antipathy glowing in his eyes? And there is always another question in the background: Why? Why is he so forthcoming with information, or why is he so reticent? Nothing

---

[15] This could also be done using the same high-speed mapping program with aerial graphics that soldiers use to map infiltration and ex-filtration routes: right click on the map, fill in the information, and eventually you have a perfect terrain map with all the grids, houses, and people in relation to one another.

can be taken for granted. Does his story have credibility, does it check out with others soldiers have heard?

It is unending extra work. But if you can manage to collate all the gossip and then go after a bunch of insurgents, it fills you with a simple sense of accomplishment and the dawning realization: Damn, the shit actually works.

❖ Big-wigs, stories, and whiskey bars

People don't want to be "informants." No one likes a rat, especially soldiers. Yet some people do rat on their colleagues, in aid of the cause. Usually the cause is their own well-being—but this is irrelevant if it might serve the purpose.

Victims of violence were always more forthcoming than others. Moreover, on the very first missions, soldiers encountered a simple truth. People may be afraid to talk about insurgents—but they always tell the truth about the *victims*. When soldiers put emphasis on finding victims of insurgent violence, people have a stake in the matter, however terrified they may be. Soldiers can become (as we liked to call it) "insurgents behind insurgents." To be insurgents behind insurgents is simply a different way of looking at the neighborhood. As counterinsurgents, we are looking *in* from the outside. But as insurgents behind insurgents, hearing the stories of the dead—through the anguished whispers of the living—we can turn it around, looking *outside* from within. We can better understand the effect of insurgent (and counterinsurgent) violence on the population and their reaction to it. It was a simple tactical concept that paid many dividends over time for some soldiers.

As one learns the neighborhood, with its loyalties, its big wigs, its brothels and underground whiskey bars, it becomes possible to pick and choose who you want to meet. Sometimes the meeting is to further the mission; other times it is just for fun, to enjoy some good food, good company, and good stories. The everyday stories people tell made it possible to get to know their relatives and friends as well.

Underlying all of these efforts to get the neighborhood under the skin is the quest for actionable intelligence: distinguishing the enemy from the innocent, locating insurgents and their leaders, collecting dirt to develop a profile and a target packet, and trying to get the hang of the changing nature of the neighborhood.

When soldiers get word that there is someone of stature in town, you cannot miss the opportunity. This was how some soldiers came to be in the doorway of Mr. Ahmad Chalabi himself. In his palatial residence, he certainly appeared to be doing well. He is affable, thankful for the services of soldiers, their sacrifices and dedication for the betterment of Iraq: His appreciation seemed genuine. But the minds of soldiers were preoccupied by the many books they had read while in Iraq. Some had just finished reading *Inside the Resistance* by Zaki Chehab, describing Chalabi as "the man who could give Machiavelli a run for his own pasta." Soldiers had to see this guy. Chalabi was certainly remarkable in managing, in just a few minutes, to drop the name of every U.S. high official in the Green Zone. He pointed emphatically to the many U.S. generals on his speed dial.

But there was the not-so-obvious concern that crept into the mind. How is it that the affable, wheeling-and-dealing corner store guy knew all about the many people going in and out of the vehicles at Chalabi's house? If he (and others, no doubt) knew so well what times he would come and go, and what other shady cats were in the house, how much knowledge did he retain of the patrols and actions of *soldiers*?

People's grasp of their own neighborhood was mind-boggling. Holy shit, came the singular thought: How to get a glimpse into that rabbit hole?

❖ Start walking

The only way to do it is to start walking. Walking is the best way—the only way—to do counterinsurgency.

Soldiers walk, walk, and walk some more in the heat and the bone-chilling cold, despite the fatigue. In army speak, that means *dismount*: Get off the damn trucks, Bradleys, Strykers and tanks. Keep looking for stories, head on a swivel, eyes open, ears alert.

Whatever the deep-seated cultural differences between American soldiers and Iraqis, if we walk, we will be forced to interact. Both sides begin to see each other as people; they learn to navigate the differences without getting hung up on them. But the burden of properly navigating a prohibitive cultural terrain—as a foreign intervention force waging a counterinsurgency—lies with the Americans. Some do it better than others, but every soldier on the ground, operating outside the wire, keeps trying.

Yet throughout these encounters, from all the stories they heard in the first few missions, soldiers had a nagging feeling that there was something missing, something vitally important. Ah, of course: Iraqi women.

PART II

THE CIRCLING SONG: IRAQI WOMEN

What could a bunch of enlisted grunts—Airborne Infantrymen from small towns of America—possibly have to say about Iraqi women?

Certainly, Iraqi women presented a mystery. At first sight they were abstract entities, black-clad creatures scurrying about in abayas, showing only shifty black eyes. The official Army PowerPoint on culture was memorable, mainly for its soporific effect. Basically, it conveyed to us that Iraqi women are "religious and conservative"—i.e., women in Iraq are trouble and leave them alone. And Iraqi men are even more "conservative"—i.e., they get really pissed off if you talk to Iraqi women.

But soldiers had to walk the streets, and some of us soon came to terms with a different reality. Iraqi women (and most men) are not the boogeyman abstractions depicted in the Power-Point slides. And many Iraqi women were extremely effective in helping us hunt down insurgents.[16] Strangely enough, some of them hated the insurgents even more than we did. That always produced a very pleasant feeling in soldiers' hearts.

The first-ever encounter with an Iraqi woman is utterly puzzling. The women at first seem to be standing in the shadows of men. In public, this is the standard, though it is often different inside their houses. Yet even inside the house they often stand in a corner constantly displaying a conscious, almost judicious, sense of subservience.

You look closer at the deliberately subservient yet constantly moving eyes of young girls and wonder, "What exactly is going through their minds?" You scrutinize the faces of older women, some with so many deeply etched crevices in their faces they seem to count off each year of their life. Even faces as bland as the stucco walls have something going on in there. Soldiers are instinctively aware of their own peculiar situation: They are men with guns, standing unwelcome in a house. They would wonder, "What the hell, man, these women are they acting like this because we're in the house, or is it because of the other Iraqi dudes in here?"

What do you do? The rulebook suggests showing respect, which translates into leaving the women alone. To talk to them deliberately would only mean more women would get smacked in the head while further pissing off those petty men.

Culture and religion undoubtedly have an immense impact. But it seems to be the men that define and enforce those standards, the majority of women are simply complicit in it.

---

[16] In fact, more Iraqi men than women helped us; we made a deliberate decision to include more stories and impressions of Iraqi women in this book, as they are so absent from general awareness.

"Values" and "morality" are the greatest excuses to become the worst of men.[17] Culture, religion, and men may authorize it, but men can get away with it only if women acquiesce to it, as most do. But some, and they are formidable women, sure as hell don't.

---

[17] Here, the references to men refer exclusively to the minority of religious fanatics and militias, not the vast majority of decent and educated men. However, they too, in their comfortable silence, remain thoroughly complicit in the situation.

3

ALONE WITH THE DAYS: ASPIRATIONS AND DEAD ENDS[18]

No one can make a fool out of a man better than a woman. Being effective and staying out of trouble always requires coming to terms with our own imperfections as soldiers and men. This is not only a time-honored truth—it is also a word of advice.

As long as we are wearing a uniform and carrying a weapon, *romance is on hold*. When deployed, it is a line that we never—ever—let any of our soldiers cross.

Given the anonymous existence of women in the shadows of men, it is difficult for soldiers to have meaningful conversations with women. Yet difficult does not mean impossible. Adapt, overcome, and "Charlie Mike"—Continue Mission, soldiers joke sarcastically. But no matter how cynical or jaded, there is no sarcasm among infantrymen when it pertains to meeting a woman, American or Iraqi.

The situation is hardly normal. An American soldier and an Iraqi woman are mutually ignorant of each other's realities, and most

---

[18] *Alone With the Days*, a novel by Fadwa Touqwan.

conversations are based on assumptions and prejudices on both sides, bringing about a mild concussion: "What the hell is going on?"

Encounters

An Iraqi woman finds herself face-to-face with an American soldier. Her justifiable apprehension is palpable. These are foreigners, armed to the teeth. How many Americans would welcome armed police officers into their own homes for coffee? How many would welcome armed foreigners, in uniform or not? Moreover, stories of abuse of women by American soldiers are actively propagated and are widely believed to represent a norm rather than some horrendous exception.

A woman confronts armed, sweating men standing in her doorway, their faces burned from miles of walking, their clothes unwashed and stinking from funk; even their deliberate smiles look menacing. At first, the woman understandably worries about her life, security, and personal dignity. The only common ground is their prejudices and ignorance concerning one another. An uneasy moment passes. Depending on the context, soldiers will show a little humility: With the asymmetry of power, they know they can always control the nature of the encounter. An Iraqi has no way of refusing, and we must show respect when we can. Generally, it is not too difficult.

Then there are moments when one gets completely star-struck. A beautiful and elegant Iraqi woman with eloquent eyes, perfectly defined features, and disarming eyelashes speaks English with an incredibly alluring accent. A woman so completely feminine, with such an obvious sense of modesty; once again we ask, "Is this real?" To someone completely deprived of any feminine presence, not having slept in three days, and sent on a mission in the middle of nowhere, it is a sublimely hallucinatory moment.

She is well aware of her own beauty and the power it engenders. She is subtly but effectively coquettish—as long as she is surrounded by other women. Soldiers really want to capture the charm of the moment. Fatigue does not help; "God damn, where is that smattering of Arabic I learned?" Too late; the soldier quickest on his feet, with

46

better Arabic skills, captures the moment. You silently curse him and wait for your turn, Charlie Mike.

Countless Iraqi women have described to soldiers their precarious existence. Some unfortunate ones live in a world that is forcibly pious and puritanical, enforced by insurgents, militias, and the militias affiliated with the government. Preachers, insurgents, and militia leaders have inspired village idiots and sexually repressed young men to become AK-47-wielding enforcers of religious piety. Men that embody the worst of men act in the name of god, their actions sanctified by some cleric; failing that, the AK-47 they have in their hands is sanction enough. Many women pointed out this stark reality to soldiers. One only has to listen to understand the details.

An Iraqi woman would launch into passionate diatribes against insurgents and would point out how insurgents are responsible for most of their misery. And Americans are responsible by extension, *by not being in control*. It is not a statement of support for our invasion, only a reflection of their miserable situation and their understanding of the changing dynamics of the battle space. Yes, their lives were not much better before Americans came in, but now, with the lack of security and with the unleashing of religious zealots, their lives had become even worse. They highlight their desperation with a fervor that fills the air. Only the gleaming eyes and their words express their true sentiments: By virtue of their sense of modesty, they sit still with a minimum of movement. The comportment of some of the women quickly became incongruous with the sentiment they tried to convey.

Focusing all their frustrations at the soldiers, they would ask, "Why, why, why?" with the tips of fingers tightly clenched in a raised right hand. "Why you don't kill these people, you American soldiers, you need to be strong, *strong*, you need to kill," and the hand would gesture with a pointed finger—jab-jab-jab—"why do you let them go?"

It is a peculiar moment. These women really want some people dead, perhaps more so even than the American military lawyers who verify and approve the target packets. Some of the women have so much anger in their eyes that their usually lyrical-sounding Arabic takes on

47

a distinctive edge. There is a little opening, and you must capture it. The frustrations of these Iraqi women and their deep-seated hostility to the insurgents become a clear tactical advantage in a counterinsurgency centered on a population.

But many Iraqi women, like many men, also drive you nuts with their prevarications. Sometimes they are genuine supporters of the insurgents, but, more often, they have no choice but to be complicit with the insurgents in order to save their own skin. And many women were surprising and disarmingly unpretentious. Some consistently engaged in acts of subversion and resistance, running circles around the insurgents, their own parents, and their prohibitive culture. Some women impressed and humbled us with the clear, cogent articulation of the freedoms they sought, and their sense of optimism and aspiration. Others broke our hearts with their stories of despair.

The Feisty Progressive: Miramar[19]

An Iraqi girl asks, "Do you read Dostoevsky? I think he is a great man." Again, you do the crab walk. Are you serious? What the hell? And her shiny eyes suggest that she has read a whole lot more than a page or two of Mr. Dostoevsky. The trick in talking to her is always trying to anticipate the next question, but no one expected this.

But it's the army, and as unbelievable as it may be, even some of enlisted humanity has read the good Russian.

"Hey, you ever read Dostoevsky? *Notes from Underground*? Well, shit, come on, man, this is your moment." A lot of laughter.

"Well, Miramar," (soldiers gave her the pseudonym for her own safety, taken from one of her favorite stories)—"yeah, we have guys who love Dostoevsky. I mean, who *hasn't* read him?" She laughed, well knowing

---

[19] Given Miramar's family's prominent position and her own precarious existence, we have considerably altered her background and her story. And we have permission from her to use her emails; as she pointed out many times, the situation of women in Iraq "is terrible, sooo terrible, someone needs to write about it."

he hadn't read a lick of the crazy Russian. "Oh that is wonderful, my dear, that is so wonderful; I love this writer!"

Soldiers would joke: "Miramar, what's with you and the Russians? You've got no love for Americans. And this just breaks our heart."

"I like Russians and their stories maybe because of Dostoevsky. He had a strange effect on me, and I loved his writings and always saw myself as one of his characters. My mother first led me to his writing as a teenager." She comes from a long line of accomplished family members: writers, painters, even poets. She is a teacher by profession, a painter by passion, a writer in her soul, and a feisty woman with an attitude of resistance in everyday life.

She is also in love with Naguib Mahfouz. "Miramar, how come you are so in love with dead men?"

She agreed with a laugh. Yes, Dostoevsky and Naguib Mahfouz are her lovers, adding, "It is *better* to be in love with dead men, my dear."

Soldiers, perhaps being men and giving into their own prejudices, had missed the obvious. It took an educated, feisty Iraqi girl with an attitude to elucidate it for us. Miramar posed her opinion in the form of a question: "You know why these stupid men [the Iraqis] don't want Americans to talk to Iraqi women and don't let Iraqi women talk to Americans, you know why—you know why?" And here she paused, elongated her accent and raised her pitch: "Because they are afraid you will learn the truth about these stupid, s-t-u-p-i-d men."[20]

Her joking comment had some validity in relation to the primary job of soldiers. Soldiers are always looking for information concerning the local men. Soldiers seek information on the insurgents, on the evolving situation in the neighborhood, and on the changing dynamics of the battle space. If you strip away the complexity of the military and legal jargon in the operations order, it simply says there is some fat guy we are going after—some guy with a wife, or a few wives, who

---

[20] She was convinced of it, but conceded that some are worse than others. She and some of her friends actually read this section and gave us insights.

also happens to be an insurgent or an insurgent leader. Not all of the multiple wives are as happy and content as the men would have one believe. And neither are the many children from multiple wives all content with their situation, nor the families of the many wives. Usually it is not one big happy Brady Bunch family.

It was the women and girls who articulated this background for a bunch of wide-eyed soldiers, listening to the volleys of neighborhood gossip and getting a very rapid education. Soldiers are dependent on village gossip for information to learn of the whereabouts, effectiveness, and actions of powerful men and their allies in order to catch them at the most propitious and least expected moment. The information can come from a myriad of sources. But women, it seemed to the soldiers, did have a peculiar advantage in Iraq.

Being ascribed a marginal position in their own society has caused Iraqi women to redefine the ideas of subtlety and nuance. It has made some of them incredibly astute students of men, both American and Iraqi, as well as experts on their own surroundings—which in Iraq was also the battle space of soldiers. One began to see how at times they retained an element of resistance against Americans as well as against their own men, and how they precariously navigated multiple forms of authority, the contesting claims of control, and various forms of violence they contended with. Some especially impressive women, as we'll see, even volunteered to provide actionable intelligence and take risks in support of soldiers.

It seems that to live without being true to oneself is to merely exist out of habit. A man or a woman forced to live in an oppressive atmosphere many choose to be complicit, all the while engaging in a desperate attempt to find meaning in their complicity. A very few refuse this complicity and find meaning instead in acts of resistance, no matter how trivial. Miramar has found a delicate balance. She does not seek to change the world with her small acts of resistance, but she refuses to be defined by the environment surrounding her. In that refusal she makes others uncomfortable, rattling their cages by stating the obvious. Of course, this being Iraq, that's not always the best

50

idea. To her credit, she is still doing it with a smile; she is not yet a victim of the religious thought police who are the bane of her every-day existence.

To an American unfamiliar with nuance, she comes across as contradic-tory. While she has no place in her heart for clerics, religious zealots, or anyone implementing religious edicts in social life (she calls them the Taliban), she remains a devoted Muslim. Although she despises insur-gents of any sectarian identity, she is proud of her own sectarian identity, and she laments the inability of Iraqis to fashion their own destiny. She appreciates the efforts of the coalition but feels they should not be in Iraq in the first place. Yet for all her criticism, she would assist the Americans in order to get rid of the insurgents. She only wished that Americans were stronger and delivered more often on their promises: *"What is wrong with you American soldiers?"* she would staunchly demand.

It slowly sinks in how some women navigate the oppressive attributes of culture and religion when taken to extremes and imposed by vio-lence propagated by zealots. Here is Miramar, an educated woman full of character and passionate opinion on every conceivable topic. Yet the moment she steps out of the house she is forced to wear a headscarf she detests: It is not the scarf but being robbed of the choice that angers her. So her mission is to irk the militiamen, not to walk around like just another frightened little bird. She refuses to be an indistinguishable creature with hunched shoulders and shifting eyes, deliberately sub-servient and stripped of individuality. (Of course, this is an Iraqi city, not a city in Saudi Arabia or a Taliban-controlled enclave.)

Women without choice embody the ideal world of religious fanatics. For a woman to exercise choice, even at the margins, constitutes resis-tance; and in a neighborhood run by zealots, this can be a death-defy-ing sport. Miramar seems oddly astute in her ability to irk them. But a remarkable number of young women were equally determined to say the hell with it, always trying to irk the zealots and laughing uproari-ously about it later. Soldiers would get entertaining e-mails describing the moment of walking next to the militia hangout wearing jeans and the resultant looks of apoplectic men.

51

The question inevitably came up, for such a beautiful and a charming woman: Why is it that you don't have a boyfriend or husband? She responded with a long e-mail that captures the attidude of a teacher trying to instruct some ignorant American soldiers:

"NO, NO No . . . Now, here, the men have so bad thinking, so bad view about the women. I'm sure you met many Iraqi men and you felt that maybe you felt you couldn't like them, or maybe you hated them, and if you really felt like that I will agree with you. I think, no, I'm sure, those men are afraid of the women, they think women maybe will take the jobs and the positions, and then take the lead.

If you lived in an Arabic country, you will see and feel it firsthand, you will understand why all that happens. In most Arabian families, the boys are treated so different from the girls in the same family. The boys have absolute freedom to do everything they want, they can do, go, think, even dress, as they want; any boy can take his decision himself, but the girls don't. Every girl can't do what she wants, can't go when she wants, can't dress or even talk and think as she wants, the women and girls here live in a cage, in prison, they don't have the freedom. . . . I think these societies will not be developed until liberated from religion's control.

Maybe you will find it strange, but I decided to stay single because I don't want to chain myself; I want to still be free and marriage will chain and stop me, and I have many other aims in this life.

On the other side, I hate the men here, all of them are narrow-minded; they look at women's faces not at their minds, they treat the woman as slaves not as human. They even don't understand the meaning of friendship, so it's difficult finding a man as friend here, but I'm forced to work and talk with them. Where can I run away from those stupid men? The people here cannot imagine that someone dares to refuse all their old traditions, refuse this reality."

That was a beginning. Miramar also explained two realities that we never knew.

First, there are countless women in Iraq who organize conferences and practical organizations to help out the many young women who were abused or raped, the victims of violence, as well as the many women and families harassed by insurgents and militias. These organizations are scattered all across Iraq, founded and run by women. Miramar would attend the meetings, and we would get calls and e-mails with the latest information.

Imagine for a moment if soldiers could be lucky enough to find the names and contact information for some of the women who were victims of insurgent violence—there is a source of intelligence (contingent on its verifiability). Many woman would provide that information after you have known them long enough.

Miramar also explained to us a peculiar poignancy: That a woman's beauty becomes, in the eyes of the religious fanatics and pretentious moralists, her greatest sin. Her point was simple. No matter what happens to a woman—raped, abused, groped (things that happen more often than men would like to acknowledge)—it is always interpreted by the religious crowd as *the fault of the woman*. It was her modesty and virtue that failed! The simple reality that some man forced the act is quickly discarded. Instead, the issue is that the woman wore jeans or was not dressed modestly enough. In Miramar's opinion it has nothing to do with religion and everything to do with "these stupid, stupid men. It is terrible to be beautiful here; I worry so much about my sister, oh, you know my dear, she is such a beautiful girl." She was not talking about some abstract idea but a reality she contends with on a daily basis, walking down the street in her own neighborhood. She would not give in, resisting in her own small ways, and she generated much respect in the eyes of these gun-toting, sweaty foreigners.

Since she has resigned herself to a single woman's life of intellectual pursuits, soldiers always joked, "Well, Miramar, no problem; I think it's great, you can scare away all the men you like. Hell, even we are pretty scared." She appreciated that sentiment.

53

Today Miramar is wearing her tight, long black skirt, a tight purple silk shirt with white stripes, short dark hair scattered, looking stunning in her Sunday best.

"Hey, Miramar, you look very elegant today, dressed to kill as they say."

"Oh, thank you, my dear, I had to go to a party, a wedding party actu-uually, my friend got married."

Smart-ass grunts can't resist. "Ha ha, so tell me, should I be happy or sorry for your friend?"

Miramar laughed, "Oh my dear, yes, love and marriage, this word scares me, but this poor girl, she decided to fall in love"—and then comes her sideways glance, quietly shrugging her shoulders. "Now she will live in hell with her lover." Everyone was doubled up in laughter.

It was surreal: The world of American soldiers and that of an Iraqi girl who has never left Iraq, strangely collapsing into one, converging upon numerous common points of reference and their own sarcastic humor. Especially surreal: That she feels more comfortable with a bunch of armed foreigners than in her native world as she steps out of her house.

"Miramar, what do you want to do, other than start a woman's revolution in Iraq?" No, no revolution, she wants to do a Ph.D. "To do some good in this earth. That's my inspiration."

"Damn, well you could do some serious damage then." But it is true: When so many people worry about which road to take, which road has the most roadblocks, no one worries about the "earth ball."

Miramar's upbringing in a family of scholars and professionals has molded the way she looks at the world around her. "Ever since I was six years old, I have been painting, and painting is my true passion. But I always loved reading. I grew up with war, many wars, too many wars: the Iran-Iraq War, then the Kuwaiti War, then the 1991 War (the uprising against Saddam), then sanctions, then the 2003 war, and now this. But reading always helped me. I first read *Les Miserables* when I was eleven years old and ever since then I have been reading."

As she became acquainted with soldiers, she would constantly be in touch by e-mail and cell phone. She would get into lengthy arguments and debates on every conceivable topic, commenting, "Ooooh, this is terrible, why I must teach these Americans! You should *know*, you should know this." She was a teacher by profession and always acted the part. That was perhaps her problem. Soldiers found it humorous, often educational, and always insightful. It was insurgents who saw her as a threat. Soldiers would end an e-mail, an Internet chat, or a phone call by telling her, "Please be safe and don't do anything crazy"—and she would break into a laugh, "Yes, we are all crazy, my dear."

At first she seemed the exception to the rule. But many Iraqi women, especially the young girls and university students, shared similar aspirations. Many harbor deep convictions but very few act on them in the face of such overwhelming odds. Miramar and a few others were different in their willingness to take risks, following through on their convictions. Their penchant for subversion and resistance was infectious.

Many Iraqi men, as you get to know them—especially the young students who want to escape Iraq—would inevitably ask, "How can we come to America?" Soldiers had a standard response to that question: "Go to America? Man, we are wondering about that ourselves!" It generated lot of laughter among the soldiers, though not many Iraqis understood the humor.

But this was a question no *woman* ever brought up, no matter how well they came to know the soldiers, Miramar included. But if there was any Iraqi who deserved to be in America studying (besides some of the Iraqi interpreters, who continually risked their lives), it was Miramar. Her intellectual curiosity and broad knowledge far surpassed that of most American college students. The soldiers were always googling shit in Iraq to impress her, not the other way around! Soldiers would ask if she had ever considered studying in America.

She had not, it was not possible, she said. But she had considered Lebanon and Egypt, since some of her family members had visited those countries during Iraq's glory days. She was afraid to consider applying to school in America because of the war. Soldiers tried their

55

best to explain that in America no one really gives a shit about Iraq or Iraqis. "Sweetheart, it wouldn't matter if you were an alien from another planet, that's one of the great things about America!"

She was intrigued but not convinced. "I need to think about it."

A few months later, after much prodding, she was willing to check the websites, explore some opportunities soldiers suggested, and eventually she even let the soldiers have copies of her official papers so they could make inquiries on her behalf. Of course, to hand over one's papers in Iraq is to hand over one's life.

"You know, Miramar, you're absolutely crazy—now we have all your papers! You're crazy to give them to us and trust us."

She readily agreed, laughing, "Yes, I think so, I am mad, a little crazy." Yes, we are all crazy. Being crazy (as Waylon Jennings said) keeps us from going insane.

So Vast the Prison: Lubna[21]

An overwhelming amount of misery, except for those directly affected by it, sometimes has the strange effect of losing its meaning. It is no longer real. Strange to realize that an abundance of misery becomes a spectacle, and we could be indifferent to misery and laugh at the spectacle.

However, that was before we ran into Lubna.

Thousands of Iraqi men have died—mostly at the hands of other Iraqis but also at the hands of American soldiers—and have left behind thousands of widows to tend to families. Iraq has over two million internally displaced people, not counting another two and a half million Iraqis living abroad as refugees. (A consistent joke with the soldiers, why are the figures always so round—how come it is 2,500,000 and not 2,500,001? We want to know the story of that *1*.)

Many widows care for their families with the help of extended family. Others have to do it alone. An invisible casualty of war is that families

---

[21] *So Vast the Prison*, a novel by Assia Djebar.

are torn apart, traditional forms of safety nets cease to exist, and people become helpless and then hopeless. Thousands of women live in abject poverty with their children in makeshift shacks, bombed-out abandoned government buildings, or hastily constructed mud or plastic houses. The worst-off live in the middle of garbage dumps. There, the threat is usually only the smell of garbage and oozing sewage— something people can get used to. Soldiers know this firsthand.

At first it is unbearable, but if there is no choice, and if you have to walk, crawl, and hide among sewage-infested garbage mounds, spending hours in it, you do it and get used to it. Soldiers spend countless nights, crawling and hiding and hanging out in these shit holes in the hot summer nights and on muddy rainy nights. On freezing cold nights, they snuggle next to each other, spooning with one another to use body heat to stay warm. They live covered in mud and garbage, smelling like sewer rats while they try to kill insurgents and contemplate the meaning of life, confiding in each other their dark secrets and darker fantasies. The surrounding miserable stew becomes an abstraction; it even begins to develop a perverse charm. In this catatonic and fatigued state of mind, it is easy to disregard the immediate reality that surrounds us: kick the dirt, hop over the garbage, and ignore the people living in misery. Yet this fantasy of indifference does not last long.

A soldier was scanning his sector with his NODS (Night Optical Device), leaning on a mound of dirt and staring at the dark silhouettes of people walking across the mounds, through the smoke of the intermittent fires burning in this ocean of garbage. Then he spat, almost talking to himself. "We need to go talk to these people. Who the hell are they anyway? I mean, what brought them to this shit hole, where do they work, how do they get paid? And the kids!"

He bellowed, "I mean what the hell, look at those kids, the kids have no life. You know man, the kids! That shit pisses me off, I mean—fuck."

Two soldiers nearby turned lazily. It was as if they had never seen the place before, the place they were becoming intimately familiar with yet knew so little about. The people living there were just an abstraction, images that flashed by but were never seen, and until that moment, no one had given it much thought. It was on that day that they first tried to see.

"You're right, man, what the hell do they do, how do they live, how do they get paid, where do they get money to live? We just need to go talk to some of them when we get a chance."

They never did get the opportunity to talk to very many people or visit many houses in the garbage dump. It's hard to do courtesy calls when you are laying an ambush with the hope of killing people, and it is damn near impossible to do so when you are freezing your balls off and eager as hell to kill somebody just to get to a warmer place.

The place stretched for miles, bordered on one side by a Shia militia stronghold and on the other by a Sunni militia (recently converted to our side). In this shit hole lived a strange mixture of Iraqis—not in any way happily, but amicably enough—while mortar rounds flew over them. They lived together irrespective of sectarian identity or clan loyalties, a perversely peaceful community linked by a shared, unique, all-pervading misery. There was a common cohesion: displaced people trying to eke out a living and survive. Tensions certainly exist. As the soldiers learned, there are rules, norms, a semblance of an authority structure, and lines one does not cross. Even in the garbage pit there are men who run the show; men who are liked or hated, dim-wits and cock-suckers. They're everywhere.

There is a sense of community between people from the same provinces, but the abject poverty of the pit seems to have formed its own bizarre kind of universe. It has always been a place where the itinerant have found refuge. But the massive influx of displaced people was recent, a result of post-invasion violence. You run into people from as far west as Anbar province, as far east as Nineveh, as far southeast as Maysan province. Almost everyone has a similar story of destitution, death, and displacement by force and threats of violence, with extended families that would have helped but are by now equally destitute. The men, women, and children sound, look, and smell the same. They are undernourished, thin, burnt by the sun, and weathered beyond their age. The kids: thin, matted hair, dirty clothes, runny noses, covered in mud or dust; and everyone emanating a putrid smell that one eventually gets used to. Differences between people are mainly a matter of their features, degrees of misery, and distinctive smells. One is always left wondering what the children might grow up to be: criminals, thieves, insurgents?

And what about the little girls?

No education, barely a family, they spend the formative years in a garbage heap they call home. How many prostitutes can a country sustain?

The stories of despair and grief were so similar that the mind often refused to make sense of them. We find ourself making a conscious effort to empathize. Then we just shake our head. The soldiers may be crouching inside one of the houses, sitting on an empty olive oil can in a corner, listening intently while someone speaks, only a few inches away so that you smell the body odor slathered in layers over their skin for so many months, perhaps years. It takes effort—a tremendous effort—to truly grasp their precarious existence. It's easier to ignore it and be indifferent, to imagine that we soldiers are just as miserable. Their stories seem too removed from this earth, too removed from any point of reference soldiers are familiar with. It is strange to be in the middle of it and be unable, or unwilling, to completely open our eyes.

Then we ran into Lubna, a prematurely aged, undernourished mother of three who resembled a matchstick. She began enlightening us simply through the twist of fate that she could speak some halting English. That blew us away. She explained her story simply, with no flair, conviction, or vivacity. Her subdued monotone voice was lifeless. Having heard countless sob stories, it was this monotone that soldiers found distinctive, and it made her story all the more compelling.

Her ability to speak halting but coherent English (interspersed with Arabic) made it easier to grasp her story, but it also made her existence in that tiny twenty-by-twenty shack with flapping plastic sheets amid the rotting garbage all the more incongruous. Our own prejudices had led us to expect that English speakers are usually better off. She was a woman from Ninaweh province, the wife of a schoolteacher turned small-time entrepreneur who was displaced, and she moved to be with her family. She was displaced again and eventually found a home here, in this shithole, as a temporary place to live on her way to a different town.

Why would you move across Iraq? She did not say. But her husband had disappeared, along with one of her older kids. Perhaps he left her and the family. Unable to provide for their families, many men have chosen to simply abandon them instead. Perhaps he was killed with the kid, or perhaps he was apprehended and was languishing in some prison. Only god knows the answer, if there is one, but even he seemed to be hiding. She did not believe that her husband left; only that he was either killed or apprehended.

"Please find him!"

As incredible as it may sound, some Iraqis still saw American soldiers as supermen, capable of anything. It was more a reflection of Lubna's own hopeless condition than a real perception of American soldiers. There was something strange in the way she made the request. It was as if finally some determination had infiltrated her voice. That was a good sign. She was past the frantic, almost fanatical period of pointless hope, of refusing to come to terms with reality. Lubna would always hope, even if it's a hopeless hope, but she sounded smarter than to hope foolishly.

This was not the first time soldiers were asked to find missing Iraqi family members. Who keeps a roster of missing people in Iraq, or the names of civilian deaths? No one we know. If only soldiers could do it, they would—especially as it would be an enormous enhancement to our credibility on the ground. For over a year, Lubna languished in that shit hole with her three children, ages four to nine. The question in everyone's mind was: How does she manage to live? What does she do for a living? How does she make ends meet? If she was at least passably good looking she could sell herself. But that appeared to be a hard sell. Then again, there were undoubtedly less attractive prostitutes

60

than Lubna. One can always count on men; desperate men and women are everywhere.

She claimed that she sold gasoline by the side of the road to make ends meet. That story is not very plausible. The local militia controlled all the gasoline distribution, as well as the black market. It was not easy to buy gasoline, and it would be doubly difficult to buy enough to sell it on the black market without connections to the local militia. She certainly did not have the money. Furthermore, a quick scan of her shack did not reveal any gasoline cans or bottles. If she was telling the truth, gasoline cans would be her most precious possession other than her kids, she would never leave them outside. They would be inside her shack and she would guard them with her life. Most likely, during the day she walked to some black market vendor and sold it by the side of the road on his behalf, getting a commission of sorts in return. That job she might be able to do, even as an internally displaced person with few connections.

"Lubna, do you have any papers?"

It was the only time she became animated during the soldiers' numerous visits. Visibly excited, she exhaled in that dejected way people would speak of death after they come to terms with it, explaining that she had lost all her papers. When her husband disappeared, all the family's papers were in his possession. From her body language and eyes, that was very believable. It was likely that, after having found a temporary refuge in this shit hole, her husband left with their papers to find some sort of assistance. Despite the fact that there is virtually no assistance, everyone tries anyway, going to the Iraqi Red Crescent Society, the myriad ministries, and any number of local assistance groups run by Iraqis to assist internally displaced people and refugees. Mostly they try to use their papers to obtain food rations. If that was what her husband was trying to do, he may have taken a wrong turn and ended up dead; it happens more often than one would like to admit.

It is strange being displaced. A person's life and all of its meaning comes down to the papers that say who you are. Every internally displaced person or refugee holds on to their papers for dear life: Only death would force them to relinquish them. They do so precisely to avoid Lubna's fate. Displaced in her own country as a result of violence, trapped in a strange town and in an incomprehensible level of poverty—not knowing anyone of importance who could help. And soldiers knew to expect the next question, one for which they again had no answers.

"Can you get me papers?"

How can you possibly say no to such a seemingly simple request? But soldiers can only make promises they can keep, and bad news never, ever gets good over time, you just have to say it.

"No, Lubna, we don't know how to get you papers or where to find them." She did not look disappointed at this; nothing could disappoint her any more.

In each and every encounter with displaced people, soldiers are constantly faced with the dilemma of what we can possibly do to help. On countless occasions, soldiers and officers have assisted Iraqis with their own money. It does help, and destitute people are glad to get anything free. But it is only temporary gratification; it does not fundamentally alter the situation they are in. And the fact is, there are so many that deserve assistance. Where do we begin and where do we stop? How do we pick between one miserable family and another? The depth and intensity of the misery can't help but make one humble.

It was like a pig oven inside her shack. There was no ventilation and it was steaming. One kerosene lamp always twinkled in a corner atop an empty five-gallon oilcan. This weird contraption consisted of an empty light bulb with thin metal straps tied around it to hold the wick and keep it steady.

A soldier sat in a corner, another in front of her, and the third adjacent to her, all sweating profusely; it dripped down onto their pants. We could occasionally hear the sounds of the individual drops. Sometimes the sweat hit a cigarette dangling from a lip and you heard a barely muttered "shit." The air was saturated with cigarette smoke, with the smell of burning kerosene, feces, rotten garbage, all of it baking in intense heat. The faint light of the tiny flickering flame made the constantly moving eyes of the three dirty kids sparkle from time to time. They were sitting in a corner, wide-eyed under matted hair and wearing tattered rags for clothes.

Lubna was sitting next to the lamp covered in a black gown that had turned brown from dirt, her face glistening with sweat, hair greasy and matted, her teeth a brownish black. Intermittently, she would, with visible effort, take a deep breath, hold her chest, and emit a deep gurgling noise. Her odd monotone voice had an otherworldly quality. She certainly appeared to be living in hell. Soldiers were tourists in this hell, traveling on a luxury vacation package. There was no comparison. If soldiers live, they will get their glass of bourbon, maybe find a woman, and perhaps try to live for the moment. Not so for her. They kept smoking in that steamy shack staring at her eyes; it was the eyes that made her distinctive and disturbing.

The eyes of the living have an unmistakable glow that one takes for granted. When living a lifetime in a second, some eyes move rapidly, some move slowly about in desperation, and some try in vain to scream while nothing comes out. In the case of a three-year-old girl caught in the blast wave of an al-Qaeda suicide attack, the eyes looked peaceful and full of life. As a soldier picked her up, she was delicate, alive with no apparent injuries. But one look at her eyes told you that the blast wave had destroyed her internal organs. The eyes were beautifully bright and wide. Then she slowly stuck her tiny tongue out, letting out a faint, almost inaudible cough. That was all she had in her, and it was over. Her eyes were still open but it was as if someone turned the lights down slowly inside. The shine went out.

Lubna's eyes resembled that little girl's after the shine was gone. It was the first time soldiers had seen the eyes of a dead woman still among the living.

Soldiers pulled their wallets out; they gave her some money and promised to come by again. Lubna had no pretensions of pride and she took the money. But the soldiers were hoping—because she seemed so out of place in this shithole, spoke English, and seemed to have her wits about her—that it would at least help her get in touch with some family members. They hoped the assistance would somehow alter her situation, not at the margins now but fundamentally.

Sometimes even the most jaded and cynical man wants to hope—that is, wants to be human.

Lubna did not give soldiers any meaningful tactical information because she had none. She was too busy surviving. But she did make them see things differently and helped them better understand. Walking out of her shack in the middle of the night, you saw the same distant intermittent burning fires, smoke, mounds, and silhouettes of people in the green haze. The silhouettes were people now, coming back to life: People with stories, just like Lubna.

Is it stories that make people, or people that make stories?

Soldiers continued to zigzag through the dump, stepping through shit-infested mud toward the expected ambush line a few miles down. Waiting for an ambush is a comforting feeling. The many little people recede and become silhouettes again, and soldiers just wait. It's a different time. Soldiers see comfortably again with clarity as life reverts to slow motion and presents itself in a series of continuous freeze frames. It is possible to find peace at the ambush line, much easier than trying to understand Lubna's vast private prison.

Just as she came to life, she was gone. One hopes that if she is dead that she died with all her kids, preferably a good quick death, even if violent. If she is alive, one would hope she has returned to some family member and not moved to a different version of the same hell. The greatest thing Lubna ever did was to point out that so many other women were living under similar circumstances. Women widowed, abandoned, and displaced from war, now living all alone and struggling to make ends meet while caring for their kids. They precariously navigate insurgent and counterinsurgent violence, militias, zealots, criminals, and a society filled with men who ascribe them a marginal place at best and prevent them from truly living. The fact that despite the odds they soldier on is the greatest testament to their spirit, but the Iraqi women will always remain the greatest casualty in this war.

Soldiers want to believe that if she's dead, Lubna died like a soldier, trying her best and fighting to the last breath. One can only hope: Sometimes one has to.

Sweet Tea and Konaffe: Good-Hearted Women

Where there are men there will inevitably be brothels, no matter the location or the religious piety of the region. After thirteen years of sanctions, after destitution and intense violence, Iraq was filled with displaced people—and yes, there are lot of prostitutes and a lot of brothels. There are stories of mothers letting their daughters sell themselves so the family could live.

These women, oddly, had a unique advantage within the counterinsurgency. Insurgents live a subversive existence, hiding amid the innocent. Yet there is another group that, by virtue of their profession and the nature of the society in which they live, has a similar subversive existence: Women of the Night.

Many Iraqis refuse to come terms with their existence. And, of course, at the mention of brothels by enlisted soldiers, people who are quick to prejudge will hop to the predictable conclusion. Alas, such absurdities reach new heights in Iraq. There are no brothels in Iraq. Of course not, it is a Muslim country!

Oh, really? Yet the Iraqi men always refer to them: *sharmuutha*. They may be Muslim, but everyone is human.

If there is a brothel in the neighborhood, soldiers need to find it. It is tactically important. Some Iraqi men readily agreed that they exist, but they just did not know the location. Of course, no one knows anything, ever. Fine, forget the hypocritical men, turn to the women the soldiers know and ask, where are the brothels? A chance bit of information from a woman, along with a soldier's hunch, led to the discovery of a brothel in the middle of a zealously Muslim, insurgent-controlled neighborhood. Of course, it did not exist, insisted the neighbors. But two other women—one a college student and the other a professional—disagreed.

It was a gray, nondescript two-story house that looked like any other: walls, metal gates, a little yard. Walking into this house was odd and strangely heartwarming. Women walking around with their hair flying all over the place, with coquettish movements and unabashed, excited laughter. It was the absence of any pretension to modesty, the essential honesty, that made the place wonderfully respectable. It is as if the women were unequivocally saying: Yes, this is what we do, and we are not hiding it—not inside this house, anyway—and you are welcome to the house.

The women would greet the soldiers with a smile, saying *Ahlan wa sahlan,* "My house is your house." Yes, the soldiers understood: *Ahlan wasahlan* takes on a whole new meaning in this house. The soldiers walk in with an answering smile, *Shlonak habibi,* "How are you, my dear?" and everyone shakes hands before sitting down.

It was perfectly normal and decent inside the house, in stark contrast to the world outside. There is a strange connection, it seems, between soldiers and whores—but not in the way the stereotypes might suggest. It was a quick realization: Soldiering and prostitution are the two oldest professions on the planet. Both have lasted from time immemorial. What is the connection? Perhaps it is their dispensability that makes both professions indispensable?

Both evoke the worst sentiments in people who would like to eradicate these two professions from the planet. Such people may have the best intentions, but perhaps they live in a dream world, a bit closer to heaven than the rest of us. Focusing on the imperfections of others is the wet dream of perfect hypocrites. Iraq takes this concept to an even higher level.

There were all the women in the house, chatting amiably, offering tea and sweets, saffron-colored Konafa. Perhaps a house specialty, or maybe it was part of the package; regardless, it always tasted very good.

The dampness of humidity and the mist of fried oil seemed to be stuck in every piece of fabric, especially the heavy blankets, piles and piles of them always neatly stacked. The first place soldiers secure after they clear a house is always the most comfortable corner, no matter how musty it smells. But not in this house: The blankets were a strangely ominous presence; the imagination of soldiers ran amok. No one said a word, it was instinctive, everyone knew they needed to stay away from those blankets.

So they were sitting on the straight-backed chairs as the women sat on the couch, giggling and smiling coquettishly at the American soldiers. Despite the irreverence of everyone concerned, the soldiers and the women, there was a strangely respectful sentiment inside the house, one set of professionals to another.

One constantly encounters sensible and sincere people in Iraq, but you always wonder whether they are telling the truth. Most of the time they don't; the search for the truth is maddening. Encountering prostitutes in a brothel who make no pretensions about who they are was always enlightening.

Some insurgents apparently die in search of virgins in heaven: Where women of the night do not command any premium, virgins are all the rage. But here is an unassuming house filled with available women. Of course, the insurgents in control are aware of its existence (and it is not the only one in the neighborhood). Some of the insurgent leaders and members were certainly patrons, but the prostitutes would not let on who they were—only acknowledging that "some of them occasionally stop by, some pay, others leave without paying."

Yet, looking at these women, you realize that it cannot be their looks or their sexual prowess that makes it possible for them to survive in their profession. Something else gave them credibility and made them formidable women of the night.

It is not the looks or the sexual prowess that comes at a premium. It is a whore's discretion that comes at a premium, their ability to keep secrets—the simple, the absurd and the absolutely perverted— that makes them who they are. How else could they function and survive in a world of hypocrites that deny their existence but cannot survive without them? It is the ability to guard secrets that is their singularly important professional strength, the singular element that engenders professional credibility. Sex is the job, but *secrecy* comes at a premium.

These women of the night would not provide actionable information, would not divulge their client list—not even for money, and never immediately; they were professionals. What they do have is gossip, neighborhood gossip about men: Who runs what, and how someone is related to someone else. Seeing no danger to themselves, and no tactical value—and that will all depend on how soldiers pose the questions, without interpreters—they tell stories and gossip about random people. And they were always more animated storytellers than most, at least to the soldiers. They had an intimate glimpse into a subversive reality that others did not.

For the soldiers sitting in this house, there was a palpable irony. The armed American soldiers remained the only men who went into the house at night, spoke to the women and impressed them with simple human decency and respect, and yet always disappointed them as men. That was the only strength the soldiers had, that they did not need them as women, only as decent people—a unique group who could tell them stories and from whom they could glean actionable intelligence.

And soldiers always had someone reliable to summon if they ever needed a man to step up to the moment. At the sight of him, most women (and men) tremble, and some even salivate. And yes, some women in this house would hold their breath as their hearts undoubtedly skipped a few beats: at the sight of Benjamin Franklin.

Soldiers needed them for their stories. Some became obsessed with listening to them, as they brought the neighborhood to life in a tantalizingly vivid manner. These women know the worst of all the men in the neighborhood. Maybe the good man Waylon Jennings was right when he said,

> Right or wrong a woman can own any man,
> She can take him inside her and hold his soul in her hand

Then leave him as weak and weary as a newborn child
Fighting to get his first breath and open his eyes.[22]

Well, soldiers guessed that some of these women had the souls of the worst of the men in the neighborhood in their hands. Soldiers will always have Benjamin Franklin to do the man's work. And maybe, over time, the women serving sweet tea and konaffe will also spread rumors and stories on behalf of the soldiers in the neighborhood.

_____

[22] "If You Could Touch Her At All," Waylon Jennings.

4

DISTANT VIEW OF A MINARET: RISKS AND SUBVERSION

> She turned her head to one side and stared up at the ceiling, where she noticed a spider's web. She told herself she'd have to get out the long broom and brush it down. . . . She stared up at her foot, that now pointed towards the spider's web, and noted her toe nails needed cutting.
>
> —"Distant View of a Minaret"[23]

Warda was a lively, wildly unpretentious, irreverent peasant girl, weathered beyond her age. The encounter with her was as unexpected as she was, when a squad of soldiers walked out of a pear orchard only to meet this Iraqi "cowgirl" standing in front of them. Now what?

The Irreverent Cowgirl: Warda

Three days earlier, on a hot humid night, the UH-60 Black Hawks had dropped them off in a muddy field in an insurgent-infested enclave. They had already had numerous direct fire engagements, cleared countless houses, and sent a mess of insurgents higher for further rigorous

---

[23] "Distant View of a Minaret," a short story by Alifa Riffat.

questioning. By now, they are unshaven, disheveled, fatigued, irritable from adrenaline while simultaneously "amped up" from enemy contact. Their ears ring; their noses and mouths are filled with the sweet caustic smell of cordite from too many C4 demo charges. All the faces are caked in sweat, dust, and mud; their pants, once covered in mud, have now dried, giving them the peculiar feel of paper maché. The water in the camelbacks is near boiling, and nothing is more disheartening than drinking hot water in the heat when you are fatigued. But the weather is not really so hot—only one hundred some degrees, and that's bearable, everything is bearable, sometimes even perversely charming. What really pisses you off is a cloud of annoying flies that follows you everywhere in the orchard. Alas, they are tiny, that's their strength.

And then there is the cowgirl.

You can't just leave her be. Who knows what the hell she is? Maybe she is a forward observer for insurgents or maybe she is just a peasant. How can you decide with any sense of certainty?

Everything in a counterinsurgency, in combat in general, is best assumed to be uncertain and significant, even the banal and the trivial. That is the only way not to get blindsided. The seemingly simple becomes complicated because nothing can ever be taken for granted, and it alters the way one operates. So it was with her.

What do we do? Do we leave her? Do we ignore her? We can't take her with us. This complicates matters and soldiers get aggravated. In combat, whether it's a raid, a mission, or a patrol, you are constantly making decisions with the limited information you have. There is no escape. Some sort of decision must always be made.

Warda's body is partially covered in a black gown, but not deliberately or purposefully, it's all over the place. Her headscarf is bright orange and lies on her shoulders. She does not look like she gives a shit. She is standing in an awkward pose, looking curious and amused and staring right at the Americans. Then she grins widely, raises her hand and waves at them. Perhaps she is happy that the soldiers seemed to have no intention of harming her; maybe she is just curious, naïve, and amused. Perhaps she is just human.

Soldiers motion her to come forward. She walks with a purposeful strut, hands swinging from side to side, her dress waving in the wind, her bright orange headscarf falling to her back. She looks the soldiers straight in the eyes, completely irreverent. She has none of the pretensions of modesty you find in most of the women in the cities. She walked up to the soldiers and greeted everyone, smiling all the while. Her intense black eyes don't shift about randomly, as with most other girls, but instead follow her will. She seemed completely aware of her surroundings.

She was about one hundred and ten pounds, five feet three inches, well-endowed with a wiry build, sharply defined features weathered beyond her teenage years. But it's her feet and hands that were defining. She had the strong fingers of a mountain climber, nimble yet feminine, with cracked nails that had rarely been cleaned. Her feet were the size of an average man, with star-clustered toes and numerous calluses. She appears to have never worn shoes, certainly not in her formative years. She appears to have been working the fields ever since she has been able to walk. And yet there was something that made her look truly unique, an aura about her that sank in and lasted. And there were no pretentious or ingratiating moments; she was confident as well as irreverent.

After the greetings she fired off a volley of nonstop questions:

"Ah, the Americans are here; are you here to kill insurgents? We have lot of them around here; I have not met any Americans before. Where are you going, when did you come here, and what are you doing in the orchard? There are no insurgents in there, only terrible pears, oh yes, there are some dates too. No one takes care of the orchard now, it is abandoned, even the house inside is empty . . . How long have you been in the orchard, why did you not come to the village? It is not a nice orchard."

At first, it seemed she was asking questions out of nervousness, but later we realized that's simply the way she was. Quickly scanning those nearest her, she broke into a laugh and asked, "Oh, did everyone fall in a canal? In the mud? How did you all manage to get in the canal?" This was, in fact, a question soldiers kept asking themselves. The bane of a soldier's existence: newly ploughed muddy fields surrounded by canals.

No one had a moment to respond. She kept firing questions as if she had just run into a bunch of long lost cousins, as if it was the most normal encounter in the world. To say it was utterly unexpected is an understatement; everyone had no choice but to laugh. But there was that one undisputable point: You can't let her go because no one knows who she is, yet you can't keep her because it limits mobility—so what in the hell do you do with this girl?

Soldiers follow common sense, a key principal in patrolling. (It will always be heartwarming when an upper echelon leader authorizes common sense.) It was decided that soldiers should locate her house—somewhere nearby, as she is running around the fields—take her there, secure it, and set up a new patrol base inside. Containing her was imperative. She looked like she couldn't keep her mouth shut in regard to either Americans or insurgents. Actually, no one could contain her, the only hope was to keep her occupied.

When you're fatigued and have been walking nonstop for three days with little to no sleep, an extra four hundred meters feels like four hundred clicks.

"Warda, where is your house at? We need to take you to your house; it's not safe out here for you."

"Oh," she exclaimed looking from one soldier to the other. Then she raised herself very straight, thrust her chest out, and clenched her hands on her hips. Her trademark pose.

"It's for your own safety, Warda," she was assured. "It is very dangerous to be out here."

"Oh, OK. My house is just across the canal that way," she pointed before offering another bit of information. "My father has met Americans before, but my sister no, my mother no, and my uncles all have met Americans before. OK, let's go to my house." She turned around and took a few steps as if she would gladly lead the way, strutting off ahead by herself.

A soldier quickly stopped her. "No, Warda, you tell us where your house is, OK? Tell us where it's at and we will walk you to your house. You walk in the middle of us—do you understand?"

"Oh," those curious eyes flared again.

"Warda, it's for your own safety, you know there are many insurgents around here, and it will not be good for you or your family to be seen with Americans."

"Oh, OK, no problem, let's go to my house."

This was done as much for the soldiers' own safety as for hers. The last thing anyone needs when they're a little over twelve hours from getting on a bird to the safety of a majestic base is to be led into a well-laid ambush by a peasant girl. Whether she would or not is beside the point, one must assume that she would. It's best that she is in the middle, so somebody can always keep an eye on her.

It's time to walk again: across the orchard, bordering the fields, crossing canals, through the mud, looking for her house. Warda was impressive. The soldiers were walking at a brisk pace while Warda grabbed a stick and swung it everywhere, her intense deliberate eyes focusing on all the gear, the fatigued faces of the soldiers. She kept up easily with the soldiers, as sure-footed as a mountain goat, her head constantly swiveling about.

They reached the house. It was big enough and at a relatively good tactical disposition. It was a spacious house for a peasant family, mainly because it wasn't theirs: The owners of the field and orchards had left for Syria. As sharecroppers, Warda and her family merely worked the fields. They had been asked to move in and keep an eye on things. Warda kept beaming at the sight of Americans in the house. Her father, his brother and mother, the mother's sisters (four of them), and a well-worn older grandmother—none of them shared Warda's enthusiasm. They had the more familiar look soldiers were used to: apprehensive, a bit scared, they generally wished the Americans would simply leave. And yet we couldn't.

The family had no choice in the matter and had to deal with us as best they could. Soldiers receive the wary welcome with a sense of inevitability: "Welcome, welcome, mister, this is my house."

You can hardly blame them for their apprehensions. For one, it is an inconvenience to the family. Also, given it is an insurgent-infested neighborhood, the knowledge that Americans were in the house for an extended period of time could be enough to get the family killed. No matter that they did not have a choice in the matter—most insurgents do not take that into account.

"Sir, we found Warda in the field. We wanted to bring her here and perhaps stay for a little bit."

Soldiers go through the rote actions of securing the house and setting up security around the perimeter. Some continue on the follow-on mission; the others, luckier, wait and relax, prepared to move on a moment's notice as the Quick Reaction Force. While some pull security, others are sprawled across the floor wrapped in blankets provided by the family, passed out from fatigue. This is the standard: Get some rest when you can because you never know when you will get a chance for the next nap. This is a strange sight for Iraqis. These are American soldiers, not getting in their face but staying in the shadows. Nor do the soldiers look as if they care; it is more as if they are in a dream world and have perhaps lost their way. Family members slowly begin to resume their daily chores, cooking and tending to the two cows in the back.[24] The two men in the house were sitting around watching TV and some soldiers joined them, while the rest slept on the floor, their gear within arm's reach as if this was a completely normal situation.

The two kids in the house were the first to warm up to the soldiers; they find soldiers an exotic and exciting curiosity. They run around,

---

[24] Whether to allow these tasks is a judgment call; one lets it happen depending on the level of hostility emanating from the household and as security allows.

hopping between the soldiers racked out on the rugs. Some soldiers make funny faces and offer to give them a ride on their backs: "Do you want a camel ride?"[25] It is usually more for soldiers' own entertainment than for the kids, acting like clowns and making fools of ourselves.

There is nothing more bizarre than the sight of a six-foot American soldier with red hair, on all fours, crawling around and snorting, while the Iraqi kids laugh hysterically. The men and women do not know what to make of it, except for two certainties: The soldiers look as if they have lost their minds, and they evidently mean no harm.

As this circus takes place in the background, everyone else maintains a watchful eye. One can never take things for granted, even when drinking chai and salivating over the meat the women are cooking in the kitchen. "Hey, check whether we can buy dinner here, that shit smells a lot better than the goddamn MREs."[26]

The men and women are evasive on the question of insurgents. "Yes, there are lots of them, it is a big problem, but we don't know anything."

That is the standard claim. However, there remains the obvious point that if every Iraqi were as detached and uninvolved as they claim, then there would not be an insurgency in Iraq. Each of us has our own prerogatives, of course: For soldiers it is to find the insurgents, for them it is simply to live and try to stay out of harm's way.

A soldier who was dehydrated and afraid of being a heat casualty decided to get an IV—a lactate ringer's solution—before heading out

---

[25] An Iraqi friend, a university student who read this section, e-mailed a pointed comment complete with laughing emoticons: "Oh you Americans still think that all Arabs are nomads, live in desert, use camels, don't know about other types of animals."

[26] Before each mission, everyone would promise themselves that they will not eat any diarrhea-inducing local food. There is no escaping our own stupidity, it always smells so awesome; after a few days, the aroma become unbearable, you are so hungry and you eat it. Only to regret it, as you defecate the entire digestive system, turn around and puke what was left of it, as you make a solemn promise, this is it, not again, I will not make this mistake again, yet you do it all over again a few days later.

on the next patrol. At this, Warda's curiosity reached an all-time high. She squatted next to the soldiers administering the IV, elbows on her thighs, palms cupping her face.

"What is that?"

"He is a doctor."

"Oh, you are a doctor." The volley of questions resumed.

Some soldiers sensed the most effective response: "Oh, Warda, you know you are very beautiful." This produced an infectious hysterical laugh, and she was visibly moved by the compliment, but not enough to dampen her insatiable curiosity.

But soldiers never lose sight of the ultimate job: "Warda, what about the insurgents here, have you ever been in trouble with them? Have you ever been in danger?"

"No," she responded indifferently, more interested in the radio a soldier was cleaning. "But surely you run around here, maybe you know where they live? Where they hide?" At this point, just to fix her wandering gaze, she was given an extra radio hand mike to look at.

"Warda, tell me, which houses do you stay away from in this neighborhood?"

Continuing her perusal she casually remarked, "People say the house over there, across the canal is where some bad people spend time. The farm over here, or that house near the orchard, some bad people maybe meet there too."

She was a precocious young girl who has spent her entire life in this neighborhood. She had an enviable grasp of the physical terrain and an intuitive understanding of what was happening around her—where she would be safe and where she would not. On a different day she could have been appointed an honorary fire support officer and she would have been very good at it.

Warda had actionable intelligence on possible insurgents' hideouts and locations of possible arms caches. Yet there was one problem.

There was no sense of direction in her description, at least not in the way soldiers were used to. No sense of cardinal directions, no aerial graphics. The way to figure it out would be to find common physical points of reference. We had to take her to the roof.

The rooftop provided a good vantage point. Using her house as the still point, the huge house to the north across the vast field and the orchard to the south across the canal were reference points Warda could easily understand and use. She explained in great detail where she would run around, where she would not, and the houses that she steered clear of because "bad men" and "people who get in trouble" are reputed to stay there. An immediate sign that this girl's information was credible was that some of the places and houses she described matched the target houses that soldiers had been to earlier; they were in their aerial graphics. This proved that she knew what she was talking about.

Also, and more reassuringly to the jaded and cynical grunts, this showed that despite the difficulties, our armed forces still manage to refine and improve their capacity to collect actionable intelligence against al-Qaeda and Jihadists in the furthest reaches. To be on the ground and have a random Iraqi girl tell us stories of insurgent safe houses, to follow her story using her landmarks and find out that half the places she is talking about match the Geographic Reference Grid (target list) is a moment that raises your morale. That is actionable intelligence from higher at its best.

With less than ten hours to go before the soldiers were to be picked up, they put Warda's new information out over the net, giving possible coordinates and descriptions of caches and insurgent hideouts. In the end, the few squads on the last follow-on missions did not catch any new insurgents based on her information. After three days of missions in the neighborhood, the insurgents had already scattered to new (and unknown) safe houses. But they did locate two arms caches, including a farmhouse with a buried weapons cache and a Vehicle Borne Improvised Explosive Device. They were all abandoned; it was clear the insurgents had left in a hurry. With a series of big, gratifying booms, the soldiers watched all of it go up in smoke. Oh Warda, sweet Warda, if you only knew how good you are.

It is that time of the day, past midnight. Warda has yet to flag in her enthusiasm and inexhaustible energy; everyone else is tired. The soldiers are eager to get to the PZ—the pick-up zone—while the family members are eager to get the soldiers out of the house. As soldiers were getting their gear ready,[27] Warda became curious about the Night Optical Devices (NODS). The thought that the soldiers could truly see at night was unfathomable to her. Yes, soldiers could indeed see at night—but it's a weird, green, video-game haze, and trying to navigate with night vision across fields and canals all night just means more time on their asses and faces than on their feet.

"Yes, Warda, we can see at night, come here, take a look."

This evoked the best laugh she had all day: Warda wearing a soldier's ACH (helmet), looking through the NODS and grinning from ear to ear, talking non-stop. It is a moment with American soldiers she would never forget. She had to show her mother, "Look, I can also see at night!"

Soldiers started cleaning up and tidying the house, collecting every bit of garbage they brought with them and putting it in their rucks. Some swept the place they slept in, others folded the blankets the family was kind enough to let them use—standard operating procedure for soldiers on every air assault mission all across Iraq. Of course, there is a tactical reason for collecting every bit of garbage. There is no reason to leave anything that could be of use to insurgents. But more than that, it is the decent thing to do, to clean up our own damn mess. After three sleepless nights and a number of firefights, the last thing soldiers want to do is clean up some Iraqi household. But it must be the rule, not the exception.

The family is visibly moved by the sight: American soldiers in all their gear, sweeping and cleaning up garbage. It may not win any hearts, but it makes damn sure that they recognize the soldiers are decent

---

[27] Taking accountability of sensitive items before the final movement, checking and double-checking the serial numbers of every little piece of equipment to make sure everything is accounted for. Accountability, accountability, and accountability: the ultimate watchword for every soldier. You lose it, you own it.

people. In the unlikely event that soldiers show up in the same neighborhood again, they will most likely be welcome. Leaders offer the family members some money for all their hospitality. They adamantly refuse, "No sir, it was our pleasure." You quickly learn how to overcome this hurdle of Arab hospitality: Give the money to the kids. Soldiers pull their wallets out—the wallets they are not supposed to carry with them on missions but invariably do. "Here, use it for school, buy some books. Here you go, Warda, buy some new clothes." The parents are always smiling, they are thankful. One by one soldiers move out, bidding farewell to the family and thanking them for their hospitality—never mind that they had no choice: They were decent enough. Warda was standing right in the middle, smiling, and one offered his hand. "Thank you, Warda, you are beautiful; Thank you for your help."

With a beaming smile she took his hand and shook it vigorously; everyone followed suit. About a hundred meters passed her house, walking through the field to the PZ and looking back, you could see the house through night vision. There was a faint light emanating from the house and you could see the silhouettes of the family members in the doorway. The faint figure of Warda was right in front, still looking at the soldiers even though they were passed the distance where she could see them.

Soldiers are at last in the PZ, waiting for the bird. They are almost home, but not quite, you never let down your guard because the insurgents are a bitch of a cunning bunch. Then comes the most anticipated magical noise on the planet. Not even a good-hearted woman's voice professing undying love sounds as sweet. Soldiers' hearts warm up and begin to beat faster with excitement. The deep thumps of an approaching Chinook CH-47 banking right to pick up the rest of the guys at the other PZ, and then the clunky rumble of three Black Hawks in their final approach. You resist the impulse to smile, you're not home yet and you're trying not to let your guard down at the last moment, but life is certainly beginning to fall into place.

Everyone sits on the door before lift-off, and then the rotors thump faster, the bird shakes in steady motion and your heartbeat gets in sync with the thump of the Black Hawk. All the noise is drowned out as one no longer hears but feels the noise—and it is sublime.

Sitting on the bird at night with legs dangling over Iraq at a hundred miles an hour is not a moment of celebration; instead it is happily serene. It is the sense of not having any responsibility that makes it so perfect. Every second and every minute of every day on a mission, the lowest to the highest level of soldier and leader walks with a burden of responsibility; the higher the rank, the bigger the responsibility and the heavier the burden. As men, soldiers may be imperfect, but during a mission, the decisions each one makes impacts the lives of all those around. Leaders have to live with those decisions, and they will take them to the grave.

The moment the bird lifts off, the heart feels lighter as the sense of responsibility eases. Soldiers have put their lives and responsibility in the hands of the Black Hawk pilot and the Black Hawk crew chief, sitting behind his machine gun. The wind hits the face. The fatigued guys on the bird all have the same distant stare and the same sentiment, powerful and peaceful. The feeling pervades the bird. Soldiers lucky enough to be in the corner get to lean their heads against the side, letting their minds wander aimlessly and looking forward to that bottle of ice-cold water they will grab the moment they land.

The Black Hawk keeps moving. Torrential wind is slapping at faces, trying to grab the tobacco wedged in the lower lip. Warda has receded as one of the many fleeting memories of this counterinsurgency. But she also left an indelible mark—so genuine, so unpretentious, and touchingly irreverent. How long will she be like that? You keep staring at the distance as you feel the thumps of the rotors in your gut, thinking about the twelve hours in transit before getting dropped off in a different place to do more of the same thing. But some ice cold water . . . man, that will taste so perfectly transcendent and heavenly.

The Black Hawk is in its final approach to the majestic base and soldiers see the many lights, blinking and lighting up the Disney World below. The birds came in almost as the sun was rising, just a little more than twelve hours before the next one was due.

After a twelve-hour break in this majestic base, soldiers will again be dropped into a different version of the same neighborhood, in a different part of Iraq. In transit, the mini-suburb of a base presents a transplanted and perverted version of America. The incongruity of everything inside the base is shocking, coming from the world that surrounds it. Next to no sleep, no proper food, dirty with mud and with the blood of a few critically wounded soldiers being evacuated; soldiers carry with them the rage of so many days. You walk into the dining facility with a single purpose: eat, get out, and get some sleep. You do not want to deal with any people. But that is almost always impossible.

It is both exciting and enraging.

Even though the majestic dining facility makes one salivate, it also makes you queasy and extremely angry. The grotesque lavishness of everything baffles the mind. "Who in the fuck thought of this ridiculous shit?" you wonder. It's supposed to be a war zone, but the food inside is better than any chow hall inside any army base in the United States. The myriad choices of food, piles and piles of it—and the place is even *decorated*. Indians, Sri Lankans, Pakistanis, Africans and Nepalis—men in crisp uniforms sheepishly serve the food, the cheesecake, a wide variety of pies, cookies, fucking ice cream, all of it piled sky high.

Then the soldiers notice the cheesecake-eating fat bodies sitting around, getting fatter, yapping incessantly. The worthless bastards who give the army—*us*—a bad name. You know they would be the first to call their congressman if someone took ice cream and cheesecake off the menu, never mind that the majority of them never leave the wire. You want to stuff an entire cheesecake down their throats and then drag them outside, put them in all your gear, and take them on a hike . . . what a dream. Jesus Christ, why would you be such a disgrace to the uniform?

The lavishness, the purposelessness, the general lack of testosterone that you smell in the chow hall—it's surprising and disgusting but, like everything else, you slowly get used to it. Perhaps it is the grunts who got off the bird that are strange.

There is no denying that the food looks gorgeous, and while soldiers criticize the ridiculousness of it, they pile it on with no sense of irony.

83

But it is not the aroma of food that strikes you, it's the *people*—their fresh deodorant, the body wash of the women, occasional whiffs of perfume that get lodged in your nostrils. Probably this is because soldiers smell like sewer rats,[28] alien bodies next to all the clean men and women in clean uniforms. The impulse is to eat and get out of this surreal place.

But just then, a leader who was dreaming and salivating about a cup of coffee moves to the coffee station and finds something far more perfect and astonishing. She looks so perfect holding the coffee creamer, pouring it carefully. The well-kept, delicate fingers make you feel envious and self conscious. Even in her off-putting army uniform, her red hair seems to glow, her curves look stunning. Yet strangely, it's her body wash that gets etched in your mind. A deep breath and ahhhhh, the smell of a woman.

And far more astonishing is the glance that tells you, "yes."

Now, again sitting in front of your food, arranging it as if with a purpose, you again battle all the rage. Now you really want to choke. You stuff down the food without enjoying it: The craving is to enjoy it manically and go absolutely insane, treat every second like it's the last and grab everything as if it's the last time—all the while agitated that every second you spend awake is a second of lost sleep. You eventually leave without being fully content; you never will be. You run back to the makeshift cot in the transit tent, back to the rest of the guys, away from that dream universe and back to the familiar one.

But her screams and moans will remain with you until they get drowned out by the noise of the rotors, and the sweet-salty-taste of her sweaty skin will remain until you start tasting your own sweat in a few hours. But that's later. For now, you crash next to the few guys who are still awake, and you have to put up with a volley of jeers.

"You did good, man, damn good work. You even eat??"

---

[28] NO soldier in Iraq can complain about lack of showers; we have colleagues in Afghanistan averaging no showers for fifteen to twenty days, and some of them had to go fifty-five days without a shower!

"Nope, but who gives a fuck? I could still be laying next to a woman right now, but no, here I am cuddling with you sick bastards."

Not to be outdone, another smart-ass pipes up, "Hey, don't try to lay next to me, I'll probably end up with some goddamn VD. And I don't want none of it—she looked the type too, better go see doc after the mission."

"Shit, come on, you know she wasn't that bad."

"What do you mean not that bad, who you kidding? This is Iraq motherfucker. All these Army women, if they can just breathe and be a woman in uniform they look like playmates."

Everyone is awake, there is no escape, and the charm of enlisted life is that even in one's moment of small triumph, someone will always bring you back to earth.

Yes, it is Iraq. Almost every American woman in uniform has more choice, in terms of who they want to sleep with, than they ever would again in their entire life. Yet precisely because of that, everyone understood: It was very well done, pulling it off covered in mud, smelling like a rat, looking like an animal, spontaneously and with no time to spare. That's saying a lot about this guy.

Lying down by the guys, he mumbles, "She smelled so good as she walked by, you know . . . you know, man, she smelled . . . she smelled just like a woman, you know?"

Everyone lies there with a half-grin and half-glazed nostalgic eyes, trying to remember the smell of a woman.

And then, inevitably: "Hey man, get the shit ready, the op-order is in half an hour, the birds will be here in three to four."

So it goes again, but you still want to lie there for a minute, to let the imagination have the best of the little time that is left. A luxury. Luxuries come at a premium, so the brain for a split second freezes with a grin, thinking of the red-headed stranger asking, "Can I sleep in your arms tonight," and wondering, "Will you remember me when the candlelight is gleaming?" But nostalgic dreams and imagining the smell of a woman will have to wait for another time.

"Hey, grab the shit! Let's move, let's go, let's go!" So it is, on to another Jihadi-infested theocratic enclave, away from the dream world of the majestic base to the real world on the ground in Iraq.

Women of Sand and Myrrh: Hamida Is a Woman[29]

Some women are absolutely stunning, and that beauty engenders a distinctive power that makes them formidable. Some women, comfortable in their beauty, are able to use this power astutely, making them even more breathtaking. Hamida was the most stunning woman the soldiers had met in Iraq.[30] Ahh, she even smelled amazing, none of the musty smell of cheap perfume to cover up lapses in bathing that tainted so many others.

Yet another mission in the heart of a Sunni Jihadist insurgent enclave. The soldiers had been in the neighborhood for a while. Since they got off the bird there had been a number of direct fire engagements, mainly random firefights, nothing of import. But they had been clearing houses, detaining insurgents, sending them higher, using demo-charges to breach countless doors. When they walked into this house around eight in the morning, they were already expected.

It was an affluent house with a lot of men, women, and kids. All the men and boys were gathered in the living room and were already being interrogated by some high-speed people—professionals at one of the three-letter agencies out of Washington that soldiers had accompanied on the mission. Grunts and their leaders left them alone to do their high-speed work and moved to the back of the house.

"Let us find some food, maybe get some tea, hey! Where are all the women in this house at?"

---

[29] *Women of Sand and Myrrh*, a novel by the Lebanese author Hannan al-Shaykh.

[30] It took a lot of deliberation, weighing multiple stories and a whole lot of bourbon, to come to this rational consensus about Hamida.

All the women were in a bedroom. Four older women and a menacing looking grandma stood in a row, shielding the three younger girls in back. The older ones were dressed completely in black, their faces uncovered. The three young girls had their faces covered. You could tell by looking at their eyes that two were teenagers and one of them was considerably older, in her mid-twenties perhaps. The younger two had eyes that darted in all directions but generally kept to the floor—standard procedure. The older girl wore a tightly wrapped black gown that traced a well-endowed figure, and a red veil covering her face; she was clearly staring right at one of the solders, apparently even smiling behind the veil.

The soldier was staring right back at her, past the four women and the grandma (the impenetrable shield). In the background, far off, one could hear intermittent gunfire and explosions. Suddenly, in a swift but delicate movement, Hamida reached up to the veil covering her face. With deliberate control she slowly—one might even say seductively— pulled down the veil, revealing her face and her smile.

She was stunning, and she knew it.

Her gesture was so incredibly unexpected that the soldiers' jaws literally dropped and they lost all sense of tact and subtlety. Hamida's smile grew even bigger: yep, she had 'em. Seeing the soldiers' faces, the older women sensed something amiss and whirled around to look at their daughters. Yet in that split second, Hamida managed to cover her face completely and return her gaze to the ground like the other girls. Holy shit, what a facility for situational awareness.

The older women were at a loss. As they turned back to look at the soldiers, Hamida raised her head and again pulled down her veil to reveal that enormous, beautiful smile. This time the soldiers were smarter: They stayed put, looking unperturbed. They gathered from Hamida's gestures and smile that she understood English and asked her whether she did. Hamida now covered her gorgeous smiling face, and nodded: She did indeed speak English.

A quick tactical decision had to be made. This is as critical a point of decision as it ever gets: A gorgeous woman that speaks English. How in the hell do we get these older women out of the room without pissing them off or making them nervous? Drawing on all their combined tactical acumen and combat experience, the soldiers made a decision.

"Look, leave two guys here to pull guard outside. No one can go in or out, especially those three-letter civilian cats in the front of the house. Everybody else go find cabinets and closets that are locked." Then we get the older women to open them; they invariably have the keys or know where to find them.

The soldiers leave the room, then come back to explain the situation to the women. "Look, we'll leave two soldiers outside the room, as our job requires, and your daughters can stay inside the room, where they are safe. We'll make sure no soldiers go into the room without your presence."

The soldiers pull out chairs and two of them sit outside, out of sight of the girls.

"Madam, we in no way mean any harm to you, your daughters or anyone in your family, everyone will be safe with us." That's all you can say, and it must be stated with conviction.

"You have to find the keys, show us everything in the house, and open every closet because we don't want to break them, it will serve no purpose. Please, please do it for us." The women nod their heads vigorously; they buy it. A bunch of soldiers are assigned to go with the older women and keep them busy for as long as possible. Two others are sitting outside the room, out of sight of the girls inside. As the older women waddle out to their spacious kitchen, some soldiers sneak back into the room with the girls. Over the secure net on their own channel, they demand: "Hey, make sure you keep all the women together in one place and tell us if they're coming this way."

Two soldiers outside the room keep a look out for the high-speed civilians in the front of the house.

As the others walk in, Hamida is laughing genuinely; she has none of the apprehensions of the two teenage girls, whose eyes keep darting about. The soldiers ask whether they can sit down, cautiously grab some chairs and place them in a corner as far away as possible, just to make sure the girls are not worried. It is imperative to show that they are treated with respect, that their personal space is not crossed, and that soldiers understand their need to display the requisite modesty. After all, one can still hear intermittent firing and explosions in the distance.

The smiles of girls can never be confused as a typically "normal" interaction; it never is, not as long as one side is armed with a weapon and wearing a uniform.

Hamida sat down on the corner of the bed, motioning the other girls to sit down. She was visibly relaxed. Her veil was completely pulled down, her hair partially revealed, and she knew that the gaze of every soldier was on her. She was running the show and she knew it, comfortable in her own element. Soldiers have ceased to be seen as a threat. If a soldier manages to overcome that perception and establish that they are not a threat unless they have to be, an encounter can begin to have some semblance of meaning.

No one ever found out why Hamida pulled her veil down and defied her mother, aunts, and grandmother. Perhaps she was just being mischievous. Perhaps she wanted to talk to the soldiers—or perhaps she took pleasure in being defiant and subversive of the strict cultural norms.

Or perhaps it was something much more elemental and human.

She was sitting with most of her brown hair revealed, holding the black gown wrapped around her well-endowed figure nonchalantly, yet with perfectly dignified comportment. With her sensually accented English, the deliberate movements of her hands and body, she knew what she was doing; she could feel the eyes of the soldiers.

She said she was pleased to talk to the soldiers, but she had not had the opportunity before and had only seen them in passing. She learned English in school, at Baghdad University, which she attended while living at a relative's house in Baghdad. After the invasion she stopped going. Her parents do not want her to go anymore. She was upset and angry at this turn of events. She wanted to finish her degree and eventually work in the government.

"The government"—that's strange, one rarely hears that. Everyone complains about it, and a lot of men want to work in the government, but a woman?

At least, that had been her plan before things went sour.

"Well, Hamida, you speak English, why don't you work for the Americans? They'll pay you well too."

"Huh? No, I don't want to work for Americans, besides my parents will never let me, and it is not safe, the insurgents will kill my family. I just wanted to work in the government." Her grandfather, her father, even her mother at one time, they had all worked in the government.

"Are you serious, your *mother* worked in the government?" She did not fit the soldiers' conception of what a civil servant looked like: covered head to toe and trying to bar her daughter from talking to the soldiers. Jesus, she looks like she was present at the creation. A civil servant, are you serious?

"Yes, she used to work for the education ministry, then at the culture ministry, but not now. . . . " Obviously, she is out of a job. Many of her family members had worked in the government, and even studied abroad. One recognizes that Hamida may be living in a provincial town, but she is from a family of professionals and she shares those aspirations. "Yes, my family used to have a house in Baghdad, some relatives used to live there, I think it is abandoned now, some other people live there. The situation is terrible."

Soon enough, the soldiers got advance warning: The others had reached the limits of their imaginative capabilities. The women were on the way to the room—but they were now relaxed and laughing; even the menacing grandmother no longer had the evil stare of before. They seem to be laughing at the soldiers' ability to make fun of themselves, goofing around and acting like clowns. What to make of these soldiers? The situation was very different from an hour ago; soldiers are still a nuisance in the house but are no longer seen as a threat. One woman offered to make some tea for the soldiers. "Yes, we would love some tea actually, it sounds great," but the soldiers really needed to get out of the room. It was too hot and stuffy.

In this affluent house, there were a number of rooms that served as living rooms, each one with a TV and satellite connection. Soldiers decided to ask that the women move to one of the spacious living rooms, well out of the sight of the men—both the Iraqis and the American three-letter guys who occupied the front of the house, interviewing the men. It was time for the soldiers to have some tea and enjoy the company of Hamida. The generator was running, one woman was making tea, and the rest of them, including Hamida, moved to a spacious room with many seats, couches and chairs. Soldiers sat in the straight-backed chairs, making certain that the women sat on the more comfortable couches, that they were relaxed enough to move around without any fear. The soldiers have traveled many miles from an hour and a half ago.

Everyone was comfortable in the living room and the TV was on. Soldiers requested they turn it to a music channel, with Lebanese and Egyptian music videos. The last thing anyone wanted to watch was the news or anything else serious. But there was also another reason, a trick soldiers had learned early in the deployment. How do you get to talk to women, and how do you get on the good side of young Iraqi girls? Start talking about popular Middle Eastern singers.

It was an eleven-year-old Iraqi girl who taught the soldiers that trick. During a conversation when asked what she wanted to be, her answer was that she wanted to be like "Elissa."

"Hmm, interesting, who the hell is Elissa?"

Well, we were happy to find out who she was and watch her music videos with the interpreters. She certainly has a nice voice, but it was her scanty costume, skin-tight leather pants and gyrating nubile body that really piqued the soldiers' interest. But the insight was, of course, more valuable than just appreciating Elissa's tantalizing endowments.

Just as soldiers are pleased when Iraqis ask probing questions about America and about issues relating to American pop culture, Iraqis are pleased when soldiers ask about bits of Iraqi history or about famous stars that they admire. It provides a basis for conversation—and the Iraqis are surprised and impressed that soldiers actually know about them. Every Iraqi girl and boy has their favorites: asking about them— Elissa, Laura Khalil, Cheb Mami, Mustafa Amer, Amer Dyab, Hani Shaker or Kazem al Zaher—is always a way into a great conversation. Some affluent Iraqis even listen to, and made soldiers listen to, Algerian/ French Rai singers—Cheb Khaled, Cheb Mami, Faudel, Rachid Taha— and some even listen to the Turkish pop singer Tarkan. Soldiers were told, "You should listen, oh you should, they have some goood tuuunes." And they certainly did. A sullen-looking older Iraqi man or woman would often lighten up at the mention of Fairuze and Um-Khalthum. Fairuze, a seventy-year-old Lebanese singer, may be long past her glory days but is apparently one of the most admired and listened to singers in the entire Middle East. As for Um-Khalthum, she seems to be in a pantheon of her own: She seems to have a near magical effect on many an Iraqi patriarch. In a way, we owe all of them!

So it was, playing music videos and asking about the Middle Eastern singers in Hamida's house. Each soldier trying to outsmart the others, making Hamida the center of their world. Hamida, being Hamida, enjoyed the moment and played them like a musical genius. She was obviously impressed with the soldiers' knowledge of Middle Eastern pop culture. Everyone was drinking tea, having a chat, and even the older women chimed in occasionally with laughter as some soldiers decided to reenact some music videos right there in the room.

Hamida's mother, the former culture ministry worker, could speak English haltingly, and she began to explain her time in the government. The old days were not always good, she said, but they were better than the situation now. For this family at least, the older days were certainly better: They were a family of senior Baathist bureaucrats since the beginning of the Baath party, since the time of its formation. That explains the wealth and the affluence, the many houses in Baghdad, the farmhouses, and this palace in their home town.

Just then, two young boys snooped around the room: These were clearly spies, sent by the men to watch the women. Soldiers politely ask them to come and sit down—and now soldiers have positive control of them. They cannot return to their fathers, uncles, and the high-speed Americans at command central in the front living room. Contain the flow of information and you retain a tactical advantage.

A soldier keeping an eye on the hallway said, "Hey, one of the three-letter guys is snooping around."

"Hell mother fucking no, that fucker is not coming in here!"

"Well, it looks like he's coming this way."

Another point of decision, because technically he has all the authority and power, but in reality, soldiers do not like these three guys they had to accompany—annoying know-it-all pricks. So they resorted to a more common-sense approach that noncommissioned officers and young leaders—the good ones—eventually master to avert precisely these kinds of situations.

Yes, these three cats may have all the power and authority, but it is the leaders and their soldiers that control the context. The cats will strut, but they are prisoners of this context. They are inside a bubble soldiers create, and they can be as powerful as they want inside the bubble. It is the same trick some soldiers used when they were unfortunate enough to escort embedded reporters.

A digression. Of course, many reporters are good people, and some of them (though not all) bravely take enormous risks. But they are also living a vicarious experience free of charge, with better pay and infinitely more choice. They never have to carry the burden of decision or the responsibility for men who look to them for guidance. At the point of decision, the objectives diverge: The reporters will always be careful observers, looking for truth, and never active participants.

The best of our journalists are fully aware of this perpetual grunt sentiment and can navigate their peculiar situation astutely. Which makes it twice as hard—because their bullshit trackers are very good.

This mission, however, was particularly bad.

Among all the people soldiers have had to work with and learn from, there were many brilliant people from three-letter agencies (and other high-speed agencies and organizations) that served as inspiring examples. But this mission had been assigned the worst of the bunch. They had to be dealt with accordingly.

The leader stands up. "Hell no. You and you—go out there and keep him busy, take him to the other side, show him the cupboard full of books and some random shit, you know—something that will get him excited. None of 'em speak a lick of Arabic, just keep the retards excited."

Two soldiers quickly step up and out. "Hey, stay on the radio, use this channel, alright?"

Yeah got it, we're tracking.

"Hey, don't let us down, be fucking smart."

"No man, we got this shit."

Situational awareness and maintaining control of all moving parts at all times is critical. The reason was simple just now. Soldiers have built a rapport with these family members. They might be able to provide some tactically valuable information to conduct follow-on missions. But there are some men, like these three cats, who believe that the Iraqis are as impressed with them as they are themselves—and the shit does not work that way. If they come into the room and start throwing their power and authority around, regurgitating tired anecdotes and slogans about our magnanimity with that condescending tone (no matter whether or not they are true), the opportunity will be lost. It is best to keep them on a tight leash.

As Hamida seemed comfortable, the conversation now turned to the most important and pressing topic that soldiers had been gradually working toward: the insurgents in the neighborhood. She was precise and to the point.

"I don't know much, but I will tell you what I know."

Her mother and aunts were visibly uncomfortable and suggested that Hamida cool it. Hamida turned to them with a defiant stare and nearly snapped at them: "No mother, let me talk to them about the insurgents; I want to tell them what I know."

Oh, what a woman!

Hamida explained the many killings in the neighborhood, the specific vehicles insurgents were using, how some insurgents had come from outside, how they killed some innocent people for collaborating with the government, the houses where victims of insurgent violence live, which houses the insurgents frequent—everything in precise detail, using her house as a point of reference. She did not know as much as she would have liked because the situation was difficult and she was not even allowed to go outside the house alone. She always had to walk with a couple of older women or with her father. She was decidedly angry about how her freedoms were circumscribed. She talked and the soldiers listened, for perhaps two hours; she talked and talked, and she drew places and directions on one soldier's green all-weather notebook.

Then the radio crackled—the sound was dreadful and heartbreaking, for every second spent with Hamida was worth a million others the soldiers had spent in Iraq. As the soldiers left, they thanked the women, including Hamida. One soldier said to Hamida's mother—but really trying to ingratiate himself with that stunning creature herself—"You have an incredible daughter; you should be proud of her."

She smiled, "Yes," and looked pleased—not at the compliment, let's not kid ourselves, but at the thought that the soldiers were finally getting the hell out of the house. Another soldier, always trying to capture the moment as a clown, blew a kiss directed at all the women: "Thank you, for everything, the tea, the bread, the company, hey we are going to miss you." Another soldier grabbed his heart, imitating being struck, staggered back and forth on buckling knees, and collapsed on his buddy, giving him a big hug, to all-around laughter.

"Ooooh I am in love—ohhh Habibi, bahebbak."

Even the women were laughing, especially the menacing grand-mother; either she found it truly funny (a remarkable breakthrough of cosmic proportions), or she was so happy to be rid of the soldiers that she could not help laughing. Most likely a mixture of both. They were perhaps all wondering, are these soldiers really supposed to kill insurgents? They act like bunch of clowns who have lost their way.

Hamida was standing bidding goodbye, poised as always with a smile, all her actions deliberately subtle. A soldier walked a little closer to Hamida, looked back at the other women, and then, staring straight at her, proclaimed loudly so everyone could hear, "Hamida, thank you, thank you, for your help. Good luck with everything and please be safe, maybe you will work for the government and we will see you on TV?"

She had a smile, but she was not moved by the compliment. She was a woman who knew exactly what she had and she was not about to be moved by the pathetic flattery of a soldier. But one must try nonethe-less. She raised her hand slightly, a deliberately subtle wave, with a smile, and wished the soldiers good luck "killing insurgents." Soldiers, responded with laughter, "Yes, Hamida, we'll kill some insurgents and we'll do it just for you."

Then Hamida raised her hand further, and with a slow deliberate slic-ing motion of her hand—a wonderfully chilling gesture—she said, "You should kill them, one. . .by. . ..one. Yes—*one by one.*"

At that moment, you wanted to stay longer, to hear more of her story. She looked just as gorgeous, but now her honey-colored eyes had no smile. They gave the impression that if soldiers had given her some insurgents and a weapon she would have personally laid waste to them herself, "one . . . by . . . one"—and enjoyed it.

On the third and final day of the mission, taking a circuitous route, soldiers were utterly exhausted when they came up upon a large abandoned farmhouse across a canal. After a few hours' rest, one of them walked past some nearby mounds, covered with palm reeds. He turned back to check it out, commenting, "Dude, something is fishy here"—and stumbled upon one of the largest arms caches they had yet found.

The blessing of an arms cache is that you have done your job right, but the curse of it is, if you follow the book, it creates a nightmarish situation of paperwork, following a logical process promulgated by someone who, however well intentioned, has never spent time on the ground. This is how the army at times manages to screw up the best of wet dreams with mountains of paperwork. That cache created a lot of laughter: It contained thousands of rounds of heavy caliber ammunition and crates of mortar rounds—all clearly labeled as the property of the Armed Forces of one of our closest allies. Shipped, the soldiers hopefully assumed, during a much earlier time when Saddam used to be a friend.

Another digression: This find was nothing compared to another cache that one of our most respected enlisted leaders found. It was so huge that, in addition to everything else, it had "Made in USA" anti-tank weapons of the kind that we still use. It was so large that, at the point of detonation, a river next to it actually *changed its path* momentarily. Soldiers had to be about four clicks out, just to be away from the blast wave—it was that big. This one was nowhere near as big as that, but it was big enough.

With only a few hours left before getting on the bird, soldiers collected all the explosives and stacked them in the farmhouse abandoned by the insurgents. A soldier hopped over and pulled out the all-weather notebook with Hamida's handwriting and pointed out that this was one of the houses by the canal she had mentioned, with everything drawn in precise detail. Through night vision you could see the house balloon to twice its size; then it imploded in a cloud of dust with plumes of smoke over thirty feet high and multi-colored fireworks exploding. The loud boom and the concussion wave warmed the heart. Everyone grabbed their stuff, stepped out in the night through the fields on a strut towards the PZ, thinking: almost home but not quite yet, and time to get on a bird again.

The Answer Is No: Aminah[31]

> It is often said that Heav'n has no rage like love to
> hatred turn'd,
> Nor Hell a fury, like a woman scorn'd.[32]

Maybe, but the real genius of some formidable women is not their fury, but their capacity to create a living hell—and make you like it.

A bunch of infantrymen were walking through an insurgent stronghold in the middle of a pitched battle that had raged for a while, with heavy-caliber machine gun fire, explosions, and Apaches firing, as the soldiers on the ground had requested. A soldier in the alley raised his M4 Carbine and followed an insurgent that popped up on a roof, using his laser and night vision; the insurgent fell down a lifeless silhouette, then another and another.

To the right of the soldier stood a woman, Aminah—and it was not the first night she had stood like this.

It is hard to pinpoint why some people get the strange urge to crucify their minds, make them go numb, and allow themselves to be utterly dispensable. Aminah straightened herself, grabbed her long black abaya, and started walking at a brisk pace, side by side with the soldiers, through a known insurgent stronghold. Rounds pinged off next to her feet as she kept moving without missing a step.

By any account she was an average woman, a middle-aged mother of three living in a modest house and working a series of modest jobs. She had one version of her story; the soldiers believed—and eventually learned—a different version.

In her eyes, since the U.S. invasion, she had witnessed her neighborhood transformed into the fiefdom of zealots, mafiosos, and politically affiliated local gangsters, now turned public figures. They used violence to consolidate their power in the name of the people while invoking the security of the people they terrorize.

---

[31] "The Answer is No," a short story by Naguib Mahfouz.
[32] "Mourning Bride," by William Congreve (1697).

She has no soft spot for Americans either, as she has had to navigate violence from all sides. But—lucky for us—in this neighborhood most of it was perpetrated by insurgents.

She had a fair complexion and a friendly, maternal expression. But at the mention of insurgents, her calm voice rose an octave and her warm gaze turned to ice. It made one imagine the painful secrets she must have hidden in her heart. Perhaps she had been abused and raped by the men seeking control. Everyone in Iraq, soldiers and Iraqis, has enough ghosts to haunt a good-sized American suburb.

Motives are important yet difficult, if not impossible, to assess. An Iraqi willing to help comes across to soldiers as a hoax, a trick; you wonder about the true motive. Yet that is the wrong question to ask. What matters is not her motive, but whether her information is credible and whether she will keep her word. It is a mutual bluff; both she and the soldiers can call it. If her information is credible and if she takes the risks, the hell with the wider motive; soldiers take the necessary risk and follow through.

Digression. In battles, following through at the point of decision without taking prisoners may result in civilian casualties, and may even get one in trouble. Yet the concern for civilian life cannot be a blanket excuse for not taking drastic action when necessary. It only means the significant recognition that we may be mistaken, that the application of violence may cause the avoidable suffering of the innocent, and we must have the utmost sense of humility—and responsibility—about our destructive capacity. This concern is captured as an operational concept in our rules of engagement: "the selective and proportional use of force."

Risks in battles are never equally shared. "When things go wrong, shit always rolls downhill" is a longstanding maxim of grunts and inevitably true. But for soldiers and leaders on the ground, that challenge is worth the risk in a counterinsurgency. To refuse to take risks is to be in the wrong job.

But the soldiers' risk is minor in comparison to when a civilian risks everything—especially a woman in an oppressive atmosphere. Aminah, and some others like her, rose to the occasion by risking everything at a time when most men and women would tremble at the thought of violence, hoping someone else will take care of it.

Afterwards she always thanked the soldiers and said she appreciated their efforts. There is nothing one could say, it is understood, the respect is earned; soldiers keep walking, constantly scanning the sector at night in their walk back home.

But what must have been a matter of towering importance, even if unstated, was Aminah's confidence that this particular group of soldiers would invariably follow through on their promise to lay waste to the insurgents. She was quite sure that this demented crew would do things others would not—that they would go places others refused to go and would relish the opportunity of fighting these men who reigned unchecked. With these soldiers, it was not all talk, she was certain: If she led them in the right direction, hypothetically speaking, she trusted them to be her fire and her sword.

Perhaps it was her response to the situation of a woman living in the shadow of men, forced to use her leverage with the utmost subtlety, the power of the seemingly powerless. Whatever the motivation, some remarkable women produced useful sources of actionable intelligence in this counterinsurgency. Motivations are never the guide, only the validity of the information and whether it is worth the risks. The caveat is that, just by being American, soldiers create unrealistic expectations in people; while some Iraqi women, by virtue of their peculiar situation, can be—well, breathtakingly manipulative. Soldiers see it on the ground and it ceases to become an abstract concept. It means soldiers always have to be responsible, have to recognize our imperfections and limitations and make only the promises we can keep while keeping the promises we make. Credibility on the street inevitably begets more credibility, and that is absolutely critical in waging a successful counterinsurgency.

PART III

INTO THE LABYRINTH: UNDERSTANDING INSURGENCY ON THE GROUND

Soldiers walking into a new neighborhood are supposed to secure, protect, get control of, and win the support of the population.

You got it boss, no problem, do you take sugar with your coffee or are you sweet enough?—Wait a goddamn minute!

Insurgents actually have control of the neighborhood, and the question arises: *How* do insurgents control a neighborhood? How does it transpire on the ground?

Gradually we came to understand intimately the reality of insurgent control on the ground. But as we came to terms with the insurgency on the ground, we were also presented with another puzzle. It is not *one* insurgency that we were fighting in Iraq, but *multiple* insurgencies.

Understanding the broader issues is not the concern of soldiers on the ground. They are assigned to fight the little fights on the ground while the smarter and more perfect people fight the big ones. Nevertheless, understanding the broader themes, at grunt level, always made it easier to make sense of events on the ground, and even made it easier to fight the fight.

5

THE HARAFISH:
METHOD BEHIND THE
INSURGENT MADNESS

> In the passionate dark of dawn, on the path between
> death and life, within view of the watchful stars and
> within earshot of the beautiful, obscure anthems, a
> voice told of the trials and joys promised to our alley.
>
> —*The Harafish*[33]

Becoming inured to the death of the innocent works to trivialize a horrible occurrence. The first death, and the second, *those* deaths have an impact—and then all the others merge into an abstract collage. You slowly begin to take these atrocities for granted.

The sight of the man lying in the gutter, hog-tied and tortured, appears to be without reason. The unrelenting heat makes his stubby face move in death; his skin feels warm and profusely sweaty. He seems determined to stare at the blistering sun with his dilated pupils, frozen in an unwavering gaze. There is no sense of shock: You merely shake your head with an unconscious grin. Damn, why this guy? Because no matter how everyday it becomes, the violent death of the innocent is never completely without reason.

---

[33] *The Harafish*, a novel by Naguib Mahfouz.

103

The surroundings slowly begin to come to life with people, their glances and their intermittent stares. The rustling steps of people pass the gutter, some of them trying not to look, each face a mask of terror or anxiety. The eyes and the hurried steps belie the pretence of indifference of innocent people living through an insurgency.

Soldiers idle around the gutter, casually chewing tobacco, talking about matters far removed, yet always on alert as they constantly switch their attention between the man in the gutter and the rustling steps of people. It is another desperate attempt to find some semblance of coherence and logic, trying to discover the method behind the madness on the ground.

Method in the Madness: Insurgent Strategy on the Ground

Insurgents achieve control of the population with the *support* of a minority and the *complicity* of a majority. To do this they use violence, both against the legitimate authority that they try to undermine and against the very population that they seek to control. The best of the insurgents may try to engender positive support through positive actions: delivering services or providing protection—or just promises, depending on the resources at hand. But such positive support only goes to consolidate the control that they have achieved on the ground through violence.[34] Yes, belief in a creed, ideology, traditional loyalties and kinship ties, all these factors sometimes help insurgents embed themselves in the society and gain control. But in our experience and understanding, no matter how deeply embedded in the society, it is the insurgent application of violence that plays the defining role in getting complicity of the people—the initial foothold—and in their eventual expansion of control on the ground.

---

[34] Important things are always simple, and simple things are always hard: Murphy's Laws of Combat. Insurgent strategy, while simple, is influenced by many other facts on the ground: level of popular support, military prowess of the insurgents and of their adversary, level of external support, and the nature of the political system, among other factors. These factors influence the means to achieve the end, but they do not alter the objective of control.

If we assume away for a moment all the other elements—beliefs, ideologies, kinship, and everything else that can be instrumental in assisting insurgents get control—we can see the *defining role of violence in insurgent strategy* on the ground. This assertion is rooted in the experience and observations of foot soldiers who ate the dirt on the ground—who flew into Jihadi enclaves in Iraq, who fought a deeply embedded and ideological driven Shia insurgency in an urban setting, and who fought (and continue to fight) the Taliban in Afghanistan. Sunni Jihadists, Shia militants, Taliban in Afghanistan—all of them have some support of core believers, as well as many who support them for reasons of their own.

But insurgents get the complicity of the indifferent majority by relying on intimidation and violence, as the preferred method of getting the "initial foothold"—and in some cases as the exclusive and ongoing means of control (e.g., Taliban in Afghanistan and numerous Jihadi groups in Iraq).

❖ People, power, control, and the nature of violence

In the context of an insurgency centered on a population, with competing claims for control by both insurgents and counterinsurgents, *power* is an empty idea. *Control* is the element that defines military power and gives it meaning, but control is a choice that *people* make.

Yes, people are center stage—always. *People* are the prize in this battle.

Complicity and *support* are two ways that people make the choice to be subjected to someone's control. And once soldiers recognize this reality, they can see it everywhere, they see how it transpires on the ground. It is deceptively easy to see the people as mere observers or victims of violence. But being victims of violence does not mean they are robbed of their choices; their choices merely become limited and precarious.

Insurgents and counterinsurgents constantly subject each other to multiple, contesting forms of violence. But insurgents also subject *people* to multiple forms of violence and intimidation. People are forced to navigate astutely around these forms of violence. The contesting claims of insurgents and counterinsurgents create a context that forces people to make choices and to become active agents of change. When people have a choice, however limited, power does not translate automatically into control on the ground for insurgents (or counterinsurgents). Showing up in a neighborhood with a gun in your hand means nothing: what you do with it, when and how you do it and how people react gives the moment its meaning.

The ideas of power, control support, and complicity are closely related operational concepts.

Power is the concept that represents the authority or the capacity to lay claim, make proclamations, give orders, and to change things on the ground. Power lays claim to control. Without control, it is an idea without substance.

Control is the ability to change and manipulate events on the ground. Only when power manifests itself in terms of control can a leader realize the objectives. Control comes only as long as people relinquish it because control is ultimately a choice people make.

People may choose to subject themselves to someone else's control either willingly, out of *support*, or unwillingly, by becoming *complicit*. But even in its most elemental moment—a guy staring down the muzzle of an M4 Carbine or an AK-47, licking and tasting its metal (power)—control still allows a stark choice: to subject himself to control or to refuse. Everyone in that dire situation inevitably chooses one way or the other. A few people always resist. To assume that *everyone* will meekly obey would be to deny the essence of the human spirit and ignore the history of our species. People do resist at the most unexpected moments. And when people resist, even for fleeting moments, they make power an idea without traction. At the moment of resistance, the one who claims power with a weapon down someone else's throat now has his own decision to make: Will he follow through? If he does—as is sometimes necessary—the transient moment of control and power encounters a void. No one can control a dead man! There is no control and power without people: Control is a choice people make, and control, even at its most elemental, is allowed only when a person relinquishes it.

❖ Precarious and limited choices

In an insurgency centered on people, control is not usually a choice of life or death, but only about life—how to get a sufficient number of people to make favorable decisions to your side. No one has the capability to have a muzzle on everyone's throat all the time. People have considerable choice even in an insurgency. But they constantly live on the edge, making difficult decisions every day as they navigate multiple forms of violence and claims for control.

The people occupy the frontier—the ambiguous space where the intense and bloody competition for control takes place between insurgents and counterinsurgents. Despite being at the receiving end of insurgent violence, people still end up with many choices. They may choose to be controlled after rationally taking into account the costs and benefits. Or they may choose instinctively, based on sentiments, deep-seated beliefs or prejudices. The choice they make might be steadfast, based on visceral sentiments or positive support. Or it could be a momentary choice based on complicity, reacting to the changing environment while feigning ignorance. Constantly changing events compel the people to navigate their environment carefully. Their lives depend on not being observers but *active participants*.

Violence becomes an integral element they must consider when they make decisions. Insurgent violence and intimidation is not necessarily about being personally attacked or threatened with a weapon. Violence is always a possibility when people are fighting. Someone with a gun might *possibly* use it. People try not to make it *probable*— by taking short-cuts, lying, prevaricating, or avoiding the situation.

The reality of violence is always present, both literally, in the form of dead people by the side of the road, and metaphorically, in the form of a constant concern people carry in their hearts, affecting their day-to-day decisions. Which road should I take? Should I go or not go to the celebration at the mosque? Should I, or should I not, talk to the American soldiers that patrol the streets? In Iraq, people ask each other, "Shaku-maku?"—the equivalent of "What's up?" But the meaning of the question is in the tone: On the way into town, "shaku-maku" elicits the latest street gossip about which road to take, which areas to avoid, which checkpoint has the worst sort of insurgents. People must now take into account imperfect information to make astute decisions. Faced with the probability of violence, the banalities of gossip become a death-defying sport.

The people become agents of change as the actions of insurgents and counterinsurgents affect the way they make decisions. Their decisions, in turn, have an impact on the actions and decisions of the combatants on both sides. People are the prize in this battle. That is the peculiar, unique role of the people that prevents "power" from being translated readily into the ability to control.

❖ The nature of insurgent violence in Iraq

Violence in all its forms—the killings, explosions, broken bones, punched-in faces, twisted heads, the sad, poignant, absurd, and the absolutely sick actions perpetrated by insurgents on their own people, always justified in terms of creating a virtuous society—they all have a purpose and a reason in Iraq. The intended effect of violence and resulting intimidation is about altering the way people make decisions, altering the way they behave, live, and navigate life.

These lasting ramifications of violence are very much in the minds of people. Those who are not directly on the receiving end are also affected in the way they think and make decisions, how they behave and navigate life, and that is perhaps the greatest effect of violence.

The perverse genius in the deliberate application of insurgent violence is to engender the *expectation* of violence, and thus to affect the way people make choices in the short-term, immediate moment. It is not abstract.

- A Shia family tells soldiers they have decided against attending the Ashura festival for fear of suicide bombers, despite their yearning—they can see the minaret and sparkling lights from their second-floor balcony. They have altered their behavior because they have internalized the threat of violence.

- A Sunni family tells American soldiers pointedly, "Yes, we know about the insurgents, but, please, no we will not talk to you because they will kill us"; they, too, have internalized the probability of violence.
- Many young women and students purchase abayas, and the price of abayas increases in the neighborhood—a sure sign that many women have internalized the threat from the proliferation of armed virtue enforcers in the neighborhood.

Internalizing the effects and implications of violence into their decision-making alters the way people act; it affects all their choices related to control and power. Thus, violence for insurgents becomes an instrumental means of getting a foothold, a semblance of control on the ground. Insurgent violence is never random but always deliberate.

The selective murder of an opponent, either real or imagined, is far from random. It is intended to deter like-minded people from making similar decisions. People may not think in those terms, but when they begin to avoid certain routes and particular checkpoints, when they begin to be careful about who they talk to, that is precisely what they are doing to minimize the probability of being affected by violence.

Overwhelming amount of violence applied against a population could, one assumes, subject them to total control regardless of political judgments. At the point of a muzzle, with the credible threat of being killed, the majority of people will walk lock-step with a minimum of resistance. Breaking bones and punching faces gives a fleeting moment of control—a foothold, a starting point. But unless one quickly and astutely expands on that foothold, the moment will be lost; inevitably people will resist, no one wants to be bossed around—whether by foreigners or by their own people.

Insurgents have consistently shown their willingness to resort to overwhelming force when they have it. This is amply evident from the neighborhoods they controlled. They have the *willingness* to expand on their gains, but they may not have the material *resources* or the *capacity*—especially in a context when Americans constantly challenge them and support other groups who oppose them. Insurgents compensate for lack of firepower by using violence: the threat and the ability to use coercive, destructive power ruthlessly and with no compunction.

They apply it at times judiciously, at times maintaining the pretense of randomness. But the point is made. We exist, you shall not ignore us. Look, we just kicked the shit out of a guy in the market; or better, the teacher is now in the gutter with his wife, with two rounds in the head. Numerous captured insurgent leaders emphasized (spend a few days with these leaders, it's an enlightening experience) that they decide whom to eliminate, and also *how* to do it, in order to get the maximum bang for the buck. The demonstration effect is crucial.

The way insurgents inflict violence, the level and frequency of violence, the difference in public display—it all varies from group to group. It depends on differences in neighborhoods, the level of American involvement, the level of internal fighting among insurgents, and a host of other factors. The violence has the effect of bringing the people center stage, creating a peculiar context that people must keep in mind constantly as they make decisions, however trivial.

The nature and the form of control also affect the way people make their decisions. In an insurgency, the choice is constantly between two *different and contesting forms of control.*

Contesting Claims: Legitimate Control and Insurgent Control

There is a conceptual and qualitative difference in the two forms of control people are subjected to in an insurgency: legitimate government control and insurgent control. *Legitimate control* is the formal recognized authority—the government—that exerts control backed with all the tentacles of formal authority and the state's coercive machinery, along with some semblance of institutions to provide basic services to the population. *Insurgent control* is a challenge to existing authority. The distinction is important, as it impacts the way people make decisions regarding complicity, support, and control.

❖ Legitimate control

Legitimate control is *not* synonymous with righteousness. It does not matter whether it is a democracy, a theocratic clown show as in Iran, an entrenched colonial plantation like British Malaya or French Algeria, a roman-tunic-wearing freak show as in Libya, a leopard-hat-wearing freak as in Congo, or the delusional senile tin-pot Robert Mugabe in Zimbabwe, who has single-handedly destroyed a country.[35] It only means a *government*, with its coercive machinery and some semblance of institutions. The idea of authority, and the many expectations it engenders, affect the way people make decisions in terms of control.

With legitimate control, people—whether or not they support the government—are complicit in maintaining its control. They have to turn to the government for services: security, jobs, money, and even sometimes for food and cooking oil. Legitimate control carries a heavier burden. If you are the government that is claiming control, you are everyone's favorite whipping stick. People who refuse to grant the government an iota of support will nevertheless turn to it for basic services and then bitch, moan, and gripe at its failures with no sense of irony.

Everyone hates the government until they need it. A Sunni man, who is complicit with the Sunni thugs controlling the neighborhood, harbors no support for the Shia-dominated government of Iraq. He will gripe all day about both the insurgents and the government. But he will highlight the inability of the government to provide electricity, give him a job, or "fix the country," and he does not expect the insurgents to do any of those things. That is the qualitative distinction, the difference of expectations.

Given that he is a Sunni man, our prejudices would suggest he is a diehard supporter of insurgents—viscerally connected with his Sunni

---

[35] The leopard-hat-wearing freak show is the former Zairian (now the Democratic Republic of Congo) dictator Mobutu. This serious nut-job was the formally recognized authority for thirty-two years over a landmass the size of all of Western Europe. He was the formal authority; it did not matter that he was a freak (in fact, our own freak). One can also imagine other freak shows still on display.

brethren out of sectarian loyalty. He supports them all right, but it is not written in stone; and he is surely not fighting on their behalf, he is just going along. But this guy and many others like him would quickly become complicit with the government if the government could provide what he seeks. This may create the conditions for engendering complicity (although in his case, he may continue to gripe).

With legitimate control is expected a sense of predictability. Predictability minimizes the number of variables in people's decision-making; it makes it possible to lengthen the time horizon of their decisions. It makes it possible to dream of the future. But this sense of predictability wanes as an insurgency gains strength. When young Iraqi girls and boys wonder aloud whether or not to go to university, not knowing how things will be in the future due to the violence and instability, they have lost their capacity to dream: The time horizon in their decisions is too short. Predictability is gone.

The yearning of average people for some semblance of predictability cannot ever be taken for granted. There is a sense of complacency inherent to living in a predictable environment: In a nice suburb, people like to spend some time at Trader Joe's, save some money at Walmart; a latte at Starbucks is tastelessly bland yet safely predictable. People take the same road to work, and they are instinctively aware of the nuances of traffic and get pissed off at unexpected delays. But with an insurgency in swing, to assume predictability would mean complacency; it could mean an ill-informed decision that may cost a life. In an insurgency, with contesting claims of control and violence, that sense of predictability and complacency comes at a heavy premium.

In Iraq, our friends would launch into diatribes: "We Iraqis—I know my people—we need a strong leader, we must have a strong leader." Some would pointedly claim that democracy cannot work in Iraq. It is not a statement about their preferences for a system of government, for a dictatorship, democracy or theocracy. They are pissed off, and they assume that "a strong leader" would bring some stability and predictability to their lives. People's yearning for the predictability that comes with lasting stability is intense and real.

Insurgents, as part of this society, are well aware of this sentiment. With their first volley, the predictability is shattered: The beginning of the attempt at insurgent control. At that moment, people find that the unknown suddenly looms larger than it used to. The imagined reality of peace is no more. As soldiers would express it, this is the "oh shit moment."

❖ Insurgent control

At the beginning of an insurgency, tactics aim at chipping away the legitimate control exercised by the government. Unless insurgents have overwhelming popular support, or can usurp power through subversion (for example, by infiltrating the state apparatus), it is damn near impossible to single-handedly defeat a legitimate government and take control.[36] In trying to chip away at legitimate control, insurgents alert the government that they can no longer take their control for granted.

An insurgency usually begins with the deaths of random soldiers, policemen, bureaucrats, or politicians. The first death is always perceived as random, the avoidable and bewildering death of the innocent. Predictability is intact, but people wonder about the death. They assume that, thankfully, it does not pertain to them: The complacent state of mind is still intact. Insurgents understand that people desire predictability and stability, and, therefore, they start by rattling cages. And after numerous deaths, people cease to see these acts as random, they wake from their daydreams.

If the insurgents have done their job well, people need not see or hear anything in order to feel the waning of legitimate control and the increasing unpredictability; it begins to crawl on their skin.

---

[36] Examples of how to usurp power through subversion: the Free Officers Movement led by Nasser in Egypt managed to topple the king and eventually get control of the state apparatus that continues down to this day; the Free Officers in Iraq, led by Colonel Abdul Qarim Qasim, kicked out the imported King of Iraq; the Baathists in turn kicked out Abdul Qarim Qasim and took control of the Iraqi state.

People now have to make a conscious effort to anticipate future events; the element of the unknown begins to loom large in their decision-making. The insurgents challenge existing forms of authority, norms, rules, and laws both written and unwritten. They get their supporters to engage in symbolic acts of resistance against the existing order—something as simple as raising a flag, reading pamphlets, putting up posters, enforcing a small scale curfew, or (the all-time favorite) walking down the street chanting slogans, throwing shit and burning things along the way. It does not give insurgents lasting control, but it makes certain that the government cannot take for granted the people, its control, or its legitimacy.

Soon, the authorities lose the ability to say, "Let there be light." This is because the insurgents can turn light into darkness by cutting electricity pylons or bombing the electricity distribution system. Insurgents also have the ability to punish, and they compete with the authorities for the right to murder. At the same time, the insurgents promise the people an alternative reality, a reality where they can "dream with open eyes to make it possible." People understand that these are contesting claims to control, competing for their support.[37] Insurgents appeal to kindred spirits. They claim to offer an alternative reality better than the one that exists, and the competition between insurgents and counterinsurgents begins.

It will not be possible for insurgents to solidify the fleeting moment of control unless they somehow manage to defeat the government militarily or gain control of the state coercive machinery or foment a large-scale uprising that forces the government to abdicate. Instead, they chip away by being a deadly nuisance and making it clear to the

---

[37] Nothing is without its ironies. The insurgents that offer an alternative reality also claim a *monopoly* on that alternative. That's why they fight with each other. The moment insurgents get power, it becomes the insurgents' turn to say, "I will strike down upon thee with great vengeance and furious anger." In our readings, more often than not, in their attempt to solidify their gains, insurgents-turned-rulers fast become a reflection of their former adversaries, just as ruthless or worse. Very few have avoided being the victims of their own success, but why?

people that the government is not in full control. They find ways to project their power and authority symbolically. If insurgents declare a curfew in a neighborhood, or ask people to put up flags, *and people obey*, insurgents have managed to project authority and power that has traction on the ground.

However, insurgent control also engenders an expectation to deliver on some promises. Insurgents create shadow governments. They attempt to provide basic services, sometimes subversively using the very system in place, sometimes creating a parallel realm challenging existing authority. They claim to provide security—usually as protection from their own associates. And sometimes they instigate their own shadow laws for people to abide by.

In the many Jihadi enclaves of Iraq, local insurgent leaders would mete out medieval punishments in broad daylight. And in the absence of any system of maintaining order, some people did appreciate the swift delivery of justice by Jihadists, in family feuds, real estate issues, and monetary matters. Soon, of course, the swiftness of Jihadi justice reached absurd proportions. (The same pattern can be seen in Afghanistan at present.)

People only know that they need to be cautious in granting complicity. They must consider their rational and irrational preferences and pay attention to their surroundings, the time and place. Complicity becomes a more deliberate choice, no longer to be taken for granted. The people feel the distinction on their skin as they walk down the street. They now have to navigate the struggle, choosing to be complicit with either legitimate government control or insurgent control, or at times both.

❖ A storm is coming: Support of the people

Support is easier to recognize than complicity. People act in support of the cause, following their visceral sentiments or rational preferences. Voting provides a quantified index of support. But the most recognizable form of support in an insurgency is the willingness to fight and die for a cause. Those dedicated supporters are a tiny minority. Equally important, however, is the wider population that is *not* willing to fight on behalf of the cause—and they are the ultimate prize in the battle.

People walk down the street ranting and raving, beating their chests, gyrating down the street, screaming their own version of "hell yeah, this is the shit, we got this down, bring it on." But people who do not walk down the street screaming, who stay inside drinking a nervous glass of tea, tell the soldiers: "We will not leave the house tomorrow, there is supposed to be a storm."

A storm indeed: A show of support by the select group that supports the insurgents' cause, a loud demonstration to challenge government control and to project insurgent authority and power. Supporters are willing to defy, resist, take risks, and take part in these public symbolic acts.[38] Engendering active support among the people who are merely complicit, and turning the minority of supporters into a majority, are key to consolidating control.

The other element of support that distinguishes it from complicity is *time.* Complicity changes much more readily than support because the changing context plays a much bigger role. A decision out of support will be far less conditional on the circumstances of the moment.

The Time and The Place: Complicity of the People[39]

If the insurgents can gain the support of the majority of the people, they could, technically, force the government to abdicate if the people are willing to act on that support. The reality is that amid the many groups and claims for control, obtaining the support of a majority remains a tantalizing wet dream. The more realistic objective is to gain the *complicity* of the majority.

---

[38] Political rallies in the U.S. are symbolic acts that show a group's support. The vote count in an election quantifies that support, measured against contesting claims. But how would these same people choose in the context of contesting forms of authority and violence, when people with guns rule the streets?

[39] "The Time and the Place," a short story by Naguib Mahfouz.

Complicity occurs when people relinquish control; they make a choice disregarding their true sentiments, in reaction to their immediate surroundings. They obey dictates by feigning ignorance, claiming indifference, or pointing to the threat of violence—or any number of real or imagined excuses. They have become active agents of change. They have willingly become subjected to the control of one side or the other.

But complicity grants only momentary control. The decision to comply is influenced by the immediate situation. Time and place are defining elements of complicity and that makes complicity very fickle. The trick, then, is to get enough people to choose to be complicit by manipulating their surroundings, creating a reinforcing cycle: Complicity of some of the people fosters complicity of others, which in turn generates control on the ground. A person being compelled to choose may become complicit, but with apprehension: head bowed, eyes darting about, wondering, "Oh shit, is this a good idea, holy shit, this is a bad, really bad idea." But they look around and wonder, "Are the other people doing the same thing? Oh thank god, there are some others." Individuals choose to be complicit with one side at one moment, and with another at a different time and a place, reacting to a different surrounding. Soldiers saw this situation often.

Complicity of the People: "This Area Is Very Safe"

All the men were walking in line to the front of the house. Soldiers ordered them to move, and they quietly obeyed. It certainly looks like control, total and absolute. Is it?

❖ The Time

The IED had gone off not fifty meters from his house. There he is, the man of the house, the patriarch, meekly obeying every order from soldiers. Does he know anything about the IED that went off? No, he does not: "The area is very safe." Of course. It is safe every time.

"Look, sir, the IED that went off, it was right across from your front yard."

"Oh, that. Well, mister, that is not my area." Of course, it is not his area.

117

Just then, a kid—perhaps ten or twelve—comes around the corner. He sees the soldiers and freezes in place. The old man and his family are visibly agitated and call to their son. This is a propitious moment. "Excellent, let's put the family in the house, separate them, and then let's start with the kid." So the soldiers isolate the family and ask the kid about the IED, and he gives the most amazingly nonchalant answer.

"Oh, well, my father told me to stay away from the house, just keep all the windows open because there might be an explosion, so I stayed away. But I did not do the IED, it has nothing to do with me." Soldiers had no reason to doubt him.

"Please believe me, all I did was to open all the windows in the house as my father asked me to do." Then he starts to cry. The kid was not in any way incriminating his father, his family or himself. He is just being truthful for whatever reason.[40]

"Jesus, where in the hell did this kid come from?" The soldiers, despite being ambushed just a few minutes ago, look at each other and bust out laughing. The simple unvarnished truth sounded so out of place. Prevarication is an art form: The truth is so rare that when it comes into your face so effortlessly it sounds absurd.

The laughing of soldiers made the Iraqis fear for their lives. The laughs, it became obvious, sounded more ominous than any threats. But no one was threatening to kill innocent people. After all, people in a neighborhood don't usually plant IEDs next to their own houses; only insurgents do. And they plant them especially near their enemies—the very people who might be helpful to the soldiers.

---

[40] The way American soldiers react to roadside bombs differs from unit to unit. Most simply fire off some rounds and keep driving away, "get out of the kill zone." But that is the wrong approach in reacting to an IED. It is far more important to quickly assess the situation, cordon the area with the resources one has, and quickly try to follow through and look for the perpetrators, start tactical questioning of the bystanders as a means for further investigation while others attend to the casualties.

But soldiers also knew that some of the people in this gathering were aware of the IED all along. Every ambush by insurgents is always known by some people in the neighborhood. Soldiers learn these simple truths slowly. Why are the gasoline cans of the roadside vendors unattended? That is their most prized possession, why would they leave them to be stolen? Why is the corner storeowner not there today, leaving the store open with all his shit inside? Why are the vegetables vendors not in their usual place—but their wares are?

❖ The Place

Well, because they know there is an ambush ahead. Either insurgents warned them or they knew somehow and got the hell out of Dodge before things went haywire. For soldiers steeped in an insurgency, this is a reality as simple as walking down the street. But if soldiers could get to know enough people in the neighborhood, *somebody* would call before it happened. At a moment when soldiers smell something fishy, it is time to take a step back, reassess, send an element to go around and flank the insurgents' flank.

But today, it is time to call the father and have another chat with him. Now he is repenting, expertly neither lying nor telling the truth. Withholding what little he actually knew and "cannot recall."

Who is in control, who are the people complicit with?

He did what he was told, did what soldiers ordered. Soldiers could have ordered him to march like a frog and he would have done it. Yet he is looking straight in the eyes of the soldiers and denying the little truths that he knew, withholding any information he might have had. People were subjected to control by soldiers, but at the same time they were complicit with the insurgents in their own little way. It was their decision to make. Soldiers had only an illusion of control: People were not willing to give them what they wanted. The choice of complicity was a decision to save their own skin, a choice they made taking into account their immediate surroundings.

They were, of course, afraid to give out the little information they had for fear of being branded as rats, of having insurgents hunt them down.

❖ The Time and the Place: Complicity

Some of the people who refused to be complicit with soldiers during the day, in front of their fellow citizens, did comply at night, in the safe confines of their own homes. People will often tell stories and offer information when they are quite certain no one is around and listening.

In the middle of the night, soldiers walked into the house. They jumped through the roof and apologized for sneaking into the house without being invited—insisting that they mean no harm. It was only that they wanted to resume the conversation they had left off during the day, a week ago, after they got ambushed fifty meters from the house.

The people—when convinced that it is just them—share information. That is, they tell their own story, as best as they know it, and it is up to the soldiers to make sense of it, to assess its credibility and find common themes with other similar stories. The people are now complicit with the soldiers. The surrounding has changed, the context is different, and they have decided accordingly.

They could have refused to be honest. It is not likely that soldiers will inflict any physical harm on people in response to their dishonesty. Dishonesty and prevarication arise from the context in which people live, trying to navigate multiple forms of control and threats of violence. It is always a puzzle: people, having woken up a few teas later, are now willingly cooperating (in that hushed conspiratorial voice, and with a lot of humor) as if it is the most normal condition—cooperation they adamantly withheld during the day just a few days back. It's the same soldiers, the same people, the same laughs and the same jokes, but the people have chosen differently, to be complicit now with the soldiers.

What changed was the *context* that people had to take into account when they made their decision. They were afraid of being branded as collaborators; they were afraid of possible actions (and inactions) of their neighbors. Above all else, they were seriously afraid that the insurgents would get the word and might physically harm them or their family. And they knew that American soldiers, no matter how pissed off, almost never randomly shoot people execution style the way insurgents do, and one can actually get away with lying to them. Whatever the efficacy of the differing methods, this is a fact of the way the U.S. military has decided to act. There is no choice, of course, because it represents a fundamentally different philosophy.

The logic of complicity plays out in how insurgents get control of the people in a neighborhood. It plays out in the streets, in the restaurants, the stores, schools, mosques, checkpoints—and in people's homes. In a neighborhood under insurgent control, the insurgents are constantly among the population, though unseen by the authorities. Insurgents have mastered the art of being subversive. This lethal drama, not without its charming moments, plays out in real time in Midaq Alley under insurgent control.

6

MIDAQ ALLEY UNDER INSURGENT CONTROL

> Although Midaq Alley lives in almost complete isolation from all surrounding activity, it clamors with a distinctive and personal life of its own. Fundamentally and basically, its roots connect with life as a whole and yet, at the same time, it retains a number of the secrets of a world now past.
>
> —*Midaq Alley*[41]

Walking down Midaq Alley at sunrise, you see the expected faces and hear the expected din of a bustling neighborhood. But paralleling this illusion of normalcy is a different reality, the realm of insurgents—hidden, but retaining control and manipulating events and people, leaving only traces of their fingerprints. Control through subversion.

They have the support of a minority and the complicity of a majority, based on the effective use of violence against the authorities—and against the very people whose complicity they seek. Insurgents have somehow managed to create an impression of solid control, effectively challenging the attempt by Americans and the government to instill a semblance of legitimate control. There is genius in the insurgent madness.

---

[41] *Midaq Alley*, a novel by Naguib Mahfouz.

Americans only feel the insurgents when they witness the outcome of an insurgent action aimed at themselves or at the neighborhood populace. Iraqis, of course, feel the insurgents' presence when they are subjected to the results of their actions; but some people also *see* them, just as they see the Americans. Most try to ignore both, feigning ignorance because insurgents have control of the place.

We can begin to see past this illusive reality only when we learn to make sense of the obvious in terms of the "not so obvious." Then we come to understand the congruities by paying attention to the many *incongruities*, by seeing one in relation to the other in our long patrols.

The Long Patrol

The early morning start of a foot patrol in the spring—the best time of the year and of the day. The air is crisp, with no humidity; the sky is free of smoke from gasoline fires or burning trash. People walk with a purpose, with determined eyes. They even look fresh now, before the full fury of the sun can beat them down. The beginning of the morning patrol is never too exacting on the soul. Soldiers are almost tempted to enjoy the moment.

Nothing in Midaq Alley looks out of place, compared to any other place that has seen years of intermittent violence and is filled to the brim with people. A space filled with blocks of gray two-story houses, with satellite dishes and bullet holes. The main avenues of approach are always filled with blocking positions: various roadblocks and check-points placed by Americans and insurgents.

The street has its fair share of stores and restaurants—once bustling, no doubt, but people now seem weary of the place. The stretch of farmland on one side appears out of nowhere, looking as out of place as the canal running alongside the bustling part of town. At the far end appear little peasant houses, separated by the canal. The outskirts of town—a middle class, even affluent, neighborhood—has recently filled up with the shacks of internally displaced people. The kids run about at all times shouting, "Mister, mister, mister." People occupy a group of abandoned government buildings.

124

Soldiers notice the distinctly familiar smells of the neighborhood: garbage, spices, cooking oil, gas fumes and sweat, mixed with whiffs of sewage here and there, merging with the muffled whirring of generators. Men, women, and children go about their business in this setting, effectively hiding their concerns behind dispassionate and determined faces. They walk under the crisscrossing electricity wires that look as if a giant spider has woven its webs from roof to roof. Among the populace, some are insurgents, some are supporters, and some are merely complicit. But who is who? No one wears shoulder patches except the U.S. soldiers.

The Iraqi policemen patrol in their blue and white land cruisers. Wearing light blue shirts and dark blue pants they linger in one street, yapping, smoking cigarettes and joking at passersby. Soldiers look at them and wonder, how in the hell could we distinguish the police who are innocent from those affiliated with insurgents? Some of the same guys who attack soldiers at night are sitting there laughing right now. We have to pick them out and send them packing.

But how?

In another avenue of approach are a bunch of Iraqi Army soldiers, doing the same as the police—but at least they maintain a show of hard work. Iraqi Army soldiers become assiduous in their inspection of vehicles whenever American soldiers are in sight. The man in charge even gives orders. The rest of the Iraqi soldiers are in the back lying on mattresses, trying to catch some sleep. That is a core principle that binds grunts the world over: getting some sleep. You feel envious of the sleeping Iraqi soldiers. A few of them are making tea outside in a massive pot as others are just waking up. A bag of fresh bread sits next to it, and we are eyeing the bread. Iraqis notice and offer: "Sir, have some tea, some bread," always a tempting offer.

Next to them is a barrier. Americans have emplaced massive concrete barriers, miles and miles of them, along one side of the neighborhood in an attempt to control and secure the population by minimizing the avenues of approach. Soldiers sarcastically comment that the greatest U.S. contribution to Iraq is "concrete, baby, concrete as far as the eye can see."

125

But is it the insurgents in the neighborhood that are contained inside the barricade? Is it the *people* in the neighborhood who are now contained? Or is it the Americans that are contained? After all, any time they walk to the neighborhood they have to take the self-restricted roads. More often than not, they decide to take a longer route—otherwise, the insurgents immediately know when Americans pass their forward observers.

Yet soldiers are proud of the barriers, proud of the soldiers who did it. Mainly, they are grateful *they* did not have to do it. It was a battle building these walls, with soldiers shot at, threatened, doing it all at night. Soldiers would comment, with a slicing hand motion, "YES, it is contained, hoooah!" mimicking someone higher, and everyone would laugh. Only—who has contained whom? There is only one certainty for soldiers: There are plenty of insurgents outside, inside, and at times literally amid the barricades.

A bunch of soldiers who always patrol this neighborhood are lingering around, eating some falafel sandwiches next to a barrier and chatting with some Iraqis. One Iraqi asks with evident displeasure, "Sir, what is this?"—pointing at the barrier. Iraqis have to navigate our well-intentioned, logical actions that sometimes do not have the expected traction on the ground. So you know the Iraqi posed a valid question. Although the logic behind the containment is impeccable—it is intended to make people safe, and in some ways it has in fact improved their safety—but there are certainly issues.

His once open neighborhood is now chopped and isolated. He is genuinely tired of dealing with this war over roads between insurgents and counterinsurgents. His family is now forced to take a longer route, skirting a neighborhood they would rather avoid. No matter what you do, how well intentioned or how impeccable the logic, someone will always be unhappy. Try to make everyone happy and you end up like the neighborhood whore with the kindest heart, always broke, in constant pain, and with someone always at the door, knock, knock.

So the soldiers want to answer, "Well, what the hell do you think it is?" Instead, they ask, "Well, sir, what do you think?" They offer to buy sandwiches and tea and ask him to sit and tell his story.

❖ The art of never lying

There are insurgents, but you can't see them. There are Iraqi Police and Iraqi Army; you see them easily. There are American soldiers, and everyone can see them a mile away. And the people clamor on about their own business, despite and amid everything.

An Iraqi doctor (still working) and his wife, a geneticist (now out of a job), explained their point of view cogently. Some of the insurgents were neighborhood boys, they said. As someone who has lived there over twenty years, he knew almost every one of them. Some local insurgent leaders came from other neighborhoods, but most are from here. Yes, some of them were lunatics—"animals," his wife pointed out—so they have barred their daughters from going out without an escort. But "these people," the insurgents, keep other groups from coming into the neighborhood. It makes the people feel safe, even if they don't support them. Yet they constantly live in fear because some insurgents come to them for assistance. "I am a doctor": it is the worst job in Iraq. So they ask us, please, don't ask about the insurgents and don't come to the house again. It puts them in danger.

The man is a doctor, from an affluent family, and doctors are a choice target in the criminal world, the easiest people to kidnap for ransom. So he needs the protection of the insurgents, regardless of how much he may hate them. Besides, they have two beautiful young daughters, one in her mid-twenties and the other a teenager. Women are the easiest targets of all; they are a liability.

But the distinction between criminals and insurgents at times ceases to exist, as they both challenge formal authority. They become one and the same. Criminals can legitimize their businesses by buying into an insurgent franchise; they are then seen as something larger in the eyes of the people. Transitioning from criminals to insurgents adds only a few extra elements. They might get paid for an occasional attack on American soldiers or the murder of some opponents if they buy into a good franchise.

Iraqis in this midst walk around wearing a mask of indifference and ignorance. They call the thugs criminals, but word it differently.

When the nut-jobs run the nut-house, the doctors can't call them nut-jobs. The doctor calls them the neighborhood "boys" while his wife calls them "animals," or hooligans with guns—not a term of endearment. Iraqis fear the insurgents and they may even be complicit, but it does not mean respect or support.

But support for insurgents does exist. You hear it, you see it, and when shot at, you actually feel it.

❖ Stories without details

A soldier's patrol through a neighborhood may appear random, but you walk with a list of houses and people to visit to glean what is possible from them. Sometimes it is in preparation for soldiering at night. If the weather is perfect, soldiers want to enjoy the moment—but you cannot because insurgents are enjoying it too.

Soldiers walk into one of the houses they planned to visit. Walking into the house, they receive the usual apprehensive welcome, encountering the fraught smiles of a family completely at a loss. The faces look eager but the eyes are desperate, the brain searching furiously for a suitable opinion.

They hear a loud boom in the distance, the rat-tat of insurgent AK-47 fire. Goddamn, only ten in the morning and it's already started. In that split second, soldiers pay close attention to the distance and direction and try to distinguish the subtleties in the noise of the explosion. The entire neighborhood, a maze of grid-squares in three dimensions, flashes in your brain, registering all the possible sites where your colleagues could be scattered about; you think of the fastest way to get there as the radio crackles.

The Iraqi family members have heard the same noise. They try to mask their fears with unperturbed faces, but fear oozes out of every pore. The Iraqis in the house were not involved; but the thought crosses their minds, what might these Americans in the house do if some other Americans were hurt somewhere? It's a fearful moment.

Radio traffic explains that a convoy of National Guard units was hit with an IED along the edge of the neighborhood. A couple of

American soldiers guarding the convoy—the worst job on the planet, driving around until you get blown up—a couple of the soldiers were seriously wounded, some others not so seriously. Colleagues conducting a patrol nearby had rushed to the scene to help with the casualty evacuation. The incident took place, predictably, between two Iraqi police checkpoints, checkpoints that had disappeared only moments before. Soldiers share a sarcastic chuckle, commenting as they always do, "Man, we need to go whole hog on these IP guys; believe me, before I go I am going to take care of a whole lot of them."

Soldiers listen to the radio, shrug their shoulders, and turn back to the Iraqi family with a nonchalant grin. The family was always helpful with stories since the first meeting, and soldiers know enough to reciprocate by bringing random shit—books to the children, pain medication to the grandma—because these people certainly know a thing or two. Of course, they confirm that some insurgents from the neighborhood were probably responsible for the big boom. They have mastered the art of agreeing emphatically with the broader points while avoiding the specifics. Yes, they tell you, the insurgents definitely control the neighborhood. They are everywhere; "Oh, but it is difficult to know exactly where they are"—or what they do. Of course, soldiers agree completely with the family.

Absolute genius. How do they do it with such emphatic conviction, avoid the truth without actually lying? Yet you know that the insurgents could be the neighbors in the house across the way or in the next street, and you know the family has a pretty good idea who they are. For the moment they will stick with the broader story. That's fine, the specifics will come later, they always do. Soldiers step off and start walking again.

❖ **Honest men**

A few streets down is the house of an unequivocal supporter of insurgents, the vocal opponent of Americans. The only reason to go there is to be a nuisance: The mere presence of Americans irritates him. But in his irritation, you get glimpses into his nightmares. It is always entertaining to be a burden, to drink his tea, and he is not without his charming aspects. He is intriguing despite all his vitriol.

129

He is everything: a businessman, political operative, part-time cleric, community organizer, and, most certainly, insurgent middleman. On the last score, unfortunately there is nothing to link him. He is smart. If the gossip in the neighborhood is not enough, the flags, posters, memorabilia, photos on the wall and propaganda material show quite plainly that he is more than just a supporter of insurgents. He is one of them, and one of the smartest—which means he will not fit into the legal criteria Americans seek in order to capture him. Even if captured, he will most certainly get out. He is trying to be a respectable politician. His suave manner and his standing in the neighborhood show that—unlike many—his aspirations are in line with his capabilities. And that makes him dangerous. He is an opponent deserving of respect; to underestimate him is to be blindsided.

He is honest with his opinions, telling soldiers on numerous occasions, "We appreciate what the Americans have done, but now it is time for you to leave." The fiery intensity in his eyes shows he means more than what he says. Then a joker among the grunts would always advise him, "Tell you what, sir, why don't you tell your buddies to save the ammunition for the real fight, the big war that's coming after we leave."

And everyone would laugh at the hackneyed joke that never seemed to get old in Iraq. The sarcasm and macabre humor of soldiers mask the feelings running through the head. You want to drag him to the back room, hose him down, make him wish he were in living hell and get the real scoop. Instead, you grip the pistol grip of the M4 tighter. To drag him to the river would be murder and to let him go is to let him get away with murder; you look for the delicate balance, if it exists.

For all his faults, he has endearing qualities. Though a part-time rabid anti-American cleric, his wife is a school teacher and the oldest daughter is a second-year university student, now living at home given the security situation. Both women speak English—and this guy has no problem with them talking to soldiers. That is a big step up from many others, who lock their wives and daughters in the closet at the first sight of Americans.

His brother is the ultimate character soldiers wanted to like but were careful not to: a former Iraqi national hero, long past his day in the spotlight. He is a former member of the Iraqi national soccer team, a middle-aged guy with a wiry build with the wild enthusiasm of a precocious toddler. He always brought so much energy to the room. Of course, he supports the same political party his brother supports, that of the insurgents. But this guy, if he spotted the soldiers far off, he would dash over and start talking. The constant topic of debate: American football versus soccer. Soccer is "the world sporrrt!" Yeah, yeah, OK, soldiers get it, but can soccer ever beat the sensation of Friday Night Lights (high school football: the myth)? Soldiers don't think so; for them it's a religion, just as soccer is in Iraq.

Never mind, he always had his posse of followers and would snappily send a couple of minions to bring us some drinks. He is wildly enthusiastic about the state of the Iraqi national soccer team, and he admits that the Americans saved the team. He is ecstatic with the improvements. Here's a guy that should be given a few soccer balls, no joke, he would certainly put them to good use. He talks like he coaches every team in the neighborhood. He is a local celebrity. In this town, as the good ol' man Waylon would say, he is still the king, just like Bob Wills in Austin. Every guy passing by would acknowledge his presence. When the Iraqis won the Asian cup finals, beating Saudi Arabia, he was carried away in all the joint celebrations. He was a transformed man. You hate to burst his bubble, how could you dislike this guy?

We strangely want to like him, but his unequivocal support for his brother's political party made us wary. Soldiers continue on their long patrol.

Demonstrating Control

Insurgents cannot merely exist: They constantly have to prove, justify, and project their authority. Their ability to dramatize power with actions on the ground reinforces and gives traction to the authority they claim in the neighborhood. Military attacks are an obvious tactic. Symbolic actions aimed at impressing the people are another trick in their playbook.

Using the support of the people and projecting it to maximum effect is standard fare. They do it with no subtlety, right under the nose of Americans, which is precisely the point. If Americans find out, they in turn face another predicament: How can you tell people that they cannot have a simple demonstration in the neighborhood when Americans claim to fight for Iraqis to have that very right?

The guys gather around the mosque and decide to chant down the street after the prayer, yelling and screaming. They make enough of a ruckus that people in the neighborhood notice it. It is a demonstration against the GOI and the Americans, and it seemed to appear out of nowhere. The spontaneity is pure genius because it is a façade. It is a sweet lie, as sweet as the pretense of coincidence when jumping into bed with an old girlfriend. Insurgents and their supporters do it well, while people who are complicit feign ignorance.

That is not to say that spontaneous demonstrations are absent: Something sparks the moment, and people go haywire. But people don't spontaneously draw slogans on pieces of cardboard and fabric or walk around with flags stuffed inside their bags and clothes in case they want to have a demonstration. It was locally planned and executed. Just as quickly as it appeared, it soon fizzled out. But the point is made: Insurgents exist, they have their supporters, and they are not afraid to show it off right under the nose of Americans and Iraqi authorities. It was aimed at the people in the neighborhood as much as at the authorities. (The locally recruited Iraqi Police had conveniently disappeared while the Army soldiers sat on their mattresses.)

People who did not want to be part of it reacted the way they react when faced with any difficult situation they are unable to avoid. Expecting that such a circus portends more trouble, they tried their best to scatter—fast but quietly, without being conspicuous. Those who were not genuine supporters did not deem the risk worth it, so they got the hell away: The distinction between complicity and support. But though they knew some of the guys present in it, they would not tell soldiers who they were. "Oh, they are not from the area." Of course not.

The point was made clearly: The insurgents are around, and they have power and control and core constituents who are unafraid. Watching from a distance, soldiers wondered, how many of the people present at the demonstration would actually risk their lives, would pick up arms and put up a fight? A demonstration during the day is different from actually risking one's life. How many would walk the walk? Not many; posers are dime a dozen. But the key to getting a grasp of the real combat strength of insurgents is to be able to answer that question.

The Mosque

The mosque where the demonstration began is now back to its usual gray nonchalant self, empty and lifeless.

The mosque. "Well, everyone goes to the mosque, insurgents too, lot of things happen in the mosque," people comment in the neighborhood. Soldiers resist the temptation to answer, "well, no shit." Instead, they try to walk the inoffensive middle ground, so they can get to the mosque later.

A lot of shady shit goes on in that mosque, maybe not in the prayer room, but somewhere on the property. It makes impeccable sense: the mosque is the center of the community, and it is immune from American encroachments.

Even the people who talk of the mosque in ominous terms—"oh it is terrible, what they [the insurgents] have done to the mosque"—would rant and rave if Americans walked into the mosque to clear it. And there is no better way for a soldier to get in trouble than to walk into a mosque without permission from higher up. But higher ups in turn need permission from higher, and on it goes into a universe far away. Permission is hard to come by—unless soldiers and their young leaders on the ground figure out innovative ways.

Yet, that's the place you want to go, at the right time, with discretion, and it is the one place that you cannot go. Looking around the neighborhood, the reasons why we should not go are also obvious. Besides being a public relations nightmare for higher up, and, therefore, counterproductive, there is probably no better excuse for the insurgents to rally a crowd in the neighborhood than to claim Americans went into a mosque—disregarding the fact that insurgents were inside. That bit of information will be conveniently omitted: People who detest the insurgents want the Americans to get the insurgents out of the mosque, but they would not want the Americans to actually *go* to the mosque. The mosque is a godsend, and you can begin to understand why the insurgents say thanks be to Allah.

Soldiers keep walking and wondering how to beat it—both in the neighborhood and with our own higher. So the soldiers on this long patrol now shake their heads as they walk by the mosque, thinking that there has got to be a way.

And they reach one of their favorite destinations, the former Iraqi army officer in his corner store, who regales soldiers with valuable stories.

The Fox and the Hounds

The former Iraqi army officer who lives by the mosque was always full of insights. So the soldiers walk into his comfortable shop for a chat, listen to some of his stories, maybe even have a cold drink to mitigate the early afternoon sun.

Retired after an illustrious career that has spanned thirty years, the former officer now frequents the mosque near his house. He had the deliberate insouciance of a man privy to many secrets. And he had the scars to prove every war he had taken part in—al-Anfal campaign against the Kurds, Iran-Iraq war, and the Kuwait war and 1991 uprising. Soldiers always gave him professional respect, or maybe they appreciated the great stories he told. This makes him welcome the soldiers to his house.

"Well, the mosque." A deep grunt, a shake of the shoulder and another grunt, "For our people, the mosque, it is everything."

"Yes, it is understood." And indeed it is.

The guys who run the black market rackets, control the fuel distribution, run the extortion rackets and the insurgency are sometimes all one and the same, or at least interconnected. Everyone who is anyone gathers at the mosque. It is not that the sheikh in the mosque is running the show, he is not. It's just that the mosque provides one of the great venues for everyone to get together in a safe confine. They have guarantees from the government and the Americans that they will not walk in—or if they do, at the behest of Iraqi authorities, they might as well not bother because insurgents always know a few days in advance.

The cleric in charge of the mosque, for all his craziness, is a rather affable guy in his own house. He is way too demanding—no matter what you deliver, nothing seems to satisfy him, and he complains almost out of habit. To utter a positive word even by accident seems tantamount to blasphemy. He is a buzz-kill, born to be a preacher. The former army officer asserts, in a rare moment of certainty, that the cleric is genuinely clean. He shrugs his shoulders, almost with pity: "He is just a cleric."

Then he speaks of his neighborhood and its people, every day a different story, and it eventually dawns on you that you may be in the presence of a true fox—a man who knows many things and is utterly comfortable in his knowledge. He is a family man, a grandfather, a retiree from the army, but without his due pension. Once a high-ranking Baathist, today he is reduced to wheeling and dealing in his prosperous-looking corner store day and night. Neighborhood boys turned insurgents are also his customers. He states unequivocally that insurgents are in full control of the neighborhood, and he appears utterly comfortable with that idea. Just as he is comfortable in his many jokes with Americans, predicting that Americans will not be defeated in Iraq. You wonder whether he is being sarcastic, and he adds with a sly grin, "You are *Americans*," with that certain intonation that soldiers have heard before: the Americans, the strongest and most powerful army ever. As a former army man, he has been on the receiving end of it, and it is nice to see he has a bit of humor. Soldiers always add, "Sir, Iraq has some good fighters too!"

Then he would add, with a twinkle in his eye, "But you Americans, you need to be strong." Meaning: "You Americans need to *kill*."

135

But you can easily picture this fox commiserating at the death of his insurgent buddies, telling them to be strong. This sneaky bastard is a true genius. He is either working with insurgents or has enough credibility with them to get away with anything. A man with so much experience presents a justifiable concern: He could be of great service to the insurgents (and also to counterinsurgents).

Dealing with the reality of insurgents and Americans, he seems not at all perturbed; there is no hint of apprehension in his eyes. He is a man of experience, he has seen his share of events, this is just another one. He is either fully in control of his own destiny or utterly resigned to being at the mercy of circumstances. He is comfortable either way, ready to drift with the drifting sand.

Some soldiers always joked that they wished for a USB cable to plug it into his head, download everything, and watch it on a flat screen TV. Damn, what a movie that would be! He only runs the corner store today, but he knows every Neighborhood Advisory Council (NAC) member and some prominent members of the District Advisory Council (DAC)—the gatherings of local movers and shakers who are supposed to allocate resources to provide basic services to people. This fox is well plugged into the current system, a sign of his past stature and present genius.

Officers' nightmare: local politicos

Accompanying officers to a NAC meeting, never a pleasant moment, is an assigned duty on this long patrol. It is educational and gives a glimpse into a different world—but you walk away wanting to punch holes in the walls.

NAC and DAC members are a group of guys you want to do without, but you cannot and should not. Sitting there observing, the mind wanders. You begin to ponder the best place to put some explosive charges to blow up the whole damn thing. But you are pulled back into reality when a true battle of wits ensues between American officers and local politicos. Soldiers, as good enlisted men, see its peculiar charms. You begin to have a good time, adding peanut gallery comments throughout, whispering into the radio for added effect and sharing your suicidal thoughts with those listening in, who keep coming up with better ideas. NAC and DAC meetings, playing local politics—a necessary nightmare for our officers in a counterinsurgency.

The Iraqi local officials come across as cynical caricatures of a complex society. They are also some of the most astute people you will run into in all Iraq. The instinctive impulse is to scream, "You are the government now, you run this show, come to terms with it instead of making excuses, take some ownership goddammit, what the fuck."

Instead, the officers assigned this un-enviable task put on their most reasonable officer face. They work the part with conviction, controlling their inner rage: "Well, sir, absolutely, I understand your concerns, they are all valid points, but let us consider the alternative"—and the local politicos would put on their most intense obsequious face as if listening. How quickly they transform, much like a bunch of grade school boys who suddenly quiet down when they catch sight of the shapely new student teacher. But it is only momentary. Like bickering grade schoolers, they quickly revert.

As much as they like and respect their superior officers (sometimes), grunts are amused at their discomfort and call them on it: "Hey, sir, you are going to have a panic attack soon"; "Hey, sir, wouldn't you rather be in a firefight than this shit?" It's a welcome moment of humor, but seeing the officers' controlled frustration you realize their blood pressure is rising to unhealthy levels. The worst part of their new job description is there is no escape; they must play local politics as best as they can.

To assume that the Iraqi NAC and DAC members are easily manipulated caricatures would be foolish and dangerous. They are very good at straddling all worlds. They slow things down to their own pace. While the Americans are always in a hurry, DAC and NAC guys are not. We like to sprint; they prefer to take a leisurely walk absorbing it all. Americans come and go, while they are there to stay.

So you keep running circles around each other, even while you fight some of their own affiliates on the ground. Sooner or later they will probably come around. The best of all outcomes is when they take ownership of some American idea and propound it as their own. And at that point, as the powers that be, we resist the impulse to claim it as our idea and instead show a little humility. Officers quickly take the next steps, set up the mechanism to hold them to the plan, and congratulate them on their ideas while Americans assist them in implementing those ideas on the ground.

NAC and DAC members have perfected an art form. Americans playing local Iraqi politics may not be as perfect, but they have three advantages: power, money, and bunch of disciplined soldiers that can stare at the screaming eyes with callous indifference or kick in some faces if necessary. With a little reasoning, some cajoling, and some genuine give and take, something just might be possible.

DAC and NAC members do what they do because they simultaneously straddle four different worlds: the Americans, the local people (to whom they are supposed to provide basic services), the insurgents, and themselves (their own self-interest in consolidating their power). Retaining their own authority and consolidating it further is very high on the agenda. Yet, given the changing context, this requires some form of give and take with the insurgents. Everyone has to go home sometime. They go home to sleep and wake up and scratch their balls and slurp their morning chai-tea like everyone else. They are alive because those who are contesting for power allow them to live, for the moment.

They may not be completely beholden to insurgent interests—some are, but not all. Nevertheless, at some moments they will manipulate the agenda at the meetings to allocate the limited resources on their own behalf and that of the insurgents, whether out of support or complicity or pure self-interest. And with that action comes money and possible actions on the ground to enhance services to the people that may engender support for the insurgents. And the true goddamn genius is that they do it all on the American dime.

That insurgents inadvertently benefit from our largesse is not a contentious argument but a simple fact. Friend, foe, the innocent and the law, all are at times governed by the context in which they operate, not by the labels we attach for our own convenience.

How do we release the sensible ones from being beholden to insurgent interests, so they can act on their own—at least partially mindful of the greater good? So that they can take actions that engender support for them and for the *government*? It's not about absolutes; it's always about degrees, a delicate balance again.

Leaving a NAC or DAC meeting, however frustrating, one is always impressed with their sense of certitude. Is it real, is it a façade, is it merely imagined? Soldiers step-off as their patrol is now almost over.

❖ Insurgent control: Mr. Arif and children

An insurgent murder is (sometimes) anything but secretive. You hear the shooting in broad daylight. Every inch of your skin has an astringent tingle as you control the reaction to run toward the noise—an instinctive impulse. Then the radios crackle: None of the Americans in the area were hurt. Soldiers closest to the incident start to sprint in the direction of the shooting. Weary looking people, a wailing woman, hurried steps, claims of ignorance, a few men trying to control the situation the best they can, and everyone simultaneously firing disjointed requests at soldiers, the loudest using hand gestures as well: "You need to bring a helicopter!"

In the middle of the busy thoroughfare of restaurants and shops lies a middle-aged, heavyset man in brown pants, tennis shoes, and an off-white shirt (now covered in blood), sprawled on the ground with multiple chest wounds and gasping for air. You recognize the expressions and the subtle desperate contortions. By now you know the air is getting sucked into the chest cavity, the lungs are collapsing, and the heart is the next to be choked.

Soldiers approaching the place, absorbing the events, do what they can. Some secure the area in a tight 360, some push the crowd further back, as a guy with Combat Life Saver training and Emergency Medical Technician begins to attend to the victim. They provide some basic first aid: covers the chest wounds with plastic from MRE packets and tape, does a needle chest decompression, controls bleeding and stops the arterial bleeding in bicep, simultaneously gets the blood pressure up and gives him a whole bag of Hextend Intravenous fluid to increase the blood volume. He has lost loads of blood. Damn, this guy is in the worst shape, if we can get control of the wounds, perhaps we can buy at most a half hour of life, that is the best case scenario.

Other soldiers are watching the crowd like hawks. You have two guys on their knees helping the Iraqi, they cannot worry about security; there is a crowd, and here is a perfect moment for someone to take a shot. There is no escaping it—no matter what the situation, being on one's toes, maintaining situational awareness, taking nothing for granted is the only way to have sense of security on the ground.

The two soldiers on their knees look at each other. The little failures—it is a disappointing moment. Just as little accomplishments warm the heart, the little failures momentarily put you in a funk.

"Fuck man, we were a bit too late." They look at each other. "Fuck it."

The two soldiers look at each other and shrug the shoulders. They look up slowly at the desperate Iraqis and the woman eagerly watching. Bad news never gets good over time, it is an ingrained maxim, a law of the heart, and it's best to come clean sooner rather than later.

"We are very very sorry, he is gone, Afwan, habibi, afwan?"

The inevitable moment of the loved one refusing to come to terms with the grim reality. A long moment's pause, and you know next will come the wailing, loud and shrieking, and more people will inevitably gather.

It is time to finish the business and get out, things could get ugly. The Iraqis who were present know that Americans did not shoot, but the gathering crowd may not know, an angry crowd that is filled with incomplete information is a situation best avoided.

A soldier securing the perimeter noticed a car with a girl about twelve years old and a boy about eight, looking, whispering, and mumbling to themselves. In the pandemonium no one seems to have noticed the two kids. He walked over there, leaned on one knee and talked to them. It's their father. The kids, perhaps already in shock, grabbed hold of his left forearm. He looked at the kids, at the gathered crowd and at the man on the ground, what in the hell do you do?

It was the strangest sight as he slowly took the kids, walked with them holding on to their shaking hands straight to their father lying on the ground. The soldier knelt on one knee as the kids sat, and the kids grabbed their father's right hand, raised it, and whispered, with faintly audible cries ba . . . ba . . . ba, and released their father's arm as the chubby warm hand dropped listlessly. The children would raise it again very delicately and again one heard the soft desperate call for their father.

The two soldiers knew, it's a voice they will hear in their heads for a long time, an anguished face they will always remember.

One can never know whether the children, if they live long enough, would be glad that they were beside their father at his last moment or regret that they had to live a lifetime with the memory of their father violently torn apart. Sometimes there is no right and wrong, you decide as you decide and live with it. It is what it is.

The Iraqi police—having conveniently stayed away while their insurgent colleagues carried out the murder—now show up. It's time to hand the scene over to them, that's how it is done sometimes, the perpetrators, the police, the law all become one: The nuts running the nuthouse. As the soldiers are about to step off, some soldiers who have always kept tabs on the Iraqi police in the neighborhood walk up to the head guy. He is one of the worst. The soldier talks to him smiling, offering him a cigarette, sharing a smoke and taking in his hearty laughter as if they are best friends. Then he walks back, commenting with a smile to his soldiers, "Yeah that guy, he is one of the worst, he was behind this and half the other shit that goes down in this neighborhood. I had to go say *Shlonek habibi*! We have to greet him sometime."

Then he adds, grinding his teeth, "That motherfucker man, I tell you what, some good things are going to happen to him in a very bad way, baby, we will make it happen," and everyone joins in the laughter. As soldiers step off, the marked man is assiduously trying to control events, putting the dead father that his men just murdered in the police vehicle while trying to calm the relatives who have now arrived at the scene. Soldiers wave at him, thank him loudly and effusively, as he waves back with his usual smile. A soldier comments, "Yeah, we are definitely going to have some tea with him."

But they have stayed around longer than they anticipated, and they know that come nighttime there will be a raid, it is inevitable.

The father of the two children, a Mr. Arif, as soldiers learned, was someone who had intermittently worked for the Americans, and at times for the government. But that was only the easiest of excuses: He was an easy target, and they managed to put an end to him in the middle of the thoroughfare to make a point—this is what awaits the person who crosses the line. His death has more validity than his life. He is only one poor guy, but his death makes multiple points on behalf of insurgents. That they exist; that they know who crosses the line; and that those people will not go unpunished. The demonstration effects of murder, of force, aimed at the population the insurgents seek to control goes a long way towards obtaining complicity. People take those hurried steps passed the scene, keeping in mind the reality of the time and the place. The insurgents exist, and they manifest themselves only at the moments they choose. Getting to them at the moment they appear, or *before*, is the trick.

All day one can choose to pay attention only to the illusion of normalcy, to be blinded by the illusions. At night things change, and soldiers get a firsthand glimpse into the alternative reality. The place is infested and crawling with insurgents, like rattlesnakes in a snake farm. Rattlesnakes come to life out of hiding, to span the terrain with confidence, having wallowed in the shade all day to escape the full fury of the sun. They crawl out hissing to get some fresh air and look around, the goddamn rattlesnakes.

Get Up! Get Your Shit On! TST!

> "Hey listen up! This is what we do, what we are good at, let's do this shit right. Mark my words men, let's do this in goddamn style—are you with me?"
>
> —A Staff Sergeant (11B3P5V)

Soldiers get their final mission of the long patrol. It is the middle of the night by now: a TST (Time Sensitive Target Acquisition). It is a very precise mission, put together based on all the high-tech and low-tech intelligence capabilities. Soldiers know, "TST's the ultimate money-maker." It's the moment when soldiers get to do what they are trained to do: a strange feeling, complicated, exhilarating. So much for that deserved break the soldiers were hoping for. Well, at least they managed to get some chow and relax for couple of hours.

A TST: catch some insurgent leaders in a sticky part of town, at a time and a place of *our* choosing, with the certainty of a firefight. Get a rattlesnake in his own snake farm, his own terrain and natural habitat. The moment the mission comes down (always in the middle of the night) you hear intermittent curses of soldiers awakened from a restless slumber after a day of walking. You hear the soldiers from night patrol hurry back to base to put their things together.

The place slowly transforms into controlled pandemonium. For an outsider looking in, the buzz, random curses, yelling and moving about may seem as if soldiers have lost their minds. But there is intense purpose and focus. Everyone runs, yells, walks with a purpose, checking and double checking: equipment, maps, photos, geographic reference grids, radios, batteries, night optical devices, weapons. Eventually everyone sits down and reviews the operations order, everyone with their own little piece to execute; you study it in the brief time you have. It is, after all, time-sensitive. The clock is ticking; soldiers know they are about to go out and stop some fucker's clock from ticking. You look at imagery, at the plan, look at it inside and out, imagine it, and try to get it into your bloodstream because no one has any doubts as to what awaits and you want to be ready. Sarcasm and humor is on hold during the operations order: This is it, this is the job. The intensity and purpose inside the building becomes so thick you can flick out your tongue and taste it, smiling inwardly.

Officers command the fight, but it is the enlisted leaders who control the fighting. They are in the middle of it. A noncommissioned officer in his fourth deployment—a man who lives for this moment—looks at his guys rallied around him:

"Look, you know this neighborhood, you know how this will go down, this is what we do, this is what we are good at and let's do this shit right. And remember men, if anyone does anything smart or stupid, first fucking call comes to me, understood?"

The leader of the main assault element replies simply, "You know it, Boss, it goes without saying, brother, we are doing the assault, we got this, and you just remember the channel on the radio if you have to switch to it."

A few strange cackles and laughs, and everyone steps off. With a steady heart, the bones feel heavy, the blood is warm and the walk has a strident purpose as the ground envelops and swallows each step.

This is it.

❖ Night vision

Soldiers head into the neighborhood. They step off, determined and masking their apprehensions, fears, and doubts—overpowering them with logic and trusting only each other. Soldiers come to terms with fear. The sooner you do so, the better you will perform.

Having decided on the best form of infiltration, soldiers take a circuitous route. Entering the neighborhood, they see it in the surreal green images created by their night optical devices. It seems strangely familiar but unreal, even as you hear the first rat-tat burst of insurgent AK-47 fire, the tracer rounds tearing through the air. Fucking rattlesnakes, crawling everywhere.

Insurgents in their own habitat are tactically proficient, and they pay attention to detail. Every insurgent leader places forward observers and security elements in good tactical dispositions to provide early warning. These forward observers—usually with the Iraqi Police—make phone calls to inform them of suspicious activity. But they cannot know the soldiers' precise location.

So the burst of insurgent fire serves two purposes. It warns others of the danger and gets them ready for a possible fight. And it is a form of reconnaissance: Firing at random, they expect soldiers to return fire. But soldiers know that the moment they fire, muzzle flashes will give away their position. So, if soldiers fire, it must be deliberate, controlled, swift, well-aimed and never random.

❖ Greetings!

Soldiers split as pre-arranged. The main effort moves to the location at a fast but controlled pace to secure the house with the rattlesnakes. Others fight the insurgents at large, buying time and making sure the place is in complete lockdown. No one can go in or out for the next hour or two, it is absolutely imperative, lock it the fuck down! There is the rat-tat and clanking noise of weapons, intermittent explosions from RPG fire (Rocket Propelled Grenades).

The main assault element is now at the insurgents' door.

The world slows down, all the noise is now muted. You grip the pistol grip tighter; soldiers stack tightly next to one another. It is the house of insurgents. Inside could be an insurgent leader, surrounded by his acolytes and family, armed and ready for a fight to the death. Or the house could be filled with explosives, rigged and ready to blow the moment you bust in; it has happened to some brothers. There is only one certainty: You can't know what awaits through that door, but you will go through it nonetheless. You hear the boom, you hear your own breath, and you walk through the door into the house, swiftly, deliberately and with a sense of purpose and focus, inhaling the cordite. That is violence of action. Everyone walks into the house with a greeting: Peace, Love, and Happiness—m-o-t-h-e-r-f-u-c-k-e-r.

Soldiers walk in, moving from room to room around furniture, knick-knacks, scattered chairs and carpets; the world in slow motion now, everyone has their assigned part, each on the other's heels, ready to pick up any slack in a split second.

Two soldiers walk in the narrow hallway, shoulder to shoulder in a "rolling T" with weapons at the high-ready. Some others walk behind.

Steady, deliberate steps toward the two doors at the end where they can see a shirtless insurgent, AK in hand, trying to step out in the dark. He is disoriented. In a split second, the safety levers turn from safe to semi, and four controlled rounds are expended in slow motion, tap-tap-tap-tap. The AK drops first, his body slowly follows. The soldier to the left kicks the weapon, hops over the warm rattlesnake, who is fast losing his life. They keep taking the steady steps in the hallway. Nothing is over, the house is not cleared. Another one pops his head out for a second and aims his AK; two lasers are on him in an instant, making his balding head glisten in green. Four quick rounds and he, too, slowly drops.

Now two others come out begging for mercy, hands in the air. "Please, mister, please, mister." Soldiers put them in a corner, clear the rooms, and the building is clear.

The guy on the ground is writhing in pain with a muzzle on his navel and a boot on his neck, facing the moment of truth.

In order to lie effectively, people need to have their delicate internal balance intact, have some form of control—or the pretence of it. In a startled state of mind, with the world turned upside down, lying is very difficult. Soldiers asked a few short questions to verify his identity and he answered truthfully, shivering in fear, his moans getting louder each second as his brain processes pain.

Everyone comes downstairs dragging three rattlesnakes. The guys are on the list, all positively identified, as are the two killed in action—a rare moment of simple successes. Other soldiers start a quick hard search of the house. The world once again turns at its usual pace, nothing in slow motion.

Outside the house, in the distance, insurgents would fire a burst on auto; it would be quickly followed by a single deliberate shot, our strategically placed snipers in action. There is the slow drawl of a sniper on the radio, one of the best, an international award-winner. He always had that nonchalant calm voice as he rattled off the enemy dead. He announces that he anticipates the enemy to pop up on a different corner, so he is moving to a different position. We know from experience that he has that sixth sense—the ability to correctly antic-ipate the movement of the enemy like no one else. In a TST, he turns a rattlesnake hunt into a turkey shoot.

The innocent are contained in a corner room, out of the way. But now an older woman (the mother of one of the rattlesnakes) grabs her chest and collapses on the ground, dry heaving and panting, out of breath.

"Goddamn, hey someone check her, what is her problem?"

Two soldiers watch the rest of the family in the room while two soldiers kneel down next to her in the hallway as the rest of the family peers from the room, terrified and wondering what is happening to her.

"What's up?"

A soldier explains, "Oh dude, she is just having a panic attack."

It is not the first time soldiers have encountered this; it is common for women and some men who are unable to handle the situation.

"Well, time for her to pop some Zanax, brother," a leader laughs.

She is panting on the ground, short of breath. A soldier retorts, "Dude, if anyone gives her Zanax, I will personally shoot you on general prin-ciple, *I* want that goddamn Zanax." Everyone laughs in agreement.

The moment soldiers subdue the enemy and get control of the house, the enemy and the innocent inside become the responsibility of sol-diers. Only a few minutes earlier, soldiers were fighting their way in, subduing crawling rattlesnakes; now, having attained control of the place, they are expected to be the decent human beings that they are and protect the innocent, who are unaware of what precisely has taken place upstairs in the house. The responsibility for controlling the situation always falls on the soldiers, part of the job description of soldiers in the front lines of a counterinsurgency.

She is panting on the ground; the sight makes the others nervous. Soldiers cannot leave her, but there is more work to be done. Elsewhere in the house, soldiers with specialized weapons still need to bring

147

their stuff down, and it is always better to have the place calm and not become a pandemonium of innocent people freaking out. But if everything takes a little longer because someone is having a panic attack, there is the danger of such a situation developing, and people may do something stupid out of fear.

One soldier calls the oldest daughter out of the room and hands her some pills to give her mother. He helps carry the mother into the room with the rest of them. Then the soldiers take turns trying to keep it calm as others continue searching the place for insurgent secrets.

Just at that moment, a loud boom rumbles the house, rattling and clanking the pots and pans. The soldiers grin, but with each noise the women and children look increasingly terrified. So much fear, they are unable to speak. You hear involuntary moans, see the constant spasms and shivering fingers: debilitating fear.

One of the rattlesnakes now decides to resist, cursing profanities at soldiers and wiggling about vigorously. Resistance, no matter in what form, is always admirable. It takes a person with a different heart, with a set of convictions and intestinal fortitude, to be able to stand up to authority. Though nothing good may come of it (as in this instance), it is their moment under the sun, and no one can rob them of that moment.

Soldiers walk day in and day out with no sense of time, at times fatigued beyond belief, mostly in a trance. You feel alive only when you momentarily realize the constant inner struggle to control the rage inside. It is pure bound-up energy: an intense fire inside the gut, waiting to burst out, screaming to escape; the entire body a raging inferno.

Now—when an insurgent with blood on his hands resists rather than surrenders—comes a moment of unmitigated, justifiable rage. The moment and the resulting violent action create an unapologetic sense of intense visceral gratification. The raging soul finds a momentary still point.

The soldiers get ready to step out again. The night is far from over. You can hear intermittent fire in the distance.

Every innocent family member is now inside the house—except for one little boy who stands at the doorstep, transfixed, terrified, eyes bulging out. Too petrified to move, his limbs jerk involuntarily, his jaw chatters from so much uncontrollable fear.

He will relive this moment. He will live it alone and carry it to the grave.

A lot of this kid's life will depend on how he somehow comes to terms with what happened on this dimly lit night, how he can find some balance between logic and emotion. Logic could tell him that his father had a lot of innocent blood on his hands (though he will never know the truth about those other children, like the ones left in that car). But along the way, he will carry in his heart overpowering feelings— feelings of utter humiliation and powerlessness, an overwhelming feeling of being utterly worthless as a human being, at the mercy of American soldiers.

Soldiers didn't wonder whether he would have a soft spot in his heart for the Americans. He will not.

Catching rattlesnakes and doing it well is the job of soldiers. What happens to the insurgents and others, the second- and third-order effects of soldiers' actions—well, it is sometimes not the job or the place of soldiers to worry about it. Counterinsurgency is different, but it is still a war.

"Hey, man, we are linking up with the others about a hundred meters out, we need to wrap this shit up."

"Hey, goddamn, everyone inside the room, right fucking now, move, move! Hurry the fuck up, throw that kid in the room, close it, we need to go."

There is no time for social etiquette or kindness of heart before stepping into a possible firefight, it's all about making warm-hearted cold decisions. Everyone checks their gear and steps off, locking the doors behind. Soldiers can't have anyone come after them, whether out of spite or fear: Nothing is over yet, there's never a moment to be complacent. Complacency is a fool's errand.

❖ Fighting your way out

The rattlesnakes are caught, and soldiers step out into the different reality of the street. It's time to fight their way out. A well-planned and well-executed combat mission is a graceful lethal drama, with death hovering throughout. Apache helicopters whir overhead, and the faint mosquito noises of unmanned aerial vehicles warn of impending dangers. The night, we own it, but has an eerie calm; everything is deserted. Now there is no humor, no sardonic comment. Weapons are at the low ready as soldiers walk down the street in night vision. Any vehicle along the road may be rigged to blow. Every goddamn thing is always possible.

Being aware of the situation and anticipating the point of view of the enemy is the only way to minimize the probability of getting surprised. Soldiers do not actually think as they step, they simply follow their trained instincts. With every swivel of the head, apprehensions and doubts yield to the inferno inside as the raging soul seeks a still point.

And in this neighborhood, one finds it fast.

With each scan through night vision, you survey the innumerable alleyways, the buildings, the walls. It is not the alley you look for, it is the incongruities in the shadows. The wall is irrelevant, but the jagged edges of a wall are always relevant. The roof is irrelevant. But the straight edge where the wall meets the roof and missing a wedge, *that* is relevant. The closed wooden doors of the corner store are irrelevant, but the door panel slightly out of place is relevant. It is in those incongruities that one may find rattlesnakes lurking.

So you keep walking, making sense of the obvious in terms of the incongruities, constantly trying to see the world differently without getting wrapped up in the obvious. Whether it's assaulting a house and having to distinguish the enemy from the innocent in quick succession, or walking down the night street during a firefight, the essence of close-quarter battle must always be how to capture that one incongruous detail in a fleeting second. Remaining steady and calm, refraining from momentary impulses is the test of tactical acumen.

Two brave insurgents pop up on a roof while two more move along the shadows in the alley. A split second later, the lasers of soldiers are trained on them, another split second comes the fire. The ones on the roof edge lose their balance and fall while the two in the alley make a futile attempt to crawl. Soldiers hop over the warm rattlesnakes and continue their slow delicate movement, scanning the sector and looking for more incongruities in what they see and feel.

About fourteen rattlesnakes with lot of toys that go boom are waiting to ambush the soldiers. Soldiers know. That's the beauty of walking at night with extra eyes in the air: some soldiers had followed the entire movement from helicopters and gave the others warning about the rattlesnakes waiting to strike. The big guns in the air—two Apache helicopters with their heartwarming noise—clear to engage. They do a gun-run, annihilating the entire ambush-line in a perfect simple swoop. It's sublime through night vision, the slow elegant movement, the steady stream of 30MM cannons and all the rattlesnakes scattering about in little pieces. Then they hear the sweet, steady, calm voice of the female Apache pilot on the radio. A woman's voice has never sounded so breathtaking.

Nightcap at Dawn

The dark night is a different reality from daytime. The people are nowhere and the insurgents are everywhere. The streets are dark and empty, and you hear only the rustle of your own and your colleagues' footsteps as you walk the last couple of miles of the long patrol.

But people are here, in the seemingly deserted neighborhood.

With the naked eye, no light comes from the houses. Yet through night vision, you see faint green luminous streaks that glow along the edges of doorways and windows. You know from experience that some people are not worried about the danger; they sleep on their balconies and roofs, saying the hell with it. But the vast majority stay still and very awake. The entire family will huddle inside one room, everyone staring at each other; some whisper phrases from the Quran in fear, praying, utterly at the mercy of circumstances. Hoping no one, insurgent or American, will show up at their doorstep. They have small candles or homemade lamps or little kerosene-fired contraptions for faint illumination—they've turned off the lights. People are never really absent, they are only absent from the streets, knowing that soldiers and insurgents are fighting it out.

You pass the neighborhood and get to an area with less danger. Looking back, you know without a doubt that the neighborhood is teeming with rattlesnakes. They have the place, the people and everything in it on lockdown. Insurgents have power. They have traction on the ground in this neighborhood. They have control because some people support them, and they get the complicity of the rest with the use of violence. They constantly attack and challenge the local authorities, keeping them from getting a foothold to instill a semblance of legitimate control.

The neighborhood has a very different reality from the early morning bustle, the illusion of normalcy. The alternative reality of the day is the reality of night. Come morning, the situation will revert: air crisp, sky clear, the hushed voices of people, their steps, their glances, the distinct smell of spices, oil, and sweat while the rattlesnakes crawl inside and under rocks to escape the fury of the sun.

They will come out at a time and place of their choosing. That is the way of insurgents, the method in the madness.

Soldiers need to get control of the neighborhood. Tomorrow's mission will be the same—to slowly make inroads, taking it to the enemy without mercy while distinguishing the enemy from the innocent. The steady accretion of small gains on the ground will bring the necessary change. The day will be day, and night will be night, with no illusions in between. It's a slow road, but it is what it is.

Back in the tent and shucking off the heavy gear, the sun is almost rising. Someone else will take the early morning patrol so those returning from the raid can have few hours' rest. Those on the late morning patrol will walk around, drink tea, laugh, joke, and share a story with an Iraqi family.

But that is a few hours down the road, and a few hours for soldiers on the ground is an eternity. The present moment is everything: utterly exhausted but completely awake, still intense at the end of a successful mission. The utter fatigue creates a feeling of peace, a graceful calm— soldiers too tired to want to revel in the moment. Tomorrow will be the same, and to be a couple of sorrows ahead is to stay sane.

There is time only for one quick cup of coffee (in a water bottle cut in half) and a quick AAR (After Action Review) while the memories are still fresh. Talk about what we did right, what we did wrong, and what we can do better: always, the only way to do it better.

Then everyone can crawl inside his sleeping bag, put on head phones, take a nap, and let the mind wander far away from Iraq for a few hours as you snuggle into the silk army poncho liner, the infantryman's dream catcher. Peaceful sleep: a simple pleasure. But first, try to gratify the heart's intense craving for some semblance of normalcy if only for one fleeting moment. Here you go, brother: "Simple pleasures of life man, and let's have many of them," and soldiers inhale the sip of sweet ice-cold Tennessee whiskey while taking refuge in the early morning hours of Iraq. A nightcap at dawn. It is what it is, today is today and tomorrow will be tomorrow.

But the question lingers, what kind of a soup-sandwich are we in the middle of? Exactly what the hell is going on in the streets between these people? What are their motives and desires? What are their histories, and most importantly: Why do so many seem as intent on killing one another as on killing us?

7

SOUP SANDWICH: THE MANY INSURGENCIES IN IRAQ

Many regard subversion [insurgency] as being
principally a form of redress used by the down-trodden
peoples of the world against their oppressors, and
feel, therefore, that there is something immoral about
preparing to suppress it. Undoubtedly subversion is
sometimes used in this way, and on these occasions
those supporting the government find themselves
fighting for a bad cause. On the other hand, subversion
can also be used by evil men to advance their own
interests in which case those fighting it have right on
their side. More often, as in other forms of conflict,
there is some right and some wrong on both sides,
and there are high minded and base people among the
supporters of both parties.

—General Sir Frank Edward Kitson[42]

If you walk the streets long enough you learn the surroundings
intimately. On many a night, during raids and time sensitive target
missions, the familiar, overpowering smell of burnt garbage,
raw sewage, and the pervasive mist of fried cooking oil and spices

---

[42] *Low Intensity Operations: Subversion, Insurgency and Peacekeeping.* General
Kitson often uses the terms subversion and insurgency interchangeably.

would be enough for a soldier to recognize the precise intersection they just passed and the neighborhood they had entered. The squad leader of the main assault element hollers to his guys, "OK, man, here you go, get ready, it's about to start!" In some neighborhoods it always started quick.

Yet there was also a strange disconnect, another serious concussion, that some soldiers and young officers would discuss in between chasing insurgents: This was the startling difference in the levels of American and Iraqi deaths. In July 2006, for example, the death toll of American soldiers was forty-two.[43] In that same month, there were over three-thousand reported deaths of Iraqi civilians. The disparity between the numbers always remains the same—and that is *a lot* of Iraqi people dying.

The soldiers on the ground, if they had learned anything by this time, well understood that most of the Iraqi deaths took place at the hands of other Iraqis and not Americans (although Americans were responsible by extension, for being unable to stop it). Deaths of Iraqis from vehicle bombs and suicide bombs averaged around ten to twenty per day, while the deaths of Iraqi civilians from gunfire and executions averaged around forty to fifty *per day*.[44] Of course, "we don't do body counts." But nothing better captures the absurd nature of the reality that Iraqis live through and soldiers have to navigate on the ground than the contrast between American deaths and Iraqi civilian deaths and the fact that most of the Iraqis are killed by their countrymen.

How to make sense of this absurdity? Soldiers on the ground look up at the heavens. Understanding the wider events help them to make sense of their immediate surroundings, and strangely has the effect of making it possible to fight better.

And, looking up from the ground, one could see the reality that made the American counterinsurgency effort unique. It is not a single insurgency that the Americans were fighting, but several. In fact, Americans were fighting a counterinsurgency in the midst of a

---

[43] www.globalsecurity.org
[44] www.iraqibodycount.org

sectarian war—involving gangsters, extortionists, and assorted socio-paths who were having a field day in the guise of an insurgency. The Iraqi government had next to no legitimate control on the ground. Its institutions either did not function at all or had been hijacked in a power grab among the various contingents (including political par-ties) fighting for their share of the gravy train.

So, as they looked around as well as upward, some soldiers labeled the insurgency a "Soup Sandwich." How to get a handle on *that*?

Yes, there are the Sunni, the Shia, and the Kurds, as everyone keeps hearing, but nothing you saw on the ground fit neatly into those three boxes. That enviable sense of clarity in the heavens is something that soldiers on the ground never get to experience.

The Sunnis were an eclectic group. They included the Baathists them-selves, who had already embraced insurgency as a military strategy. They also included the Tribes, as well as al-Qaeda and its many allied Salafist brethren. The assortment of insurgent groups kept multiply-ing, each coming up with its own innovative name and absurd claims. At the height of the Sunni insurgency, a neighborhood gangster might cut the head off a neighbor, steal his BMW, call him a collaborator, and upload a video clip onto a website (labeled with some name that evoked medieval warfare)—and he would become an insurgent group. And another bunch of guys might get their fifteen minutes of fame in cyberspace by following up with a religious disquisition in an Internet chat group: "So, my fellow lunatics, is it right or not right to behead the Iraqi collaborators?" Unfortunately, this is not a joke.

Then there was the Shia insurgency. Supposedly, they had been liber-ated by the U.S., yet some felt the need to fight the liberators. The Shia insurgency was led mainly by Jaish al-Mahdi, a group unique in its astute manipulation of political realities and sectarian divisions, man-aging to get control of neighborhoods while fighting the government it was a part of. And on the side, they would kill Sunnis and cleanse neighborhoods—in the guise of redressing old sectarian grievances.

There was another strange reality that soldiers came to terms with. Many an Iraqi, of whatever sectarian identity, held deep-seated suspicions of Kurdish intentions, and some considered them insurgents. Yet all the soldiers' Kurdish friends were quite happy with their own fortunes at the moment. (The Peshmerga fighters have now become part of the Iraqi Army, and some soldiers fought side by side with them.) But they always had forebodings about their future after the Americans leave.

Iraqi people—the many children, women, and men that never asked for any of this—happen to live in the middle of all this absurdity, with us soldiers walking in their midst.

How to make sense of this soup sandwich?

Every insurgency is different (says the field manual that some friends sent over). Nevertheless, every insurgency also has many components that are similar (FM 3:24): *Organization, Tactics, Strategy, Believers,* and an *Insurgent Narrative*—the ideology or story line to justify the fight.

There might be some underlying structure to the chaos after all.

Clarity in chaos: Seeing the many insurgencies

Soldiers by training, instinct, and experience quickly come to terms with insurgent *tactics*. It takes a little longer to comprehend their wider *strategy* and the nature of the *organization*. And soldiers certainly get the opportunity to learn a lot from the *believers*.

Whether it's some rag-tag bunch of guys with AK-47s or a nationwide insurgency with tentacles reaching every part of the country, there is always some semblance of an *organization*. A bunch of pissed off guys with AK-47s stumble on a 155mm artillery shell, but they cannot do a damn thing with it without some rudimentary organization or without learning the *tactics* to emplace the thing. And even if they know what to do with the artillery round, they need *believers*—the men and women willing to take a risk in order to make it happen.

Soldiers can see how insurgent *strategy* plays out on a daily basis, as a struggle to get control through complicity and support of a population even as they try to undermine the legitimate government through the use of violence. And it is the job of soldiers to become instinctively and intimately familiar with insurgent *tactics*. But the best of the insurgents always innovate tactically; it is their greatest strength. To innovate requires a good grasp of their surrounding, their adversary, and the strategic objective on the ground. The effective innovation of tactics on the ground also improves the wider strategy at the margins, both for insurgents and for counterinsurgents.

The best of the insurgents make the broader strategy and tactics on the ground congruent. The bigwig leaders and talking heads of an insurgency may provide strategic direction while middlemen keep it alive and bankroll it. But it is the foot soldiers and local leaders that put their ideas into action. At times they do so astutely, at times not. It becomes the job of the counterinsurgents, the soldiers and leaders on the ground, to discover and exploit any incongruities between the wider organization and the local cells, and between strategy and tactics.

Soldiers also become familiar with the believers, in all sorts, shapes, and sizes—though in Iraq, they are rarely women. The men who are willing to risk, resist, and die for the cause are the best of them. Then there are those who show support in other ways—they may flip the finger, or put up billboards, or join a protest, but they are not too keen on dying.

Despite the abnormal conditions under which the believers and supporters meet the soldiers, they all have stories to tell. Sometimes they are even charming. Other times, reading and watching insurgent propaganda until the brain goes numb, soldiers begin to hear a different dimension.

Of all the critical components that sustain an insurgency on the ground, this one defied all expectations: the insurgent *narrative*, or the Insurgent Ideology—what soldiers eventually called The Insurgent Sob Story.

In Iraq, the stories come in so many varieties and versions, you wonder if they are real, imagined, or simply some absurd joke. But that is the wrong question. Some of the insurgent narratives do have traction for some people, they resonate with them. How is that possible? Why do *some* people always believe it? So soldiers listened harder and longer.

The sob story, the insurgent ideology, the narrative—whatever one calls it—becomes one overbearing, low-hanging storm cloud that is everywhere you turn once you have learned to recognize it. You begin to hear it, feel the results of it, and see how it transpires on the ground. By learning to pay attention to the insurgent story, you also get glimpses into the dreams and nightmares of the enemies that we fight.

❖ The sob story: The insurgent narrative

The ideology lets insurgents justify the fight. It helps the believers find meaning in killing and being killed, helps them make peace with themselves and their own actions. And helps insurgents make peace with the wider society, the men, women, and children who live amid the violence propagated by their sob story.

If one listens well enough to the narrative, it is possible to glimpse the dreams and nightmares of the guys embellishing the story. There is no better way to find the strengths and weaknesses of an adversary than to know their dreams and nightmares. It is difficult because it is easier to hate viscerally than try to understand an enemy. But by listening, one can see and understand the elemental reality embedded in any sob story.

Every war inevitably results in a lot of death, but wars are always fought invoking peace, love, and happiness. Insurgents fighting their own war, invoking their own version of the greater good, do the same.

The genius of a good sob story is its ability to rob the dead of their death. It is a simple, painful reality. An average Iraqi looks down at a dead guy by the side of the road; she sees a neighbor, or perhaps an unknown soul but an Iraqi nonetheless, lying in this street that she always frequents. She tries to make sense of it, but to understand, she must decide for both today and tomorrow: Why? And the insurgents provide a ready-made answer. They may appeal to her reason or her emotions, but it appeases her fears.

160

A sob story robs the death out of the dead in a peculiar way. A death is still a death, a murder is still murder, but insurgents justify the death in terms of something else. They wage their righteous fight. The man lying by the side of the road is portrayed as an opponent of their righteous fight. Maybe he is branded as a collaborator with the Americans or he worked for the government or he was simply against them. It is irrelevant whether the woman buys into the story. If she is a believer then there is no argument; but even if she is not a believer and detested the insurgents, the death is now posited in relation to something else. So now the dead guy must defend his innocence—quite a difficulty. The man is now robbed of his death.

The moment people see the death of the innocent in relation to something else, that life has lost bit of its validity.

True or not, if the story has traction, it resonates with the emotions, the instinctive fears associated with the death of an innocent. No matter how absurd or despicable, it is foolish to underestimate the strength of a well-told, often-repeated narrative. The resonance it has on the ground reinforces the story as the relevant parties interpret it their own way. At that point, the sob story becomes self-perpetuating. Those who believe it dogmatically become happy prisoners of their own sob story, and everyone who does not buy into it is instantly wrong.

The story may contain only some elements of truth; it never has to be the complete truth. When people believe, the story becomes valid and insurgents score points. In Iraq, with multiple groups waging multiple insurgencies, one hears a number of insurgent narratives. But there is a singular theme that cuts right across them: That of victimhood. Being perpetual victims is the never-ending sob story of every insurgent group in Iraq.

❖ The never-ending story: Claims of victimhood

Yes, Sunnis, Shia and Kurds all have their own version of the narrative based on their unique history and collective experiences and infused with a lot of myths to justify their own insurgency. But the one foundation on which everything is predicated is that of victimhood: The stories of how they got shafted repeatedly.

161

Of course, many of these stories have large elements of truth. Kurds claim repeated persecution at the hands of the Arabs, and they wonder when the Americans will forget about them once again. Shia invoke years of persecution at the hands of the Sunni rulers, and some Shia also wonder when the Americans might forget them again. The Sunnis claim, not without truth, that they were also victims of Saddam, and that at present they stand to be persecuted by a Shia-dominated government in cahoots with Kurds—who, they fear, will try to redress their grievances at the cost of Sunnis.

The exception to these standard narratives is the Salafist Jihadists, of which al-Qaeda is the most popular franchise. Salafist Jihadists have their own version of the sob story, the Salafist ideology, based on a unique claim of victimhood which they take to cosmic (and even psychedelic) levels.

Salafist Jihadists, the top of the line in Sunni fundamentalist thinking, embrace a literal interpretation of the Islamic religious texts: That is, the Koran plus the many sayings of the Prophet Muhammad that are enshrined in texts called the Hadiths. The thousands of sayings and actions of the prophet and his followers—like any ancient religious text—are at times inconsistent, at times defy logic, and very often contradict each other. But inconsistency is the singular advantage of religious texts, giving the ability to pick and choose.

Salafists infuse the texts with their Jihadist fervor, with the explicit aim of emulating the early Muslim communities in Islam, the *Salaf* (hence the name). Failing that, their ultimate dream is to instill their Salafist version of Islam in the entire Muslim world, with guns in hand. And oh yeah, while creating the Salaf, the perfect community, there are a few minor details: let us also destroy America, the state of Israel, Beirut, and, of course, convert the Shia people back to Sunnis. And make sure all Sunni Muslims adhere to the cosmic narrative, that would be just outstanding!

Here is a mission statement whose cosmic aspirations are so obviously out of line with capabilities, it becomes pathetically funny. Yet it is also not at all funny because a very tiny minority of Muslims actually

162

believes it, and some of them are willing to act on it. And then there is the sizable number of Muslims—in other Arab countries as well as in the West—who are complicit by serving as apologists because they have not had the good fortune of living under Salafist rule. As funny as it is, that is the story line the extreme Salafists and other Jihadi groups keep repeating and soldiers kept hearing.

Some soldiers came across some propaganda material of Ansar al-Sunna. (A crème-de-la-crème Salafist group, as we learned from some Kurdish people who knew them intimately.) As always, a bunch of the soldiers with some young officers were going through the stuff, watching the video clips, with all the speeches, moans, bitches, gripes, and vitriolic rants coming through the laptop. A young officer had a smirk as he watched; he shook his head, "Dude, are these guys on a bad acid trip or what?" Yes, indeed, it is an acid trip, only for some of them, there is no coming down.

Of the many Salafist movements and communities scattered around the world, not everyone is a militant. But a lot of them tend to be apologists for the militants. And—perhaps no irony here—the loudest apologists tend *not* to be living close to them.

Salafists and nearly all the extremist Jihadi groups take the idea of victimhood in a peculiar way. In the Salafists' attempt to create a society that mirrors the early Muslim communities, they have embedded the sentimental idea of the "pure Islamic believer" as a consistently persecuted victim, from the time of the prophet down to the present day. The pure believer is constantly fighting actual armies—the temporal side of the fight. But he also fights against the many corrupting elements in society, and that is the "moral" side of the fight—in the obscenely perverse way they define the word. And this fight comprises an endless list of enemies: the many Muslim men and women who look to the future and not the past; the Shia people; the Americans, the Jews, the British—the list is really endless. The Salafists constantly subsume any additional real and imagined grievances, incorporating them all into this psychedelic myth. That makes it possible for even some ostensibly sensible people to hear them out with a sympathetic ear; and, though they may not support them

163

in any fashion, they may end up being complicit by being apologists or merely being silent. Perhaps that is the genius of a good sob story no matter who propagates it. It has an inherent ability to trap people inside it, make them happy prisoners until too late, when they experience (as soldiers would put it) the "oh shit" moment.

It is a self-serving argument that reinforces a narrowly defined parochial view of the world, a view that conveniently omits any transgressions or atrocities committed by Muslims over the centuries. Everyone who does not buy into their version of the story is quickly defined as the enemy. The greatest irony is that sensible Muslims have been their greatest victims: They are treated as enemies more than anybody else because they, the Muslim majority, remain the ultimate prize in their cosmic battle.

Which is a very favorable situation for those fighting against them, for it means that in the long run they will have few allies and even fewer collaborators—and more enemies.

What is the driving force behind this insistence on being miserable victims? Misery, strangely enough, has its inspiring aspect, as soldiers know intimately: That is called overcoming adversity. But the stories one hears in the myriad insurgent narratives, irrespective of creed or ethnicity, contain a different theme. There is lot of injustice, real and imagined, a lot of amputated spirits and sapped aspirations. Some of it may be historically accurate but a lot of it is imaginary and mythical. This kind of misery seems completely different from misery as we understood it.

Misery: Soldiers whose grandfathers or family members served in WWII, pushing through to Berlin, or experienced the unimaginable in the Pacific theater or the mountains of Korea; soldiers whose fathers traversed the jungles of Vietnam, or any soldier who has been to a convention and met older veterans who know what real misery is supposed to be like. Soldiers today have been fortunate enough never to experience real misery, thanks to them. If one has listened to WWII veterans who fought the Battle of the Bulge, one knows that nothing is more absolutely miserable than freezing cold. On nights at seventeen degrees with a wind-chill well below, body partly covered in mud, snuggling each other to stay warm, the cold seeped into the bones with no hope of relief. Some colleagues in Afghanistan stayed freezing all night in the snow to place a Small Kill Team to ambush insurgents in Gardez: Snuggling together when a stray dog crawled quietly into the same hole, finding their warmth while also warming the soldiers all night. Thinking of them has the effect of taking away the immediacy of the present and making it impossible to complain. Life of soldiering is not as bad as it used to be: Soldiers can eat cheesecake in a combat zone, as absurd as it is, so let's be serious.

❖ Beyond misery

Victimhood is not simply about physical misery. It is a reminder of the tragic history, but it is also about amputated souls and spirits of people, of deliberate oppression, about how human dignity was sapped from them at an earlier time. But tragically, it is also an attempt—a perpetual attempt—to make one *feel* the old pain, so as to confound justice with vengeance and to justify today's wrongs in terms of past grievances.

Yes, past misery can inspire the present. But in Iraq, listening to Kurdish, Sunni and Shia insurgent narratives, it is not only about inspiration based on their unique history. It is also an excuse. Using the past stories of victimhood seems to justify the injustices of today, an easy and righteous justification of the deaths of the innocent as well as of their many imagined enemies.

The insistence on being victims becomes an eloquent attempt to defend the indefensible.

So it is that some of the Shia groups could hunt down the families of former regime members, invoking past injustices but also announcing their own righteousness in their claim of victimhood. The Kurds do the same, a bit more subtly, in their contested lands in the north; and the Sunni Salafists and al-Qaeda bring their own cosmic version of victimhood to bear on everybody. They all seem to believe that the wrongs they perpetrate today can be exonerated based on a past injustice. And the truth of it is irrelevant, if men with guns believe in it.

165

But there is something dangerous and poignant about finding inspiration in the narrative of being perpetual victims.

How can political compromise be achieved between contending parties who are feeling so magnificently sorry and self-righteous? Victimhood has nothing to do with the balance between logic and sentiment. Victimhood engenders further suspicion all around. Because each party will reciprocate in kind, acting on their own sorry story. Soon it is a vicious cycle, a black hole with no end. Perhaps the worst of it is that the Shia and the Kurds seem unable to recognize that they are the victors of today.

The pity of being in a perpetual state of victimhood is that it robs people of their capacity for magnanimity when it is most necessary. The sentiment that sometimes you "let the high times carry the low," the possibility of reconciliation and compromise from a position of strength at the moment of victory, that is all forgotten. Hell, they might not even see it: They are too blinded by their own sob story as happy prisoners of it. That is the consistent theme one hears in most narratives, listening to the stories as foreigners, the theme that is hardest to come to terms with as American soldiers.

But the subtle differences are significant. "Average" Shia men and women do not go around beating up Sunnis, nor do Sunnis do it to Shia, nor do the Kurds. One can always find exceptions: Wealthy family members kidnapped in collusion with criminals and profit-seeking neighbors; people ratting on others due to family feuds; the men who helped insurgents kick out a family in order to grab their new Hyundai. But the simple reality is that if all the sympathizers with the insurgent narratives were acting on them on the street, Iraq would look like Gotham city on steroids. Some may claim that it, in fact, looked like this at one point. We would disagree.

There is a definite incongruity between the narratives of insurgents (and their political parties) and the actions of "the people" on the ground. There is solace in this incongruity and an opportunity—not so much for Americans as for the Iraqi government. The government has the opportunity to drive a wedge between the enemy and the innocent with a well-timed and consistent narrative of their own. Offer the people a better alternative, with traction on the ground; give people a choice.

But the effort will always imply a painful task for soldiers of paying attention to the insurgent narratives—the real, the absurd, and pure fiction. As necessary as it is, the task is taxing on the soul. Soldiers get sick of bullshit very quickly and want to say, "Duude, you need to get over it and look around."

Figure 1. The Many Elements of an Insurgency that Keep it Alive

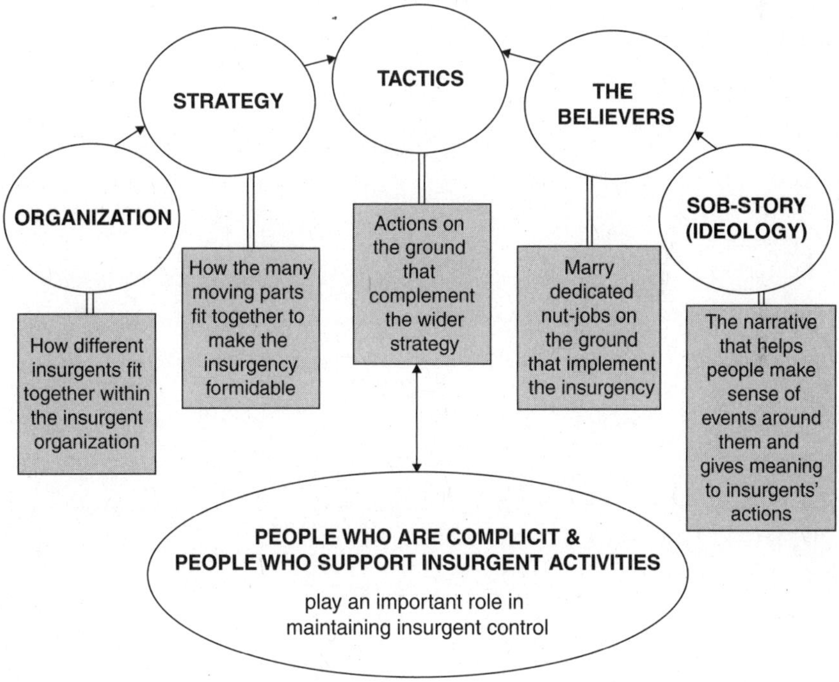

167

PART IV

CHILDREN OF GEBELAWI: INSIDE THE SUNNI AND KURDISH INSURGENCIES

This is the story of our alley—its stories, rather. I have witnessed only the most recent events, those of my own time . . . . Whenever someone is depressed, suffering, or humiliated, he points to the mansion at the top of the alley at the end opening out to the desert, and says sadly, "That is our ancestor's house, we are all his children, and we have a right to his property. Why are we starving? What have we done?"

Then he will tell the stories and cite the lives of Adham and Gabal, of Rifaa and Qassem—some

of our alley's great men. But this ancestor of ours
is a puzzle!

—*Children of Gebelawi*[45]

Flying into a new Sunni neighborhood, the questions we had
were simple. How did the former Baathists and tribes become an
effective insurgency? And a much more important question: How
did the ultra-lunatic fringe of the Jihadist community—along
with al-Qaeda, and many other Sunni extremists—manage to
get such a strong foothold in Iraq immediately after the U.S.
intervention? How did they create so many little theocratic
enclaves so quickly? What are their strengths and weaknesses,
their dreams and nightmares?

Some answers came from the Iraqis we encountered, from
other friends in the Middle East and from our own experiences
and travels. We try to bring to light a reality that people rarely
discuss, either in America or in the Middle East: How the lives
of so many Iraqis became utterly miserable under the Salafists'
medieval reign.

Chapter 15 briefly discusses the way we understood the
Kurdish insurgency. It breaks the heart to call some Kurds
insurgents: the Kurds have been the only true brothers with
us in the fight in Iraq. Many soldiers fought side by side with
Kurdish Peshmerga fighters; some Peshmerga died trying to
save American colleagues, and many a friend returned from
the mountains of Kurdistan hoping to go there again to enjoy
its simple charms. This chapter very briefly talks about the
soldiers' experiences with Kurdish people, the Peshmerga,
and the "non-insurgency-insurgency" that is taking place in
the Kurdish-controlled and contested areas.

---

[45] *Children of Gebelawi*, a novel by Naguib Mahfouz, gives an allegori-
cal-metaphorical account of the struggles among the Abrahamic reli-
gions. (Having won the Nobel Prize for it, he got stabbed in the neck
by a Jihadist.) The Sunni insurgency—as we understood it—reflects yet
another of these internecine struggles between Children of Gebelawi.

8

GEBELAWI IN HIS MANSION

> The site of our alley was a wasteland. It was part of the Muqattam Desert that stretched to the horizon. There was nothing in the void but the mansion Gebelawi had built almost as if to challenge all the fear and savagery and lawlessness.
>
> —*Children of Gebelawi*

It was a fortunate moment: the IED and the small arms fire did no serious damage to the patrol. Even better, a fire team managed to put an end to the two triggermen, as they sprinted away from the detonated IED. Now, *that* is rare.

But there is always some bad news. The two guys are undeniably from the local Jihadi cell, but they also belong to the local tribe. And the artillery rounds had been jerry rigged with the IED by some former Iraqi military. And what about the people who simply watched it go down?

Some of the people knew about it all along, and they let soldiers walk right passed and straight into an ambush. Fortunately, the black market gasoline vendors and the corner store guys gave the soldiers an accidental kind of warning when they abandoned all their shit and disappeared. Thankfully, the leaders on patrol had been walking for a while, so they had the situational awareness to take note of it.

A similar occasion in a different neighborhood—and this was funny. At the height of the Sunni insurgency, a young officer who just pinned captain looked around at his friends with a mischievous grin that hid his rage inside.

"Give me that VS-17 panel." It is a bright fluorescent orange cloth that soldiers use as a signaling device, to set up a quick helicopter landing zone among other things.

He grabbed the VS-17 panel and wrapped it around his neck, and this bright orange cloth was now covering his front and back. Everyone else was laughing.

"Sir, are you fucking serious?"

"Yes, I am."

Now everyone has that grin, and he said, "OK, men, let's fucking do it."

Then he walked straight through the middle of the road, practically screaming "shoot me," wrapped in a bright orange VS-17 Panel. The soldiers walked side by side in a staggered column through the street some called Ambush Alley. People kept looking at the spectacle, but for whatever reason, no one fired a shot at him that day. Sometimes one has to be crazy to avoid going completely insane. It provided lot of laughter afterwards—and needless to say, he remains an officer that soldiers enjoy getting into a good scrap with.

So on this day, the patrol leaders sensed what was coming and managed to flank the insurgents. But the head starts to ache again. Do we call this attack *Jihadist* because some Jihadist detonated it? Do we call it *tribal* since they belonged to the tribe? Or do we call them *Baathist* insurgents since former army guys rigged up the artillery rounds?

Who is fighting, and *why* are they fighting, and *how* are they doing it?

Baathists, Tribes, and Jihadists

In the early days, there was no resistance in Iraq and no insurgency. Then the early resistance was portrayed as regime dead-enders along with former Baathists as the front element—the main thrust—colluding with loyalist Sunni tribes who carried the flanks.

After that, it was all about al-Qaeda, the most prominent franchise of the Salafist terrorist community. Everyone seemed determined to provide the AQ (al-Qaeda) terrorist network what it desperately sought: free publicity and brand recognition.

At the height of the Sunni insurgency, the question of exactly who is at the front, the flanks, or the rear was an insoluble puzzle. It depended on who was looking and their own vantage point more than on the intricate details of the fight on the ground. But for soldiers and leaders on the ground at the height of the Sunni insurgency, the question was irrelevant. All the military leaders who walked the streets around 2005-2006 could feel it: Yes, the Jihadists were everywhere—and nearly all of them were local Iraqis. The constant puzzle, with each new story heard from an Iraqi, was this: *How* did they manage to become so effective in such a short period and get control of so many little enclaves?

Yes, the Baathists and the former military guys had a good head start in "resistance." And they were uniquely situated for it with the help of local tribes (though most tribal leaders straddled a middle ground). But it was the infusion of Salafist Jihadists, both foreign and local grown, that hijacked the initial Sunni insurgency and gave the insurgency its unique character. Including its grotesque obsession with murdering innocent Iraqis.

How did those former military guys function? And how did the Jihadists manage to get a foothold so fast?

Resistance includes acts of violence and terrorism but also demonstrations. Kids throwing stones and flipping off the soldiers, random billboards and anti-American graffiti can be acts of resistance. People are showing their true sentiments, their unwillingness to be complicit with a new regime that they believe is illegitimate.

Resistance is an elemental human impulse and an inalienable right. If there were no resistance, Americans would still be singing God Save the Queen. But resistance is not synonymous with insurgency.

173

Acts of resistance certainly hamper the government's efforts to instill control and get complicity and support. But acts of resistance become part of an insurgency only when they are *coordinated*—when the many acts begin to fit into a larger whole, moving towards a specific objective.

Former Baathists[46]

The beginning of the Sunni insurgency was sporadic resistance. Resistance in the face of an invading force is inevitable, as soldiers discussed repeatedly: If ourselves faced with an invasion, well-intentioned or not, there would be resistance. Resistance is an instinctive human impulse—even an essential one. But this time, as soldiers, the job was about how to get around it.

To learn how the former military guys pulled it off is actually quite easy. All one needs is a pack of Gauloises and a willingness to drink a lot of tea with any number of former military officers (and non-commissioned officers). They would always insist they have nothing to do with the insurgency, but, yes, they had heard that some of their friends were involved. . . .

❖ **The beginning?**

In the U.S. dash into Baghdad, we lacked a proper appreciation of the Iraqi military apparatus, and, specifically, the many shadowy paramilitary groups that functioned outside of the formal military command—reporting only to the highest-ranking Baathists. These groups were instrumental in the beginning, and they had a unique subversive advantage as secret organizations.

Other shadowy elements inside Iraq were the militias and private armies, some associated with the Baathist intelligence apparatus, others with tribal or personal allegiance. During the tail end of the Baathist regime, these militias functioned as effective enforcers, an instrument to control the population through formidable threats of violence.

---

[46] "Baathist" refers to people who were associated with the former regime, in any form—not necessarily a loyal or believing Baathist. Everybody who was somebody had to carry the Baathist card; it is unlikely that true believers exist anymore in Iraq.

There were many different affiliations within the militias: low-level and high-level Baathists; generals, colonels, and sergeant majors who have taken part in every campaign of the Baathist army; people who worked in the government; politicians and high-ranking party members. The list is unending.

The rise of these shadowy groups followed a peculiar trajectory, as explained by former Iraqi Army officers. There had been a decisive shift in the fortunes of the Armed Forces of Iraq after the 1990 Gulf War, and specifically after the 1991 uprising against Saddam, with the near mutiny of many army units. As the former military guys see it, the 1991 uprising was a mutiny by army officers and units—even though the Shia and Kurds claim it as *their* moment. The Sunni military officers contend that the Shia groups actually hijacked the mutiny.

With the loyalty of some of the army units in doubt, Saddam and senior Baathists relied more and more on the militias as trusted enforcers, shifting resources from the formal military to militias and the intelligence apparatus. This is not to absolve the formal military men of complicity with the regime, they were very much a part of the Baathist gravy train. Saddam and the Baathists followed the golden rule of any paranoid tin pot dictator: While they relied on the militias for control, they kept the military happy enough and very close. A Brigade Commander, for example, would have all the deference and pomp, the chauffeured vehicles and choice real estate that come with the position. But he might or might not have an actual brigade of men to command. And if he *had* an actual brigade, it would be without equipment. In the unlikely event he had a full brigade with the necessary equipment that he could actually command, he would also have all the intelligence guys, militias, and paramilitary officers breathing down his neck, supervising every move and reporting directly to higher, making his command into a test of loyalty. It may not be the most efficacious way to run a military, but it is certainly an efficacious way to deal with a military whose loyalty cannot be taken for granted.

The same paramilitary units were later relied on to quietly snuff out organized resistance of any sort. That was one of their greatest tactical advantages in starting an insurgency. They faced a foreign adversary

175

that was possibly oblivious to their very existence, and, in any case, utterly lacking in contextual knowledge and unable to distinguish the enemy from the innocent. So these guys simply dissolved into the population, retaining their tactical knowledge: Not only the whereabouts of safe houses, weapons, and ammunition dumps but also—and this was the most important bit of knowledge—the locations, capabilities, and aspirations of their colleagues in the military.

The former members of the disbanded Iraqi Army had a similar advantage. The vast majority of the officers and soldiers of the decrepit Iraqi Army simply changed into civilian clothes and went home instead of putting up a suicidal fight; it was a decision to save their own skin, one actively encouraged by American propaganda. Nevertheless, it is erroneous to say that the Iraqi Army disappeared or permanently dissolved.

The integrity and capability of a fighting unit does not depend solely on its equipment and uniforms. Part of its effectiveness is determined by its soldiers' loyalties and willingness to fight. A company of infantrymen that goes on leave is suspended; or, if it is disbanded by an occupying power, the company no longer exists. Nevertheless, the integrity of the company—the loyalty of the soldiers to their chain of command, to one another and the mission—may still exist in the minds of the men who are willing to fight.

As we understood it, the former officers would not be able to summon a company that is disbanded. But it sure as hell would be possible to know who to call. You know who is a good sniper, who is good at leading men, who is good with explosives, who has the best tactical acumen and who will keep their memories and information in their rightful resting place. Disbanded army officers could put together a couple of squads of motivated men who have the capacity to put up a damn good fight, defying the odds for any number of reasons. Even so, the decision to disband the army or the Baathist state should not be misconstrued as the singular reason for the many insurgencies. Some soldiers and units would have resisted anyway, and the disbanded soldiers only added an extra dimension to the situation.

The disbanded soldiers went home as former soldiers, now unemployed, with a wealth of military expertise that went for sale to the highest bidder. They had information accumulated through years of service, including information about the sea of conventional weapons scattered all over Iraq that we failed to secure. They had knowledge of the whereabouts of their colleagues and of the many tentacles of the former security apparatus. And they had contextual knowledge, a unique ability to distinguish the players, and the sides, in the ensuing insurgency.[47]

To learn about the sporadic beginning of the Sunni insurgency, how it increased in intensity, and about the infusion of Salafists and Jihadists, one only needs to sit down and smoke some cigarettes with former insurgent leaders, many of them former military men now on our payroll. They tell good stories with a lot of laughs, and soldiers listen, grasping every word. The best way to fight them is to sit there asking probing questions, always joking that this might be useful for the second inning, if it should come around.

❖ Their strengths and weaknesses

The advantage these players had—the former Baathists-turned-insurgents, the paramilitary guys and disbanded army guys—was at the tactical level. It was their strength *and* their weakness.

Their greatest tactical strength was their local level organization—an aggregation of more or less discrete insurgent cells. But this structure of independent cells without an overarching strategic organization became their greatest weakness in the long run. A bunch of former soldiers and militia men, dedicated and effective, would put together a couple of fire-teams of four to eight men, sometimes even smaller, to attack U.S. soldiers. They could be formidable in their own locale, whether or not they had any military effect. American soldiers traveling or doing patrols are ambushed, randomly shot at. The effectiveness of the attack is irrelevant. The *fact* of the attack announces the existence of the insurgents in the neighborhood, and it demonstrates to

---

[47] The ones who started the resistance and survived were well rewarded, when the best of them ended up directly on our payroll five years later as the Sons of Iraq.

the local people—and to wider media networks—that the Americans are not fully in control.

These guys had a rudimentary organization at a tactical level on the ground. Embedded in an ocean of their own people, this simplicity was their strength.

They also had a solid sob story, one instinctively understood by many people. It was rooted in the past and the present, without offering much of a vision for the future. The narrative was simple: oppose the occupying force, engage in resistance, get them out of Iraq, and refuse to subject ourselves to the Shia- and Kurdish-dominated transitional government. The Sunni grievances began with the claim that they were also victims of Saddam (a partial truth, often repeated) and that Americans were unable to provide the basic services or security or a proper livelihood. Never mind the fact that *nobody* could have gotten the basic services up and running in Iraq, given their derelict state. Add to that the colossal and inexplicable failure of postwar planning, and insurgents readily capitalized on our inability.

But while the U.S.'s inability to meet Iraqi expectations played a role, that was not the only reason the Sunni sob story had so much resonance with the people. No one appreciated how deeply embedded the state of Iraq was in the lives of the people before dismantling it. It is a singularly strange story of how people were forced to be dependent on something they loved to hate.

While the sanctions did succeed in containing Iraq in relation to other states in the region, if they were meant to *weaken* the state internally they had precisely the opposite effect on the ground. The state became the final arbiter of everything in people's lives, making them dependant for everything, including cooking oil, food, wheat flour, and medicine. But only in the *cities*. Saddam starved the provinces, especially the south, to feed the cities. And as the private economy shrank under the weight of sanctions, it was replaced with a perverse version of black marketeering and cronyism. Any businessman that flourished had to be in cahoots with Baathists, who got part of it: smuggling, extortion, black market rackets, the same old story. For those city-dwellers who were not plugged into the gravy train, the state assisted with subsidies on everything imaginable. The urban middle classes—professionals of all sorts in the cities, young and old, rich and poor—became completely and utterly dependant on something everyone claimed to hate.

Dismantling the Baath party and the state—*de-Baathification*—sounded like an abstraction on TV news. But on the ground, it meant that the calendar in Iraq turned to year Zero. Iraqis had nowhere to turn to. Nothing quickly supplanted the government: People were without money or food and could not care for their families. The human sentiment at those moments is rather simple: turn around and ask out loud, WTF?

That is the message captured by the first of the insurgents with their story of resistance. That's all they had, the Baathists and military guys: resist the Americans. They had no vision and no better alternatives. One need not look for logic when it is subservient to sentiment. That did not mean people readily resisted en masse. Some people who lost their jobs demonstrated; most stayed home. But the story found resonance.

So many Iraqis (particularly Sunnis) were simply pissed off, and as time passed it reached a fever pitch. Not much of a sob-story was needed to get the complicity and support of people in the Sunni neighborhoods. This meant, for soldiers on the ground, that people would not provide information on insurgents that attack Americans; they would prevaricate at every turn because they sympathize with the resistance.

How to distinguish the enemy from the innocent in this context? Soldiers walked into Sunni neighborhoods that have been subjected to over a decade of anti-American invective, among people who have lived under twelve years of UN sanctions which they remember well—though they were encouraged (or forced) to forget the reasons behind them. Many Iraqis believed that America was the source of all their problems as they had been constantly told, and the generation who came of age under sanctions knew nothing else. The simmering anti-American sentiment created a powerful impulse for resistance when Iraqis found us in their own front yard.

179

Many people get impulses, but only a few are likely to follow through. The smart insurgents would persuade young men to becoming trigger-men, and even pay them a few hundred dollars (the prices varied). Passionate idiots—you have to love them for their passion—assumed that their enthusiasm would compensate for their lack of training, staying by the roadside to squeeze the switch to detonate the IED. The Baathists and military guys who cooked up the plan sit in the corner store smoking, watch the whole thing go down and walk away. If the guy gets killed by U.S. firepower, insurgent leaders swiftly claim him as a martyr in the resistance against the most powerful army in the world. His neighbors will call him a hero, though they would not take part in the resistance. His parents and loved ones will be grief-stricken—martyr or not, the grief of a mother remains the same.

But there was also a practical reason for complicity, one that people highlighted often. With increased lawlessness, day-to-day life was becoming a death-defying sport for average people worrying about criminals, and the local insurgents provided security in the neighborhood. That was the first (and often the only) selling point they had. With the absence of any semblance of legitimate control on the ground when the Baathist state was dismantled, the local guys with military experience—sometimes in cahoots with neighborhood thugs—managed to turn themselves into an effective protection racket. People paid for it and were happy to do so in the absence of a better alternative. Thus it was possible for these groups to get the complicity and allegiance of their own neighborhood almost by default. There was a lot of truth in the statement, "We don't like those men, but they protect us from other groups."

And everyone knows that there are lots of these "groups," but who exactly are they? Soldiers were getting very familiar with the helpless look, the pleading eyes, and the shrug of the shoulders of an Iraqi with nothing to say.

Soldiers were increasingly seen as an occupying force, and one whose mission seemed to keep changing: They were now desperately looking for an elusive enemy that was not supposed to be there in the first place. Though the initial resistance did not immediately amount to an organized insurgency at a strategic level, and was effective only at local level, it had the cumulative effect of making it nearly impossible for Americans and the American-supported government to exert any meaningful legitimate control on the ground.

Success, it seems, breeds success. Insurgencies evolve and grow in complexity both as part of the environment and in response to the tactics and strategies of its adversary.

Many Baathists and many professional members of the former Iraqi Army were linked to the insurgency in some way, though they assidu-ously deny it. There were, in fact, many different affiliations within the militias: low-level and high-level Baathists; generals, colonels, and ser-geant majors who have taken part in every campaign of the Baathist army; people who work in the current government; politicians and high-ranking party members. The list is unending.

Sitting with a random former general, it was always painful to hear him insist he was merely being a "professional." That hackneyed comment had soldiers reaching for a pack of cigarettes to calm the raging nerves. These senior and mid-level officers started to play an active organizational role in the insurgency, attempting to coordinate between groups across neighborhoods and even across cities, making the insurgency seem more complex.

As the organization became more nuanced, the sidekicks and middle-men increased in number. They play a critical role, generally under-rated by counterinsurgents: greasing the wheels, playing courier, straddling the realms of politics, finance, and violence. They are men who coordinate the transfer of resources, peddle influence, and put people in touch across cities without getting implicated in direct vio-lence. A lot of tribal guys ended up being very effective middlemen, smart enough never to get their clothes dirty.

The Many Sunni Tribes

A bunch of men who happened to belong to a sub-clan of the Dulaimi tribe, in al-Anbar province, might attack a U.S. patrol with an IED and RPG fire. Their action does not reflect on or implicate the entire tribe. Only a few guys planned and executed the attack. But the problem for soldiers is that no member of the tribe will publicly condemn their action or help the soldiers, whether they support it or not. After all, it's their *own people*.

As the situation changed, however, these discrete acts became part of a larger whole, and tribal groups became part of a Sunni insurgency growing in strength, complexity, and determination.

Tribes and tribal leaders had their own set of predictable, contradictory, and idiosyncratic reasons to join an insurgency. Many Baathist paramilitary organizations were based on kinship, clan, and tribal loyalties, focused on patrons at the highest levels of government. Paramilitary and Baathist militias thus found automatic allies in their tribes and clans. They could switch their role from Baathist enforcers to resistance fighters—and drop the Baathist label in favor of Jihadist platitudes—knowing they could count on the support of their clans. Some of the reviled Baathist enforcers even managed to absolve their past sins by parading their new role as active participants in a resistance against the occupiers. But not all tribes were part of the Baathist gravy train: Some were heavily persecuted, and some leaders were apt to be killed if they did not hightail it out of Iraq.

Historically, the fortunes of tribes in Iraq followed the changing political landscape. In the heyday of Baath party socialism, fueled by oil money in the late sixties and seventies, the push for centralization often imposed policies against the interests of the tribes, who were seen as obstacles to centralization. Tribal fortunes changed around the time of the Iran-Iraq war. As the people increasingly realized the vacuous nature of Baathist socialism, and as the tyrannical aspects of the regime became more profound, Baathists relied on tribal leaders to keep their people in line. This reached a peak during the sanctions period (1991–2003). The Baathist state, according to some former colonels and generals of the Iraqi Army, was closer to collapse than it appeared. Following the army mutiny, the weakened Baathist regime relied increasingly on Baathist militias to maintain control. Another tactic was to include an increasing number of Sunni tribes in the

Baathist patronage system. As long as they toe the line, the tribes can make some cash, have their fiefdom, conduct smuggling and do well. Tribes with ties to the Baathist state perhaps had their own motives to actively support the insurgency against the coalition and the newly formed central government.

Those who took part in the insurgency could take for granted the loyalty, if not the complicity, of their fellow tribesmen. But tribal elders were also in a situation where they had no choice. As explained by a number of local leaders during 2006–07, unless there was a compelling reason, no tribal or clan leader was in a position to stop their men from fighting the U.S. forces, whatever their personal views. They simply played it smart. Many tribal leaders and elders paid lip service in support of the insurgency, pandering to the raging sentiments of young men who opposed a foreign invasion.

This perhaps explains why, even at the high point of the Sunni insurgency, there was no nationwide Sunni tribal uprising. Apart from the occasional hackneyed anti-American invective at a funeral or turning a blind eye when their own bodyguards might plant a bomb or two, the leadership played no active role. Pray on Friday, donate money to the anti-American cleric in the mosque who calls for resistance—and drink some scotch whiskey, hiding inside the house at night, to calm the rattled nerves. This is what many prominent Iraqis do. Take a break, visit extended family living in the condominiums in Beirut, spend a night or two in Le Meridien or Kings Palace Hotel with a view of the Mediterranean. And then come home and generally go the way the winds are shifting. These guys are too fictional to be real and too real to be fictional.

This story of the collusion between former Baathists and Sunni tribes is simple enough—but in this simplicity is a formidable challenge to the counterinsurgents. For a foreign intervention force, it is inherently difficult to distinguish the enemy from the innocent. Tribal loyalties add an extra layer of complexity: People's complicity and support may reflect traditional and deep-rooted loyalties. Getting the cooperation of the local people becomes a much greater challenge for counterinsurgents.

All of a sudden, the cliché about insurgents becomes too real for comfort. Insurgents do not need to *win*; they only need to affirm their existence through sporadic attacks. Each time they attack, they demonstrate the inability of the counterinsurgents to be fully in control, scoring points in the minds of their own people. This virtuous cycle for insurgents is a vicious cycle for counterinsurgents, a perpetual funk that shifts the burden of innovation to the soldiers on the ground.

It would be damn near impossible to implicate any tribal or clan leader directly in an act of violence by the rulebook. Not that they are innocent, but they are never guilty in the rulebook sense. The middlemen and sidekicks who keep an insurgency alive and provide its backbone are acting, often, with the tacit approval traditional leaders—as when the Sunni Baathist/tribal insurgency picked up in strength. Tribal leaders have an amazing ability to maintain a healthy distance to avoid being implicated in violence.

The perception of raging chaos by itself scores points for insurgents. Regional and international TV screens were filled with images of violence, the occasional burning humvee, insurgents running down alleys while shooting from the hip, accompanied on U.S. TV by the clichéd image of a smoke plume rising amid buildings as a reporter speaks breathlessly from a roof top—fast becoming part of the news himself as the actual news becomes the backdrop. But in the regional media one saw grisly images of dead and dying Iraqis beneath that plume of smoke, amid angry crowds wailing and ranting, images that were never shown on American TV networks. In most cases, these incidents, though shown in sequence, were discrete events with no relation to one another; but they conveyed the perception—in most cases accurate—that Americans and the new government of Iraq were unable to instill legitimate control on the ground.

Though the insurgency was far from coordinated, all its elements, whether former military, Baathists, or tribes, paid homage to Islamic rhetoric, infusing their struggle with Jihadist terms (though most did not really give a shit). There were the obligatory calls for Jihad to justify the fight and enlist the support of local clerics, but these on the whole lacked conviction.

Salafist and Jihadist insurgency in Iraq

The Sunni insurgency in Iraq took an ominous turn with the entry of Salafists and assorted Jihadists, both foreign and domestic, expertly situating the insurgency as part of their wider struggle of global Jihad. That was the moment that many refused to come to terms with.

The extreme fringe of the Jihadist alliance quickly managed to turn Iraq into an absurd inferno, justifying every grotesque act with a psychedelic sob story infused with anti-American invective. But that sob-story also enshrined a particular way of life that the Jihadists would force others to live. That was perhaps their problem.

The Salafist Jihadists, with their own insistent narrative, are a loud and self-righteous minority, a tiny sliver that sticks out among the many sensible Muslims. While there are many Salafists and radical Muslim communities dispersed all over the globe, including in Iraq, believers are not automatically terrorists willing to take up arms against non-believers. Most radicalized Muslims (especially those with the good fortune to live in the West) sympathize with Salafists for the simple reason that they do not have to live under their rule. If they did, one can almost guarantee—and some of us have seen it— they would no longer be apologists for them.

Soldiers encountered many rabidly anti-American (and anti-every-thing) men and women who believe in the creed but go about their business, praying for deliverance without turning to violence. But as part of a very tightly knit community, they are unable or unwilling to criticize those who pursue the path of Jihad. Some live the fight vicariously through their actions. Some sympathize out of deep-rooted traditional loyalties that make it difficult to disagree.

It is sometimes tempting to laugh and ask the Jihadist sitting across from you, "Come on, man, do you seriously believe that nonsense?" But it is no laughing matter. Behind the dazed stare, behind the fear, apprehension, disgust and anger, is a man who truly believes and is willing to risk his life for the cause of Jihad.

Like most Salafist-inspired and Jihadist terrorist groups, AQ is a successful global insurgent franchise. The franchise aspect gives AQ remarkable resiliency, allowing it to take its magic carpet ride under everyone's radar screen. They sing their siren song to their zealous believers and to the many apologists who do not have to live through the Jihadist dreams. Most people don't buy it—but some do, and they are deadly serious. And yes, soldiers have met quite a few of them.

❖ Insurgent franchises

The Jihad sob story—the purist Salafist version of Islam—is the philosophical underpinning for the global fight and for the franchise as well. Any successful terrorist attack that kills the innocent is justified with a cosmic sob story: That is the branding. By giving AQ (or some Salafist group) the credit, the terrorist franchise buys into the global Jihadist struggle and, in effect, pays its royalty fee.

Salafists are insurgents by franchise because there is a *territorial* element in their agenda. Attacking Western targets is only the icing on the cake, as important as it is. Their real objective remains territorial: The aspiration to create a community that replicates the medieval era. And that, of course, requires getting control of the population, through threats of violence, through complicity, or with the support of a dedicated minority. So, the territorial element of the Jihad franchise happens to be *people,* with names, voices, and families. People who resist, or even remotely disagree, are subjected to often grotesque violence.

The territorial objective is also part of the overall franchise—a Salafist version of capturing market share. Territory is at stake in Afghanistan and Pakistan and in a few Salafist communities in Iraq that center on mosques. It is also an objective in the little-noticed turf battles raging in the Palestinian refugee camps in Lebanon, between Palestinian nationalists (supported by various external actors), and radicalized Palestinians who identify themselves as Salafists.[48]

---

[48] *Everyday Jihad* (see following note).

The strength and resiliency of this global insurgent franchise lies in its capacity to re-situate these local struggles—conceptually, in the minds of believers—within the global space of Salafist Jihad. And in turn, the global terrorist acts of Salafist Jihadists become part of the local struggle against enemies real and imagined.[49]

As an operational concept for soldiers on the ground, this means that AQ and its many Salafist offshoots are neither a worldwide hierarchical organization, strictly controlled by some executive committee, nor a series of independent cells operating autonomously. The resiliency of the franchise lies in striking a balance between the two. The global movement allows the autonomous growth of dedicated local Salafist cells and unites them in a framework of shared belief. These local groups, with their nuanced local knowledge, are the best means of maximizing market share (that is, control of the population)—through preaching and conversion or through violence.

A local Salafist group may develop around a mosque, or around a charismatic firebrand Salafist cleric. It becomes part of the global struggle when they buy into the global franchise. At that point, the local Salafists may benefit from outside help in the form of strategic guidance, terrorist training, and propaganda support (i.e., marketing assistance). The global movement reinforces the local narrative, provides a forum to exchange information and ideas, and may even supply foreign fighters with experience (i.e., management consultants). (One other franchise element: There are serious penalties for early termination of any business franchise. A Salafist terrorist franchise is for life: Early termination entails a painful death.)

The delicate balance between the local cells and the global ideology *is* the franchise relationship. The franchise allows for the organic growth of terrorist cells embedded in the local environment, and the steady accretion of marginal, local gains on the ground adds to the larger

---

[49] This is an extension of an idea we got from a great book a whole bunch of soldiers read while in Iraq. We owe a debt to one of our friends, a captain, for insisting that we read it: *Everyday Jihad*, by Bernard Rougier, translated from French by Pascale Ghazaleh (Harvard University Press, 2007).

whole. A bunch of local Salafists becomes part of the wider struggle when they buy into the Jihadist franchise, bringing their local struggle into the global space of Islamic Jihad. The moment when believers identify with global acts of terrorism, at that moment, the global Islamic Jihad becomes a local fight.

The Sunni insurgency found new vigor, new determination, and strategic direction by allying with global Jihad. Radicalized Sunni groups, both foreign and local, hijacked the local resistance and claimed it as part of the global Salafist struggle—not just in rhetoric but also in action. In a short time, however, the same pissed-off Sunnis who cheered on the Salafists became trapped in the psychedelic sob story, and many (though not all) Jihadists became victims of their own success.

❖ The beginning of the Jihadi insurgency as we understood it

A partial truth, constantly overstated, is that the lawless, chaotic post-invasion environment, with no semblance of control on the ground, provided a perfect venue for all kinds of Jihadi groups to come to the party. In fact, the franchises became formidable on the ground not solely because of foreigners coming across the border but also from within. Many radical local Iraqi Muslim clerics (and their followers) quickly bought into the Jihadist ideology while those who already believed in the Jihadi creed were now inspired to act it out.

Three distinct groups of people bought into the Jihad franchises in Iraq, each for different reasons. The pragmatic Baathists and tribal members found willing partners in AQ, though they were not true believers in the Salafist ideology or even "fellow travelers." A hardcore constituency joined the fight for ideological reasons as did the desperate, quiet Salafists and clerics that stepped up to endorse the global Jihadi struggle now being waged inside Iraq. They knew what they were getting into, grasping the opportunity to chase their cosmic dreams, at the expense of their own people.

A lot of other people, however, quickly lost their dreams by supporting these nut-jobs, at first becoming complicit and finally becoming prisoners of their misplaced dreams.

9

IDRIS LEAVES THE MANSION: GLOBAL JIHADI FRANCHISES AND LOCAL BELIEVERS

> "You are not my son and I am not your father. This is not your house, and you have no mother, brother or friend here. The world is before you—go forth with my anger and my curse. Time passing will teach you your true worth as you wander forlornly, having lost my love and protection!"
>
> Idris stamped his foot on the Persian carpet. "This is my house—I will never leave!"
>
> *—Children of Gebelawi*

I n the influx of Salafist Jihadists after the invasion, it was not their numbers that mattered, as soldiers saw it, but rather their genius in organization, strategy, and tactics. And the responsiveness of local Iraqis enabled Salafists to hijack the momentum and entrench their franchise.

Global and Local Jihadists

At the end of 2003, the resistance was already evident, but the resistance fighters were incapable of marketing themselves. They failed to

189

exploit the Internet or to play on the biases and loyalties of regional media to gain traction in the region. Even at the beginning of 2004, with journalists (including Westerners) moving about the country in search of stories, the local resistance was generally clueless about making their case in a coherent fashion. By the middle of 2004, the Salafists and Jihadists more than filled that void.

The Jihadists' use of propaganda was nothing short of genius: positioning the local Sunni insurgency as part of their global struggle and customizing their narrative to appeal to a broader audience. Propaganda works only as long as it resonates with people, and Salafists and Jihadists knew how to capture the audience, displaying a nuanced grasp of the biases and weaknesses of their own societies. They aimed their propaganda at Salafist believers throughout the world and in the wider Middle East, as well as at the Iraqis.

For a die-hard believer, any Western (especially American) involvement in a Middle Eastern country—even humanitarian work—is posited as bad news. Aid workers, it must be noted, are considered fair game by Salafists as long as they are white, Western, and non-Muslim (as are most aid workers globally). Salafists decry any Western engagement as encroachment and as signaling the Muslim world's inability to rise to the challenge. The American interventions in Iraq and Afghanistan were quickly painted in those colors.

For communities of Jihadists in their enclaves scattered across the globe, this was a propaganda boon. Internet sites, propaganda material, and the diatribes of local clerics featured American tanks entering Baghdad and C130 Spectre gunships lighting up the sky over Afghanistan. Salafists exploited the resulting sentiments with panache, certain they could not go wrong with this one.

They appealed to anti-American sentiment, to the biases in the regional media, and to the instinctive human impulse to sympathize with those who resist in the face of overwhelming odds—Robin Hood, the weak against the strong. In every Middle East news channel, the American intervention in Iraq was posited as an illegal invasion, and the resistance in Iraq was seen as the righteous resistance of brave Iraqis against an illegal occupation.

This consistent story of resistance across Middle Eastern media channels had negative ramifications on the perception of Americans throughout the region. Ordinarily, a bunch of Americans could have a good time bar-crawling in Tel Aviv, ending the night (as always) in Hava's apartment on Hayarkon Street (if one is lucky enough to find parking—far more difficult than getting laid in Tel Aviv). But such a quest became all but impossible immediately following the invasion— even in Monot Street in Ashrafieh. The sudden increase in the level of difficulty was not due to a momentary increase in the modesty of the brunettes of Ashrafieh.

The anti-American sentiment in the Middle East was palpable. Propaganda manipulation—through strategically placed Internet clips and speeches carried on regional media—amplified that sentiment throughout the Middle East, with direct impact on the local Sunni insurgency. The increased propaganda, publicity, and marketing of the insurgent franchise by Jihadists of all hues had the effect of legitimizing the resistance, which was now slowly emerging as a full-fledged insurgency. It still had its Hollywood quality, the weak against the strong. For an Arab onlooker, it seemed that the Iraqis were *sticking it to the man*, a bunch of brave Iraqis fighting the most powerful nation on earth.

And there was also a tactically relevant impact for soldiers on the ground. For local Iraqis watching TV, the Sunni insurgency had strategic coherence. Perhaps the insurgency was going according to plan; perhaps it is part of a larger whole. Indeed, the Jihadist franchise was slowly getting its foothold, piggybacking on the momentum of local Sunni resistance. The perception of success begets further success and makes the enemy more determined. And a determined enemy on the ground has tactical ramifications for soldiers.

The successful global marketing strategy also had an impact on the local Salafist franchises. To make their case, they only had to show a photo of American soldiers patrolling the streets of Iraq and Iraqis fighting. Underlying the pervasive anti-American sentiment (a unique sob story in its own right) is the view that the American intervention was illegitimate—and the deeply humiliating sense that no one in the Middle East, and specifically no Arab Muslim, had been able to stop the American juggernaut as it trundled into Baghdad. Arabs and Muslims were left with a bitter taste in their mouths and impotent anger at their own regimes, governments that most Middle Easterners hate almost out of habit. They felt the regimes were either complicit or only paid lip-service in terms of opposition, a sentiment repeated endlessly on every news channel.

It is easy to respond simply, "too bad." But the problem with a Too-Bad strategy is that someone else will capture the moment—as Salafists almost did. That bitter caustic taste, the widespread popular anger provided an opening to be exploited, and Salafists seized it to legitimize their own franchise, beginning in the initial post-invasion violence—until late 2006, when they became victims of their own success.

For a fleeting moment, Salafists managed to portray themselves as a militarist alternative. In the early days, they managed to win the sympathy of many Arabs, Muslims, and Iraqis by portraying themselves as formidable fighters, men with conviction. Unlike so many posers who merely talk the talk, here are some men with conviction who will fight the fight—and fight against the Americans, the most formidable army in history. Jihadists fighting the Americans in the streets of Iraq in front of the world's TV networks allowed other pissed-off Arabs to live vicariously (just as many Americans watch the action of American soldiers and live vicariously). Even Arabs and Muslims who disapproved of the Salafists were, at the time, willing to listen. For a bunch of determined believers, every sympathetic ear just might mean an easily malleable believer, a potential foot soldier for the cause.

The Sunni insurgency, still growing in strength at this point, was generally described as either an al-Qaeda activity or merely as resistance against the invasion. The reality lay somewhere in between. The local Sunni resistance was feeding off the Jihadists while the Jihadists (local and foreign) managed to get a quick foothold for their franchise inside Iraq. It was a marriage of convenience.

By the middle of 2005, the Sunni insurgency increasingly created the perception of an elusive enemy—amid a clear sense that the American effort lacked strategic coherence. The Salafists brought strategic coherence that coalesced the formerly disparate Baathists and tribal groups, making them more formidable, while the intensity of the fight made the local enemy more determined.

The Sunni insurgency was fast evolving on the ground, growing organically. It reacted to opposition (military and non-military) with increasingly sharp Jihadist rhetoric and tactics. A handful of groups with especially effective propaganda became notorious: *Jaysh Ansar al-Sunna* (Partisans of the Sunna Army), a Salafist Jihadi organization with roots in Iraqi Kurdistan; *Al-Jaysh al-Islami fil-'Iraq* (The Islamic Army in Iraq), another organization with a rigorous Salafist discourse; *Tandim al-Qa'ida fi al-Rafidayn* (al-Qaeda's organization in Mesopotamia); and countless others, equally lethal.

The Salafist rhetoric was no longer a religious cliché. The discourse, the rhetoric on the ground, changed in substance. Baathists had invoked Jihadi platitudes, but they did not mete out medieval punishment to their own people, behead them, or stone women. The Jihadists who got control, however, lived up to the literal creed.

No one—not the Iraqis engaged in resistance, nor the Iraqi people, nor the Americans—had anticipated the tenacity with which Salafists and Jihadists would entrench their franchise. Allying with the Sunni resistance was a means to an end. The Salafists found strength in league with the local pool of homegrown Salafists and radicalized local Muslims. Through them, the Salafists expanded their presence, created pockets of theocracies across Iraq and engaged in a medieval reign the likes of which no Iraqi or American could have imagined. And it started with the local believers.

The People: Stuck in the Middle

The element missing from the standard story line is the rise of *local* Jihadists in Iraq. At the height of the insurgency, they came out of the woodwork to run the medieval enclaves. The trickiest part of fighting them remains knowing how to distinguish the enemy from the innocent when they are embedded in a tightly knit community.

In this long war, the problem arises everywhere, not just in the streets of Iraq. There are the radicalized Pakistani and Bangladeshi Muslim youth in certain slums of East London; some (not all) pissed-off Algerians in Southern France or Spain; the many refugees converted to the creed in the camps of Lebanon or in downtown Amman; Afghan and Pakistani youth similarly schooled; and tiny pockets throughout the Muslim world, from Egypt all the way to Morocco, and even in areas of Indonesia, Malaysia, and the Philippines. The vast majority of these Salafist believers remain merely a cultish religious group that adhere to a rigid creed and pray until they get a callus on the forehead. They are apologists or sympathizers—but only a handful actually resort to using arms as a means of creating the Salaf or engage in acts of terrorism as a means of redressing what they believe are their righteous grievances. This distinction is significant: It allows us to distinguish the enemy from the innocent so as to drive a wedge between them.

The growth of small Salafist and radical Muslim communities inside Iraq has occurred in plain sight but outside of general awareness in such overwhelmingly Sunni cities as Fallujah, Samaara, Baquba, parts of Yussafiya, Muammadiya, and others. These communities tend to be viewed as just another group of religious Muslims. But it was with the help of these local radical Muslim groups, based around mosques, that AQ and their allies found strength to create their reign of terror.

❖ Growth of the local Salafists and Jihadists

Many Iraqis—whether educated and affluent or destitute—express surprise at the existence of Salafists in their midst: "This is unbelievable, they are not Iraqis!" Unfortunately, many of them are, in fact, Iraqis, often born and bred in the same neighborhoods where they live. Some perhaps adhered to a very rigid form of Islam all along.

The true believers, the ones willing to fight for the Salaf, remain sparse and disparate. The difficulty and the puzzle is that they retain a tightly knit sense of community based on their beliefs, while living side by side with neighbors with different beliefs. Their sense of community is not defined by proximity or by the stereotypical tunics they are thought to wear or by the ridiculous-looking beards Hollywood likes to give them: Salafists could be white, black, yellow, olive-skinned—or even redheads, like the few from northern Syria. The sense of community exists in the minds of men and women converted to the creed. Due to the esoteric nature of their belief, even in Muslim countries they remain an autonomous community embedded in the wider society.

A Pakistani Salafist living in London's Green Street may have a hard-drinking, rave-going Pakistani neighbor with a white girlfriend. The Salafist calls the couple his dear friends, though he may disagree with their lifestyle. But he finds a sense of community, of belonging, with an affluent Indian accountant from Uttar Pradesh who just happens to be a Salafist.

The sense of community in the minds of the converted makes it possible for them to be effectively subversive almost out of habit, to exist in plain sight yet be utterly unknown. This adds an extra layer of complexity and makes it that much more difficult to distinguish the enemy from the innocent. The accountant and the guy who lives in Green Street may both be just two guys slaving away at their jobs, having nothing to do with the militants, but they may possibly have an inkling of someone among their many acquaintances who just might.

Both of them may find sympathy with the militants, being fortunate enough to live comfortably where they can live vicariously through the militants' exploits, reading their stories, watching the Salafist DVDs that proclaim, "Oh these brothers are so brave!" The believers who sympathize with the militants remain innocent. But somewhere, inside the protective cocoon of tightly knit communities, lives a nut-job—there is always one—who decides to follow through with his delusions of cosmic grandeur.

❖ Swimming with the wrong crowd

The Iraqi family is surprised, utterly disbelieving, and completely bent out of shape to find that the son of the religious family just a few doors down, a family they have known for a long time, has now turned complete nut-job. He has always been very religious, they insist, but this is unbelievable! The young nut-job is running with the wrong crowd and is responsible for a number of heinous crimes—even beheading, in broad daylight, some local people that he has known all his life and whom he now considers not Muslim enough. But his luck ran out and he ended up flowing down the tangled brown river until someone fished him out.

Now the same family conveys their sympathies to the Jihadist's family, who are in mourning, Salafist or not. There is no sense of cosmic grandeur in his mother's shrieks, only uncontrollable grief for the loss of her son. Men and women repeat in disbelief: How did a devout, friendly guy with many friends end up being implicated in some bombing plot? The sense of community of the converted allows for the growth of subversive communities in plain sight under everyone's nose.

The slow, sporadic and random growth of radical Muslim communities in Iraq took place mainly during the sanctions decade when Saddam went on a re-Islamization program, propounding his version of simplified Islam to subordinate clerics.[50] Baathists tolerated the growth of Islam as a means to legitimize the regime, not so much to supplant Baathist ideology with Islam, but to allow people enough personal space so they do not rock the boat too much.

The growth of radical Islam in Iraq is a peculiar phenomenon, given the context of an authoritarian secular regime (under international sanctions), with no serious history of Islamist violence. With the Iraqi economy in tatters—and amid the Baathist torrent of anti-American invective—radical Islamist rhetoric perhaps found willing ears among the pissed-off youth who came of age under sanctions. For many Iraqis, the revisionist history and purist vision of Islam presented a new alternative reality where they could be *men* again.

Other Iraqis were taken by surprise, astonished at the spread of Jihadist believers in their midst. When Salafists were flying high,

---

[50] The subversive growth of the many tiny Salafist enclaves in Iraqi towns and cities has yet to be fully documented.

displaying grotesque forms of violence on the Internet, many Iraqis were quick to point out (as some still do) that this was the work of "foreigners" and not Iraqis because Iraq had never had such a history. Yes, there were any number of foreign Jihadists, but they readily tapped into an existing Salafist network, easily recruiting new believers and foot soldiers. In the post-invasion chaos, foreign Salafists found strength and support among these home-grown Salafists and managed to firmly embed their insurgent franchise. The most notorious of these Jihad franchises remains al-Qaeda in Mesopotamia, partly because of their efficient methods of terrorism, but also because of everyone's need for a bogeyman. After that group bought into the al-Qaeda franchise, they became the one insurgent franchise that attained global notoriety while the others disappeared without ever making it into the news.

The Salafists/Jihadists succeeded all too well in situating the insurgency in Iraq as part of their global struggle. While fighting the Americans, they also pursued their agenda of getting control of local populations with the callous use of violence—the territorial element of the Jihadist vision, creating enclaves. And they exploited the fault lines of Iraqi society to increase instability and gain control on the ground.

❖ Franchise strategy and tactics on the ground

American soldiers flying into the radical Sunni theocratic enclaves encountered a grotesquely shocking, almost absurd manifestation of violence on the ground. Sometimes it was firsthand knowledge, sometimes it was described by Iraqis. Soldiers by profession are no saints, so shocking a soldier is saying something.

The city of Samarra, at the height of the Sunni insurgency, was a theocratic enclave run by Salafists, Jihadists, and other radical Muslim groups. Samarra remains a classic example of how the U.S. failed initially: Salafists hijacked the momentum of local resistance fighters, capitalized on American failures, and established their insurgent franchise—a reign of misery that in some ways made the Middle Ages look attractive.

Around the end of 2004 (and again at the end of 2006), both Americans and Iraqis considered Samarra one of the worst cities in Iraq. There were daily beheadings and kidnappings of local notables by recently empowered Salafists. Barbers were eliminated (because men are not supposed to shave or cut their hair), as were the corner store vendors that sold music or anyone caught drinking or even thinking of alcohol. Women were required to wear a medieval outfit, and education was hijacked as well. Young girls were raped by Salafists invoking a clause of "temporary marriage"—even though, ironically, the "temporary marriage" clause is predominantly a Shia tradition—and some girls who bravely resisted had their heads smashed. (This is a punishment righteously called "stoning.") At its height, anyone who did not subscribe to their view of the world was seen as an enemy. Those who did not comply were killed and left to rot by the side of the road, as an example to others.

These gruesome acts were rarely discussed on American TV networks. But this description grossly understates the suffering of innocent Iraqis in the Salafist Jihadist enclaves, as witnessed by soldiers and related by Iraqis.

Prisoners of the Sob Story: The Good Professors

Soldiers got to know a mixed, Sunni-Shia Iraqi family. Both the husband and wife were English-speaking professors at one of the prominent universities. They always served us great stories, sweets, tea, and many laughs.

The first encounter was not random—it was the result of using a good Rabbit-Hole Matrix. They gave a seemingly genuine welcome: Most people do welcome men armed with guns, but the genuine part is hard to come by. Their knowledge of the neighborhood, generously shared, along with their fluent English, soft drinks and jokes, made it a good place to spend time. Soldiers exchanged email addresses and phone numbers, with everyone promising to meet under better conditions.

Their own story was in essence a confession. It was a story of anger, buoyed up by living vicariously through the resistance, followed by deep disappointment and outright fear once the Jihadists got control.

It is a story one hears across Iraq. They had lived their entire life in a predominantly Sunni urban neighborhood (although the wife was Shia), not far from a prominent Sunni mosque. Their story is told in a detached tone of voice, punctuated by brief sighs that highlight an internal struggle: How could we have been so wrong, how could we not have seen it? They are too well-informed and smart to blame the situation entirely on the failures of Americans, though we certainly carry a share of responsibility for their plight.

Here is a family that unequivocally supported the resistance in its early days. They were livid at the invasion, even though they hated Saddam just as much as the next Iraqi. The good professor stared in disbelief at the destruction of Iraq by looters with American soldiers *looking on*; he describes walking into a shell of a building that once was his office. The memory is vivid: The inability of the Americans to deliver or protect, followed by their increasingly heavy-handed actions, the random arrests in search of an elusive enemy. So the couple had cheered the insurgents, at the time still just a resistance effort.

Like many others, a deep sense of frustration made the professors readily sympathetic to the resistance. They go to work in the morning managing the death-defying sport of driving, spend half a lifetime to buy gasoline. They come home pissed off, thanking god for being alive for another day: Amid rampant violence, every second out of doors is spent navigating between life and death. Any checkpoint or a wrong turn might end up being fatal. When they sit down in the evening with the TV to try to escape, they see Americans—whom they hold responsible for all their misery—fighting the Iraqi resistance. They spontaneously cheer for the Iraqis fighting, releasing a bit of the rage and living vicariously through the actions of insurgents, as many supporters do.

But the good professors' world changed quickly once the Jihadists took control. The local Sunni insurgents, whom they had supported, were now pushed to the margins. It took a little while for them to perceive this fundamental distinction.

It was the lives of women that changed first. The wife, a charming and elegant woman in her late fifties who has retained some of her former beauty, was harassed for her "western" dress, although she had never considered her dress to be western. She told of being slapped on the back and buttocks at a checkpoint manned by Jihadists. Soldiers were puzzled at hearing such stories repeatedly from women and girls. When a Jihadist man paddles a woman in public, is it religious piety or repressed sexual urges—or a mixture of both?

With unchecked coercive authority, the worst of men easily confound lascivious impulse with religious sanction. The women, of course, have no choice in the matter and are supposed to tolerate it as a matter of sanctified virtue. Iraqi women never seemed to find solace or humor in its absurdity.

At home, madam professor was unequivocal in decrying "uneducated men with guns." Female university students could always point out which checkpoints were the worst. The first call they made in the morning to their friends was to figure out which checkpoints to avoid because of "the terrible men." Jihadists certainly tapped into the lascivious sentiments of men who confound their manhood with their AK-47. Getting paddled on the ass or chased with a stick was, of course, a minor inconvenience compared to the fate of others, who bravely resisted and were raped and killed. The same grim story was recounted by numerous families: In response to abuse, a young woman slapped a Jihadist militant with her bag and spit in his face out of impulsive rage and was simply dragged down the road— hitting, biting, screaming every inch of the way—to the middle of a major thoroughfare, where they shot her in broad daylight.

So, madam professor purchased a few abayas for the first time in her life, "just in case."

Then came more ominous checkpoints that charged money and started harassing people, and then the random bombings against Iraqis, abetted by insurgents in their own neighborhoods. And all of a sudden, the landscape shifted. After the professors' family had to run for their lives from a neighborhood Jihadist checkpoint, they suddenly realized that *they actually live in a Sunni neighborhood*—something that they had unthinkingly taken for granted.

Not being especially religious, it came as a shock that their mixed sectarian identity was now a liability, that they were actually marked people. They received an explicit death threat, and now they looked around them for the first time—alas, a little too late. The local resistance fighters had moved to the shadows, replaced by new groups. They may look the same and carry similar weapons, but they act differently—zealous, uncompromising, self-righteous. There were now random killings and beheadings and bodies lying in the street. Shia families began to flee for their lives, while more and more abayas appear on the streets. By now, a Jihadist Salafist insurgent franchise is well entrenched in their neighborhood, assisted by local Salafists, thugs, criminals, perverts and sociopaths—and with the complicity of the people who mislaid their dreams, becoming prisoners of somebody else's psychedelic morality tale.

So the professor's family quickly packed their stuff and moved to a tiny rented house in a predominantly Shia section of town, near some of their friends and family. Their Sunni neighbors keep an eye on their house. Some of the young children of their former Sunni neighbors have partially occupied the house to deter squatters. In almost three years, they have never traveled the few miles to the old neighborhood to see the house.

The professor recognizes the irony: How they missed what was coming and were carried away in their passions. He fully recognizes that, whatever evil machinations he may have expected of Americans, they will eventually leave, but Salafist Jihadists will not. Soldiers always responded sarcastically, "Now come on sir, look at us—we are men of peace, love, and happiness, why can't we stay?" He would always laugh uproariously, holding the soldiers hand, and retort with a smart-ass quip.

But he always invoked two particular crimes that he seemed unable to put behind him, two defining incidents that that they believe were deliberately planned.

One was the bombing at Al-Mustansariya University, where he had friends working. He would ask in wonder, "What kind of people will bomb a university?"[51] The other was the Al-Mutanabi Street bombing in March of 2007. A winding alleyway near the old Jewish Quarter of Baghdad, named after one of the greatest Arab poets of all time, Mutanabi Street has always been the haunted heart—still faintly beating—of Iraq's surviving intellectual life. Coffee, tea, and hookahs were served in grimy old cafés, with nicotine coating the walls and chairs and fans that never work, filled with people whose brains scream louder than most. They sit surrounded by bookstores, cooking up their visions and commiserating with one another, long an art form in Iraq. The professor had friends caught in that blast, and his cool voice cracked whenever it was mentioned. It was not a random act, he insisted. The attack was deliberately planned and carried out to send a signal to the intellectuals: watch out, you have no place in our world—the Salaf, the perfect community. If Iraqis do not get these lunatics out of Iraq, he predicts, it will be like Taliban—or "maybe Iraq will be like Saudi Arabia without the king!"

Cities of Salt[52]

Soldiers have heard Iraqis use the term "Saudis" as a synonym for Salafists. But when the professor talks about Salafists, Taliban, and Saudis in the same breath, it has a more substantive meaning. Soldiers know him well by now: He has assisted the soldiers in his own seemingly innocuous ways to go after insurgents. Both have educated the other: Breaking down each other's stereotypes and prejudices, finding common points of reference, engaging in battles of wit—disagreeing on many points but always as friends. The professor, showing no mercy, will call the soldiers on their bullshit, but only after the tea, and always with a smile.

The professor is a worldly man who has traveled and read and is well aware of the peculiar realities of the Middle East. He pointed out with eloquence (with his wife filling in the gaps) how Saudi money financed many schools that spread the extreme versions of Salafism and Jihadism

---

[51] The bombing on January 16, 2007, attributed to the Salafist group Ansar al-Sunna, killed more than seventy people and injured more than 150.
[52] A novel by Abdurrahman Munif.

in many parts of the world, and how many rich Saudis (and others from the Gulf) try to funnel their zakat (charitable donations) to Jihadists and Salafists. He believes unequivocally that Saudis are as responsible as anyone for the global development of Jihadist Islam.

Soldiers are well aware of that fact, but it is very nice to hear it from a worldly and informed Iraqi. To this day, Saudis assiduously export Wahhabism: The professor is especially vexed that individual Saudis finance Salafist clerics, organizations, and mosques. He is well aware of the fatwa of a prominent cleric in Saudi Arabia on behalf of the Salafists in Iraq.

For him, Salafists were neither Arab nor Muslim—and Saudis were in a different class all together. Suppose one turned off the air conditioning and cut off the oil of Saudi Arabia: With the women all covered in abayas and locked up in harems, what is the difference between the Taliban in Afghanistan and the royal family in Saudi Arabia? If the Taliban represent super-sized Salafism (though blended with Pashtun tribal traditions), then Saudi Arabia is the diet version (blended with Wahhabism and a whole lot of Bedouin traditions).

But a Saudi Prince can keep his many wives locked up in a harem, fly in his customized Boeing 737 to the U.S., and hobnob with high and low, confident that everyone will be complicit in the charade. He might drink the place dry of Johnny Walker Blue Label and run a $15,000 bar tab at The Lodge at Torrey Pines in La Jolla, try to purchase the entire female waitstaff for his buddies and finish up the night with couple of California blondes between his legs—all with a ten-man security detail provided by the U.S. government. The bartender that opened all those bottles of Johnny Walker Blue that day happens to be a frontline infantryman, a guy that walks the streets of Iraq with an M4 Carbine.

The difference between Salafists and Saudis is that the Saudis have the political acumen (and the oil money) to turn hypocrisy into a veritable art form. The Salafists are ideologically blind rather than politically astute. They apply their literal, extreme interpretations of religion with no pretence, displaying an ejaculatory fascination with violence as they dance around headless bodies. The Saudis have struck a delicate balance to navigate two contending currents: the deeply traditional, Arabized form of Islam that is Wahhabism and the forces of modernity that come with oil money. The delicate balance is found in one word: hypocrisy.

So the kingdom that we can call Salafist-lite remains an absolutist fiefdom, where honesty might be a crime: Given the level of universal deceit, telling the truth becomes a revolutionary act. While some of the women appear to be fighting back, the men retain a monopoly on hypocrisy behind their gold-embroidered black tunics and checkered headdresses. Guardians of the holy places and paragons of Muslim virtue, they embody the holiest hypocrisy, but they do it in style. Is it the complicity of the spineless that turns hypocrites into emperors when no one is brave enough to speak of the obvious contradictions?

The hypocrisy and lavishness of the royal family also inspires the most zealous Salafist believers to place the kingdom itself in their crosshairs. Whatever slow-moving changes have taken place—at a snail's pace, Saudi fashion—have made even Saudi Arabia, incredibly, a target of the die-hard nut-jobs!

"Maybe, on the way home, Sir, we should turn the air conditioning off in Saudi Arabia and leave the king sweating a bit. What do you think?"

The professor had a genuine laugh. He has been to many Middle Eastern countries, including Saudi Arabia. But he began judiciously: "The King, I think he is trying."

He knew Saudi Arabia well, as he had seriously considered getting a job at University College at Yanbu, a Red Sea port city. "They pay so well." But he said he just did not want to subject his wife and daughters to that life—aside from his instinctive antipathy toward Saudis. He is attracted by opportunities in the United Arab Emirates, in Abu-Dhabi, and in Ras-Al Khaimah. But the allure fades when he thinks of leaving Iraq. He wants to keep teaching, but he does not want to leave Iraq and his familiar precincts, finding solace and sharing his misery with his remaining friends. "I hope, I hope, I think, things will change."

Here was a family utterly at the mercy of circumstances, two professors who had mislaid their dreams and now feel robbed of hope.

❖ Charm of Idris: See no evil

When the professors, like many others, became caught up in the passionate intensity of post-invasion violence and the pervasive anti-American sentiment, Salafists and Jihadists made common cause with local resistance fighters, winning people's complicity and even support. Building on that momentum, they achieved control on the ground—and even complete lockdown. But soon the sociopaths and criminals who found refuge in the Jihad franchise began to push the real resistance fighters to the margins, supplanting the Iraqi resistance with their Salafist struggle and turning the local enclave into a wholesale reign of terror.

The success of the Jihad franchise owed much to their perverse genius in managing perceptions. To the global audience, they posited the violence in Iraq in terms of the wider Salafist jihadi struggle while successfully masking the atrocities they committed on the ground—things that never became widely known, except to the Iraqis who lived through it and the soldiers who came across them. The sites of mass murders with fresh mass graves; entire villages cleared of people and turned into training camps; in one river valley, villages completely wiped out. A group of farmers who refused to leave their piece of land were massacred by Jihadists, who then cordoned the place with a web of IEDs and rebuilt it as a sanctuary to train foot soldiers.

The mystery is not the atrocities they perpetrated, but *how they hid them so well.* Even most Iraqis were utterly unaware of the level of violence and suffering, and perhaps they still are.

For soldiers on the ground, it remains an inexplicably bizarre puzzle, one with tactical ramifications in this long war. The Salafist reign of terror should have represented a huge propaganda advantage, yet it was rarely, if ever, exploited. Instead, this information was contained and compartmentalized. Compartmentalized information is

205

one of the elements that allowed Salafists to entrench their franchise on the ground.

Their success in containing the flow of information undoubtedly helped Jihadists in getting the complicity of the people. The unwillingness of so many Americans, high and low, to come to terms with the grotesquely under-reported suffering of the innocent in Iraq remains a sad travesty. We are partly responsible for their suffering because our early mistakes played an important role in strengthening the Salafists and Jihadists.

Prisoners of Information: Fighting Metaphors

> A foolish consistency is the hobgoblin of little minds, adored by little statesmen and divines.

> —Ralph Waldo Emerson

The peculiar reality of compartmentalized information sank in memorably at a lavish dining facility inside a majestic army base. Sitting in the dining hall, soldiers get glimpses of news. On this day, the U.S. news featured a tiny taste of what was happening in a neighborhood soldiers had recently left. One might expect the newscast to involve footage from the actual neighborhood being discussed, but this occurs very rarely. Instead, we see an iconic TV personality analyzing the situation from a rooftop, with Iraq spread out behind him. In effect, the TV personality is the news and Iraq is the background: foggy sky, a stand-alone minaret, some gray buildings.

Then we see an expert, summing up. We know there are experts who have studied much about what they are talking about, who provide much-needed nuance by placing events in context. Then there are "TV experts," who pontificate while looking pretty. The one on TV that day was a real expert: He knows his shit, and soldiers had read what he has written. He got only ten seconds before they cut to the anchor.

The anchor wears his anchor face, and everyone is telling a little bit of the little truths they know (no one can ever have the complete truth). Then comes the concussion: They show some footage of American soldiers getting off a chopper that is four years old—made glaringly obvious by the equipment they carry. We see places that are patently not the place referred to. The soldiers shake their heads, laugh, put their heads down and eat. They want to get on a bird faster, to get back to the reality they know.

It makes the heart very heavy, seeing the TV image with ears still ringing from combat, maybe wearing the same uniform covered with mud, blood and shit from soldiering for four or five days straight with no sleep. That image captures the essence of what this counterinsurgency is all about: It is a war of metaphors, with the living, breathing Iraqi people reduced to abstractions. No better place to fight an intense metaphorical fight than on the boob tube. But *people* are living in the middle of this metaphorical fight, and soldiers on the ground are a part of the contending metaphors.

What to do when the reality on the ground is not congruent with the metaphors? Generally the response is merely to increase the intensity of the metaphorical fight.

The interpreters on the ground didn't get to watch TV, and soldiers could empathize with that (even those who religiously avoid the boob tube). So, soldiers jerry rigged a system to pull in a satellite feed so some of the interpreters could watch Arabic-language TV.

And now, soldiers could see two different worlds, two sets of metaphors: Those repeated in the American media and those in the Middle Eastern media. Look to the left, soldiers hear blah blah blah; look to the right, they hear wah wah wah—on and on, back and forth.

❖ See No Evil

Some soldiers joked that everybody in the West and the Middle East has seen the images of abuse at Abu-Ghraib—but how come no one has seen the grisly images of the Iraqis suffering at the hands of the Salafist and Jihadist nut-jobs? The answer is complicated.

Jihadists, in fact, actively blocked reporters, though not necessarily in order to contain information; they also kill reporters more or less out of habit, especially if they are Western. In most conflicts, journalists (and aid workers) are allowed unrestricted access by rebels and insurgents; it is usually the government authorities that restrict journalists. In Iraq, it is the other way around: in fact, journalists became *targets* of the nut-jobs. Living up to their extreme creed, Jihadists treat all reporters—local, Arab, or Western—as part of the enemy.

When reporters are blocked, they have no way of getting firsthand information, and the little bits coming out can be controlled by the Jihadists. Then again, Americans in the early days of the insurgency also had a visceral revulsion to bad news. A metaphorical battle is far more enjoyable. The soldiers' common sense cliché, that bad news never gets good over time, was disregarded.

Moreover, the nature of Salafist and Jihadist violence is so medieval and grotesque that it is difficult to present. A shrieking Iraqi mother cradles two fresh corpses, their heads cut off. Would such an image have made prime time TV in America, even if a TV reporter had managed to capture the scene? Viewers might have choked on their McNuggets and turned off the TV, jeopardizing whatever show followed the twenty-two minutes of world news. Soldiers who witnessed this grotesquely painful spectacle could only put in a new wad of tobacco for comfort.

The tactical saliency is that the gruesome nature of these crimes makes it nearly impossible for people to absorb them—in America, Iraq, or the wider Middle East. But even the most digestible images won't make it on American TV, as long as people are treated to capsule news items in ten-second blasts.

Thus, Iraqis in some areas were subjected to a medieval reign under Jihadist rule. Iraqis and soldiers (apart from those who witnessed it) tended to turn away from the misery. It was so gruesome as to become abstract. Not so much news, it was sociopathic evidence, material for a forensic psychologist. The effect was to contain the flow of information out of Jihadist enclaves.

In any case, by the time the resistance became a grotesque new reality, most Iraqis had become prisoners of a psychedelic sob story of cosmic proportions. It was too late.

❖ YouTube

The propaganda genius of diehard Jihadists (particularly al-Qaeda) was brought home in an unexpected way when a former soldier frantically called some of his army friends.

"Duude, go to YouTube, and type exactly what I say, just check it"—a propaganda video showing bunch of Jihadists, complete with rap music. (Never mind the irony that Salafists would kill music vendors on the ground but use their music in a recruiting video!) Having seen many such videos, the soldiers were not impressed; what was the big deal?

Then he explained. The militant wearing all the muj-gear and surrounded by other militants is an *American*—and not just any American. "He was one of my best friends in grade school, dude, and we freakin grew up together."

"You've got to be fucking shittin me!" Everyone replayed the video, as he narrated.

"Man, this guy, and another buddy of mine, we used to go hunting with our shotguns all the fucking time, and now he is rolling with some Jihadists," and he laughed his usual laugh. From the same small town in America, one guy joins the army, becomes a fire team leader and a Squad Leader in an infantry unit, while his best friend from grade school appears in Jihadi recruiting videos.

"I'd love to sit down with him for an hour or so man, just to ask him, what the hell happened to you, and how in the fuck do you stay motivated to do this stupid shit?" His army friends watching the clip readily agreed, "it's a small fucking world, brother."

Jihadis go to great lengths to manipulate public perception (especially of their own people). At the height of Jihadi violence in Iraq, with multiple franchises on the ground, they had exclusive access to record and post their own atrocities. The Salafists controlling a medieval enclave in Samarra—or Adhamiya, Arab Jabur, Yusafiya, or any number of Sunni towns—might kill men, women, and children, invoking their cosmic sob story. But those atrocities go unreported. Unless they choose to record it themselves as part of their Jihadist narrative, the beheading will never get on TV networks or the Internet. And because the information from Samarra does not come out, people in Adhamiya or Yusafiya have no inkling of what may be in store for them as well.

Containing and controlling the flow of information has tactical advantages—and it has strategic significance as well—in a fight that is partially for the minds of people. Without real information, people make a choice to be complicit, yielding up control on the ground. They are prisoners of limited information.

But no advantage lasts forever. Salafists did manage to entrench their many franchises, but just at that point the inherent contradictions came into play: Their ideological rigidity, their single-minded belief in their self-righteous fight, and their reliance on the use of force as the best form of control. It was as if they assumed that the people could be reduced to a figment of their imagination.

10

THE RIGHTEOUS WORLD OF IDRIS: JIHADISTS' USE OF FORCE AS THE INSTRUMENT OF CONTROL

> Then Idris's voice reached them, as strong as thunder;
> he stood before the mansion, looking menacingly up
> at it as he bellowed, "You kicked me out to please the
> lowest of your children—and do you see how he has
> treated you? Now you yourself are throwing him out
> into the dirt, just as you did to me, and you're worst of
> all. Take notice that Idris cannot be beaten!"
>
> —*Children of Gebelawi*

alafist use of violence was a topic that soldiers often discussed. Use of force—violence—is what soldiers do: It is the job, as in any war, but it is also a discipline. For soldiers trained to do it well, there were notable, and puzzling, differences in the form of death inflicted by insurgents.

There is a difference in the logic behind the use of force in tactical and non-tactical situations. Insurgents would use civilians as a shield; they would even use an ambulance to attack U.S. forces. The acts, repugnant on moral grounds, have undeniable tactical logic. Insurgents are breaking the conventional norms of war-fighting in order to minimize the existing asymmetry of power between themselves and the counterinsurgents. No one can deny the tactical logic of such actions—especially against an adversary (like the Americans) who will always avoid the use of violence when it affects civilians.

No, the puzzle is the *non-tactical* use of force—including the choice of means, the forms of death they visited on their own people. What is the reason for slicing off a screaming man's head when a single round from an AK-47 would do the job effectively? They record many videos of this. Why bash a girl's head? And why kill the barbers, the music vendors, the purported spies and collaborators? Why resort to grotesque forms of killing, invoking Allah's name while doing it? Why celebrate the death with bloodthirsty gusto, running in circles around the dead body, doing a mad dance, stomping around holding guns and the blood-soaked knife in the air—and recording the moment with cell phones or camcorders.

Soldiers watched all too many of those videos. They would ask the Jihadists they caught what was behind their obsession with beheading and displaying the heads?

Salafists literally aim at emulating a Salaf, and, in fact, consider public beheadings a perfectly acceptable form of punishment. In Saudi Arabia People, convicted of crimes get their heads chopped off in "chop-chop square." The difference is only that the head is not displayed in websites. Everyone seems strangely comfortable with the practice. Saudis are careful, of course, not to behead any Europeans or Americans—only immigrant workers from developing countries and the occasional poor Saudi.

The greater difference between Salafists and the Saudi system is that in the case of Saudi Arabia there is a judicial system, based on Sharia law, and people have a sense of predictability in the way the system works. There is legitimate control on the ground. But this particular form of legitimate control has a built-in bias, a problem inherent to Sharia. A guy who steals a goat or camel could get his hand chopped off; but a royal prince who pilfers millions of dollars (more or less out of habit) gets a customized jet. Perhaps electronic theft is not under Sharia jurisdiction.

The Salafists, drawing inspiration from their literal interpretations, feel righteous in deciding who to kill and on what basis. But it becomes un-endurable for others when the guy who runs the enclave has sole authority to mete out punishment, making life-and-death decisions based on logic that people do not quite understand. Iraqis in Salafist enclaves were subjected to this tyranny so that the lunatics could attempt to create a perfect society, an abstract figment of their own imagination.

The application of violence is always deliberate and contains meaning. It is never random. Soldiers know this well because it is part of what they do. Shooting has a swift, surgical quality to it, even though death may be the outcome; severing a person's head has a repulsive quality. Death is death, but such qualitative differences matter. A person, a living breathing man is begging for mercy, writhing like an animal in fear, sweating and sobbing. Sometimes the beheading is completed in one swift swing, sometimes it takes more time, a series of deliberate swings, until the head is severed. Then comes the "victory tour" (as soldiers called it, watching the videos): Some nut-job walks around carrying the head, displaying it.

But the Salafists find its meaning in their glorified sob story no matter how despicable their actions appear to onlookers.

Is Idris Righteous?

There is another puzzle in the stories soldiers keep hearing each time they fly into a theocratic enclave.

Salafist militants justify their acts of beheading a music vendor, a barber, or anyone else in terms of their cosmic beliefs. The deaths of barbers, music vendors, and grotesque killings of the innocent have to be understood in this context as "punishment" for anti-Salafist activity. It is also a defensive strategy, protecting the psychedelic narrative from corrupting elements—the moralistic side of the Jihadist fight.

Salafists and most Jihadists were foreigners in Iraq. Iraqis were not enthralled with their attempt to re-conquer Iraq and remake it as a purist Islamic nation, especially as Iraq at one time had perhaps the most educated populace and workforce in all of the middle east, as many Iraqis still point out with pride.

Having established a foothold for their franchise in the form of enclaves, Salafists in Iraq did not seek to instill their beliefs in the minds of the people through conversions or persuasion. Instead, they used their power to instill it by force. The Jihadists were never apologetic for their reign of terror, justifying everything they did in terms of the sob story. For Salafists, the actions of music vendors, barbers, or any number of others were potential encroachments—not necessarily in terms of territory, but in beliefs, in the minds of men, the key battle space in this psychedelic fight.

Accordingly, the Salafists also sought to muzzle the political parties organized along Sunni identity, especially the Iraqi Islamic Party (IIP) (*Hizb al-Islami al-Iraqi*).

There is an irony. IIP, founded in 1960, was banned in Iraq until *after* the invasion in 2003, when it secured the largest block of Sunni seats in the parliament. In reaction to the secularism of Pan-Arabist socialism, the IIP was organized in the sixties around the Islamic revival movement in association with the Muslim Brotherhood, with members in Egypt, Jordan, and parts of Syria. The irony is that, while many Western and Arab governments view the Muslim Brotherhood and its affiliates with suspicion, in Iraq the IIP and its leaders were once again running for their lives—despite being officially accepted as a legitimate political party, a sort of non-official representative for the grievances of the Sunni resistance.[53] Salafists viewed them as an enemy to be suppressed—as colluding with the enemy *merely by being part of the system.*

In questioning captured Salafists, as well as their hostages and other victims, everyone spoke of the insurgent obsession with sending

---

[53] The leader of IIP, Tariq-Al-Hashimi, had his brother and sister both assassinated; low-ranking IIP members were constantly in the crosshairs of Salafists as well as Shia militias.

214

signals and "teaching lessons." The demonstration effect of death is a powerful piece of credible information that people internalize when they make decisions. Leaving the dead bodies of a family by the side of the road has the effect of making people hesitate before doing anything. Men and women simply respond, "Oh sir, please, we should not talk to you," and quickly add, "you know what happened to so and so." People become easily complicit with the insurgents.

Idris and his Garden of Earthly "Delights"

In one of those medieval enclaves, soldiers were clearing the Jihadists' safehouse when they heard a faintly audible whisper: "Mister, mister, please, mister." Inside a cage-like contraption they found three emaciated Iraqis. After being freed, they sobbed uncontrollably, yet without tears: They were so completely dehydrated that they each took in two bags of intravenous fluid like a sponge.

All three were teachers from the same school, two of them heavily tortured and marked to be killed the next day. They mentioned the ditch where their captors had dropped those they had killed. The other one—the lucky one—was to be released in order to carry the news!

The non-commissioned officer who led the assault yelled, "Are you fucking serious, that is some medieval shit!" The hostages were three of a series of victims, schoolteachers and others accused of non-Islamic practices, that the Salafists abducted and killed. In the face of such callous disregard for the innocent, how many in the neighborhood would choose to oppose them?

During air assault missions into Salafist enclaves across Iraq, countless Iraqi families demanded, "You should not leave; you should kill these people and stay here!" This was perhaps not so surprising in the middle of 2006. But we were aware that the same people would have said very different things in 2003, wrapped up in the intense anti-American sentiment.

The people in Salafist-infested enclaves all across Iraq pointed out voluntarily the impact of Salafist violence. Salafist actions had the effect of terrifying people. Of course, many Iraqis had suffered torture and mass murder under Saddam, but he was given to making people disappear rather than cutting their heads off in broad daylight. If the credible threat of death gets people to be complicit, the grotesque use of violence, the cosmic joy in displaying it, completely terrify the people. Salafists and Jihadists pulled no punches; they did whatever they threatened to do.

So, on countless missions into disparate corners of Iraq, soldiers listened as men, women, and girls bemoaned their earlier disbelief. Their voices cracked with fear; their faces exhibited the contorted twitches of the absolutely terrified; their sighs were utterly powerless. It was not hard to see why. Nothing was more enlightening than spending time with captured Salafists.

Cosmic Joy

The grieving parents, the angry brother and little sister, were right on the mark with the tactical information they gave about the local Jihadists. They had a personal stake in the outcome.

When captured, these Jihadist soldiers were all guts and vitriol, resisting and loudly claiming their innocence, accusing the soldiers of seizing the wrong men—and also accusing the family that they, correctly, blamed for ratted them out. (Hmm, soldiers wondered, why would they assume that?)

In their possession they found a video, the tormented death of a young girl. The man insists that this was just an ordinary video someone had sent him, and the others back him up. But soldiers have prior intelligence that these are possible Jihadists. They surround him like bunch of squirrels on a hickory nut. Every nut cracks if one approaches it right, finding the weakest link by good observation and a bit of brainwork. Separate the nut-jobs, isolate them, and do so quickly.

The obvious evidence was the video of the gruesome death of a screaming girl, begging for mercy, asking to be freed, and resisting with every ounce of her life. It is a heartbreaking moment when she finally stops resisting and gives in to the abuse, being thrown around as a bunch of men beat her to death. It is always the same way, and it is always, every single time, a group of men. She slowly accepted her fate, lying listless in her bright orange and yellow outfit.

A technical detail: This was supposed to be the stoning of an adulterous woman, but there were no stones involved. A bunch of men bludgeoned her to death with sticks.

A simple commonsense trick soldiers learned, flying into theocratic enclaves, is that, when conducting follow-on missions after clearing the target houses, the best approach is to follow the trail with the help of victims of violence—to be *insurgents behind insurgents,* as some jokingly commented. When shown photos of the captured men, the family insisted that yes, they are the men responsible.

Soldiers returned to the structure where the nut-jobs were being held. *Of course,* they are all innocent men. Soldiers had two pieces of information. First, the credible positive identification of the men by four people, including a little girl. Second, that video—but no faces appear in it.

OK, let's see how this will go down.

The gruesome death of a young girl is the obvious, important fact. But equally important are the little details and incongruities in the video: people's feet; the nature of the onlookers; the few of the group who consistently beat her; and above all, the way the camcorder moves. The man who recorded it holds the camera in his right hand, but it is not a steady hand. The guy is a lefty. As he takes part in the beatings with his left hand, you can suddenly see from the jerking footage— amid clothing, the slanted stomping of the men, their flying feet and hands—one fleeting glimpse of the left hand, maybe a tenth of a second. The image of the left hand is peculiar, it has a medical dressing, turned brown from all the dust.

It is painful and enraging to be watching this gruesome tape repeatedly, as some soldiers did, but there is no choice. Then to watch it again and again sitting in front of one of the captives, looking perturbed but still angrily professing his innocence.

217

Finally, it was decided: "OK men, let's strip them—everything, socks, shoes, everything." Everyone was brought out from isolation and stripped. A bunch of men standing with zip-tied hands, and yes, a whole different world is revealed, there are now enough little details to figure out who is who.

And there was one big detail. Without the jelabiyas, one man had a medical dressing.[54]

"What happened to your hand?" a soldier asked in his deliberate Arabic.

An accident. Oh that is terrible, the soldier agreed, "Yes, terrible."

Then the soldier raised the man's left hand, still wrapped in an old bandage turned brown, and he points to the paused screen, showing the tiny glimpse of the raised left hand holding a big stick, directed at the girl's desperate face. Stars so rarely get so perfectly aligned in a counterinsurgency, but sometimes they do, and when it does, it either warms the heart or enrages the soul.

The man tried to speak again, but the soldier simply said, "Shut up, I don't want to hear a goddamn thing."

Then he turned around, walked to the back of the room, grabbed a chair, and slammed it into a wall where it splintered into pieces, then grabbed the funky table lamp from the stool and slammed it on the wall right next to the row of men, the pieces flying everywhere.

Then he walked back to the man, exhaled a deep breath—desperately trying to spare them both from his rage—and gave him a cigarette: "Let's talk."

What kind of men would actually bludgeon a woman to death with sticks? This is what soldiers would like to ask. But it is not necessary, they are staring right at them. They look like any other middle-aged

---

[54] The jelabiya (or gelabiya) is a loose-fitting caftan-like garment for men or for women.

man, with one great exception. Unlike most sentient human beings, these nut-jobs believe in a sob story that makes them feel righteous enough to do what they did. To resist the worst impulses while looking at them is the most difficult task in the world. Never mind, there is a lot of battlefield tactical questioning to do and (one sincerely hopes) many follow-on missions.

Now they are smoking cigarettes the soldiers gave them. But their voices are different now; the insistence of innocence is gone. The faces have gone saggy, eyes turned from fiery intensity to the look of begging dogs. Their hunched shoulders make them look fatter than they are.

"Have a Gauloises." Offering another a smoke, lighting it, putting it in his mouth. "Thank you, mister, thank you, oh, thank you."

The nut-job uses his shaking hands, still tied at the wrist, to smoke it with long deep drags to calm his now completely rattled nerves. Over the next few hours spent in long discussion with the soldiers, he and his friends are now all about cooperation.

The nut-job, now a husk of a man, looks at the Arabic-speaking soldier, trying to envelop him with his dark, pleading eyes, as the man on whom he has pinned all his hopes. The soldier offers him another cigarette, intoning with genuine sincerity, "Well, sir, thank you, we greatly appreciate your cooperation, have a cigarette, take your time. Please, enjoy it."

There would be *many* follow-on missions because of their cooperation.

Soldiers quietly let them know that it was time to send them all higher for further questioning. Despite being nut-jobs, they all seemed to want to live. Of course, none them had any remorse about killing those other Iraqis, who refused to live the way they commanded them to. Their quick involuntary panting, buckling knees and chattering teeth were now identical to the expression of the young woman that they self-righteously murdered only three days earlier, in front of her shrieking parents pleading for mercy.

Slowly being led out of the musty room, now into the dark night, the captives knew that these soldiers would have little role in their future. Yes, soldiers have in their hands a bunch of nut-jobs who have murdered women—a lot of them—plus American and Iraqi men. But there is a fundamental paradox that soldiers face on the ground, after taking some risks and doing their job: Are these murderous nut-jobs in fact valid targets that fulfill everyone's legal, moral, and political concerns?

The Most Disgusting Song: Jihadists Acts of Terrorism and Sectarian Violence[55]

Acts of terrorism, bombings, and assassinations seem to strike fear in different ways. In a town full of two million people, even with a bombing every day averaging about ten to twenty deaths each, the individual's chances of being caught in the blast radius are low. People go about living, instinctively thinking and acting in terms of *probabilities*. They avoid possible places where they might be caught in a blast— even making macabre jokes; they take short cuts, minimize hanging out in the market, avoid public places, and seriously consider whether to attend the Ashura festival. However low the probability, the people are constantly aware of the *possibility* they might be next. And some- where inside, each morning when the father goes to work, the wife and kids get a knot in their stomachs and wonder if today might be the day.

Any act of terrorism, whether bombing, assassination, or hijacking, strikes fear. With each acts of terrorism, insurgents display that they exist, that they are not defeated, and that they retain the ability to disrupt legitimate control. With each act of terrorism, people find that the predictability inherent to legitimate control has been shat- tered. Jarred awake from their complacent slumber, engulfed in fear, the innocent begin to look at each other with suspicion—a great advantage of insurgents. The fear of terrorism created an opportu- nity for the worst of men to engage in turf battles, fight for control

---

[55] "The Most Disgusting Song," by Jesus Rodriguez, Live Fact (1992).

of neighborhoods, and consolidate their enclaves through intensely sectarian rhetoric.

Although there were no sectarian battles in Iraq's recent history, sectarian identity has always been socially relevant. Starting around the 1950s, sectarian identity became politically relevant, as Shia people became organized.[56] And by 2003–2006, nearly every political party in Iraq was organized along sectarian and ethnic lines. But the social and political relevance of sectarian identity does not by itself explain sectarian violence.[57] Identity is one thing but sectarian violence is quite another, as it requires actually killing people. If every Iraqi with deeply held sectarian identities began killing, things would look very different. There was some critical missing element.

For conceptual clarity, we usually identify north and northeast Iraq with Kurds, south and southeast with Shia, and the western part of Iraq as Sunni. But the reality on the ground is a little complicated. Despite the sectarian cleansing that has taken place in the last two to three years, Iraq is incredibly mixed. It was not uncommon to find Shia, Chaldean Christians, Azeris, Assyrians, and Turkomans—a colorful collage of ethnic and sectarian identities—living side by side, depending on the city. They may not be holding hands and doing the Macarena together, but they do not try to slice each other's throats either, as some of us understood—even when we saw the first dead bodies in the gutter: Another strange moment of concussion.

---

[56] The politicization of Shia identity was a direct reaction to the increased secularism of Baath party, secular Pan-Arabist and Arab nationalist rhetoric; it reflected also the inroads of the many Iraqi Communist parties inside Shia communities in the 1950s.

[57] Concepts of the social and political relevance of sectarian identity are derived from the literature on ethnic identity. See: James D. Fearon, *Ethnic Mobilization and Ethnic Violence*, Handbook of Political Science, March 20, 2006; "Violence and the Social Construction of Ethnic Identity," James D. Fearon and David D. Laitin, *International Organization*, 54 (4), Autumn 2000.

A Shia family living inside a Salafist enclave and protected by their Sunni neighbors talks about the terrible Sunnis and their death squads, all fire and brimstone. There is no love, they are asking for revenge, even while they describe how their Sunni neighbors are protecting them. They have nothing but good words about the neighbors; their sectarian identity was irrelevant. The same is true of Sunni families living in Shia strongholds, protected by Shia neighbors against the Shia death squads.

In fact, long before Salafists came onto the scene, a number of Shia death squads conducted assassinations of former Baathists and members of Saddam's security apparatus. Their agenda was more about settling old scores than attacking people based on sectarian identity. But a number of factors allowed some groups to exploit the situation along sectarian lines. At the time of the first elections in Iraq, people voted along sectarian lines, and politicians pandered to the most intensely sectarian sentiments. The election indeed empowered the Shia militias to carry out their sectarian agendas with a cloak of legitimacy.

But it was the deliberate actions of Jihadists, and how Shia groups reacted to Jihadists, that allowed every party to justify the killing of innocents by sectarian sob stories. Soldiers walked in neighborhoods "cleansed" of one group; walk to the other side of town, and it is cleansed in reverse. It was a power grab on the ground. Violence driven by a sob story quickly becomes self-perpetuating as everyone begins to believe their own bullshit. When men with guns get wrapped up in their own fantasies, the innocent always pay a heavy price.

Some Salafists openly claimed to attack the Shia as apostates (Asar al-Sunna, for example). Others, with a perverse propaganda genius, maintain the pretense that they do not, fearing an international backlash even among Salafist believers, given the level of civilian casualties. But they continue to attack the Shia people anyway.

But the actions of these nut-jobs get added meaning from the way others react. Ordinary people did not go about killing their neighbors: Most sympathized and tried to save them. Nevertheless, in abstract terms, something in their hearts also sympathized with the intensely sectarian discourse. Yes, it is Salafists and Jihadists that carry out bombings of Shia neighborhoods or mosques—but they are by now really the tip of the iceberg. Each such deliberate act creates an opportunity for zealous Shia militias—and Muqtada al-Sadr in particular—to retaliate by, in turn, cleansing Shia neighborhoods of Sunnis and justifying it with incendiary rhetoric. Jihadists and Salafists, of course, responded likewise, creating a vicious cycle, with each side becoming rhetorically trapped and becoming mirror images of their worst enemies. Archenemies in effect become allies, for each justifies its existence in terms of the other.

Looking on from outside, it looked like violence based on sectarian identity, but that was not the whole truth. It is misleading to assert that "the people" are fighting each other when groups with specific agendas are inciting and inflicting violence. The Salafists Jihadists, with their cult of martyrdom, must get extra credit for their ability to sow discord and drive a wedge between people.

Salafist Use of Fear as the Governing Principle

If violence was the governing instrument of Salafists, fear was their governing principle. Fear is an ever-reliable human sentiment. Violence instills fear in people, but grotesque forms of violence make them absolutely terrified—and readily complicit. Not everyone in a town is subjected to violence, but the overwhelming level of fear makes the majority internalize the fact of violence into their decisions. People work with the assumption that if they stay out of it they will survive. So they toe the line.

Complicity of the innocent comes cheap when people are worked up into paroxysms of fear. The Jihadists' ability to exploit their fear with callous disregard is one of their greatest strengths. But putting too much emphasis on fear is also perhaps their inherent weakness—because fear, as it happens, creates its own resistance in some people. Not everyone wants to be afraid.

223

❖ Aladdin's Castle

The Blackhawk landed in the middle of the night in the ornately manicured garden of a house in the far outskirts of a large city, in a distant province. It was a castle, but a modern one—a huge gated community, with many houses scattered about. Soldiers used it as the main patrol base and quickly dubbed the place Aladdin's Castle.

It is the castle of a clan elder, an extremely wealthy man. Weighing just slightly more than a hundred pounds, he is apparently kept alive by obscene amounts of caffeine, sugar, and nicotine. When he stood up, it was an event in itself.

In his generosity, the patriarch allows many clan members in distress, some running for their lives, to settle on his massive property as his guests. Not everyone in the clan has been so lucky. Some of the people living there have not left the compound for over a year; they live inside the gates, guarded by people from the same clan while the brave ones bring in the necessities.

The patriarch and his family are now marked people: They have not left the castle for over two and a half years! They were marked by nutjobs trying to rule the area, outraged that this clan would not toe the line. The idea of an ornate cocoon of fear ceases to be a metaphor. Hundreds of men, women, and children ensconced—entombed?—in a castle garden. The reality of their precarious existence slowly sinks in, and it is no longer funny.

The thing with patriarchs and elders is that though they may look frail and emaciated, they have twenty-five million antennas hardwired to their brains and tuned into the community. If he is effective as a leader, he will always be well apprised of the neighborhood.

Soldiers spent four days enjoying the patriarch's hospitality, gleaning every bit of tactical valuable information he graciously provided. He was a frail man with a graying but crisp mustache: Soldiers joked that if he ran out of cigarettes he could suck on his mustache to get a high. His mental agility was impressive, despite all the sugar, coffee,

224

nicotine, and an occasional whiff of hashish on the roof to calm his nerves when things are stacked too high. He had an encyclopedic knowledge of every nook and cranny of his fiefdom, now fallen into the hands of the nut-jobs. Only his right hand moved with the ciga-rette, prayer beads occasionally tinkling inside his sleeve. He always maintained the unperturbed, even-keeled demeanor of a thoughtful leader, hiding any apprehensions of life and death of his people, every word deliberate and deliberately delivered. His people looked up to him to calm their restless souls.

The patriarch was in no way complicit with the nut-jobs. He loathed them, but the fear of death has forced him and his people to hole up in the castle prison. With no power to resist, it was close to complicity—but not quite. It would be wrong to confuse his frail physique with a frailness of heart or mind.

He glided past everyone to address the leader on the ground, and took hold of his left hand. "Thank you," he said in his hoarse yet deli-cate voice. "Sir, why don't you stay longer, and maybe some of your soldiers."

The soldier took his right hand off the M4, grasped the old man's frail hands, and said, "Sir, we cannot, but we promise someone will. Tell me, are you OK, will you be OK?"

"Of course, of course sir," he responded.

There was no reason to doubt him; he knew exactly what he was doing. He then went down the line and shook hands in order of importance. And although no one wore name tapes or rank insignia, he was right on the mark, his powers of observation always amaz-ing. Soldiers run into all kinds of people, including many who believe they are important, but it is rare to experience such great power of observation, such subtlety and nuance. That was the reason he and his people stayed alive.

It was some solace, getting on a bird, knowing that the patriarch had survived in that castle, along with his people.

Salafists' self-righteous acts of violence target opponents that are real—the resisters, like the clan elder who would not toe the line (*offense*)—and also imaginary opponents, such as barbers and educated women (*defense*). And the many sociopaths and criminals who have found a home among Salafists pursue their own agendas behind Salafist rhetoric. People on the ground, atomized inside their protective cocoons, must navigate multiple forms of violence, including arbitrary forms of justice meted out in the traffic circle in broad daylight.

❖ Idris is honest: Complicity and rage

People who have lived a lifetime in the same neighborhood recognize subtle distinctions among the insurgents—the Salafists and the former army guy, criminals, and ideological supporters. They know where the "safe houses" are.

Some people are honest about their complicity, about how tired they are of being afraid and being subjected to injustice. Some break down; some are filled with rage. An English-speaking middle-aged woman responds in a soft voice (her education is enough to make her a possible target). She eloquently asserts that if she could get her hands on some of them—her eyelashes now fluttering at million m.p.h—"I will stab them!" and her hand punches out: jab, jab, and jab. Her eyes were ice, and her intense expression showed that she meant every word. It is easy to guess that she has been personally wronged sometime, somewhere. How best to capture the moment? A soldier quietly responds, "Well, ma'am, if you could give us a hand, it is risky, but we may be able to promise you the opportunity, if you want it." Of course, soldiers cannot and will never do so—nothing, nothing in life is ever that easy—but she does have a hearty laugh.

11

GENIE IN THE ROOM

> The mountains stood alone on the horizon except for a
> tall boulder in the east that looked like the head of a body
> buried in the sands, and Idris's hut at the eastern end
> of the mansion, planted defiantly but pathetically in the
> ground. The very air warned of hardship, trouble and fear.
>
> —*Children of Gebelawi*

Another nut-job-infested shit hole in a distant province. Soldiers had landed at night, to rotate in and out of a patrol base, the palatial house of a generous Iraqi family in the neighborhood.

The older woman, wrapped in her black abaya, her hands on her hips, was short but not sweet. "No problems in this area."

Of course not. The impulse is to comment, "Of course, that's why they dropped us off the bird here last night." Instead, with a sincere smile: "That's good; we are not looking for anybody here. How are you?"

The handful of soldiers laughed, standing in her front yard, but she did not laugh. She had the apprehensive stare of so many other Iraqis when faced with tired-looking soldiers. Standing in the doorway, she made it readily understood: No one was going to be welcome in her house.

House in the Orchard

Surrounded by orchards and fields, the house was visible from five hundred meters away. Soldiers had been hearing stories about this house all night, from people in the neighborhood: The family was believed to be victims of nut-job violence. A bunch of soldiers with a penchant for wandering on their own had readily taken up the hint.

Coming out of the orchard, covered in mud, they found a mid-sized house with an incredibly well-kept garden and a sandy veranda so well-swept you could see a diamond-shaped pattern in the white sand, an incongruous contrast to the muddy soil all around the house. It felt very good to be surrounded by trees, out of the incredible heat.

The matriarch's look was very clear: "I am standing in the doorway; you are not coming into the house, or if you do, it has to be by force."

One can only be polite yet determined and request permission to search the house and the premises, that's all. She took a step back, turned sideways with a grunt and waved the soldiers in; not a word was said. Delicately searching the house, they found it filled with a mother, three daughters, and three toddlers, all boys. It was a large stucco house with six rooms and a massive kitchen. The house was unique, with a cement-like floor made of a mixture of mud and cow-dung, and spectacularly clean, smelling like fresh clean soil. The temptation, partly induced by fatigue, was to lie down on that cold floor, surrounded by trees, taking in the breeze, and sleep. But that would remain a distant dream.

There is nothing of significance in the house: an old mother, obviously the matriarch; two older daughters in their abayas—initially bashful, but soon going about their business without a care, leaving the abayas to flail around. Another daughter, however, sat in the corner room covered in her abaya, never saying a word. Toddlers were running the show with the soldiers: Kids always know instinctively when they see clowns, and clowns get animated at the sight of kids.

Finally, soldiers step out into the orchard to head back. The soldier that talked the most remarked, "There is something funny about that house, I just can't figure it out. They were all hiding something, especially the mother"—and before he could finish, another interrupted, "Yeah man, I know, I know."

"Yeah, where are the men in the house?" That was it. It is sometimes possible to miss the obvious.

"Call [higher] and tell them we are going to the house again, we have to go back."

Walking back to the house, the mother noticed the soldiers from a distance with a look soldiers have seen before: "OK, what now? Just leave us be." One soldier walked straight up to her and asked her in his haphazard Arabic, with the most humble tone, "Can we bother you for some cold water?"

A straight gaze and another grunt. There was clearly much hostility to the soldiers in her heart, yet she waved her hand again. Soldiers followed her like a row of ducks back into her house. The first soldier apologized for messing up the swept sand, but she just shrugged her shoulders. He again apologized with all the sincerity he could muster. She turned, looked at the prints, looked him in the eyes, and then turned with a grunt and kept walking, with the soldiers following her, ducks in a row.

Another soldier, not missing an opportunity: "Hey, man, you just got punked, big time." Yes, getting punked is part of life in counterinsurgency. She seems so pissed off she could punk most anybody. But this time, as soon as soldiers walked in, there was a greeting—from the kids, looking with anticipation at the clowns walking in. A couple of soldiers reply in kind, kids entertained by clowns and clowns entertained by kids.

There has to be a way to engage the matriarch in some kind of conversation. Without a cue from her, no one else in the house will utter a word, she runs the show. A soldier grabbing the glass of water, thanking her, gulped it down. It did taste very good coming from 120-degree heat outside, so he grabbed another.

The question is posed: "Where are the men in this house?" The matriarch gives a concise, frosty answer in a controlled burst. "They are not here."

OK, it seems soldiers will be in the house for a bit longer. "We have been walking a lot. Can we rest here for a little bit?" She grunts again.

"Where is your husband?" Another quick burst: "He is gone."

The impulse is to ask, "Gone where, to the goddamn market, the mosque?" But instead, with a purposely vague look, a different question: "Is he going to be back any time soon?"

Another quick burst. "No." It goes through the mind, holy shit, this is one ornery woman. Forget it, let's just cut to the chase.

"Why not, is he, uh, did he pass away?"

"Yes."

Oh my god, this matriarch has built a wall that cannot be breached in any fashion. There is only one thing she wants: The soldiers out of the house, and she wants it to happen fast. Well, that is not going to happen. She is too ornery and that makes her too intriguing. What is she trying to hide, could someone here be the nut-jobs soldiers are looking for? There are women and toddlers, where are the husbands? Are there any sons? But she just would not speak.

"Well, we are sorry to hear that, what happened?"

By this time, the two daughters who were always doing the chores are standing in a corner listening; the other daughter is still sitting in her room, on a chair, covered in her abaya like a stone silhouette. One of the kids must be hers—he keeps running back and forth.

The matriarch explains in a very dispassionate tone that her husband died in some sort of an explosion. And the soldier goes round and round, trying to empathize and trying to find out who was responsible: How did it happen, who killed him?

It was a chilling moment on that very hot day, as the matriarch looked straight in the eye of the soldier, pointed her finger at his heart and said:

"*You* did."

Yet there is some relief. Now we are getting somewhere; soldiers have faced this situation before. It's a war, people die, soldiers included. Everyone's grief is the same—her grief is hers, and it is the worst in the world. The soldier looks down deliberately; it is never comfortable to be accused of murder. So the others apologize profusely saying it was not he or his friends. She concurs and explains that her husband died during the initial invasion by an aircraft. Maybe it is true, maybe it is a lie, there is no way to judge. But if it is the truth, here is a woman and a family that was profoundly shocked and awed and she still is and always will be. Soldiers apologize again, very profusely: "Is there anything we can do to help you at this moment?"

It is a very terrible thing to ask, one feels terribly guilty but that is all there is left. "Maybe we can talk to our boss, get you some compensation, money, what can we do?"

It is one of those loaded comments, the moment a soldier utters those words it opens up opportunities. But we always dread hearing the requests. It is always tricky. If soldiers can meet the call for assistance, there is a second chance, and we can go further down the rabbit hole. But if she asks for something and soldiers cannot meet her demand, there is no room for excuses, all doors shut quickly.

On an air assault mission with the specific duty of going after nut-jobs on a specific timeline, making and keeping promises is not possible, other than minor ones, and so the next few seconds were a bit worrisome. But the matriarch answers that she is sustaining herself just fine, no assistance is needed, thank you very much. Do you need more water?

There is an almost tangible, deep hostility in her voice, but at least now she is comfortable enough to be open with her hostility, which is a relief. Soldiers keep taking all her anger with as much good grace as they are capable of, going slowly down the rabbit hole.

Soldiers spend the next long moments, about half an hour, simply talking about her family and her children. And she is actually now using complete phrases of English here and there—a sign of how far soldiers have slid down the rabbit hole in that time. But her phrases of English only make her more intriguing.

The soldiers are astute enough not to start bombarding her with the important questions about nut-jobs in the neighborhood. It is better to get there later, let them take their own time; her family story is intriguing in itself, and she is angry but honest. She believes her husband was killed by Americans, but there is another question: Where are the fathers of the toddlers, the husbands of these young women? Are they dead or alive? Did they hightail it out when the soldiers landed at night, if so, where to? The place is on lockdown, after all.

Both husbands of the daughters are dead. Simple. And no going anywhere on that topic.

The matriarch is justifiably angry. She is carrying the burden of the entire family on her shoulders. Her oldest daughter has one kid and her husband was killed—"maybe" by the nut-jobs—about two years ago. But she is murky on the details. As she points to her daughter, the daughter quickly looks to the ground. The other daughter is single, she is no longer going to school; she looks far older than her age and has the bashful look of most young Iraqi girls when faced with American soldiers grinning at them. That's it.

But what about the still silhouette in the room, the one that never came out?

The mother adds, slowly, her husband is working elsewhere and no one knows where he is. Times are tough—meaning, he is dead and they have given up on him (or he is an insurgent that has hightailed it out). The two toddlers are hers. Soldiers have heard enough such stories that it requires a conscious effort to look sympathetic: By now you're pretty numb to the story in its different variations. The only way to go down the rabbit hole is to be engaged.

"Could we talk to your daughter in the room?"

"NO"—and that no was very determined and insistent. She meant it from the very depth of her being. That's it, whatever is in that room, a man, a women, a genie from a lamp, that is what she is so careful to hide. Even the other two daughters are standing still, looking at the soldiers; their eyes look apprehensive, and their smiles are gone. The matriarch looks so tense that you know in the room, covered in the abaya is a deep dark secret: a genie in the room.

It is definitely a woman, the silhouette makes it certain, and she is definitely the two toddlers' mother because they keep running in and out. Men and women can prevaricate but toddlers don't. But what is the secret? Why is the matriarch so tense at the thought of soldiers talking to her when the other two daughters are going about and talking freely? It is something the matriarch is ready to guard with her life like a venomous snake ready to attack.

The soldiers now have to choose. One can always say the hell with it, go and try to talk with the daughter because they are men with guns. But that only gains the pretense of cooperation and makes it impossible to go down the rabbit hole. As long as the matriarch opposes anything, nothing in this household will happen. But with one nod she could open multiple pathways down the rabbit hole and even reveal the secret, one that might be tactically relevant. Soldiers decide.

"OK, we are sorry, we apologize, we will not talk to your daughter in the room." She visibly relaxes.

"Thank you for the water and the pears from the orchard, do you mind if we come around again, to eat some pears in the orchard later?"

She curtly answers that it is fine, eat as many pears as you want, yes you are always welcome.

Soldiers thank her again profusely and leave. They have lot more work to do in the neighborhood, but between missions, when taking a break perhaps at night, it might be possible to come by again. Soldiers only landed in this neighborhood about twelve hours ago and they have a couple of days more. As soldiers step off, one of them mumbles to his friend, "There is a genie hiding inside that room and we need to get the full scoop." Everyone concurs. It may or may not be tactically relevant; the curiosity of the grunts sometimes gets the best of them.

233

But the matriarch is as sharp as a tack, she knows something, of that soldiers had no doubt. They will come by the house again.

At night between rest cycles a few soldiers once again emerge out of the orchard, aimlessly wandering, their mouths filled with half ripe pears. Snooping from the back, slowly looking into every room, they see all the women in the largest room inside, sitting on the floor on many blankets—and (there is always a surprise in Iraq) watching a black and white TV hooked up to a car battery!

Another thought crosses the mind: Are there TV stations that beam programs that can be captured by an old black and white TV with rabbit ears? Well, this is Iraq, anything is possible, and here is entertainment for the night.

Soldiers walk in, making some noises so no one is surprised. They stand by the door. Everyone is comfortable except for the matriarch. She is shielding the thin figure of her daughter, the genie, quickly covering her from head to toe in a black abaya. She is in a corner, looking away; there is no way to get a glimpse of her eyes. But it's the matriarch that counts, she knows what's up.

Soldiers sit on the floor by the doorway and start chit-chatting. They immediately contest the matriarch's claim that the area is safe. "No, this area is not safe. We know where a lot of insurgents are, we caught a whole bunch of them. But if you are afraid to talk that's fine." And surprise, surprise, she agrees with them. Of course. Yes, it is terrible, but no, she will not talk about them.

That's fine, that's a good start: She will talk about insurgents when and if it is time. So soldiers talk about the family in the little time they have before being called back to the next mission. It is a farming family, the family owns the field and the orchard. They work the field and the matriarch even has some people who work her fields. With a look at their fingers, feet and faces one can easily recognize a real farmer; they are telling the truth. Well, how do you sell the produce?

"Someone from the village will come and buy it and take it to the market."

234

"But could you not make more money if you sold it in the market yourself?"

"No, this is not possible."

Well, it need not be said, it's understood: The matriarch does not want to risk leaving the daughters behind. Soldiers were still sitting on the ground, and one of the toddlers began crawling on the soldier's leg, and another soldier put his Advanced Combat Helmut on the kid's head. It's so large it looks like a turtle shell, and when a third soldier would poke the helmet it would start wobbling and the kid would start laughing, and so would some of the family members. Another toddler wanted the same, so the clown doing most of the talking puts his ACH on the kid—with the night vision devices—and now it turns into a circus. Even one of the daughters gets a glimpse through the night vision devices, with evident amazement. The other daughter looks through: wow, she too looks utterly bewildered and laughs hysterically, and the toddlers now want ownership of this night vision device.

Yeah, well, no, that will not happen; we lose it and we buy it!

This is going on between conversations; the matriarch by now looks as if she is fighting off laughter. The genie is in the corner hiding, and maybe listening. Why doesn't she want to look through the night vision devices? This is clearly a determined genie with a purpose.

Soldiers ask about the old bongo truck parked outside. Loaded in its back were neatly packed greens, beets, and other vegetables ready to be sent to the market.

"Who can drive the truck?" One of the laughing daughters points to the mother, surprising in a farming community.

"Are you serious. You can drive?"

The matriarch is even more intriguing, it turns out. She used to be a teacher, a long time ago when she was young, before things turned sour and the family moved out here to their families' land. That is a familiar story to soldiers: Many professional families turned farmers.

During the sanctions decade, families that could not make it in the cities returned to their land and their extended families. Soldiers have run into farmers with masters degrees in mathematics. That explains her smattering of English. But now she does not drive. Things are not safe. Someone from the market comes and drives the truck. But now that the soldiers are here, no one will come—and the vegetables will rot.

"Shit." In everything there is an opportunity.

"OK, how much money will you lose?"

"Sir, I will lose a lot."

OK, no problem, we will take care of your vegetables. We will take care of it.

Then a uniquely American question: "Why don't you buy a color TV?" She simply looks, slowly turning to face the speaker.

"Yeah, yeah, I am sorry, we are dumb, you have no electricity." Well, why don't you buy a generator? It is not safe. What is so unsafe about a goddamn generator to watch some color TV?

Radios crackle, and the soldiers get up; break time is over. Time to go, and they barely peel the NODs off the toddlers before heading back into the orchard, dreading the muddy canal.

"Can we come back again?" There was a nodding head instead of a yes, but that's good enough.

After a night of soldiering, early in the morning the first order of business is to collect some money from higher to pay for the rotting vegetables, collect some leftover candy from MREs to give to the toddlers. Walking toward the house, one thing is obvious. This is a hard-working family, everyone is awake at the crack of dawn, and it seems the first order of business is to sweep the yard, make it perfect. The boot prints from the night before are gone, replaced with the perfect diamond shapes of the raked and ornately swept white sand. It is not even six-thirty in the morning and everyone is awake and working. Goddamn!

Walking in with a greeting, the difference is obvious. The matriarch is now coming to terms with the soldiers. They are a serious annoyance and a nuisance to her existence, it shows in her face. But they are also harmless, and the two older daughters don't run around to cover themselves. Yes, they have a half-hearted abaya wrapped around, but they are wearing what they were wearing and going about their business, cleaning and sweeping. Besides, there is more to be done in the yard than to pay attention to bunch of foreign strangers that seem to simply enjoy pears and wandering around aimlessly.

But this time they ask whether soldiers wanted tea.

The genie was in her room, covered in an abaya from head to toe, again a silhouette statue. Soldiers ask the matriarch for permission: Can we give this candy to your daughters, so they can give it to the kids?

She has that look again: What is this all about? But she says yes.

The two toddlers are awake and come running. They know their priorities. The clowns are back, let's look at the NODs again! Only someone who never had to walk the fields with them would be so enthusiastic to put them on. (And only the toddlers are so enamored with the clowns that they do not smell them. The soldiers can smell their own body odor; when everything else smells great, you know it's bad.)

Soldiers asked the matriarch if the vegetables were still rotting. She stared, as if asking them not to remind her, then answered, "Yes." Some other soldiers were being offered tea by the daughters. The breakfast they had prepared smelled fantastic—fresh bread, some greens and meat with something that looked like grits. Obviously, they had been about to eat before they were rudely interrupted yet again by these obnoxious and determined clowns.

The soldier talking to the matriarch said, "OK, so the vegetables are rotting, no problem, we told you we would take care of it." He pulled out a wad of a few hundred American dollars: "This is for you."

She was visibly shocked. Yet she quickly regained her composure, raising her right hand, palm facing the soldier and politely and sincerely refused the money. Then she raised both hands and refused the money once again, but with no hostility: "Thank you, thank you, but it is not necessary, I am fine, I will not accept the money."

Damn, punked again, and she even punked Benjamin Franklin. How often does that happened anywhere, even in America, much less in a farmer's house in the middle of nowhere in Iraq? Damn, here is a woman.

There is no choice, this dignified matriarch beat Benjamin Franklin. It is time to take it with grace; the soldier stood there with a despondent look on his face as his hamster wheels kept turning furiously inside his head. Yes, he cut quite a pathetic figure in his grimy T-shirt. He is carrying an M4 carbine machine gun with a M203 grenade launcher attached to it, about six high explosive 40mm grenades, two hand grenades, two concussion grenades, army communication equipment with a fundamental design flaw (its weight is inversely related to how well it works), and about two-hundred rounds of 5.56 ammunition that he just reloaded in the morning, along with GPS systems, a compass, a digital camera of sorts, and all the rest of the shit. But he is standing in her kitchen utterly and completely defeated and she beat him so unequivocally with such grace and style. Then she kindly offers him tea, tells him they should eat some bread, but no money is necessary. She went for the kill. She beat both Benjamin Franklin and the grunts, and did so with such elegance and grace, goddamn.

OK, well let's see, maybe not so fast, it's the grunts' turn.

"Are you sure it is OK if my friends have some food, it looks great."

"Yes, absolutely there is plenty of food," and there is no hostility in her voice. Whatever hostility she still has is hidden very well. (A lot of Iraqis are masters of that trick when faced with men carrying loaded guns and covered in dirt.)

The soldier walked near the two older daughters in the kitchen who had prepared the food, telling them, "My friends will eat, but then, we insist, we will give this money to the children, to you, to buy some things for the kids." He walked closer, with the Benjamin Franklins split equally three ways, but stopped short of handing them.

Now the older daughters are surprised, and smiling, while the soldier turned to the matriarch and asked, "May I give it to them, for the children, do I have permission?"

She hesitated with a stern look but finally said, "Yes, that's fine."

The daughters were smiling as he handed it out, telling them that one part was for the sister in the room. The matriarch can beat Benjamin Franklin any day, but it's going to take some time to beat the grunts. Touchdown, baby—but it's not the time for a victory dance: There is never a moment for a victory dance in a counterinsurgency. Of course, he walked back with the same grave face, thanking her profusely for letting him help her grandchildren, and she thanked him in return.

Soldiers have questions for this madam matriarch, she just might know some of the guys soldiers are looking for. They are in the neighborhood and the place is on lockdown, but no one knows *who* or *where* they are. But the most important fact is that everyone says this house has victims of nut-job violence, but no one gives any details. The matriarch shows nothing in her stoical face. Her words suggest that she has control of the world around her, but something in her expression suggests that she bears the worries of the world on her shoulders. And she barely says a word about nut-jobs!

Other soldiers get some food on their plates and are eating, apparently goofing around with the kids but in reality pulling security, keeping an eye on things because nothing is ever perfect in a counterinsurgency, everything is imperfect, and being on one's toes is why soldiers get paid the big bucks (as they keep reminding each other).

And still, the genie remains a dark silhouette in the room.

The women, the daughters are comfortable in the kitchen going about their business, still willing to smile, but they are in a way irrelevant. The soldier grabs his delicious food, fresh bread, and tea and sits on the ground in the corner. The big aluminum plate is crooked in so many places that it is as if someone used a hammer to make it flat. The matriarch is insisting that he sit on the chair. "No, I am comfortable here, I can lean my back on this wall, all this nonsense gear is heavy and wiggles around!" The daughters laughed while the matriarch had a slight glimpse of a smile. She was offering food, and talking; she did not have the hostility any more, or else she hid it well.

The matriarch certainly seemed to carry the whole world on her shoulders, and the genie locked up in the room is the burden she is most worried about. Maybe what she always had was the constant worry of a mother, carrying the weight of her children without a man in the house. And the many grandkids added to the sense of determination in her deep black eyes; the infinite number of etched circles and crevices in her face perhaps told a story filled with something to worry about.

Knowing the neighborhood they live in and all the travails that she has divulged so far fills the heart with great respect. Yes, respect—not sympathy or pity, for one only pities a fool. To pity her would be an insult.

For soldiers sitting on the floor and eating off an aluminum plate, the food was indeed delicious. In our starved state of mind, it was heavenly. The family and the matriarch are now talking almost incessantly about the neighborhood, and it is nice to be able to follow her story and ask pointed questions with the geographic reference grid that is now cemented in our minds. They know much about their neighborhood, including where exactly the nut-jobs hang out. Much that the matriarch shared was valuable information, given her nuanced and in-depth understanding of the local battle space, though she considered it simply innocuous village gossip about the travails of the villagers.

Meanwhile, two toddlers emerged wearing oversized helmets, laughing, and the soldier on the ground made his usual funny face and the one toddler then kicked him on the leg and ran off laughing, while the other toddler, taking the cue from his brother, also gratuitously kicks the soldier on the ground, though he did not seem to know why, and the matriarch and the mother were laughing while threatening the toddlers and asking him to stop, and the kid takes off running. The kid can keep kicking as long as he wants as long as it leaves the adults entertained; the places she knows, the routes and the houses are too valuable.

But what about the genie in the room, she did not eat yet?

Yes, the matriarch suggests that they take a plate, to her. The older daughter fills an aluminum plate with food as the soldier stands up, prepared to follow her, hopefully with the matriarch's permission. Without her permission, nothing is possible in this household. All one can do is to muster all of one's sincerity and ask.

"What is wrong with your daughter in the room?"

Everyone in the house momentarily froze in place and a palpable chill passes through the room. All the dark eyes are turned to the soldier, and the matriarch has a distraught and pained look in her eyes. With much effort, she manages, "She is sick."

The daughters, looking relieved, were looking at the soldier, worry still painting their faces. The tea, refilled only moments ago, now feels freezing. A million thoughts cross the mind. Perhaps she was mentally disabled: Soldiers have seen children, even older men, who have been bound on a leash to keep them close. Whatever it is, some deeply personal family tragedy is hanging like a heavy cloud over the house. Perhaps she was abused or raped by some insurgent nut-jobs in the neighborhood. Soldiers have talked to women who have been in such situations, though none of them were ever kept hidden in a room. They are always intense personal tragedies, of lost dignity and honor, amputated souls and spirits. And it is never easy to learn about them—but if one is able to, then very dark tunnels appear in the rabbit hole, tunnels that may turn up tactically valuable information. They almost always know who the perpetrators are, and it is often the local nut-jobs, criminals-turned nut-jobs, or both.

But why is she hidden in a room? Could this be our moment? Looking at the matriarch and her daughters, the soldier simply repeated, questioning, "Sick?"

"Yes." The pain in her eyes had not receded.

The oldest daughter carrying the aluminum plate was about to walk out of the room but froze in place when she realized that the soldier might be following her. He was not, yet—not without the matriarch's permission; neither would her daughter move an inch without her permission. So the soldier turned to the matriarch and asked with as much genuine sincerity possible: "May I speak to your daughter? If she is sick, maybe we could help. We have bags full of medicine."

The matriarch—neither hostile nor accepting—looked downcast and said nothing. She looked lost. This was the moment, as close as it was going to get. Taking her silence as permission, the soldier turned to the older daughter and she turned and started walking as well.

An Encounter with the Genie

The soldier grabbed the CLS—Combat Life Saver—bag he always carried, not that it had anything that could help, but at least it would make it look official. He walked out of the room following the older daughter and with the matriarch following them both, flashing the peace sign at his buddy. It was certainly a breakthrough of sorts.

As the soldier got close, the silhouette sprang up from the chair, wrapped herself ever tighter in the abaya and turned her face to the back wall, standing completely still. The soldier could only see her back. The abaya was wrapped so tight he could see she is less than a hundred pounds, and at most four feet ten. It is freezing in the room.

Intense anguish showed on the matriarch's face. The sister holding the plate of food now has the look of a little girl who has come across something so terrible that she might never be able to understand it. The soldier feels the chill in his bones, slowly realizing the gravity of the moment—that they are wrapped in an intense personal tragedy. The family has allowed them in: The soldiers have fallen down the rabbit hole.

There can only be two deductions, looking at the frail body wrapped in a black shroud.

She may be terribly burnt, a burn victim whose face is so completely disfigured that she has yet to come to terms with it, understandably afraid of the bewildered and shocked eyes of strangers.

Either that, or she was very recently violently robbed of all human dignity, and she now wishes she was simply a terribly disfigured burn victim.

The notion that she might be mentally disabled was discarded after seeing the look on the matriarch's face. That could never have produced this effect on the mother.

Leaning closer to the matriarch and whispering slowly, only one word needed to be asked.

She fired back in a quick violent burst, "Yes," looking straight in his eyes.

Now only a few inches from the Iraqi matriarch, so close one could smell her body odor and the generic smell of soap and spicy cooking oil, he whispered pointedly, "We are looking for the same people." It was, of course, a bold-faced lie: Soldiers were looking for a specific group of insurgents that everyone kept talking about in this neighborhood. Maybe it's the same people, maybe not. Regardless, if the matriarch starts speaking, it just might open some doors.

She slowly points to the daughter and looks at her back. Another reality quickly dawns, it is almost certain that her husband was either killed by the same guys or he hightailed out the day she was abducted and abused. Or (we could hope) he died trying to kill the guys responsible. The miracle is that she is still alive.

It is propitious that she is facing the wall. Soldiers have dealt with other people in similar situations. This experience, while not unique, is a tragedy with no end for the family concerned. The important thing is, when she does turn around, to look at her the way you look at anybody: without pity, sympathy, or a sense of bewilderment but with ordinary respect, dignity and decency.

The singular professional concern returns to the forefront, as always. Holy shit, this family may have a clue, may even have a personal stake in finding those men who drive around in a black KIA sedan terrorizing the populace (as so many families have mentioned). Maybe, maybe not, you never know. But first she would have to turn around, find the strength to face the soldiers—or perhaps to face any man, or even to speak. That strength could only come from the matriarch. The daughter is sustaining herself from the spirit of her mother. Perhaps that's why the mother looks so weighed down, pained and fatigued. She is keeping two people alive with the spirit left in one soul.

The soldier looked at the matriarch to ask another question but she simply cut him off. She called to the daughter in rapid-fire Arabic, difficult to follow. The girl responded, turning deliberately, slowly, looking down, her face completely wrapped in the shroud. It is the strangest thing—it should now be possible to ask her questions directly but this would not be possible because all her strength is with her mother. So the soldier asked her questions through the matriarch, and the matriarch would essentially repeat the question, adding her own, and the daughter would answer, looking down. It was not a matter of modesty: She wanted complete anonymity.

Soldiers find themselves in situations that are not always charming, and they always come out of it by finding some humor. But this was a singular moment when soldiers lost all their wit because there is no humor to be found when one is looking at an amputated soul.

Just as the questions and answers were getting substantive, the radio crackled. Break time is over, it's time to run, time to get on patrol. Everyone got their stuff in a hurry. One soldier, about to step out, went to the matriarch, and in the rush to catch up with his buddies he grabbed the matriarch's left forearm instead of the right, almost toppling her over; without even thinking, still holding her arm, he asked loudly, "We have to run, look, we will come back, we may be able to help, but we need your help, will you help us, will your daughter help us? We will come back we promise."

The matriarch corrected the soldier, pointing with her right hand, "*Inshallah*," and the soldier did a quick double-take: "What, oh, yes, yes, yes, you are right, god-willing, *inshallah*, we will come back, god willing, will you help us, we really have to run." Her look was intensely noncommittal.

Then one look that no one would ever forget. The silhouette that begged for anonymity now slowly raised her head, looking first at the soldiers' boots, then up further, and finally her two black eyes were straight on the soldiers. You could see fresh scars around her right eye that suggested bigger ones on her face. A tiny black mummy, tightly wrapped in a black shroud but with a pair of intense black eyes that were shining, alive, and glittering brilliantly. The soldiers, shaken, started sprinting to the orchard.

One said, as they stepped out, "We have two days, brother, maybe it's the same guys everyone talks about with this black KIA, we will find out."

"Yeah, but she will have to come through."

"We have to come by again today. It must be the same guys, the KIA cats, and these people know a whole lot more than the others."

"Duude, before we do anything, I need at least an hour or two of sleep. Shit, I am running on thirty-six hours right now, it's only fucking 0830, and come afternoon, shit will be like 130 degrees man. I will start tripping."

"Oh come on, don't be a bitch."

And amid laughter it was quickly decided, yes, definitely some sleep at the patrol base after this mission before coming back to see the matriarch.

The Matriarch's Answer

It seems like an eternity since soldiers first landed in the neighborhood. Seconds, minutes, hours, and days collapse on top of one another during any mission, good or bad. The idea was to accomplish a few specific objectives: Locate specific target buildings, clear them, talk to the captured Salafists, and eventually send them higher. All the check boxes were accomplished relatively swiftly.

Staying in the neighborhood for follow-on missions, soldiers were talking to people and listening to their stories, conducting tactical questioning, and taking nothing for granted. People's stories paint a picture on the ground that complements whatever soldiers already knew. The stories are convoluted but usually intriguing, often stories of sorrow. The tactical saliency on the ground comes when multiple, seemingly discordant narratives can be put together, to paint a picture of reality as the local people see and understand it. Soldiers manage to isolate the few consistent themes that keep recurring, and find in those consistent themes a tactical reality. And sometimes they find something new that has slipped under everyone's radar screens. That's why soldiers keep walking and talking, despite very often feeling delirious.

In this nut-job infested neighborhood, the stories complemented what soldiers already knew. But there was also a consistent recurring theme: Some men driving specific vehicles had been terrorizing local men and women, and these were the guys running the show. They are insurgents, part of the nut-job franchise—but they are also locals from the neighborhood. As in other enclaves, the lawless atmosphere provides opportunities for the sociopaths in the neighborhood, the criminals, murderers and low-lifes, who quickly get in league with insurgents. They will toe the insurgent line, but they will also use the opportunity to do what they always do, only now they have impunity and top cover. The recurring stories of these men engaging in murder, extortion, rape—and, of course, virtue enforcement—all fit a pattern. Identifying them and locating them is the hard part.

The matriarch may have the answer. The reason soldiers made a nuisance of themselves in the matriarch's house was not for the pears in the orchard nor because there was a genie in the room. It was because soldiers had learned the importance of finding victims of violence and getting their help.

They had heard about this house on numerous occasions from other people in the village. After seeing the house, there was a quick professional realization. A houseful of women and children with not a single man presents two extreme realities.

It could be a house filled with insurgents; insurgents more often than not are family men, who murder by night and play with their kids during the day. They could have run away before soldiers got to the house. Therefore, everyone in the house could be lying.

On the other extreme, it could be a house filled with only women because the men had been murdered. In that case, the women probably want the perpetrators to be found. They want justice and vengeance.

In between the two extremes lie any number of possibilities. The only way to find out is to talk and listen—following the blood trail like hound dogs yet retaining an extreme sense of humility in any interaction with the innocent.

Soldiers return to the house with notes, digital imagery, and much on their minds. They are hoping to keep going further down this rabbit hole. If the matriarch would be gracious enough, she has the power to make it happen and soldiers need to lead the way with a sense of humility. And it has to be done with next to no sleep, feeling delirious, keeping in mind the constant dangers, with feet firmly planted and a constant watch on the ground. With one ear on the radio that will crackle at any moment, and the other ear for the story people are telling.

The difference in the atmosphere inside the house compared to the first day cannot be overstated; it is perhaps best expressed by the daughter in the room. Soldiers walk in looking utterly disheveled but feeling extraordinarily well organized. The matriarch greets them, the other daughters acknowledge them with smiles, the toddlers run over to these foreign clowns—and the daughter in the room is standing by the kitchen, wrapped in her shroud. She quickly covered her face (she will be covering her face for a long time), but she is standing still and acknowledging the soldiers with her fiery black eyes.

They walk straight to the matriarch and apologize yet again for bothering her family. No problem, would you like some tea? Yes, that would be great, thank you.

As the daughter slowly walks back into her cocoon of a room, the matriarch paints a painful picture of what happened, creating the context and leaving the gruesome details to be left to the imagination. When a family invites a soldier down a rabbit hole, sharing their deeply personal tragedies, this is as deep as one can go. Yet they do so for a reason; they are expecting something in return. Empathizing should never be mistaken for reality. Soldiers are soldiers, and no matter how heartbreaking the story and how heartfelt the pleading for help, soldiers need to know that life is almost never fair. They must only make promises that they can keep, and do what they can despite the difficulties—and nothing more.

What has happened to her daughter is clear enough. She was taken to a house, repeatedly abused, and by sheer luck, was released to live.[58]

While a heinous crime, it may or may not have to do with terrorism. It is not the job of soldiers to go after rapists, though there is nothing that enrages the soul more than the sight of abused and dead children and stories of rape and the deliberate death of the innocent. But soldiers have a specific job: Go after insurgent nut-jobs.

Soldiers must keep a clear distinction between sentiment and reason. Leaders have to be able to make "warm-hearted cold decisions." No matter how enraged the soul, no soldier can ever get entangled in people's sad stories. We can only be ready to use them to our advantage: It's a war, after all. The trick is to pin down the relevant reality, isolated from the wider events. People at times feel compelled to be dishonest, confounding justice with vengeance. In the absence of justice, people feel righteous in their vengeance because that is all there is left.

---

[58] Soldiers surmised that she managed to leave the farmhouse alive when a bunch of the soldiers' friends did an air assault mission in an adjacent neighborhood about a week earlier. It seems that when the nut-jobs heard the incoming birds, they hightailed it out.

Hopefully, the matriarch's stories parallel the other stories soldiers have heard.

It is tricky. The matriarch's narrative matches perfectly with every-thing soldiers have heard. But on the specific point of where the guys might live, she brushes off all possibilities with one wave of the hand and simply says that they live in a farmhouse a little way down. This is not a possibility that anyone had considered, but she can all but guarantee that they are still there. They never go anywhere, and they stay in the area because everybody is afraid; no one speaks to or about them. For soldiers, that singular claim has quite a bit of resonance in the context of an insurgency.

Yes, a bunch of insurgents in control, no matter where, always find anonymity in their subversive capabilities, the ability to be in hiding but in plain sight. Confident in their power, they assume they can take the complicity of the people for granted. So they can stay, drink their tea, eat their fried tissue-paper pastry dipped in sugar sauce and wave at the Americans. People are afraid, no one will rat them out because they can make sure these people will wind up dead. But if they are overconfident of their abilities, one may find an opportunity.

"Your daughter, does she know about the farmhouse? Your daughter knows who they are and also where they live? Can we talk to her, show her some pictures?"

A deep sigh and a wobble of her head. "OK," and she walks to the room. Holy shit, is this going to work? That delicate, shrouded and scarred black mummy with intense black eyes, burning with her past—would she find enough resolve to look at the digital images and point out the possible perpetrators? Perhaps even help map out the route to the farmhouse on the geographic reference grid? This is not the movie where victims turn into heroes and go around blasting and shooting. In real life, most people—though not all—remain very terrified.

But first, it's time for a different question for the matriarch: is your daughter OK, is it okay if we talk to her? Yes, she is fine, she has some wounds on her hand and face but she is fine. At last, soldiers will get some positive identifications.

Blast wave: *None* of the images match the possible perpetrators, goddamn! But the farmhouse is a dead-on, and the description of the vehicles and people matches the notes in all our notebooks. If only she could give the soldiers a positive identification, point them out—otherwise, every man matches a general description—then things could so perfectly fall into place. Goddamn!

A soldier, one of the leaders on the ground, arrives in the doorway with his rooster walk. He is visibly agitated. Each bit of new information gleaned from the matriarch and her daughter has been passed on to him, and he in turn called one of his friends higher to verify. The congruity between higher and on the ground is important, though it is not always easy to accomplish and does not always work as one wishes. It helps to have friends because a million things are going on at once and higher doesn't always have time to attend to every intriguing tidbit of new info that emerges on the ground. That is the responsibility of leaders on the ground, not higher.

"Look, no one has cleared the farmhouse," he reports, "because it is in *no one's* geographic reference grids. It's not our sector, and apparently they don't know who got it."

"Are you serious?" The two soldiers look at each other and quickly come to a rational consensus. Nothing much needed to be said: OK, we have to clear the place after sundown. The leader wobbles into the room, bringing his long frame inside and wobbling his knobby head, and he smiles at the matriarch and the daughter sitting in the room. The daughter had in her eyes the closest thing yet to a smile.

One fortunate soldier is chasing a toddler with his usual uproarious laugh, making a funny face. The toddler takes off at lightning speed and hides behind a chair as the soldier circles elaborately around, laughing, "Where is he, I can't see?" Yeah, playing hide-and-seek with an Iraqi toddler in a nut-job infested neighborhood—the charms of counterinsurgency. Soldiers need whatever laughs they can get.

The daughter is wrapped tightly in the black shroud, wishing for anonymity. The scarring next to her right eye looks fresh, but what about her hand? Whatever else, she has to give some form of positive identification, and things could fall into place if the guys are who everyone says they are, and if something is found in the house, possibly even buried somewhere.

Matriarch is looking weighed down by the worries of the world, her daughter is wishing for anonymity, there is so much anguish in this room. But how resolute are the two women in their anguish?

Soldiers are trained to make life and death decisions—some do it well, some don't. But how do you get ordinary people, who have not volunteered for this, to make such decisions? There is no clear answer, you go with what you got, sometimes it works and sometimes it doesn't. All the nonsense about hanging out in the house is done for that specific purpose, to convince them, make them comfortable, help them make a favorable decision.

"You said your daughter has some wounds on the hand. May I have a look at her hand, maybe we could give her some medicine to put on them, do I have permission?"

She shrugs, yes, no problem.

The genie in the room switched her left hand with the right, now using her left hand to keep her face tightly covered, showing only her black shining eyes. She raised her right hand halfway so the abaya fell back to her forearm, showing fresh bruises and scars on her very fair skin. The soldier pulled his combat life saver bag, spilling nearly all its contents on the ground, always as clumsy as he could possibly be. He was looking for all the tubes of Neosporin.

Pointing at his own face, his own right eye, he asked the matriarch, may I have permission to look at the wounds on her face? Yes, no

251

problem. (This task would no doubt be easier with a female Arabic-speaking soldier, but you can only work with what you have.)

The daughter had kept her face tightly covered with her left hand, eyes intensely and purposefully fixated on the soldiers. Then the strangest thing happened.

She turned left, focused her eyes unwaveringly on one spot on the ground, allowing the abaya to reveal thick black hair atop a triangular, very fair face, bereft of all apparent emotion. All the bruises, scars, and wounds were now visible on the right side of her face, especially near the ear: Nothing serious but all fresh. Her gaze, fixated on the ground, did not waver once.

The soldier turned to the matriarch. Put the medicine on the cuts and wounds. They are not serious but do not put it in her eyes. And the daughter again covered her face tightly with the left hand, and the moment she found herself anonymous behind the shroud, her eyes swiftly turned right, fixed again on the soldiers.

A million thoughts cross the mind, the most impulsive being the need to blurt, "Are you serious?" But instead the soldier looked down at her hand.

He asked, let me see your right hand, and turned to the matriarch again: May I?

Yes, no problem, of course—constantly with her laser vision. Her situational awareness was simply astounding, not even a fly passed through this house without her noticing.

The daughter raised her right hand, wiggling it and pushing the shroud back. The soldier delicately grabbed her right wrist with the fingers of his right hand, while looking at the matriarch, making sure it's OK. She had so many bruises on her hand. The soldier holding her wrist pointed to the matriarch. "Put the medicine only in the places where there are cuts, most wounds on her hands are not serious in any way, and she will be fine."

There are many questions. How in the hell could she have so many cuts and bruises on her right hand all the way up? Did someone drag her down the street, what the hell happened? But one cannot let the curiosity get the best of them. There is a job at hand and that is paramount. Curiosity will have to be shoved back in the patrol-pack.

Neosporin tubes and everything else that can be spared from the combat lifesaver bag are passed to the matriarch.

The soldier looks at his friend standing at the door, and they both have the same thought, could this be the moment of truth?

The daughter, Insaf, is resting her elongated hand on the soldier's hand, poised delicately on his grimy palm, this is as deep as the rabbit hole gets. He turned to the matriarch, raising his left hand index finger: "Please, we need your help, will you help? We promise your daughter will be safe."

The matriarchs' eyes no longer have the pained anguish or worry. They are now the eyes of a woman, a mother, trying to find a delicate balance between raging emotions and good reason. Soldiers turned to Insaf; her eyes crisscross from the soldier holding her hand to the eyes of the soldier that looks like a deer, standing in the doorway with a half a can of dip wedged in his lower lip. Insaf has nothing to lose and everything to gain, vengeance in the absence of justice. But this is not the movies but real people with names; always the question, would she? Would she be willing to take a risk? Her eyes seem to say that she would, but she would not do a thing without the matriarch's blessing. Insaf is living with the spirit borrowed from her mother. The matriarch's eyes are still as she stands with her usual regal comportment.

The radio again, the soldiers were expecting it, there were many follow-on missions and patrols to do. Both held back the impulse to utter the word "shit."

The soldier with Insaf's hand looks at his friend. They both know that this was it. It is either a beginning or an end, so it's time to run with it. He slowly rests her hand on her right leg and lets go of it. Insaf remains still. As he stands up, both soldiers turn to the matriarch, mustering it all because this is it: "We swear to you in the name of Allah, your daughter will be safe, and god willing, justice will be done."

The matriarch has the eyes of a person processing too many logical hypotheses that keep popping up in her head. It is a risk. Soldiers will soon be on a bird to go elsewhere doing the same thing, trying to be insurgents behind insurgents. And the family has to live. It is a risk they have to recognize and take on their own.

"Please think about it. We will come at night. We have to run." She nods, yes. Both soldiers turn to Insaf and ask if she would think about it, about helping us. A tiny woman, wrapped in a black abaya that has seen better days, sitting still like an unmoving silhouette—staring with her shining intense eyes at two grimy American soldiers covered in mud. But it is the soldiers that have the look of pleading in their eyes because she just might be the one person who could help the soldiers distinguish the enemy from the innocent, identify the local insurgents that terrorize the place in their KIA. She has in her eyes what could possibly be a "yes," but would she really be willing to take this risk, with this bunch of strangers?

The matriarch will give the final blessing, but it is Insaf that will have to decide and she will have to convince the matriarch, and the family will have some decisions to make. The hope the soldiers held to is that the blood running in the veins of Insaf's cold hand will stay cold enough to help the soldiers send these bastards higher—the primary job function of soldiers on the ground, all else is irrelevant.

The radio is loud, and soldiers are about to step off on another follow-on mission that came down from higher. They might round up every man in the entire neighborhood, but it would mean nothing if they do not know who is who: They might be facing the innocent, and in their midst could be some of the worst of the nut-jobs. They all look the same. Unless soldiers find some people willing to distinguish them. Victims of nut-job violence were always willing, though they are also completely and absolutely terrified, and it takes time. And at times, it hurts the head and pains the heart.

254

But the soldiers need to get the guys driving the KIA vehicles; that's the only way they will find some peace of mind after this mission. They have invested too much time, effort, and brainpower on them.

The tactical reality is simple: Soldiers have two choices. Soldiers could catch what they believe are the bad guys based on her information, get pictures of them, and trundle back and verify it from Insaf—but it can only be done once, and it is hit or miss whether they round up the right men. The other way is for Insaf to walk with the soldiers and lead them to the series of safe houses that she is confident they use, and the series of mud huts where she knows they store their many goods—and pick out the men from among a lot of other men, always anonymous in her abaya in the dark night. That would be our best shot.

It is simple, soldiers can round up the men from the houses and she just has to point out whatever she knows.

Ah, but if everything were that fucking easy. It is a grave risk for her. But she has lost everything, including her own sense of self-worth, and she wants justice. She would have to trust the soldiers, at least the two that spent the most time with her, those two grimy, smelly and retarded looking foreigners that treated her with simple human decency. She has to have enough confidence in herself and the soldiers to trust them with her life. That is asking a lot of reciprocity for simply being decent. She has to choose, and get the matriarch's blessing.

Soldiers get ready to leave. The soldier with the deer eyes begins to be assaulted by three toddlers from all sides; he is laughing hysterically, snorting, and the other soldier is laughing at his snorting. The family laughs at the spectacle of foreign clowns.

The soldier tells the matriarch, "We will come by later, do not worry," and she nods with her kind eyes. She says how afraid she is of these people—everyone in the neighborhood is afraid. Here is a giant of a woman in her five feet three inches and hundred and forty-two pounds, carrying the burden of the world, afraid of the nut-jobs. She posits the ultimate paradox soldiers for chasing nut-jobs: "You must kill these people."

The soldier walking next to her nods, saying with all sincerity, *Bismillah ir-Rahman ir-Rahim,* "In the name of God, the most Gracious, the most Compassionate," and touches his heart. "But we need your help."

She nods with the intensely pained look of a grieving mother. She realizes what is necessary, but she has by no means decided what to do.

Crucify Your Mind: Damned If You Do, Damned If You Don't[59]

The encounter with madam matriarch posited a fundamental puzzle that soldiers on the front lines chasing nut-jobs always face. Men and women, wanting to assist the soldiers, would pointedly request that soldiers *promise* them—"Please promise, promise"—to kill the insurgents and *not let them go.*

But soldiers cannot be the judge, juror, and executioner. It is not a promise soldiers can make, even if at times one wants to, because it is complicated and never done unless it is a direct fire engagement where the enemy and the innocent is as clear as day and night.

No soldier has the right to decide the life or death of an unarmed man, even if it is a wanted insurgent. When an insurgent is captured and disarmed, he becomes a responsibility first, an insurgent second. Soldiers are responsible for his well-being, the rights and wrongs of the matter are irrelevant. It is that way for a reason. Men with guns have to be held accountable, the U.S. Army would not be what it is if it did not hold its foot-soldiers accountable. Therefore, to circumvent the laws and do it would be murder, even though not to, more often than not, is to let the insurgents get away with murder. And all of a sudden soldiers are sitting, staring at the Iraqis, drinking their tea, realizing that there is no escape, damned if you do, damned if you don't, what is the right answer?

But even to be quiet and not promise is also a lie. It gives the impression that soldiers can kill the captives and that may end up getting the family killed. Because the insurgent may get released, come right back

---

[59] "Crucify Your Mind" by Jesus Rodriguez, Cold Fact (1969).

and kill the family that assisted the soldiers. That has happened too often with too many blundering idiots. Decisions are made by the guys who process insurgent captives; they decide on the basis of legal criteria, lawyers making the decisions, they do not meet or deal with the people on the ground, they are only following the rule book. Everyone knows they try their best, but each has their own protocol, and at times their protocols have far-reaching ramifications on the ground.

The soldiers on the ground have to answer to the Iraqis. If they get some innocent Iraqis killed, they carry the responsibility. The mistake inexorably saps soldiers' credibility on the ground; one would have to be a raving lunatic to commit the same mistake more than once. It is a reality that soldiers can neither explain nor expect Iraqis to understand: The risk and the responsibility is their own and no one else's.

In contrast, insurgents find it absolutely imperative to maintain the overcast cloud of fear, hanging ever closer to the ground, to make people constantly feel that their sense of predictability and complacency comes at a heavy premium. Yes, some of the people do rise above this reality, following their sentiments despite the pervasive fear, and these are acts of resistance in themselves.

12

IDRIS IN HIS ELEMENT: SUICIDE FIGHTERS AND SUICIDE BOMBERS—A DISTINCTION[60]

> Idris burst into laughter . . ."You hate me Adham, not because I was the cause of your being kicked out—you hate me because I remind you of your own weakness. What you hate in me is the reflection of your own sinfulness. . ."
>
> —Children of Gebelawi

Yes, a suicide bombing, the wholesale slaughter of the innocent, unleashes sentiments of disgust and leads to a question: *Why*. It raises psychological, sociological, and moral questions about *why* men and women want to kill themselves while killing the innocent.

But a different question crossed soldiers' minds every time—question that only concerned tactics.

---

[60] In the discussion below on suicide bombers and fighters, we owe many insights to our discussions with a number of soldiers who spent a life time dealing with suicide fighters.

Some soldiers managed to escape some nut-jobs by only a few seconds, escaped by the skin of their teeth. One moment it was the usual bustle and din of the marketplace, and the next moment it was a boom that shook the earth.

Innocent Iraqis and their vehicles were charred and splintered. The smoke blackened walls, and the smell of explosives, burnt gasoline, burning rubber and plastic—everything moving with a life of its own—tangled up in the nostrils along with the metallic taste of vaporized blood, permeating the tightly closed quarters. Then, mixed with everything else, came the caustic overpowering taste of sulfur. The soldier closest to it escaped by only a few seconds, and announced in a daze, "Duude, I am going to find me some drugs. I am getting high tonight."

The next second he was instinctively sprinting headlong to the scene with every other soldier following.

People were everywhere now, some sure-footed but disoriented, as if they'd been dropped into an unfamiliar land and spun around; some doing the crab walk because of the concussion—reason, emotions, and body at a complete disconnect. Some are without life but still warm; some have not quite come to terms with the extreme pain that awaited them. A few children—and a half: Some beginning to scream with the last of what they had in them. The senior enlisted leader on the ground came to a screeching halt.

He looked around and swiftly set the priorities, taking control as he only knows how, having done it consistently through five deployments.

"Hey, where are my squad leaders? Look, I want security and make sure you know where every one of my soldiers are at, every one of them, and you keep your goddamn eyes on them, look, make sure no one does anything retarded, keep it fucking tight."

Then he turned looking for the medics: "Hey, doc, listen, you do what you can with aid. Everyone with a CLS bag, get with the medics and help him out."

Then turned to his leaders again: "Look, I am fucking telling you, no messing around, make sure you keep your eyes open. Watch out, in about two minutes, lot of guys will be freaking out." He meant civilians, not soldiers, would be frantically running around.

"I want security on the medics and all the guys doing aid, understood?"

Then he stopped and grabbed a wobbling and bleeding Iraqi man, using his left hand, and took him carefully to the pavement, right hand still gripping the M4. The man, seemingly with no life-threatening external injuries, had that haunting serene of someone who has been too close to an explosion. The absence of external injuries masks a wicked reality inside: So many of his internal organs destroyed that he was living a lifetime in a dazed second. The leader took it all in and slowly helped him sit.

The blast wave got the best of a middle-aged woman. She got thrown and tangled up on barbed wire, wrapped around her right ankle as she dangled up side down, swinging like a pendulum under the bridge. She was dead. Then he picked up a dazed little girl, not a scratch, but she only had one cough in her and her eloquent eyes lost their shine as she lay in his hands as he watched. He put her down, looked around as he stood up again, teeth clenched, and he captured out loud what was going through everyone's mind: "*These-sick-mother-fuckers.*"

The sight of the innocent, the injured and dying and dead from the blast makes the heart ache. The deliberate death of the innocent can never be excused by any sob story, and those who excuse it need to be skull-fucked down the same road so they can lick the ground and taste it. The innocent look so defenseless, so out of their wits, so completely helpless. Looking on, the screams and the last gasps of the innocent feel as if pointed at soldiers, saying, in that fleeting moment, that the soldiers had failed and the nut-jobs had succeeded. Yes, no excuses, to say anything would be an insult to the screams of the helpless. The last respect to be paid is to make the words sparse, give them dignity and accept that surreal sense of responsibility, rage and disappointment.

But the brain assiduously concentrates on the present: tourniquets, dressings, and intravenous fluid—what is necessary is obvious, but which of the innocent among so many deserves it first? Triage.

The decisions may not always be perfect; nevertheless, soldiers must now decide based on the limited information they have, knowing that one can never have everything anywhere, we can only do what we can. There will be little accomplishments mixed with large failures. The failures bring a feeling of grit that steadily lodges in the bones; the bones feel harder every second. Yes, everyone has their moment, the nut-jobs had theirs, and soldiers will find theirs and make it count.

To find that moment, the question soldiers always posed was not *why* some people will kill themselves in pursuit of killing the innocent. It may be relevant but not as soldiers. It is assumed—some indeed are willing to kill themselves. The relevant question instead was *how* they do it and the ramifications on the ground.

The acts, however macabre, are an undeniable tactical innovation, a way to minimize the asymmetry of power between the strong and the weak. It may be morally repugnant—but it is not a *moral* reality soldiers contend with but a *tactical* one.

Suicide Fighters as a Tactical Innovation

Formidable women and men make a choice to come to terms with death on their own terms. They have signed a prenuptial agreement with death. They will attack a "military target" with all the conviction and strength they can muster: Taliban fighters in Afghanistan, charging at Americans in Dohuk; Salafists running at American soldiers in the Diyala river valley in Iraq; a company-size element of female fighters doing an infantry charge at a Sri Lankan army base, while another flanking element tries to breach the defenses—each fighter wearing a cyanide capsule around her neck. Hizbullah fighters charging Israeli Defense Force tanks in the city of Eintaya; and Bint Jbiel in south Lebanon during the second Lebanon war (2006), with the near certainty they would be annihilated, all share a fundamental similarity, regardless of their creed or cause.

First, they are fighters with conviction attacking military targets, and they have to be taken seriously with a cool head, devoid of passion.

Credit should always be given where it is due—especially to the enemy, so as to understand and fight them better. Second, their pre-nuptial agreement with death makes them very formidable opponents. They have forgone loss, they fight with nothing to lose; it gives them fortitude and makes them formidable in battle. Third, for soldiers trying to counter them, this only means they may be formidable fighters, but it does not in any way alter the underlying tactical reality in battle. It is a fight, and they are mortal. To prevail will take strong resolve, tactical acumen, and resources; the side that makes and implements the best tactical decisions will eventually prevail, whether soldiers or suicide fighters.

As some soldiers always joked, there is a simple, almost appealing clarity in the use of suicide fighters to attack military targets. Wars are about killing; life and death—it is so close that at times they overlap. And suicide fighters have come to terms with their fate in advance. Hence, using people willing to die as the main assault element in a battle is a tactical innovation that goes to the heart of war fighting.

Deploying men and women willing to die in direct fire engagements, rushing headlong one after another, is intended not only to kill the enemy but also to sap the resolve and weaken the heart of the adversary to minimize the asymmetry of military power that exists between the strong and the weak. If one can weaken the heart of the adversary, half the battle is won.

Facing a firefight, some soldiers will turn their trucks around and hightail it out of the place. But most stay, get on their feet and stay in the fight, and they react to contact. With every round, reason guides your decisions, but it's instincts and heart that give you fortitude. Every second reduces itself to will and resolve.

Soldiering in its essence is a matter of the heart. In the face of danger and at the point of decision, soldiers must have resolve to keep taking the next step. Reason will guide—but the brain is worthless in battle without the heart, what soldiers call intestinal fortitude: Either you have it or you don't. It is the heart that gives the soldiers the ability to say the hell with it and walk with resolve and stay in the fight. Many soldiers have family members who have dared far more and fared worse: There are countless stories of running headlong at German machine gun nests, of the sheer insanity of the Pacific theater in WWII, of the cold mountains of Korea, and the mud, blood, rain, and guts in Vietnam. Even in Afghanistan and Iraq, a colleague saw a hand grenade thrown at his hide site and instinctively jumped at it, grabbed it and threw it, saving his colleagues' lives by risking his own. He was lucky enough to live and laugh about it, and at any mention of the incident he would simply shrug, "Well, man, we all do stupid things." The famous last words of one of the leaders on the ground as he lay dying: "Listen, I don't need a goddamn medic, OK, I am fucking telling you, make sure my guys are OK."

Behind each such instinctive act is a heart, one that is a cut above. When a soldier says with humility that he was stupid to jump onto the grenade—yes, maybe so. No sensible person, and barely any soldiers, would jump toward a grenade. Or run at a German machine gun nest. Or walk down the street in a rage towards incoming fire, suppressing the enemy on the roof, explaining when he returned, "The mother fuckers, man, they just pissed me the fuck off"—as if he had just returned from a bar fight. It was not deliberate but instinctive. Those simple acts defy all sensible logic and reason, and those lucky enough to live can always call it stupid in retrospect—they have earned the right. But it was the heart, not the brain, that gave them the resolve.

But for those men and women fighters who have signed a prenuptial agreement with death, that sense of responsibility for each other is forgone. Instead, you have corpses walking with fire power. It has its tactical advantage. Suicide fighters have a good infiltration plan—but *no exfiltration*, as one leader commented: a formidable advantage because they only do half the usual operations order. It is a fight to the end, kill or be killed.

There is no tactical difference between fighters who very much want to live and fighters who have forgone life; both are mortal. But the one who has forgone life makes not only an attack but also a statement—the loudest possible statement, that he or she is not afraid of death.

A suicide attack is meant not only to inflict damage but also to strike fear, display better resolve, and highlight the intensity of their conviction to minimize the asymmetry of power.[61]

As a tactical reality a suicide assault also carries along the weaker fighters who derive inspiration from leaders who have forgone life. But this reality also engenders a sharper sense of resolve in the opposing side. The moment rounds start pinging off, a direct fire engagement has a mutually constitutive effect. Each side reacts to the other's actions, and the final outcome is the cumulative result of everyone's actions, with the better soldiers prevailing.

Soldiers faced with suicide *fighters* (both the assault element and the flanking elements) have the certainty, a sense of clarity, that there is no likelihood of the enemy cutting and running, it will be a fight to the end. That creates its own sense of resolve.

But suicide *bombers* who attack the innocent are in a different fight altogether—a different reality with a different objective.

Suicide Bombers: Plotting the Death of the Innocent

The deliberate death of the innocent is morally unacceptable. But that means nothing as an operational concept. Suicide terrorists who kill the innocent are using a tactical innovation. And figuring out innovative ways to fight is what fighters do.

This innovation is a formidable concern on multiple levels: the act itself; the deaths of the innocent; its effect on how people react; and the way soldiers react to counter them. And in a counterinsurgency centered on a population that depends on engaging the innocent as much as on vanquishing the enemy, these effects are all the more critical.

Suicide bombers kill the innocent to highlight their own existence and to make a statement; they attempt to justify the indefensible with a

---

[61] Mongols before a raid would scar their faces to strike fear into the enemy; the news of their ruthlessness reached towns before they galloped in. Salafists cut heads to display in the traffic circle as a signal to the people. Is there much difference, apart from a span of time?

self-serving sob story. Every moment of carnage creates increasing fear and rage. It pierces the feeling of safety and the sense of invincibility inherent to living in a free country or a free city. The terrorists who plan and execute the act are targeting not only the blast radius of the bombing itself but also the eyes, ears, and minds of the people looking on.

Murdering the innocent both validates the nut-jobs' existence and pits the innocent against the innocent, as people now look at each other with increased suspicion. A bombing that kills twenty Shia people in Baghdad creates suspicion and rage in Basra (a majority Shia city in southern Iraq), where images of the dead and dying are carried into homes on satellite television. It is easier to hate than to understand. If the first-order effect of an act of terrorism is the dead and dying, then the second is the reactions of "the people."

Without this ability to instill the sense of unpredictability, magnifying its impact through mass media, the terrorist act would have no wider meaning. Fortunately for the Jihadists, every suicide bombing makes it to the news, even though their other accomplishments—beheading and tormenting their own people in their enclaves—never make it to the news. It is obvious that the Salafists are very media savvy, both from the way they conduct suicide terrorism and from the way they contain the outflow of information about the atrocities they commit in their controlled enclaves. A bombing in Baghdad near the Khadim shrine will not go unnoticed in Basra or any other town or in the U.S. or the U.K.

The Salafists' and Jihadists' greatest claim to fame is fame itself as terrorist celebrities, and each act is aimed at establishing that image and with it the self-serving sob story.

When passions are running high, logic falls short. Terrorism creates the image of a formidable enemy—often, an image that is larger than life. With rhetoric that panders to the worst in people, the perception becomes the reality. Paroxysms of fear, real or imagined, can lead people to self-destruct in unexpected ways.

During a Shia religious festival on August 31, 2005, hundreds of thousands of people were marching across the al-Aima Bridge that spans the Tigris River in Khadimiya. There had been a number of indiscriminate mortar attacks that morning, aimed at Shia by Sunni groups—attacks that were claimed by a Salafist group. As thousands of people started walking across the bridge toward the al-Khadimiya shrine, all it took was a rumor that there was a suicide bomber about to blow himself up. The resulting panic started a massive stampede; over a thousand people—children, women, men, and the elderly—were either trampled to death or fell off the bridge and drowned in the Tigris.

The Salafist and Jihadists nut-jobs who seek to sow discord and instill fear could watch the carnage and chuckle, without lifting a finger. The photo of the al-Aima Bridge, completely filled with shoes and slippers of people who are no longer living, was one of the most poignant images of the war in Iraq. An Iraqi who was there collected every news story and every image, saved them in his computer, and showed it to soldiers—it has become his personal obsession—explaining the event and reliving it minute by minute.

It is a convoluted and perverse reality that Jihadist create. Instilling fear, murdering the innocent simply to point out that they exist—in order to perpetuate a self-serving sob story that allows them to wage war with utter callousness on innocents who do not conform to their view. The irony of ironies is that it is their own people who are most often the victims, the same Muslims that they try to reduce to a figment of their imagination.

Yes, the Jihadists invoke a laundry list of grievances: the most popular theme is blaming the Americans, the British, the Jews, and the Arab governments allied with the West. When Salafists make those rhetorical linkages, mixing the foreign and military policies of other nations into their sob story, they hide the real threat they pose to progressive Muslims throughout the Middle East. Jihadists talk a big game against Americans, the British, and the state of Israel and do find moments to murder the innocent from these countries, but they stand no chance of fundamentally altering their way of life or militarily defeating them. Suicide terrorism cannot alter a way of life or change a political system: That is merely the wet dream of nut-jobs and not a realistic possibility. Their operational targets are found elsewhere among their own people.

13

IDRIS'S FOIBLES: SUICIDE TERRORISM AND ITS WORLD OF ENEMIES

> Idris fled into the darkness, shouting as loudly as he could, "Hind! Hind!"
>
> —*Children of Gebelawi*

Moral and psychological aspects aside, from the soldiers' point of view, suicide terrorism is a tactical innovation of perverse genius that must be contended with on the ground. Any tactical innovation can always be countered, and it is possible to defeat them.

The image of suicide terrorism and the deliberate death of the innocent is powerful. But behind each act of suicide terrorism is a long line of people who make it possible and very much want to live. These are the administrators, the gatekeepers, who so readily turn their own believers into a figment of their imagination: The sick genius of a sob story that makes their own soldiers' lives dispensable, as well as the lives of the innocent.

Finding the gatekeepers is a matter of deepened intelligence gathering. Their mortality is a tactical matter to be dealt with by good soldiers, quietly and with a sense of humility. As a very wise man once said, "why use tanks to catch rats, when alley cats would do the job better?"[62]

The Logic and Process of Suicide Terrorism

The prenuptial agreement with death gives them an advantage: It allows for secrecy, anonymity, and subversive capacity, restricted to men and women who self-righteously believe in the act. The terrorists' subversive capability to be non-existent in plain sight makes the innocent look at each other with suspicion. No one can guess who is going to be the next suicide terrorist, and that is their greatest strength. That is also their greatest inherent weakness.

As a tactical matter, the logic and process of suicide terrorism remains the same, no matter who conducts it. Suicide terrorism is an act carried out by a man or a woman totally indoctrinated, convinced of a cause. He or she has forgone any sense of self-worth; dying becomes the only way to regain life! Certain features of Islam (and its various interpretations) may make it easier to indoctrinate a Muslim to become a suicide terrorist.

The group that has turned suicide terrorism into an impressive tactical art are the Tamil Tiger rebels in Sri Lanka (the LTTE, Liberation Tigers of Tamil Elam)—who, as it happens, got their head start in suicide terrorism in the Hizbullah training camps in the Bekka Valley in the eighties.[63] Today, they have an army of men, women, and kids who walk around with cyanide capsules. The majority of them are Hindus and Christians by birth (atheists in practice), who believe fiercely in their ethnic narrative of separatism, with its cult of martyrdom assiduously constructed over the last twenty years. The power of a well-cultivated idea that is captured in a sob story, no matter how ridiculous or ill-conceived, can never be underestimated.

---

[62] A maxim of General Grivas (*Guerrilla Warfare and Eokas' Struggle: A Politico-Military Study*).

[63] Thanks to some officers in the Sri Lankan Army for information on the beginning of LTTE suicide terrorism.

When men and women are blindly convinced of an idea, at a moment of visceral reaction (anger or rage) they may be turned into suicide terrorists. When Iraqis would risk their lives to take revenge on insurgents who had abused or tortured them, soldiers would comment to each other how easy it would be to persuade (or dupe) some of these men and women, with raging passions, into being suicide terrorists.

Peculiarities in a faith or tradition may make it easier to exploit people's sentiments, but at the end of the day, that is only an added advantage. As long as there are men and women willing to follow through with powerful sentiments defying reason, and as long as there are men callous enough to exploit people on behalf of a dogmatic scheme, there will be suicide terrorists, irrespective of creed, nationality or sob story.

As an operational concept, suicide terrorism is meant to strike fear. Trying to strike fear in the heart of the adversary is as old as warfare itself—but the unjustifiable feature of suicide terrorism is that it is aimed at murdering the innocent and not at military targets. Terrorists justify the acts of murder by telling the converted that "The Other"— Americans, British, Jews, secular Iraqis, Shia, etc.—are all their mortal enemies.

Whether it is a Palestinian man or a woman who walks into a Tel Aviv pizzeria or a Salafist who walks into a market or a Shia mosque or a police recruiting station or Tamil rebels in a crowded market, the terrorist bomber walks in with the single-minded objective of murdering the innocent people surrounding them. The moment becomes possible because most people are not paranoid, they give benefit of the doubt. Suicide terrorists prey on the basic human expectation of normality.

The seconds that follow are inevitably about blood, guts, and carnage. The survivors of the bomb are crying, hollering, and even asking soldiers to deliver the dead. They, as well as bystanders watching with mouths agape, will have indelible images seared into their minds. Being good, normal, and unsuspecting is now a weakness that allows suicide terrorists to capture the moment. The act of suicide terrorism is not a matter of genius but of callous disregard for everything so perfect about being human.

Their genius lies elsewhere, in the tactical reality. The tactically proficient suicide terrorists—the best of them—have very refined subversive capabilities that allow them to capture that one fleeting moment of murder. Their subversive strength lies in their ability to be submerged in an unsuspecting population, to be anonymous in plain sight. Thus, the very things that define a global city—its crowds and its anonymity—also serve the purpose of a suicide terrorist preying on the innocent.

Terrorists need a foothold in an area before they can start working on their objective. One of the easiest means of getting a foothold in a new place is to prey on the unsuspecting diaspora or ethnic community. (That is not always essential: in a free society, filled with foreigners from every conceivable ethnic background, anyone can move about freely and remain anonymous.) Having a local foothold gives contextual knowledge of the strengths and weaknesses of the innocent target the terrorists plan to decimate. And in a society with conflicts, where people are inclined to notice a new guy in town—in Iraq, for example—local networks and communities become essential.

A successful suicide terrorist attack illustrates their tactical refinement.[64] LTTE, for example, will have one or two men or women who will actually carry out the attack; they live in the capital, immersed among the thousands of unsuspecting Tamils. No one would learn of their intentions or motives until after the fact. A soldier that captures one *today* has captured an innocent man or a women. But *tomorrow*—and here is the paradox—the terrorist is dead and the soldier has failed.

Therefore, the trick is identifying the others: The brains who do the background work, the men and women who actually want to live,

---

[64] Again, we thank some Sri Lankan Special Task Force officers for their information. As it happened, lot of those soldiers do contract work in Iraq, and they were always a great repository of information, advice, and even assistance.

operating a series of independent cells that function autonomously, usually without knowing of the others' existence. There is always at least one gatekeeper who is privy to all the moving parts. And the one most valued secret is the identity of the group working on logistics, the group most likely to be caught.

The would-be suicide bomber, too, is always closely monitored. That person could live an autonomous life for many years until the propitious moment arrives. Of course, not everyone is filled with such conviction. Any number of men and women get cold feet at the last minute and take refuge in a Western European capital.

The gatekeepers go to great lengths to guard the secrecy of the many moving parts by compartmentalizing the information. As they move away from targeting civilians to focusing on the assassination of high-value individuals—a much harder task—they need a higher level of subversive faculties and tactical refinement. (Salafists in Iraq were never subtle. They were crass but effective, aiming simply to instill fear and counting on the reaction of people and groups to exploit the moment.)

The guy who wants to kill himself is an important but not a critical element. Since there are no contracts bearing his signature, he remains innocent, so to kill him would be murder. And as a tactical matter, he is worthless. There will always be someone else to be duped. In the popular imagination, of course, he is portrayed as a martyr; reporters will chronicle his story or even make a movie out of it. He will be put on a pedestal by the smart nut-jobs—precisely because such martyrs are the least important and most dispensable players. The ones who create the context are far more important.

Indeed, there are many stories of supporters being duped into becoming suicide bombers without even knowing it. Someone would be transporting a vehicle or some ammunition, and it would be remotely detonated so he could become an inadvertent martyr on the Internet.

It is not difficult to kill or abuse the unsuspecting innocent. But violence creates its own counter-reaction in the hearts and minds of people. Each act of terror creates a constituency against it. Some people oppose it as a matter of right and wrong, many are scared, and—most important—some hate terrorists viscerally because they have been at the receiving end. Those men and women have a personal stake. And they are usually the ones who will assist the soldiers by taking risks on their own.

Power is always held in place by a series of tiny sinews—and terrorists and insurgents tend to forget how delicate these sinews are. Terrorists, no matter how resolute, innovative and subversive, have to be embedded in a community of people Their subversive capacity depends entirely on the people who surround and interact with them. If people are not on their side, the terrorists, no matter how skilled, completely lose their advantage.

Opportunities arise from within their own midst that make it possible to out-flank the flank, as some soldiers learned in Salafist neighborhoods. While all the high tech wizardry may help, the key is the women and men who are willing to help the soldiers by identifying opportunities to break the seemingly autonomous cells.

Subversion and secrecy are paradoxical tasks. The more effective the insurgent or a terrorist is, the more careful he has to be, living among unsuspecting people. The moment he becomes convinced that he is actually good at his job, he may begin to forget the many delicate sinews that hold his position together. Every terrorist and insurgent, even within a protective cocoon in his own community, must constantly look over his shoulder. Catching one at a complacent moment is fundamentally a question of time-sensitive information.

❖ Idris is fallible

Sometimes the best information about a terrorist comes from someone with a stake in his demise. A soldier walks nonchalantly to the back of the restaurant that sells falafel to look for the two most wanted guys on the block. Walking in, he is well aware of the risks—it may be or may not be an ambush. But if reciprocity has been established between the soldier and his source, the risk is less; and in the end, taking that risk is essential. It is the job of soldiers. When the information is perfect and stars are aligned, one can either capture him in an ornate drama or take the risk and capture him (with far less drama) with a ball of falafel in his mouth—when he is at his most vulnerable. Insurgents who are comfortable in their own element, confident enough to take people for granted, have forgotten their vulnerability. They do not expect any of the insignificant men or women at the receiving end of their handi-work to be brave enough to walk the soldiers into a restaurant.

Another paradox. To send a terrorist to detention requires writing a novel—a report that might or might not meet the standards set by perfect people. If the suspect gets released, he will certainly kill the people that helped the soldiers. And to put him on trial has the effect of turning a callous murderer into a folk hero among the believers of the sob story. But to rob him of that last moment of publicity that he badly seeks, to assure his anonymity by simply killing the captured terrorist—that, no matter how much blood he has on his hands, would be murder.

Soldiers on the ground do not define the way they fight, and they only fight the way that is defined to them. And that is as it should be.

❖ **Blood meridian in the triangle of death**

> The air was cold and clear and the country there and beyond lay in a darkness unclaimed by so much as an owl . . . war waited for him. The ultimate trade awaiting its ultimate practitioner. . . . Only that man who has offered up himself entire to the blood of war, who has been to the floor of the pit and seen horror in the round and learned that it speaks to his inmost heart, only that man can dance.
>
> —Judge Holden, *Blood Meridian*

The anonymous death of the insurgents is the one thing—*the only thing*—that will make the moment sweet for the seething Iraqi man or for the woman with a steady death stare and frosty black eyes or for the grieving father who cannot fathom how the heads of both his sons appeared displayed on the traffic circle.

Or for Insaf, wrapped in her flailing abaya, stepping outside her tidy orchard and gliding through the field.

After the capture of the men in the farmhouse, it was her choice to be escorted to identify her tormentors; soldiers wanted verification before sending them higher. But such moments are never easy. Victims are almost always terrified. Insaf froze for a second, walking flanked by soldiers on each side. With her right hand, she kept a death grip on the soldier's rack-system until it was cutting into his forearm, but who cares? Soldiers had one single-minded thought and really nothing else mattered: The guys in the black KIA have to be taken care of and sent higher, and it has to be done swiftly.

Flanked by the two smiling American soldiers that she decided to trust, Insaf was taking the risk on herself—why do people do what they do, who the hell knows? Holding tightly to her abaya, peeking out of it, she would nod at each of the men in turn, her blood still running cold: this one, this one, and this, and on and on and on. The men watched in excruciating bewilderment while a third soldier, with a smile and a joke, made each of them stand up from their squatting position. Having killed and abused so many people, they could not know which of their victims this was or see the importance of one frail woman in an abaya. Judging from the pure horror in the eyes of the men, there was no certitude left in them to lie—perhaps seeing themselves reflected in her scarred face: Afraid not of the smiling soldiers but of a resolute heart they did not have.

She did not say a word. It was not necessary. With this simple manifestation of a resolute human spirit, some of the worst of human beings became nothing as the relevant truth slowly filled the space left behind by a row of pathetic men.

Did this row of pathetic men, with Iraqi and American blood on their hands, constitute legitimate military targets that could be summarily dispatched on grounds that fulfill everyone's legalistic, moral, and political requirements? Perfect people, who fight this fight armed with metaphors, decide how soldiers actually fight on the ground, and they are the ones who will have to answer.

The greatest weakness of the self-righteous men who enshrine a self-serving sob story—the Salafists and radical Jihadists—is their cavalier assumption that people are ordinary, that they are always fearful. People are never ordinary and some have the capacity for the extraordinary in the worst possible moments when things are stacked against them. People can play an extraordinary role in advising how to dismantle an insurgent/terrorist cell for good.

One of the charms (and challenges) of a counterinsurgency for soldiers on the ground will always be how to give people the opportunity to help us. It may require playing into people's prejudices, biases, and raging sentiments. The task is not to pass judgment but to follow through when people take those risks.

Using tanks to catch rats is to act like a scared juvenile who has never been in a brawl—to confound shit-talking with fighting and to alienate the men and women who might help soldiers. Quietly letting the alley cats go after the rats is the work of a grown man who possesses the humility that comes from unwavering inner certitude.

At two in the morning, Insaf finally walked back to her house escorted by a handful of soldiers, walking through the orchard where it met the white sand. She looked at the grimy soldiers wearing their night vision. A faint light glowed in one room of the house—one could imagine the family sitting in trepidation. She slowly turned away, took a few slow steps toward the house, then strutted, then broke into a run. She disappeared into the house with a single glance backward, as the soldiers watched her receding silhouette from the orchard. Yes, beyond the many brave men who assisted soldiers in nut-job-infested shit holes, Insaf will undoubtedly remain an indelible memory for some of them, a woman who defied everyone's imagination with the decision she made and the risk she took.

But soldiers also felt a sense of accomplishment. They had pulled off something nearly impossible in persuading an Iraqi woman to identify her attackers.

The nut-jobs always hand their adversary a great advantage. Being convinced of their own perfection and righteousness, they consider other people to be ordinary—but there are always some people, like Insaf, who are extraordinary.

Waking Up From the Mislaid Dreams

> They beat people with sticks for a look, a joke or
> a laugh, until the alley endured a nightmarish
> atmosphere of fear, hatred and terrorism. Yet the
> people bore the outrageous steadfastly, taking refuge
> in patience. They held fast to hope, and whenever they
> were persecuted, they said, "Injustice must have an
> end, as day must follow night. We will see the death of
> tyranny, and the dawn of light."
>
> *—Children of Gebelawi*

These isolated successes, however, could not fundamentally alter the situation on the ground. Air assault missions were never the central front of the fight but only an augmentation at the margins.

The brunt of the burden and the losses of fighting the Sunni insurgency was borne by the countless Iraqi landowners, and by the many military units—Army and Marine Corps—tasked with controlling the vast swaths of land infested with innumerable Jihadi groups who tried to create tyrannical enclaves. These units worked to capture the moment when many Sunnis woke up from their mislaid dreams, rubbed their eyes, slurped their tea, looked around and said, "Oh shit!"

But the efforts of soldiers on the ground, no matter how hard they work, may not achieve very much as a foreign intervention force until the host nation population takes ownership of their destiny. Soldiers can only assist them. When some Sunni Iraqis, waking up from their mislaid dreams, were willing to take risks, some daring officers managed to capture the moment. That singular element decisively altered the dynamics of the Sunni insurgency, in a cascading effect that is now called the Sunni Awakening.

The key advantage was the radical Islamists' overzealousness, enforcing medieval codes with modern weaponry; they overplayed their hand perfectly, turning people against them. At their height, they also managed to disrupt the old loyalties and power relations, giving tribal leaders and local notables a stake in reclaiming their position. Perhaps most importantly, even those who despised the Americans understood that they would eventually leave—but the Jihadists would not, claiming Iraq as an Islamic theocracy.

The awakening, while a real accomplishment, also brought a sobering reality. It created a ladder of tribes loyal to the Americans (to Benjamin Franklin, to be specific).[65] Even former Baathists felt they had a stake in this game, finally fighting off the remnants of the Jihadists and Salafists (mostly local men). The Sunni Awakening allowed a reassertion of traditional authority based on tribal and clan loyalties, but it also created new power relations that undermined traditional loyalties and authority.

The many firebrand clerics and insurgent leaders had their rings of acolytes—and some of these men are now on our payroll and controlling neighborhoods (and at times also enforcing their brand of virtue). The difference is they no longer shoot at the Americans or their own people (because Benjamin Franklin has that effect on people). This is good: The innocent are no longer dying as often as before, and people have less violence to contend with.

Yet this is a tactical reprieve, and whether it can be turned into a strategic one depends on how well the government of Iraq integrates these players into the new regime, retains suzerainty over these disparate groups (whether through the electoral process or through patronage arrangements), and how well American soldiers can assist from the margins. It is certainly not an end, but rather the beginning of a whole new set of challenges.

---

[65] This is somewhat similar to what Lt. Col. Lawrence did, leading an Arab Army from Hijaz to Damascus. Note what happened to his Arab Army when Lawrence went to Oxford to write his seminal classic, and General Allenby came to Damascus and took over.

14

GHAZALNUS AND THE GARDENS OF IMAGINATION: THE KURDISH INSURGENCY[66]

For practical purposes, there is no Kurdish insurgency. Yet the concerns, stories, and myths about the Kurdish people—stories that many Arab men and women kept repeating—seemed to fit perfectly with our understanding of the soup sandwich. They had organization, strategy, tactics, believers, and a story.

Later, some of us had the pleasure of working and running around with the Kurds. It is strange that the Kurds' activities seem to fit the bill of a separatist insurgency, but no one actually calls it by that name. Perhaps because Kurds fight on our side?

Brothers in the Fight

Our own bias is unequivocal: Kurdish Peshmerga forces are very good fighters, and they were the only true brothers with us in this fight in Iraq. On numerous occasions when soldiers fought with them

---

[66] *Ghazalnus and the Gardens of Imagination*, a novel by the Kurdish author Bakhtyar Ali.

side-by-side, the Kurds impressed them with their tactical acumen, tenacity, fortitude, and the steadfast way they stepped into the fight.

On this day, the urban neighborhood looked like a fireworks factory in flames. Tracer rounds filled the air, with non-stop gunfire, the yellow glow of intermittent explosions from misdirected insurgent RPG fires, and low-flying big guns hovering in the air.

There was an unforgiving minute in this melee. A leader from a different unit, on his first deployment, had gotten lost along with his men—as lost as one could be. A senior enlisted leader on the ground on his fifth deployment heard his erroneous radio transmission to the big guns in the air; he then checked his geographic reference grid and said simply, "Goddamn this stupid motherfucker." Rounding up some of his men, he ran over, pulled him aside, and told him to sit tight.

He knelt down amid the 7.62 rounds pinging by. While his soldiers set up a tight 360-degree security perimeter, he contacted his commander, then the birds in the air and moved them into position, then got locations and situation reports on every one of his enlisted leaders and their men. He then asked the Kurdish Peshmerga Officer Nakeeb Karzan for a detailed account of the situation and the location of his men, scattered about in the flaming neighborhood. (The Kurdish unit was part of the Iraqi Army, but they were all Kurmanji-speaking Kurdish fighters.)

Then he got the commanding officer on the radio and gave him precise, succinct and detailed accounts of the situation on the ground. Only a few minutes after he moved in, the commander is now fully apprised, enlisted leaders have control on the ground, and it only remains for the enlisted men to wrench the initiative and get control of the fight.

He had one request to his Commanding Officer: that the lost leader and his men will have to be stationary unless it is absolutely necessary they be moved. The Commanding Officer (who always enjoyed being in a good fight) replied with a laugh through the static, "You got it. Those guys will be stationary and pull security, an important function by itself; it is perhaps best that those guys stay off this fight tonight unless their help is absolutely necessary, so they don't do any unnecessary damage." Everything is simple until Murphy kicks in: "No plan survives the first contact."[67]

As he and his men were about to move out, numerous rounds hit the wall next to them, spattering cement pieces and ricocheting by their feet—and the leader in charge was laughing. So many rounds, all kinds of weapons firing, explosions. In night vision, the neighborhood looked as if every nook and cranny had come alive and was scowling and cackling at the soldiers hunkered down in an alley about to move out. And he was *laughing*. That is why he is a combat leader.

There are four kinds of soldiers. Those who never leave the wire; those who cower when rounds start pinging off, and they never leave again; and those that wrench up the fortitude to take the next step, hiding their apprehensions. And then there are those that get animated as the rounds ping off and the air fills with noise and fire, when the uncertainty is the only certainty and the unknown looms large. That's when these soldiers come to life. This leader belonged to the latter group because he has a formidable heart and the necessary intestinal fortitude and also because he is a little crazy, though not insane. He remains one of the most outstanding young combat leaders the army has produced—certainly in the minds of the soldiers who walked into many alleyways with him and got lost in them on numerous occasions.

Now he is standing and laughing, his hulking figure hugging a wall, tracers flying by him, cement pieces splattering, while he is on the radio moving another bunch of men, getting the rest of his men behind him.

He laughed again: "This is it man, be ready"—and the stage for this lethal ornate drama was perfectly set.

The commander is in full command of the fight while the enlisted leaders are in control on the ground. The American soldiers will push

---

[67] Murphy's Laws of Combat.

from one side while the Kurdish fighters will push from the other. It is beautiful to see a group of good soldiers steadily take control of the situation, using the requisite amount of force, using it with caution, but being steadfast and committed all the way—as the Kurds did on that night.

❖ Nakeeb Karzan

Soldiers were good friends with Nakeeb Karzan and his friends. His story was much like many others they had heard. His family was originally from Sulaymaniyah; his family escaped to the northern mountains at the time when the Baath Party attempted to resolve the Kurdish grievances once and for all—with a military campaign to eliminate the Kurdish men primarily, and, when possible, women and children. The campaign was named, perversely, after the Eighth Surah of the Qur'an, al-Anfal (The Spoils of War). (The Eighth Surah describes in detail the righteous way to fight non-believers when Muhammed and his followers won a battle against pagans despite overwhelming odds—though, this being the Quran, the turning point in the battle is accredited to divine intervention and not to the tactical acumen of the men or their leaders.[68]) Nakeeb Karzan's brothers all fought as Peshmerga, and one died fighting. One of his sisters remains a leader in one of the female units of the Kurdish Peshmerga.

Soldiers had a running joke about him. After 6.00 p.m, he was inebriated to the point of incoherence, but there was one part of his brain that always functioned irrespective of the blood alcohol level. The part that made the tactical decisions. Nakeeb Karzan was no different on this night. He was drunk as a skunk, and his sweat probably contained more alcohol than you'd find in an American beer, but he led his men brilliantly without missing a beat or running out of breath.

Soldiers were getting fire from a decrepit structure, and some were about to go inside and clear it while others put down suppressive fire. In a neighborhood full of civilians, it was not in the books to drop a

---

[68] *The Meaning of The Holy Qur'an, in English and Arabic*, by Abdullah Yusuf Ali, American Trust Publications, 318–340.

bomb and demolish the house. No one could know how many innocent children, women, and men were inside along with the insurgents
unless someone goes inside. It is the job.

As the soldiers were about to go in, Nakeeb Karzan yelled something in Karamanji and three Peshmerga fighters ran headlong into
the house. He followed them in, rounds went off, some explosions,
and a few minutes later all four come out, one with a minor wound,
repeating, "No problem, no problem." American soldiers laughed and
everyone went inside the house to find the two insurgents that did
the shooting lying by a window, now without life. In another room
children, women, and men huddle together, as is common in such
moments.

Soldiers were back out on the streets. One pointed to the Peshmerga
soldier with the shrapnel wound, walking without his helmet, weapon
in hand but no night vision. An American leader asked him, "Hey,
where is your helmet? Look man—you need a medic?"

"Oh, no problem, no problem."

The enlisted leader answered, "Look, it's good, no problem, but you
need a damn medic, and I cannot believe you forgot your damn ACH,
what the fuck!"

He got the same smile: "No problem, it is me, it is me, you are good,
I am good, no problem, no problem."

Soldiers forced Mr. No Problem (as they dubbed him) into the makeshift command post to get some medical attention, so others could
continue on the night. For the rest of the night, they all lived up to the
name Peshmerga, "Those That Face Death."

Three hours later, the urban neighborhood was quiet. It was two in
the morning; the American soldiers had suffered only a few scratches,
and several Kurdish fighters had minor shrapnel wounds. One heard
only the slow rustling footsteps of American soldiers and the cackles
of the Kurdish fighters. How different the neighborhood looks, how
peaceful and still, compared to three hours ago.

When some enlisted soldiers and their leaders walked into the make-shift command post that day, they found the American Commander as giddy as a kid in a toy store. He had just lived through a good fight; that's all he ever wanted, it's why he joined the army. He was sharing a laugh with the senior Kurdish commander and some others.

The leader on the ground quickly grabbed Nakeeb Karzan by the neck and put his sweaty head in a headlock, and said with a laugh, "This guy, this guy is fucking good, y'know, he is fucking good."

The Kurdish commanding officer (a Major) laughed too. "Of course, of course, he is very good, he has been fighting since he was fifteen years old, and all his family, brothers, sisters, everybody is a fighter."

Yes, Kurdish fighters will always have a special place in the heart. So it is heartbreaking to consider them part of the insurgency, but it is imperative to state what we honestly understood. It's the least one can do for friends—tell the little truths as we understand it.

Coming to Terms with the Kurdish Insurgency

Soldiers now had to walk those same streets during the day wearing an ignorant grin, insisting to Arab friends in the neighborhood that they had *nothing* to do with the events of two nights before! Iraqi people are, of course, smart, especially the ones that soldiers could call friends; they had some inkling of what happened. But soldiers relied on this neighborhood, to drink tea and spend time chatting, so the whole truth is best left unspoken. After all, professionally dealing with the truth is not part of the job—that is for perfect people. Soldiers merely listened to the accounts given by people the next day when they came out to clear the streets of litter after the sun came up. They did not have many kind words to say about the Kurds, and they were filled with foreboding. Some gave explanations that bordered on the absurd.

The northern provinces have a Kurdish majority, and one hears about the exotic charms of Kurdistan. But hundreds of thousands of Kurds live in urban centers all across Iraq, living side by side with Sunni and Shia Arabs. So one wonders: If there were ever a partition, how would these hundreds of thousands of people fare—especially when the nut-jobs would quickly portray them as the new boogeyman? Iraqis have been told for decades, after all, by Baathist state media and government-sanctioned clerics, that Americans, British, Jews, *and Kurds* were behind all their problems.

Some Iraqis certainly looked askance at the sudden rise of Kurdish fortunes, riding the coattails of the Americans. But there are also many Arab families (especially Chaldean Christian Arabs) with friends and relatives who fled to Kurdistan to escape the worst of sectarian and nut-job violence when the nut-jobs roamed the streets. In any case, one issue always animated everyone—the city of Kirkuk. Many Arab friends, both Sunni and Shia, had a simple thesis: The Kurds are trying to grab the oil fields, and Americans are supporting them. Soldiers shrugged their shoulders. On top of the contesting claims of Turkomans, Assyrians, Sunnis, and Shia living in Kirkuk, the fact that the Kurdish city is sitting on a ton of oil perhaps does not help matters.

The Kurdish Insurgency

The northwest of Kurdistan, centered on the city of Irbil, is the domain of the Kurdistan Democratic Party (KDP) while the northeast, centered around Sulaymaniyah, is run by the Patriotic Union of Kurdistan (PUK). Some say that the Tweedledee and Tweedledum of Kurdish politics are Mazoud Barzani (KDP) and Jalal Talabani (PUK). Joined at the hip, they are best friends yet archenemies; each has made the occasionally necessary bargain with the devil against the other—but both have managed to survive, their greatest accomplishment. If politics is an imperfect business, they have mastered the imperfection. The Kurdish people have great stories and they share them, despite the deep sorrow often buried inside.

Like the other insurgent narratives—sob stories—the story Kurdish people tell is of being perpetual victims. Mostly, it is the story of amputated souls of people and a lot of systematic death, destruction, and destitution, as well as internecine fighting between the two main groups. The narrative, like most stories, also gets infused with self-serving myths and legends, especially pertaining to the city of Kirkuk. How Kurdish is this city? What about the claims of Turkomans, Assyrians, the Sunnis, and the Shia? Everyone has arguments, counter-arguments, and more stories.

Strategically, KDP and PUK have seemingly reconciled their differences, and each has its area of control. They astutely navigate ambiguity: KDP officials express a willingness to stay within a unified Iraq if given the autonomy to continue their way of life; PUK would occasionally muse about getting as many political concessions as possible for the Kurds. When push comes to shove, they both quickly step back from any claims of Kurdish independence, at least for the moment.

It is undeniable that the Kurdish regional government, whether controlled by KDP or PUK, does a better job of addressing the immediate needs of the people than the institutions of the incipient Government of Iraq. Each party has its own Peshmerga units to keep overt control while the secret police and intelligence agencies of both parties maintain a covert control. They managed to keep the people relatively safe even at the height of the insurgency. But the ever-skeptical enlisted mindset asks, is everything so good? There is always a catch.

Soldiers who were lucky enough to fly into Irbil (the regional capital) on escort duty had one thing to say every time: "Damn, it's like flying into another planet!"

Walk around Irbil or Sulaymaniyah: Buildings are going up, the sky-line is dotted with construction cranes, luxury vehicles whiz over the potholed roads; restaurants and innumerable tea shops are filled with people who know how to tell a good story, and maybe even splash it with some Arak. Many a soldier who had the fortune to visit the Citadel in Irbil, to walk the streets and take in the charms of one of the longest inhabited places on earth, came back smitten. *Why can't I go to Irbil for R&R?* That's the place to be.

The soldier stayed in Irbil for a few days and was fascinated. "I actually went to a damn *bank*. I mean, it was a state-of-the-art bank called the Emerald Bank. Imagine that, a bank that is actually working,

288

not trapped in blast walls! Damn, I mean, it was a beautiful bank!" Then there are the mountains that warm the heart, so perfect that even the laziest must get the impulse to climb them. Kurdish people actually walk around and take family vacations in the mountains despite the risk of landmines—inherent to enjoying the natural beauty of Kurdistan. Yes, the mountains of Kurdistan are spectacular, and spectacularly difficult, and that engenders respect in soldiers that fought in them. It also reminds soldiers why the Peshmerga was never defeated despite the repeated attempts to destroy them. They had the mountains on their side: "We Kurds, we will always have the mountains."

But despite the sense of creeping prosperity, there are concerns, complaints, and stories of despair. There is the rising disparity between the newly rich, living in Western-style gated communities and well plugged into a system of nepotism and patronage, and there are the destitute who are left behind. The minorities of Kurdistan fare no better than minorities elsewhere in Iraq. The Assyrians have had their land appropriated by Kurds from time to time, and the Turkomans have had their own difficulties. The Yazedis, adhering to a heterodox form of Islam often derided as "devil worship," occasionally seem to get shafted by all sides.

The group of Kurds that once had it worst, however, has now been liberated: the unlucky inhabitants of a Salafist nut-job enclave controlled by Ansar al-Islam. Women, of course, were generally forced to cover head to toe or were locked up in their houses; girls' schools were bombed and destroyed; music vendors, barbers, and teachers were either killed or ran for their lives. Any family that lived through Ansar al-Islam's puritanical rule can tell harrowing stories of what lunatics armed with a cosmic sob-story are capable of inflicting on the innocent.

Another Massive Concussion!

A few lucky soldiers, standing idle on the streets of Irbil, encountered an inexplicable sight. "Are you serious?"

Women Peshmerga fighters, from the female-only unit.

Soldiers know that the PKK (Kurdistan Workers Party), fighting the Turkish state across the border, has female-only fighting units. Those women are no showpieces. They traverse the mountains, fight, kill, and die. So maybe this is the real deal, the women Peshmerga fighters that everyone has heard about! There are many moments in soldiering that one feels very fortunate to have signed that enlistment contract without reading the fine print. This was one of those moments.

To soldiers accustomed to delicately navigating the sensibilities of Iraqis, and seeing women maintain a rigid comportment of virtue and modesty in public, this is, to put it mildly, a massive concussion. A whole bunch of Kurdish women in olive green Kurdish battle fatigues, some with black checked keffiyehs around their necks, their thick black hair pulled back, their skin weathered and brown from dust, and holding onto their AK-47s. Some of them wore bandoliers filled with ammunition. Their eyes, brown, black, green, or hazel, shone out of a permanent squint, accompanied by casual cackles. No, they were not pretty, but these weathered women looked very beautiful, some of them absolutely stunning; every one of them warmed the heart and generated respect. Especially knowing the mountains and the terrain—holy shit, these women actually walk the mountains, fight, and die fighting. And with no body armor!

Greetings, shaking hands, smiles, laughs, coquettish cackles; much mutual respect and bits of broken English. Soldiers are wondering, why in the hell doesn't Rosetta Stone come up with Karmanji language programs? Hell, maybe they do, but we never looked, goddamn!

One could only wish for time, time to actually sit down and listen to their stories from the mountains, especially the older women with their stern looks, damn. A soldier who always had a soft spot for anyone with black or brown hair let his imagination run wild, but that's why soldiers have good friends to bring them back down to earth.

"Man, I am going to marry me a female Peshmerga fighter!"

Others glanced over at him: "Yeah, what do you think she'll do in West Texas? She'll be bored out of her mind, no mountains, remember?"

"Well, I'll get a ranch in Montana, how about that?"

"Oh, yeah, on your army paycheck? Besides, what's she gonna do up in Montana, fight the Canadians? You planning to start your own militia?"

Everyone laughed at his despondent look; he had reached the limits of his dream world. "You are shit out of luck buddy!" More laughter. It is important to infuse a sense of reality, that's why one needs good friends.

The older fighters look far older than their age, some with a stern squint: They should not be messed with. One older woman was the undisputed leader, who had control of the entire moment, even from a distance. She kept a laser eye on the young girls, now talking with the soldiers in their broken English. Soldiers could feel her laser vision as they try to ingratiate themselves with the younger fighters. One leader decided to go over to the female leader and calm her down, explaining "I am in charge of some harmless clowns, and we will be leaving soon, please do not worry." He always took responsibility for his actions and those of his men, and so had to forgo the opportunity to ingratiate himself with these beautiful mountain warrior women. But despite all his combat experience, he looked nervous, or perhaps it was just his attempt to maintain a sense of humility. Soldiers asked him later, "Yeah, you looked afraid and nervous talking to her, buddy, what happened?"

He had his usual cackle: "Well, did you see that big ol' knife she had hanging on her belt?"

One of the fighters quickly became everyone's favorite. She spoke decent English, was outspoken, and soon became the interpreter for all her friends. Of course, it goes without saying, she was also beautiful, in her funky green battle fatigues with an AK in hand and black-checked keffiyeh wrapped around her neck, with constantly smiling black eyes and a big grin. Thick black hair covered her angular, weathered face.

Soldiers promised her, "It does not matter who you fight, we will come and fight with you, just tell us, give us the word, and we will be in the mountains!"

She had an uproarious laugh.

As they left this heartbreakingly brief encounter, soldiers did the crab-walk, waving back to convey the heartfelt regret of having to leave them so soon. A young leader again walked over to the stern-looking older woman. In the event these young clowns ever get lucky enough to come by this neighborhood, it would be wonderful if she remembered us.

Leaving this place, seeing their waves and genuine laughs and smiles, one soldier expressed himself honestly—and loudly: "Oh my god! Those women! Man, I need to build me a woman just like that!"

You let out your heartfelt, honest, momentary impulses sometime or another, and it always works against you. But it would be blasphemous to let go of that moment and not give him a hard time. His life was quickly made miserable.

Kurdish women in urban centers have aspirations that remind soldiers of their dear friend Miramar and her friends. Young girls want to go to college—university—or if they have college degrees, it's all about graduate studies as the only way out for them. Most Kurdish women live in rural conditions, trapped—yes, that is the word—trapped and oppressed by traditional codes of honor, loyalties, and lack of choice. And so many Kurdish women, children, and men still remain completely illiterate, even aside from the particularly unfortunate ones who lived under Ansar al-Islam rule.

Choice and Insubordination: Honor Killing and Self-Immolation

But there is also a sobering, more sinister reality that soldiers learned almost by accident: The violence against Kurdish women, the honor killings. And, strangest and most heartbreaking of all, self-immolation: Women burning themselves alive.

Honor killing is generally associated with sex and adultery, but as we understood it, whether among Kurdish, Sunni, or Shia families, it has little to do with either. In reality, honor killing is not about sex, adultery, or any of it. Rather it is an issue of *choice*.

A woman who is brave enough to exercise choice, in matters pro-scribed to her by family, by tradition, by religion or whatever—even if she exercises her choice by *refusing*—that choice is tantamount to insubordination. It is this insubordination that is defined as dis-honor. Insubordination of women, in deeply patriarchic and conser-vative Muslim families, infused with local traditions, immediately becomes a matter of dishonor. That apparently makes it possible for some men with little spinning hamsters in their hearts and heads to tolerate hideous crimes against women, confounding the little spinning hamsters in the heart with honor! So, an angry little man can feel self-righteous in murdering some woman—a family mem-ber, most often trying to escape a forced marriage, sexual abuse, or domestic violence. And for some women, the only remaining choice she can impose on this gruesome reality is to kill herself with the only weapon she has at hand.

Most of these acts, given the conservative nature of the society, go unreported anyway. In Islam's Sharia law, which most tribes follow in the absence of formal judicial process, *one* male witness is worth *two* female witnesses! Does it mean a woman is worth only half a man under Sharia and in Islam? Thankfully, many decent and educated people have a subtler interpretation, but there are nut-jobs who live by the Sharia code and take it literally, and soldiers have seen how it manifests itself on the ground.

That simple reality perhaps explains a lot. How can a woman liv-ing in a deeply traditional society, surrounded by people seeped in such thinking, manage to report *anything at all* (to either traditional authority or formal authority), if a man's word is equal to the report of two women? (In the case of rape, absurdities multiply. The rape victim becomes twice a victim and faces stoning as due "punishment.")

There are many educated Iraqis who disagree with this situation. Soldiers carrying guns are no experts on the issue of Iraqi women's rights, but they did not miss this situation because they were willing to listen. A husband and wife, both doctors, pointed it out, and it was the beginning of a different education, another counterintuitive les-son in this counterinsurgency.

293

Many reports of women's suffering trickle out of Kurdish areas, but it should not be concluded that women are in fact worst off in Kurdistan. On the contrary, those reports are the clearest sign that they are doing far better in Kurdistan than in other places. In Kurdistan, many formidable Kurdish (and even some Arab) women have organized women's shelters and non-governmental organizations to assist women, conducting literacy campaigns and trying to get the word out as well. Kurdish women in desperate situations thus have someplace to turn to, even though that act also puts them at risk.

These first steps have been possible because Kurdistan has remained relatively stable and free, and both KDP and PUK remain staunchly secular. The women's organizations in Kurdistan have increasingly become advocates for women's issues throughout Iraq. But real risks remain. Most Kurdish people live in rural areas with little access to education and some are actively resisting these efforts. There are any number of calls for Sharia; in the rural areas, the law remains the traditional codes, which always deal women a terrible hand.

And the situation is, in fact, far worse in other areas of Iraq. Given the nature of the insurgency, violence against women has been subsumed into the general level of violence. Of course, the nut-jobs (both the Sunni and Shia) detest no one more than the women and men who actively work to make women's lives better; they will always be under the greatest threat.

For soldiers, it is a simple education: Abusers, rapists, and nut-jobs can always feel protected hiding behind pretensions of honor, religion, and divinely sanctified law. Yes, Sharia may have its nuanced and subtle interpretations (as many sensible people try to point out). But nut-jobs are immune to nuance and subtlety, and they insist on the basics to be thrown in the face. If two female witnesses are worth one male witness, a complete woman, in the stultified minds of nut-jobs, must only be worth half a man.

Yes, soldiers felt justified for feeling absolutely enraged at this absurd idea because they have seen this thinking become manifest on the ground in very grotesque forms. One unfortunate incident (among many) became notorious worldwide.

Doa Khalil Aswan became well known as the victim of an honor killing in Bashika (Nineveh Governorate). A seventeen-year-old Kurdish girl of Yazidi faith was stoned to death on April 7, 2007 for the sin of falling in love with a Sunni boy. The incident became known when someone happened to record it on a mobile phone, and it went all over Iraq. Soldiers walking the streets in Iraq also saw it, as enraging as it was to watch. But they had seen many, many such videos made by nut-jobs using their own cell phones and cameras, and those atrocities never made the news, even locally. *Why not?*

Despite the burning rage in the gut, the only comfort is that, despite the misery, there are women and men, mostly in Iraqi Kurdistan, who are willing to take great risks and slowly try to alleviate the situation. Three cheers to them, respect always.

But then, soldiers came across another phenomenon that seems utterly inexplicable. Kurdish women, older women as well as young girls, sometimes commit suicide by self-immolation. The numbers are low, ranging annually from single digits to just double digits—but death by being burned alive is the worst and even one such death is one too many. Soldiers have had friends, colleagues, and a mentor completely burned to death as the result of an incendiary grenade. It is a death that one does not wish even on the enemy.

Some guy seeking martyrdom, seeking virgins in heaven, drives a vehicle full of artillery rounds to be exploded at the checkpoint. But the car itself immediately becomes a torch, and the man stumbles out of the front seat, flailing about and covered in flames. Whoever rigged that car failed to read the fine print: These were white phosphorous shells, not high explosives. Yes, the mistake is undeniably funny and one is tempted to call him a dumb-ass—but then again, he is actually on fire. So the soldier closest to him looks at this fast-burning human spectacle and decides to put him out of his misery. It is painful to see another human being burnt alive. It is an excruciatingly slow, painful death that seeps from the outside in.

Nevertheless, some do it deliberately to themselves. Some Kurdish women, even young girls, lock themselves in a room, douse themselves in kerosene, light a match, and wait to be burned alive. But the tragedy does not stop there. In the hospital morgue it is likely to be classified as an "accident," as no one wants to come to terms with self-immolation; as the burned women lie in a morgue, families more often than not lack the fortitude even to come and pick up the body. Iraqi doctors and nurses who have worked in the north tell these stories of anguish.

The Kurdistan region has fared far better than most other regions of Iraq, and it continues to progress, slowly but surely. But Kurdistan will remain a land of the imagination until the issue of the disputed territories is resolved in a manner acceptable to everyone—and good luck with that. With every group digging in their positions—the Kurds, Arabs, Turkomans, Assyrian-Chaldeans, and Syriac-speaking minorities—it will continue to remain tense, though it gets little attention. As the Iraqi government forces regain strength, they will become more assertive, while the Kurds will feel more nervous. However, the constitution gives the Kurds leverage: With a built-in minority veto in the Iraqi legislature, they have the capacity to block progress on myriad issues. The trick with the disputed territories will remain how to fashion a compromise when every group has its own contending sob story with its own facts, myths, legends, and hallucinations: The many gardens of imagination.

PART V

ARABIAN NIGHTS AND DAYS: INSIDE THE SHIA INSURGENCY

Soldiers had to come to terms with an entrenched Shia insurgency in an urban setting. We began to understand the broader Shia struggle and how it related to us on the ground through the stories of our many Shia friends in Iraq.

A peculiar difficulty arises in fighting an insurgent group that has political legitimacy. Jaish al-Mahdi remains a political military organization with religious convictions. It was, in fact, part of the government while we fought them.

It was a very strange fight; some challenges we overcame and some we could not. The ones we could not, we allowed to flow into hallucinations. The constant question we asked ourselves was simple: If the Americans liberated the Shia people, then why in the hell do they keep trying to kill us? And, the logical next question, how exactly do they do it?

It was a serious question, not in any way academic or abstract, and we felt its repercussions intimately.

15

NIGHT BECOMES DAY AND DAY BECOMES NIGHT: ANOTHER BEGINNING

> Following the dawn prayer, with clouds of darkness
> defying the vigorous thrust of light, the vizier Dandan
> was called to a meeting with the Sultan Shahriyar.
> Dandan's composure vanished.
>
> —*Arabian Nights and Days*[69]

A simple question had to be asked for purposes of humor and sanity: If the Shia people in Iraq were liberated by the Americans from the grips of a tyrant, why is it that some of the liberated Shia people feel the need to kill Americans?

But, as soldiers walk the street, there is also the more immediate question: *How* do they do it?

For some soldiers who transitioned from fighting Salafists in theocratic enclaves to fighting Shia insurgents in an urban setting, there was a palpable difference between the two insurgencies. The subtleties on the ground are the key to figuring out the best way to distinguish the enemy from the innocent before taking the fight to the enemies' doorstep.

---

[69] *Arabian Nights and Days*, a novel by Naguib Mahfouz.

There was much for soldiers to learn about the JAM story—especially because a lot of people in the neighborhood were listening to them.

Soldiers had found a quiet corner to commiserate at sunrise, sitting in the back of a tent by some concrete barriers inside a luxurious army base. A non-commissioned officer was repeating to his closest colleagues a maxim familiar to those stuck in a counterinsurgency: It's a different fight, a shady fucking fight.

He spoke in hushed tones (as they were also inhaling illicit sips of whiskey, having a nightcap at sunrise): "These guys are good, and this is a shady fucking fight we have to fight."

He spat his tobacco spit on the ground, grinning his trademark determined grin: "To do this shit right, we have to make goddamn sure we do it quietly. But we have to do it in style." He ceremoniously raised his cup—a plastic water bottle cut in half, packed with ice cubes and filled to the brim with alcohol bought in the streets of Iraq.

The job of soldiers on the ground is not to transform a war but only to worry about their own area of responsibility. Even so, the little area of responsibility remains part of something wider, and to understand the wider insurgency better is to fight better on the ground by taking it to the enemy's doorstep.

First Impressions in a Shia Neighborhood

During 2006 and 2007, American soldiers flying into Salafist-infested enclaves heard a consistent theme repeated by Sunni people living under Salafist rule: "You should stay and not leave." A sentiment they would not have heard in 2003 and 2004.

The Shia insurgency is similar and it is different. There is certainly an element of resistance in the Shia insurgency, just as in the Sunni insurgency. But it is not as simple as resistance against an invading force or an abstract cosmic sob story like that of the Salafists. The Shia insurgency is a struggle for an idea but a different kind. It is about the future of Iraq as envisioned by various segments of the Shia people. Soldiers began to understand that the Shia resistance against American forces is part of a wider internal power struggle between contending Shia parties that represent very different ideas.

300

The resistance by Jaish al-Mahdi (or JAM) is partly real; many JAM soldiers genuinely despise the Americans and are steeped in anti-American, anti-Jewish, and anti-Western invective. To hang out and have some good chats with some JAM combatants (many of them have legal immunity) has a perversely enlightening effect. The hard part is resisting one's worst visceral impulses while listening to them.

The anti-American invective is usually justified with something that to us seems old and abstract, though most Iraqis feel it as very recent and felt it intimately. The poorest Shia suffered the most under thirteen years of UN sanctions, and they were repeatedly told to blame the Americans for their suffering.

But at the end of the day, the JAM resistance against Americans is a cover story. The real objective is getting control—outsmarting not only the Americans but also their own side, the ruling Shia parties. Much like Salafists, one sees callous indifference toward their own people (Shia) and organized campaigns of murder against the other (Sunnis); plenty of men with delusions of cosmic grandeur, trying to reduce men and women into a figment of their own imagination.

And something else, it never fails. Some of the worst of them confound their manhood with AK-47s and confuse lascivious impulses with religious mores, making the lives of many Iraqi women a nightmare. And many sociopaths and criminals bought into the JAM franchise to extort, rape, and kill, and get away with it.

But there was also one very important distinction: the Shia insurgency was far more entrenched and embedded in the Shia society than were the Salafists in Sunni communities. JAM has a solid story with traction on the ground.

The JAM insurgency relies far more on the complicity and support of the people than on violence. Understanding the Shia insurgency meant understanding the *ideas* behind the struggle as well as the contradictions within the Shia community.

301

Soldiers' education began with seeing certain contradictions that hang on the walls of nearly every Shia household.

The Patriarch

> His dreamy gaze was reflected in the hearts of many of his old and more recent students and was deeply engraved in the hearts of his disciples.
>
> —*Arabian Nights and Days*

A few details easily reveal the sectarian identity and ethnicity of a household. Some themes are consistent: Pictures of ayatollahs on the wall, along with religious scriptures and verses from the Quran; books and newspapers lying about; the ceramic blue eye that hangs by the door to protect against evil spirits.

Walking into the house, a glance told us it was a Shia household, a very affluent one. The family always welcomed the soldiers they knew, and soldiers immensely enjoyed their company, as well as the tea, sweets, and an occasional grand meal. In that palatial residence one could find the past, the present, and the future sitting side by side.

The patriarch was a walking encyclopedia of modern Iraqi history, having lived through many incarnations of his country. Soldiers knew of his importance from the word on the street. It was not an accident that they knocked on his door. He remembers the last (imported) king of Iraq and his overthrow and tells stories of living through the political instability as an impressionable kid. Coming of age under military rule, living life as a Baathist bureaucrat—despite being Shia—and retiring with a golden parachute, Baathist style. He became the managing director of a government-run factory.

Alas, soon after he began in his new position, the Americans fired him for being a Baathist. But he was a smart man. He said to hell with the Americans—and kept going to work. Here was a bureaucrat that knew his stuff: Edicts have validity on the ground only if people abide by them. He ignored it, kept going to work, kept his job, and now he actually gets paid again. Americans are even helping him revitalize the factory. He has the institutional memory and connections to get a thing

302

or two done when needed. His complaint now is not that he lost the job, but that the help from the Americans remains too slow. And even worse, the insurgency makes it difficult to get the factory up to speed. Such complaints about the insurgents were always music to the ears of soldiers, auguring a future tactical relationship.

The patriarch knows the JAM guys who are making his life difficult; and he could also introduce the soldiers to friends in many different places. But it will take time. He has to come around to it as if it's his own idea, and then it will be smooth sailing. But the insurgents always help on that score by overplaying their hand.

The patriarch always reminded soldiers of a wealthy, affable grandpa who looked dashing in his day—someone who got laid a lot in his youth—but never talks about it. The kind and hospitable grandma always welcomed the soldiers with a heartfelt smile and treated them to animated stories and, at times, incredible food. Grateful for her kindness, one almost wants to call the patriarch a narcissistic prick, but he is too valuable and too slick.

The well-kept gray hair, the solid, if frail body, the worn argyle V-neck sweater and matching socks were distinctive on the first meeting. A worn-out blazer and tinkling prayer beads in his right hand completed the ensemble: Crisp-looking at age seventy-three, looking more like sixty. (It is doubtful he did much actual praying, but he certainly knew that the prayer beads enhanced his image.) His sons and daughters were all educated and married, and some of them live in the palatial house for security reasons. Some of the sons now also work for the current government, and a few work with the Americans.

Visiting soldiers always remained standing until he would walk in and give a nonchalant wave of the hand with a smile. The soldiers would sit down after he did, first asking his permission, which he would grant very loudly—"Of course, my house is your house," *Ahlan wa sahlan*—and ostentatiously shake each hand. One soldier who went to great lengths to charm the patriarch always said, "Man, this guy has the loudest handshake." The handshake was deliberate, purposeful, implying, "I am going to get you somehow"; it always kept the soldier on his toes. Maybe he was sincere, but it is best to assume the worst and stay safe on the job.

He is the man in this palace, and when he passes from the scene he will leave a void that will not be filled. It is absolutely critical that he is always given due respect because he may have some of the clues soldiers seek.

Some of the patriarch's contradictions are hanging on the wall of the comfortable living room, highlighting the travails of the Shia community. Shia people see the political landscape as a large family struggle, with good guys, bad guys, shameful uncles, distant cousins, and plenty of betrayals. The problem with this Shiite family struggle is that it involves guns—against the Sunnis, the Americans, the government, and even against one another.

One wants to ask the pictures, "What sort of Iraq will come out?" The past stares down from above the patriarch's shoulder. The present is out on the street: At the height of the insurgency, soldiers always heard an explosion or two, the rat-tat of gunfire either near or distant. The future: His children and grandchildren, or perhaps the Iraqi men that roam the streets with guns, will eventually decide.

❖ **First of the Shia martyrs: Turning and burning**

Like most Shia houses, the patriarch's walls display images of Imam Ali, the son-in-law of Prophet Muhammad and the last of the rightly guided Caliphs (though Ali apparently never liked the title Caliph and called himself Commander of the Faithful, or *Imam*).[70] Then there is a painting of Imam Hussein, the second son of Caliph Ali, depicting his last fight near Karbala against an overwhelming adversary—the armies of the Umayyad Dynasty that eventually became the Sunnis. This is the iconic Shia image that adorns many houses: The

---

[70] There is wide variation in the pictures displayed, in addition to the main ayatollahs. Some houses display pictures of the members of the Supreme Iraqi Islamic Council (SIIC); some display the murdered ayatollahs of the Hakim family.

innumerable incoming arrows will surely seal Imam Hussein's fate, but he looks unperturbed even at the point of decision.

He is undoubtedly a solid and inspiring leader, but clearly going down in a very bad way. Being soldiers, and taking the picture literally, a tactical question naturally came to mind. He is certainly in a very bad tactical disposition. And he faces an overwhelming enemy—the largest Muslim army commanded by Muawiya, the Sunni ruler who controlled both Syria and Egypt. Sunni forces had laid siege to the city, so mercilessly that Imam Hussein's first son died of thirst. Imam Hussein decided on a "turn and burn" (as soldiers would say in an Infantry battle drill) and "assaulted through."

Turning and burning is good and has its charms. Any soldier who has had to turn and burn can attest: Letting loose all the fire power, with 240B and M249 machine guns rocking in unison, 40mm grenades coming out of M203 tubes with the whoosh and the loud boom, the constant muzzle flashes of M4 carbines and the noise of spent brass casings dropping with the spent ammunition links and making the clink-clink-clink-clink noise, it all begins to sounds rhythmic. When you start turning and burning, someone else is running and dying—but only if you do it right. Turning and burning could be good, but to assault through without a good flanking element and without good support by fire is nearly suicidal, though at times necessary. And that is what Imam Hussein did. He turned, burned, and assaulted through, without any support by fire.

It was a suicidal tactical decision, but once the decision is made, as any soldier who has made tactical decisions knows, it is imperative to follow through unequivocally to the end. You turn and then you burn and burn with everything you've got, because nothing else will matter for the next few minutes. He committed and stayed committed. It did not work out too well but deserves respect without question because he was a fighter to the very end.

But looking at the picture, it raises a question. Facing an overwhelming adversary that guaranteed the death of those around him, why would Imam Hussein decide on a turn and burn when one can instead take a step back, assess the strengths and weaknesses, and thus put up a better fight. Even an overwhelming adversary has its weaknesses, and you just have to find them.

It became a quick lesson in metaphysics when the patriarch pointed out that some things in life are beyond our comprehension: It is God's will.

"YES, yes, yes, absolutely true." He is absolutely right, Imam Hussein was battling a cosmic reality and not a mortal one, and it is not within the realm of soldiers' little tactical minds to come to terms with cosmic realities.

But one can always discuss the fate that befell the larger-than-life mortals who adorn the wall. Nearly every one of them, as it happened, also ended up in a very bad way, faced with overwhelming adversaries. They were also inspiring leaders that put up a fight all the way to the end. One begins to see the poignant consistency in the pictures hanging on the wall. These were men with conviction and they stuck to it to the end. The men are gone but the convictions are still alive, and these mighty men from the past still inspire people.

❖ The pantheon of private heroes

These would have been very formidable adversaries while alive, when they could inspire so many. But talking about it is a delicate task. In this world the soldiers must tread carefully, asking their questions with appropriate gravity. It is the world of the patriarch's personal contradictions, and he navigates it with clarity.

The wall is the pantheon of his private heroes who will always remain larger than his own life:

- Brigadier Abdul Karim Kassem
- Grand Ayatollah Sayyid Ali Husiani Ali-Sistani (the preeminent Shia cleric at the moment)
- Grand Ayatollah Sayyid Muhammad Baqir al-Sadr (the father of the Sadrist movement, who founded the Dawa party)
- Grand Ayatollah Muhammad Mohammed Sadeq al-Sadr (the father of Muqtada al-Sadr)

306

They represent contending political and religious currents that Iraqi Shia have had to navigate throughout the last fifty years.

Brigadier Abdul Karim Kassem, the first military ruler, was a secularist and close to the Communists of Iraq. The son of a Sunni father and a Shia mother of Kurdish origin, he came from a destitute background. He was a brilliant student and military man who rose through the military ranks, becoming part of the military group that became the Free Officers Movement (the movement that started in Egypt under then-Colonel Gamal Abdul Nasser). In 1958, Kassem and his friends ousted the last of the imported Saudi kings of Iraq installed by the British without much opposition. Kassem's main constituency remained the Shia, Kurds, and Communists of Iraq. Like most military men who come to power through violence, he ended up being a despot. But he is remembered by his admirers as a leader who tried to improve the lot of the common people and of women.

Kassem started the public housing project, the Revolution City, (Madinat al-Thawra), which today is the Shia stronghold of Sadr City, overflowing with over two million Shia immigrants from other parts of Iraq. Many Shia houses in Shia strongholds still display his picture. For them, he was the beginning of Iraq, their own story, until it was rudely interrupted. Some are old enough to remember the glory days, and others hear about him from the older ones—but only about the good times, of course.

The passage of time seems to make heroes out of despots: No one remembers his repressive measures. When things are bad, people may wish for the strong hand of a despot, but they quickly repent the mislaid dreams. The Patriarch is unequivocal, however. Growing up he was the product of Kassem's social reform. He would not have achieved his education, or even a middle class existence, without the reforms and land redistribution programs begun by Kassem. Many houses display his picture; fathers and grandfathers talk about him. Everyone has forgotten his injustices because he, alas, also got killed— a political move that guarantees near immortality.

307

The Sadrist ayatollahs are considered highly political, in contrast to Ayatollah Sistani, who represents the non-political brand of Shi'ism (called the quietist Hawza). In fact, *both* parties are very political, but they have different constituencies and subtly different objectives.

Sadrists are unafraid to be seen as firebrands, and use their clerical position to mobilize the people along a Shia sectarian identity. They do acknowledge Ayatollah Sistani as the supreme religious authority, at least nominally. But they are ever mindful of the fate of their own ayatollahs: Ayatollah Baqir al-Sadr and his sister Amina Sadr bint al-Huda, and Ayatollah Sadiq al-Sadr—they all paid a high price for their political activism.

Being quiet has a peculiar meaning in Iraq. When a quietist like Sistani speaks, the politicians may or may not follow his lead—but no one can afford to ignore him, as he has the ability to throw a wrench in their plans.

What are the real distinctions, and how can one find out? We'd have to ask their pictures. The two Sadrist ayatollahs lived their lifetime in a second very painfully, and that was a long time ago. The other one, Grand Ayatollah Sistani, apparently lives in a shack even more tightly defended than the Green Zone; no soldier can get near enough to have tea and enjoy the good company of his Eminence.

❖ **The jaded realist**

Sometimes, among the array of photos, one sees another picture: Ayatollah Yaquibi, a former Sadrist ayatollah who is now the spiritual head of the Fadhila Party. The term spiritual leader was explained by a dear Iraqi friend, someone soldiers loved for his honest outbursts of jaded realism.

The jaded realist was intent on damning the one group that holds a monopoly on damnation. He wanted to damn the clerics—*in life*, not afterwards. "Spiritual head," in his understanding, meant that they can get away with murder because no one blames them for anything. He pointed emphatically at the soldiers: "*They* are the trouble with everything in Iraq, *every*thing," and he shook his finger at the soldiers, adding in all seriousness, "*They* are the people you should kill."

The soldiers burst out laughing, but he ignored them and began to tick off names, one after another. His wish list was long, and the soldiers laughed even harder. They have heard it so often, in so many different houses. If American soldiers were to carry out the heartfelt wishes of every Iraqi, it would mean getting rid of the entire spiritual and political class of Iraq. Soldiers answered with a laugh, yes, there may be many people who deserve that fate, not just in Iraq, but it is a decision that others need to make. If soldiers get those orders they would be happy to carry them out. A soldier then asked, wagging his finger in imitation of the jaded realist: "Why don't *you* do it, if we give you a hand?"

The realist burst into laughter, "Of course I would, but I have family to take care of," and he laughed even more. But there is another reality glimmering in the minds of the soldiers. He knows all the connections and the enforcers: The guys who serve the clerics with guns in hand. His innocuous stories, in the hands of soldiers, might be turned into an effective tactical reality later on.

❖ Where is Muqtada?

At the patriarch's house once again, one soldier was emboldened to ask, "Well, why don't you have Muqtada al-Sadr on the wall, you have everybody else." Their host, always sharp as a tack, seemed a bit annoyed at this. He looked at the soldiers like a wise grandfather regarding an unruly adolescent, as if to say, look, kid, you are all right, but there are some things you will only understand when you become a man, and you are not quite there.

One always has to be grateful for that honesty. Everybody needs to be put in their place sometime, especially if they are soldiers with guns in hand.

Then he simply said, "Huh, Muqtada, he is a boy," and gave a wave of the hand that suggested that was the end of that topic.

"Uh, sorry about that, sir."

Ouch, that was coldhearted. Not for the soldiers, soldiers are merely students, but for Muqtada. For some Shia people, Muqtada is an adolescent in cleric's garb, not deserving of sharing the same wall in the mighty company of others. But one must not be misled: The people who call him a kid unequivocally respect his Sadrist family lineage and what it represents for the Shia people of Iraq. Muqtada is a symbol. Some astute Shia people believe he should have used his leverage better than he has. But there is also an undeniable element of grudging respect because he stood up to the Americans and continues to do so. People will not oppose him in public despite their private musings.

The Sadrist grand ayatollahs in nearly every picture embody a consistent theme. They look learned, unperturbed, dignified but also pained. As people would say, they were always pained with the turmoil of their people. They lived it; they were not posers. They commanded no armies, they only had conviction, yet they all followed through to the end despite the constant foreboding that they might end up in a bad way. None of the Sadrist Ayatollas ran away in the face of adversity. That is a rare trait, and lot of Shia people have not forgotten it.

Muqtada, however, has a very different image. He looks like a drunk kid from a wealthy family who has woken up hung over, pissed off, and trying to figure out how his front tooth got knocked out. Muqtada is a kid from a very good family with much to learn, but he also has some smart people working with him. Otherwise, he represents clerical mediocrity.

Then the patriarch gives some tactical advice, naming high-level Muqtada supporters that soldiers need to pay attention to. Soldiers respond, yes they will pay attention—but what to do with them is for others to decide. What matters more: The patriarch also knows the *minions* of all the leaders he ticks off on his wish list. That's the more immediate reality for soldiers. Eventually, if one is lucky enough, he will get a list together and soldiers will have to verify it.

Patriarchs' History Lesson

❖ **The family saga: Political saliency of Shia**

The patriarch now has an unbelievable suggestion, but one soldiers had heard before. The patriarch suggests, with his casual wave of the hand, what to do with Sadr city and how to do it, Iraqi style: A massive crater in the middle of Baghdad, minus a lot of innocent people. He doesn't mean it literally. Today he is angry. He has had a bad day from the JAM boys in the street—he was nearly extorted for money at a JAM checkpoint—and that often means a good day for soldiers.

A soldier responded with a laugh, "Don't you still have family living in Sadr city?" "Of course" (shrugging his shoulders), he has lot of family in Sadr city, "but the place is trouble." Some soldiers would have loved nothing more than to see a coordinated sweep into Sadr city; some soldiers were obsessed with it, and they would sit around looking at the aerial images, fighting their virtual battle and imbibing illicit alcohol and tobacco. The patriarch is letting off steam. But he has a point: Sadr city is its own universe, a Sadrist universe filled with its own ideas.

But using tanks, air craft, artillery in one of the most densely populated alleyways of the world? Targeting an enclave of over two million people, the vast majority merely trying to sustain themselves, when the world is watching every move of every American soldier? The common cliché was very true: "Remember, we can do a thousand things right, even *ten thousand* things right, but you do one thing wrong, just one, that's all people will ever remember, *and you don't wanna be that guy*."

Yes, it is a war, but a different war; bad things on the ground can happen only if they happen in a very good way.

One image of a shrieking Iraqi woman or wounded child on TV is all it would take to bring everything to a screeching halt. Not on American TV: There are no actual Iraqis on American TV, as they remain a metaphor. But real Iraqi people are all over Middle Eastern TV, and the images are deeply felt. On the ground, it has the effect of setting the soldiers back; perception at times is as important as the reality.

Soldiers cannot explain these subtleties to the patriarch, who is ranting about the JAM militia. The soldiers laughed at the absurdity of his suggestion, but the patriarch cut them off: "It has been done before, I remember," he said wagging his index finger, "it was done before, and I was there."

The patriarch was an impressionable young man with strong communist sympathies when Colonel Abdul Karim Kassem took control of the country. His family had just left the Madinat al-Thawra (Revolution City), to move nearby to some wealthy relatives in the Shia neighborhood where he still lives. Baathist officers took control, relentlessly attacking the supporters of Colonel Kassem. The Baathists used tanks, artillery and everything they had to quell those Shia and Kurdish neighborhoods of Baghdad that rose up in support of Colonel Kassem. Parts of Revolution City, he recalled, were engulfed in black smoke for days.

Now he was reliving the moment with the soldiers, his hands waving about, his eyes speaking of a soul stuck in a different time and a place. The characters in the story become animated, their gleaming eyes and shaking heads present in the living room as the patriarch transplants his American-soldier-students to the bleak days of Revolution City in 1963. Soldiers sat wide-eyed, mouths agape and cigarettes dangling from their lips, invited to share in a riddle that Iraqi people are living.

But his anger at JAM boys does not equate to antipathy for Muqtada al-Sadr or for the Sadrist movement. Muqtada may be the revered symbol of the movement, but the patriarch fears the guys in the street and what they want to create. That is another subtle distinction in the Shia-family story: many who honor the Sadrist Ayatollahs and what they have done for the Shia people of Iraq may have a visceral dislike of the young JAM foot soldiers.

Another piece of the Shia internal struggle is essentially a class struggle, with two very different core constituencies. Sadrists see themselves

312

as men of the people, drawing their support from the urban slums, the youth, and urban immigrants from outlying Shia areas. Thus, the same core constituency that Kassem relied on in his day today supports the Sadrists. SIIC and Dawa, in contrast, draw their support from the remnant of the Shia middle class, the professional class, and the Shia tribes loyal to the Shia clerics in the holy cities. SIIC and Dawa can be seen as the conservative traditionalists, while Sadrists and JAM are the radicals who seek to rattle cages and change the status quo. In the Revolution City that Kassem established, the dreamers of revolution still find a home today (though they may seek a different kind of revolution). The Shia insurgency on the ground is very much about an idea, and for most Shia people, Americans are a footnote to a story that started around the mid-1950s.[71]

"Power To The People": The Beginning of an Idea

> Along its sides were couches for higher-class customers, while in a circle in the middle were ranged mattresses for the common folk to sit on. A variety of things to drink were served, both hot and cold according to the season; also available were the finest sorts of hashish and electuaries.
>
> —*Arabian Nights and Days*

In long conversations, telling stories to soldiers, Shia friends never missed an opportunity to mention their "imported Sunni King" and his overthrow in 1958. From 1920 until 1958, Iraq was ruled by a monarchy from Saudi Arabia, installed by the British after defeating the Ottoman Turks. The mid-twentieth century ushered in secular, pan-Arabist and socialist rhetoric. Kassem's 1958 coup d'etat that threw out the king relied for support on both the communists and the military. The most vocal communists were mainly Shia people of working class background. In reaction, the Shia clerical class founded the Dawa party in 1957, to combat the increasing secularization of the Shia community and especially the Communist influence.

---

[71] Or even earlier: The first rebellion against the British in 1920 was headed by a Shia ayatollah, Muhammed Sadr (of the same Sadr family).

Another peculiarity: It is rare to see pictures of leaders of the Dawa party on the walls of Shia homes, even though this represents the true beginning of Shiite political salience. Nearly every Shia political party in Iraq traces its roots in some fashion to the "founders" of the Dawa party.

Grand Ayatollah Baqir al-Sadr is considered the philosophical founder of Dawa, revered as the man who managed to mobilize the working class and poor Shia people. His greater achievement was to synthesize a number of disparate themes into a coherent whole. His revolutionary thesis was simply that people have the right to take an active political role and to define the way they are governed. And Shia clerics (he said), given their unique position in society, had a duty to help people be heard. Sadr's religious text was a pathbreaking justification of the Shiite revolutionary political claim.[72]

Many Shia people had been forced to the margins, even living in the woods—fleeing first the Turks, then the Brits and their imported Saudi king, and finally a series of tinpot dictators. The idea of power to the people based on religious doctrine was a revolutionary statement and an act of defiance.

Although significant differences divided the many clerics that formed Dawa, they were unified in one goal: to give Shia people a political voice, firmly embedded within a Shiite sectarian and political identity.

As a loose organization that slowly became a political party, Dawa changed drastically as Baathists solidified their control in Iraq. After the Baathist takeover, Dawa eventually transformed into a militant Shia alternative to Baathist rule. Dawa members were persecuted, its leaders exiled and in some cases killed abroad by Baathist agents. The party split into factions. Some exiled leaders maintained the Dawa party from exile, even attacking American assets when the

---

[72] Having said "power to the people," Baqir al Sadr remained quiet on the nature of the state that might result, a point still fought over. One approach is the Iranian model, "rule by clerics."

U.S. government supported Saddam Hussein against the Iranians. Some Dawa members continued their activities quietly in Iraq. Some Dawa leaders branched off: Ayatollah Hakim created the SIIC with Iranian support, along with its own militia, today called the Badr Organization that functions (more or less) as the security apparatus of the new Government of Iraq.

The Sadrist ayatollahs publicly distanced themselves from Dawa while carrying out a form of resistance against Baathists and maintaining the theme of power to the people. That the Sadrists stayed in Iraq fighting—and paid a heavy price for it—is remembered by Shia of all loyalties. During the sanctions decade, Grand Ayatollah Mohammed Muhammad Sadiq al-Sadr (a cousin of Baqir al-Sadr and father of Muqtada) revitalized the Sadrist movement inside Iraq, creating the groundwork of the movement that resulted in the Jaish al-Mahdi. The question of whether JAM reflects what he intended could only be answered by putting words into the mouth of a man who was killed by Baathist thugs. But it is a point people literally fight over.

There are many contending currents in the wider Sadrist movement, and amid raging passions and gunfire the sensible voices are quickly drowned. The main breakaway faction is the Fadhila (Virtue) Party that controls most of the Basra governorate in the south. When Fadhila members and Sadrists fight it out in the streets of Basra, their power struggle is often framed as a fight over metaphors—but the reality on the ground is far simpler. People with guns try to get control of neighborhoods. Ordinary people sit in their houses, listening to the footsteps at night, and find themselves in the middle of a counterfactual analysis being played out with guns.

Sadiq al-Sadr is always important. He is credited with having a sense of the common people, unlike the traditional ayatollahs who live in Najaf and dabble in esoteric religious disquisitions. His opponents may argue that Sadiq al-Sadr was co-opted by the Saddam regime, but they would never say so in public—considering that he was eventually killed for his activities on behalf of the Shia people. In fact, although the Baathist regime did recognize him as a Grand ayatollah, and he could not have preached and revitalized the movement without the tacit approval of the regime, he was nevertheless a man of integrity and not a stooge. He astutely exploited the sliver of public space that was permitted in Saddam's "Re-Islamization campaign"— the regime's attempt to mollify the pissed-off people, including many Shia, after they rose up against the regime in 1991.

Sadiq al-Sadr indeed revitalized the movement, starting his sermons with the obligatory chant, "No, no to America, no, no to Zionists," and then, "No, no to the Devil." Note that "the Devil" was never defined. The ayatollah understood the tricks of his trade. His speeches in the grand mosque of Kufa called for freedoms, rights, and the release of Shia political prisoners, until his assassination.[73] Those who protested the assassination were swiftly crushed. The movement fell quiet again, while its ideas lived in the minds of dedicated followers and clerics until the American intervention, when Jaish al-Mahdi (with Muqtada al-Sadr as the natural figurehead) made Americans the new bogeyman.

The fortunes of Shia people, of course, improved as a result of the American intervention. All the disparate groups are now back in Iraq, at times going for each other's throats, while the American soldiers often find themselves in the middle. A man dubbed the Iranian exile by soldiers—a friend in whose house they spent much time—told them the beginning of a different story.

❖ The Iranian exile

The storyteller is a man who is fond of soldiers. He has spent time in many countries, including Iran, and has returned to the hometown he once abandoned. His story traces the footsteps of some ideas—how they have traveled and the impact they have had. It is a story that runs counter to what soldiers had heard, but perhaps the story has an element of truth.

Iran (as is well known) supports the many Shia groups in Iraq as well as Hezbollah in Lebanon and has played a key role in the spread

---

[73] Sadiq al-Sadr not only mobilized people; he created a series of mosques and a network of social work programs to care for destitute Shia.

of the revolutionary brand of Shia Islam. But this affable patriarch claims that the seeds of the Iranian revolution itself originally germinated in the holy cities of Najaf and Karbala in Iraq and in the south of Lebanon. Some of the founders of the Iranian revolution actually spent time in south Lebanon before going home to Iran to head a revolution.

Recall the image of Ayatollah Ruhollah Khomeini getting off an Air France flight in Tehran in 1979—the stern look and the iconic beard, ready to launch a bloodbath in the name of a revolution. But long before he lived in Paris (the exiled patriarch pointed out), he spent twelve years in Najaf and Karbala in exile and supposedly isolated. In truth, he was not so isolated. His colleagues there included Ayatollah Baqir al-Sadr (and others),[74] who may disagree on some of the fine print of Islamic rule but agree completely on the fundamentals: The idea of rule by the people based on Shia identity as a political force and a rallying cry.

The 1960s and 1970s were a revolutionary period in terms of ideas. Shia people in three different countries found these ideas appealing: In Iraq, where they endured increased Baathist tyranny; in Iran, where a repressive monarchy forced modernization on rural people who wanted none of it. And in South Lebanon—where the Shia revolutionary idea would soon inspire the beginning of Hezbollah.

By now, the listening soldiers have been drinking way too much tea and smoking way too many cigarettes. Every time soldiers show up at this house, as appealing as it is, there was the serious risk of tobacco poisoning in the air. It is time for more cigarettes and more tea, this time with great sweets.

In South Lebanon, the exile's story again revolves around prominent men with interconnected intellectual and familial lineages. And he claims that these revolutionary ideas had already taken root in south Lebanon, long before the revolution in Iran.

---

[74] Rather than inundate the text with innumerable names of ayatollahs, we use Baqir al-Sadr as the iconic representative.

The next part was even more astounding. Prominent Shia in south Lebanon, frustrated by a Lebanese government that had marginalized them for so long, embraced the ideas of power to the people. They then found themselves in the middle of an imported fight between Palestinians in central Lebanon and Israel in the south.

The spiritual leader for the Shia people in Lebanon was also part of the Sadr clan and studied under the same clerics: Musa al-Sadr. Based in Tyre, he started the Shia movement today known as Hezbollah by bringing together assorted Shia groups. But at the same time, Musa Sadr was serving as one of the main points of contact for Ayatollah Ruhollah Khomeini, living in exile in Najaf and Karbala (Iraq).

Our exile insisted that half of Iran's revolutionary clerics (and their aides) spent time in Tyre in the seventies, and *all* had close ties with Imam Musa Sadr. (He mentioned Sadeq Tabatabai, the Deputy Prime Minister and one of Ayatollah Khomeini's closest aides; Mahdi Bazargan, Prime Minister; Mustapha Chamran, Defense Minister, and many more.) After the revolution, the Iranians used their new power, material resources, and weapons to support the Shia ideology else-where in the region, and especially in southern Lebanon. But this assistance was by no means the genesis of Hezbollah: It was provided (he insisted) in recognition of what people in south Lebanon had done to inspire and support the revolution in Iran. In blunt terms, progeni-tors of today's Hezbollah fostered the Iranian revolution rather than the other way around.

It is true: *Ideas* are far more dangerous than fighters and weapons. The blast radius of an explosion is limited, but the blast radius of a well-conceived idea with traction on the ground can be limitless, and that is the business the Sadrists are in. The links created by families and teachers are important for understanding how ideas travel, how they become reality on the ground.

In the West, the influence of Shia ideas—traversing this universe that spans five cities, Tyre in Lebanon, Khadimiya, Najaf and Karbala in Iraq, and Qom in Iran—is rarely discussed amid the obsession with weapons and IEDs. The flow of weapons is certainly important. But the struggles on the ground are in the service of powerful ideas, and understanding how these ideas proliferate is equally important.

❖ A bloody soap opera in the making

Prominent Shia clerics and their families are inextricably linked to politics. Shia politics in Iraq resemble a bad family saga, revolving around the Sadr family and the Hakim family (and to lesser extent the Khoei family[75])—both political institutions, each with its own particular style.

The Sadr family traces its lineage to Prophet Muhammad's bloodline. It is a learned, scholarly family that espouses a radical form of politics—a revolutionary dynasty. Their loyal supporters make it a well-established brand name: Muqtada and the other Sadrists always trumpet the heroic sacrifices of the Sadrist ayatollahs.

The Hakim family also traces its lineage to the Prophet's bloodline, but it represents a more traditional, conservative style of Shia politics. This family of prominent clerics has also established its own brand, its own devoted following, and its own history of travails. The Hakim family has made as many sacrifices or even more because the Baathists feared them more. (Saddam, according to common knowledge, wanted the Hakims extinct.) But the Hakim family seems to have the decency not to make martyrs out of their assassinated family members.

Of course, there are any number of political dynasties on the planet that have become political institutions. In the U.S., the Bush family and the Kennedy family come to mind as well as political families at the state level. But, unlike Iraq, no American political dynasty has gone on to create its own militia, nor do their family members claim special moral or spiritual authority.

---

[75] They are less influential only because the prominent Khoei ayatollahs were killed allegedly by both Salafists as well as Sadrists. Muqtada al-Sadr still has an arrest warrant in Iraq for his alleged involvement in the killing of Ayatollah Abdul Majid al-Khoei.

But the Iraqi Shia family saga is also a soap opera of epic proportions because the Sadrists and Hakims are interconnected. The word on the street is that the leader of the Hakim's SIIC is actually married to a woman from the Sadr family. So the heir apparent of SIIC, Amar Hakim, is the progeny of a Hakim *and* a Sadr, while the two families are locked in a power struggle! If you were making a grand soap opera about the Shia family travails across five cities and four decades, with revolutionary ideas and a lot of bloodshed, here's your leading man. The American soldiers found themselves smack in the middle of this bloody family saga. And they kept wondering, how do these Sadrist ideas fit into the fight on the ground?

The Jaish Al-Mahdi Sob Story

> All sense of security had vanished from his world and hope's lamp had been extinguished. Though he was Qamar's husband, she was more distant from him than the stars. He was rich and yet he was threatened with death.
>
> —*Arabian Nights and Days*

There's another funny thing about the current Shia power struggle. While the Sadrists are trying to impose a fervently held idea, "power to the people," the Shiite ruling parties—SIIC and Dawa—are simply trying to retain power while searching for an idea.

On the ground, however, there are more practical and less cosmic objectives. Get control of the people; mobilize people to win elections; get control of state institutions; and then use those institutions to enhance support and power on the ground—and *keep fighting.*

The Sadrists are thus the "non-ruling" party in power, publicly denying the obvious fact that it is now part of the government gravy train. The Sadrists are attempting to carry the revolutionary mantle—*power to the Shia people*—without ever defining the objective of their struggle since they now in fact hold political power. They are in trouble in a way they had not expected: They now rule the country, thanks to the Americans!

"Oh shit."

The idea of power to the people would lose its meaning if Sadrists came to terms with reality and recognized the authority that has been handed to them. It would be tantamount to abandoning the revolutionary agenda. Even worse, they might lose their core constituency if they become pragmatic partners in a ruling coalition.

The easiest way to keep the revolutionary flame alive is to pick a new bogeyman, to identify the Americans as invaders, which they are, and as occupiers, which they are not. Most Iraqis are well aware that American forces will leave because they pay far more attention to world news than most Americans do.

But Americans will always be defined as occupiers in the minds of the die-hard Sadrist believers because, even after the Americans leave Iraq, the idea of *secular democracy* is meant to stay. Sadrists, therefore, subsume every action of Americans into their anti-American sob story. They placate the diehard followers by flanking the political process—by creating constant crises to show them, "we are not part of this. We hate the Americans." Never mind that they get paid by the Government of Iraq that America helps sustain, or that Americans have indirectly armed and trained many of the Sadrist infiltrators that joined the Armed Forces of new Iraq.

In the raging passions of teeming urban Shia neighborhoods, which remain the core Sadrist constituency, this central absurdity of the Sadrist sob story tends to be missed: That the Shia, in fact, are in power, they run things and only have to take ownership of it and be responsible. Walking through any urban Shia township, one can feel the immediacy of the present crawling on the skin, enveloped in the heat and the loud rancor, mixed with the oozing smell of raw sewage. The smell is enough to drive someone to be a revolutionary or an anarchist, burn some shit down just to get the rage out. So the Sadrist pretence can be maintained. But not with everyone; because ordinary people tend not to be so ordinary, and there is always some competition.[76]

---

[76] Fifty years ago, the same constituency in these teeming Shia townships used to cheer the secular agenda of Abdul Karim Kassem, and was willing

The competition comes from the ruling parties supported by the Americans. Those ruling parties, of course, have problems of their own. SIIC and Dawa compete in terms of power, guns, and money. But they are both also searching for an idea because they had defined their existence in terms of opposing the Baathists. Dawa evolved as a militant Shia alternative to Baathist rule while retaining its conservative Shia identity. SIIC was founded by Hakim, with the assistance of Iran's clerics and militia, and it became another militant alternative to Baathist rule. Having come to power working with the Americans since the beginning, SIIC integrated its paramilitary Badr organization into the Iraqi military establishment. But now it finds itself stuck, like Dawa, as a pragmatic ruling party.

Beyond their deep-seated Shia political identity, there was no over-arching story behind SIIC and Dawa other than opposition to the Baathist state. And now, with the Baathist state collapsed, Dawa and SIIC have collaborated with the Americans. And it is never a good thing to be seen as collaborators, working with the enemy, who (it is always told and believed) is the source of all problems.

The Sadrists, on the other hand, despite being in power themselves, have consistently maintained the narrative of being outside the process—so they can always point blame at others. It does not take much in Iraq to blame the ruling parties for incompetence: Only ask how many hours of electricity they receive or about the sewage in the street or simply ask, "Do you have a job, what do you do other than sit around and smoke?"

But the Sadrists are offering no new jobs, except perhaps to create opportunities to engage in extortion. Nor do they have better plans for governing. But it is only necessary for them to point out that SIIC, Dawa, and the Americans have failed without offering any practical alternative beyond the sob story.

---

to die for it. Today they cheer for the Sadrist clerics and are willing to die for them—the power of very different ideas.

The Sadrists are very much beholden to the inflamed urban constituency they have created and to be seen as settling for pragmatism would be to abandon them. In contrast, the core constituency of SIIC and Dawa remains the professional middle class, who are not revolutionaries. Indeed, they worry and anticipate the pain of the penicillin shots that might be needed if they give in to the revolutionary idea.

Everyone is well aware of the Sadrists' links to the halls of power in Tehran, paying homage for having taken care of them during Baathist tyranny. But Sadrists remain the last of the group to carry the revolutionary mantle in Iraq while SIIC and Dawa merely pay it lip service, remaining stuck in their position as ruling parties. But despite all the ideas, compelling stories, and firepower, there was always one who could, it seems, throw a wrench at any plan, whether cooked up by Shia, Sunnis, or Americans.

The Benevolent Gaze From Above: Having A Chat With His Eminence, Ayatollah Sistani

> "We wage a continuous struggle with ourselves, with people, and with life," said Gamasa al-Bulti entreatingly, "and the struggle has victims that cannot be numbered, and hope is never lost in the mercy of the Merciful."
>
> —*Arabian Nights and Days*

The people's reverential attitude to the Grand Ayatollah Ali al-Sistani raised some questions: What sort of power does he have? How does he fit into the struggle on the ground? But he is in nearly every house, the benevolent grandpa looking down from every wall, the guy who says hello to soldiers as they walk into the living room.

In nearly every Shia house, regardless of their loyalties in the political struggle, Grand Ayatollah Sistani remains the prime Object of Emulation. After a while soldiers began to feel his presence from the wall and would even miss his gaze if he was not there.

On this day, soldiers are sprawled in a Shia family's living room, tired, fatigued, goofing around with the kids as always—and there he is again, Ayatollah Sistani, looking sternly down at the soldiers.

323

Sistani is a learned religious scholar and authority on moral matters who stays high on everyone's morality chart, much like the Pope in Rome. Some Shia take his moral exhortations literally, some not so much, and some simply don't give a shit. Nevertheless, he symbolizes years of tradition, scholarship, and beliefs, and a lot of people look up to him.

OK, but soldiers wanted to ask the picture, "Your Eminence, how do you fit into what is happening on the streets that we have to deal with, how much authority do you wield?" Three soldiers, Gauloises cigarettes hanging from their mouths sit on the carpet and stare at Ayatollah Sistani with bloodshot eyes.

The kind eyes and immaculate beard of Ayatollah Sistani also represents an institution called Hawza. Hawza is the forum of traditional Shia scholarship, an institution that propagates not only an idea but also clearly delineated interests, a time horizon, and the resources and people to sustain it.

In fact, Hawza has consistently disagreed with the "rule of the jurists" as espoused in the Iranian constitution. As the supreme Shia religious authority in Iraq, they seem to have no reluctance to make the state deeply Shia in character. But they also seem to avoid traditional politics for fear of the corrupting effect that politics could have on the clerical class (as it seems to have had in Iran). To become engaged in politics would be to undercut their primary business model: Retaining a monopoly on moral authority in people's lives.

To be in the morality business requires a man to be perfect; it is not a job for the faint of heart. Unfortunately, preaching morality also becomes the business of charlatans who hide their imperfections behind righteous rhetoric, projecting their self-loathing onto others with a straight face and no sense of irony. But in either case, the fallacy of preaching morality from a political pulpit with real *political power*—as the ayatollahs in Iran have done—has the effect of turning people's lives into an excruciating comedy. It corrupts politics and makes a mockery of morality while forcing people to navigate the absurdity. This is an absurdity that the Iranian exile and his family were very familiar with.

❖ Women without men: The illicit embrace of Iran[77]

> She had a thirty-two year old habit of not moving. She had gotten used to immobility. She knew only this, and she knew instinctively, that when Golchehreh went out, mobility and happiness would come to her. She used to be happier. . . .
>
> —*Women Without Men*

When dogmatic men attempt to enforce the absurdity with temporal authority, as in Iran, the enforcers claim the right to define how much hair can or cannot show on a woman's head, or whether a man and a woman can hold hands. It is no longer a laughing matter.

It is not really about modesty or religion but about a simple human choice, and the human dignity that goes with the inalienable right of people to choose. Regaining that choice in subtle ways becomes a form of resistance—turning the forced scarf, for example, into an art form.

The good patriarch, who had spent time in Iran with his family, was quite happy to be back in Iraq, though he is deeply Shia in his identity. "Under the Shah, people went out to drink and prayed at home. With the ayatollahs, people drink at home and go out to pray," said the gentleman.

Amid the laughter, he pointed out another reality. In Iran, if you talk to the right people, you can find all the alcohol you want, there are parties to go to almost every day, a thriving subculture of raves and drugs, and lots of beautiful women wearing stylish outfits behind the hijab who go clubbing in basements of Tehran. Some relative of some ayatollah (he noted) is probably linked to the black market alcohol racket, like everything else in Iran. "They always get a cut, always," he insists. "*Always*, in every, everything!"

---

[77] *Women Without Men*, a novel by the Iranian author Shahrnush Parishpur.

The Islamic revolution has created all the appurtenances of an Islamic state. They even try to export the revolution—the gift that keeps on giving—to other places, thanks to the good fortune of oil money, just as the guardians of virtue in Saudi Arabia propagate their Salafist Wahhabi creed with oil money. In reality, the Islamic state is thoroughly temporal. The clerical ruling class in Iran has replaced the old royal family and is now just as corrupted by its unalloyed political power. The clerics have one advantage, however: They can hide all their misdeeds by preaching morality because they are always right. They have defined themselves a monopoly of morality, written it into law, and have the guns to protect it. But that is in no way very funny, only sad for the men and women they oppress.

The humor and the future hope of Iran may lie elsewhere, in a different set of women, equally courageous and honest. Iran, like any country, has many imperfect men who roam the night looking for a momentary imperfect union in the company of a woman of the night. Of all the cities in Iran, the highest concentrations of these women are to be found (according to a resourceful and trustworthy source) in the Holy City of Qom. This is the city of seminaries, where the future ruling clerics come to study. Perhaps the future hope of Iran is to be found in the generous spirits of women that traverse the streets at night in the Holy City.

The women of the night subversively cuddle the future ayatollahs, keeping them warm, protecting them from a bleak future of impotent fantasies by making them momentarily straight, and it is a very human moment. The women of the night seduce the self-righteous impulse of moralists by making them enjoy their human imperfections in a warm illicit embrace that touches them to their very depths. One can only hope that the impression is memorable, that this moment of illicit bliss becomes so indelible in the souls of aspiring moralist enforcers that they recognize their imperfections and aspire to be human rather than living saints. An otherwise imperfect union may become a perfect one when it is between a woman of the night and a moralist: Who is the whore in this embrace?

A heartfelt irony: The Iranian clerics who gained political power by invoking moral authority have by now lost all moral authority and have only political power. The moralists now rely on political power to impose morality in Iran, and a proud nation is reduced to an absurdist tragicomedy. Politics has corrupted moral authority and is at the same time corrupted by morality: The ultimate illicit embrace.

The failed moral authority of politicized clerics in Iran has a subtle effect on the serious Shia people in Iraq. It is apparently a lesson heeded by the traditionalist Hawza in Iraq.

❖ Feeling the gaze again

The more learned and religious Shia in Iran consider Sistani an Object of Emulation, precisely because he is not tainted with the corrupting effect of politics. Retaining a monopoly on moral authority clearly requires staying beyond the reproach of politics, and moral authority is the ultimate business of the traditional Hawza in Iraq. Even so, they are very political because they have the capacity to rule the minds of some men and women.

Religious leaders come and go, but the traditional Hawza with its moral authority must stay in perpetuity. Therefore, the benchmarks they set for themselves perhaps are not calculated in terms of years but decades and millennia. Despite the travails of Iraq, the position of the Hawza in society has remained intact. There have been Sunni Kings, Shia Kings, Turks, Brits, imported Saudi Kings, military leaders, secular Baathists, and even Americans—and now we have Iraqi politicians ruling Iraq. Throughout all these changes, one institution has weathered them all—the traditional Shia Hawza in Iraq. Keeping it that way is the institutional mandate, the ultimate task, the supreme objective.

Staring at the picture now, talking into the gaze of Ayatollah Sistani, feeling the purposeful eyes, the simple question arises: "Your Eminence, please show me the money. Where do you hide it?"

Keeping the story alive, preserving the monopoly on moral authority requires work. Iranians use the entire array of government institutions and oil money. But how about the traditional Hawza? They need to maintain consistency in the message, reach the audience that matters, maintain the appurtenances and symbols of moral authority. Otherwise everything else would fall apart. That's why, in the 1950s, the Shia clerical class were scared of the communists and the secularists. They were telling a different story, propagating a different idea—and people were buying it.

Ayatollah Sistani does not keep his money in the bank. When he is elected by peers to be their leader, he becomes not only a moral authority but also the head of a multitude of charities, organizations, and mosques. He comes to symbolize the institution that will outlive him.

❖ **The little messenger: Men in clown suits[78]**

> little messenger,
>> I do not want you
>> to fill this void;
>> to love someone
>> there is no need
>>> to share a roof.

—"The Little Messenger"

Like the Pope, a grand ayatollah evokes authority and intimidates people. But unlike the Pope, he appears regal by projecting an image of extreme humility, wearing simple clothing and living in modest housing. People revere him, forgetting that behind the outfit is simply a learned man. The people who believe in the message give the man and the institution their power.

Sitting on the carpet, staring at Ayatollah Sistani's picture with a cigarette dangling from the mouth, another question arises:

"Your Eminence, if some day you find yourself in a tight corner, can you get *this family*—the family in the house we are sitting in—to go into the streets on your behalf, just by invoking your moral authority?"

---

[78] "The Little Messenger," a poem by the Iranian poet Majid Naficy.

Because without the ability to mobilize some supporters on his behalf, moral authority doesn't count. To men with guns in hand, he will be a sitting duck without political power.

It's a tricky question. Everyone claims to revere him; maybe they would take to the street on his behalf, and maybe not. His political power lies in that uncertainty. The traditional Hawza has immense implicit power—though not necessarily to create a ruckus on the ground, the way the Sadrist ayatollahs do. There is something predictable about the Sadrists and their flag burning. But one never knows whether the traditional Hawza would stage a protest: They always retain the ability to throw a wrench in the plan, simply by invoking moral authority.

The Sadrists' problem is that the Sadrist clerics are rapidly becoming both a political authority *and* a moral authority for their people. And that puts the Sadrists clerics ideologically at odds with the likes of Ayatollah Sistani—and a whole lot closer to the ruling clerics in Iran than most people would like to believe. The doctrinal rift within the Iraqi Shia leadership is subtle but significant.

Everyone knows how "power to the Shia people" turned out in Iran. The traditional Hawza seems to recognize that people are imperfect, that politics is a business of imperfections, not perfection. But Sadrist clerics think differently. They use their moral authority to mobilize people, to play a political role. If that is not sufficient, they also have guns—they don't see anything wrong with that, it is a means to an end. That pits JAM and the more vocal Sadrists against the traditionalist Hawza.

But the Sadrist version of streetwise Shia clerical politics, played with gun in hand, resonates well with their urban constituency. The traditional Hawza (led by Sistani), though unassailable as the undisputed moral authority, will undoubtedly be challenged by diehard political clerics and their gun-wielding supporters, as happened in Najaf during 2003–2005.

Sadrists twice tried to control (and lost) the holy cities in Iraq. Ayatollah Sistani had to barricade himself in his house during that lawless period in Iraq, supported by Shia tribal fighters who swore to defend him to the death.[79] And many Sadrists were implicated in the murder of clerics and officials who supported Sistani and the traditional Hawza.

In short, Sadrists are much closer to the Iranian clerics as both a moral and political authority. As we know, they get Iranian support in the form of guns and IEDs (sometimes called "Iranian Bombs"). But the fight is ultimately about ideas—and the Sadrists' ideological ties with Iran are equally important.

That is the fundamental difference between Sadrist clerics and those who adhere to the traditional Hawza. The Hawza by now has the support of the Shia ruling parties (SIIC and Dawa), as well as the many Shia tribes. It has locked in the traditionalist, conservative constituency that opposes the street-wise Sadrist politics.

❖ The "non-political" yet political ayatollah?

By staying deliberately aloof, Hawza leaves room for a *political*, ruling ayatollah. Grand Ayatollah Baqir al-Sadr developed the idea of making Shia sectarian identity a political force. Since then, several ayatollahs tried unsuccessfully to fill that role—political ayatollahs with religious credentials. Two of them were assassinated.

At present, there is no prominent political ayatollah who is able to delicately navigate the boundaries of political and moral authority. One good Shia gentleman argues that Muqtada Sadr has what it takes, and many Iranian clerics support him. They apparently told him to go back and finish his studies, and then come back to fill the role of the political ayatollah.

Sistani and the traditional Hawza do not wield as much political power on the ground as the Sadrists and certainly not as loudly as JAM. Sistani rather employs the implicit *threat* to wield political power. Even the jaded realist, who would damn the entire clerical class in Iraq, finds it difficult to criticize Sistani on moral grounds.

---

[79] And some astute Americans did support the tribes from the margins.

The radio crackles and soldiers must leave. Ayatollah Sistani is on top of the totem pole, hanging on the wall, and soldiers are at the very bottom of it, stepping off to face a different immediate reality on the ground—as the Jaish al-Mahdi tries its best to keep on giving the gift that keeps on giving, equipped with a great self-perpetuating sob story that has traction on the ground. And the worst of the nut-jobs see no irony in trying to impose it with guns.

16

THE SELF-PERPETUATING SOB STORY: THE POLITICAL AND MILITARY STRATEGY OF JAISH AL-MAHDI

> Al-Zeini was shaken, realizing that he was being led to confess. Dandan would search out the truth at the hands of anyone he sensed had an ability to expose the secrets of men.
>
> —*Arabian Nights and Days*

Many people in the U.S. viewed Muqtada al-Sadr as an upstart; many U.S. commentators and authorities treated the Sadrists with contempt. But as soldiers, the best way to fight a good fight and enjoy it is to give the enemy his due respect, learn about him, and then go after him on our terms. In any case, the Sadrists quickly became an effective populist political movement with religious sanction, led by underclass Shia men with determined conviction and guns in hand.

There are varied explanations to explain the paradox of why they keep attacking the very government they are part of. The explanations rely on labels and metaphors: a group trying to find its way, firebrand, Shia radical. In our view, they had a coherent political objective based on an old sob story: They were determined to give a gift that keeps on giving.

❖ The black hole

The military tactics of the Sadrists were realistic and usually congruent with their short-term and long-term political objectives, making them far more dangerous. JAM's tactics on the ground resembled the tactics of Hezbollah and Hamas.

Though Hamas and Hezbollah may seem different—one Sunni, the other Shia—they are identical in the way they use political and military power to keep the sob-story alive, along the way reducing their own people into finger-puppets in their lethal drama.

Hamas and Hezbollah use the existing political institutions as a means to an end by becoming part of it. Having become part of it, they engage in the politics of constant crisis. It allows them to distance themselves from the process they are part of, both to undermine it and to maintain credibility on the ground.

The image that they are not corrupted by politics is important—though it is the greatest ruse. That is what sets apart "men of the people" from "the establishment," except that that in reality they are all part of it and fight over the gravy train.

This disloyal opposition would always mobilize supporters on the ground to flank the political process. If they can get concessions by creating some sort of crisis, it enhances their image, assures the complicity of the people, and even generates support on the ground. It also establishes more credibility in the political sphere.

If the effort does not work out the way they planned, that too has the effect of emboldening their supporters by strengthening their self-fulfilling sob story. The best of the sob stories are self-perpetuating, and JAM, Hamas, and Hezbollah have some of the best.

❖ With them or against them

Jaish al-Mahdi seizes on the long disenfranchised Shia urban ghettos and the recent immigrants, promising them the alternative reality of "power to the people." It is a populist religious political movement with military capabilities. The destitute and pissed-off urban Shia have a voice in the Sadrist movement, and the brass-knuckle politics resonate with people who are tired of their current situation.

The affluent Shia people in Iraq disagree profoundly with the Sadrists, fearful of the world that they might create, but they are in a difficult position. Because to deny the Sadrists in public is tantamount to denying everything the Sadrists have done for the Shia people of Iraq. The many grievances the Sadrists highlight are real, and their quiet resistance against Baathist tyranny will always remain undeniable. That simple reality made fighting JAM a greater challenge and required our combat leaders to be doubly astute because they constantly face a paradox.

❖ Paradox

The genius of maintaining a convincing sob story lies in highlighting the immediate issues while masking the long-term objectives.

Being part of the political process gives the group legitimacy, bargaining leverage, and a stream of resources they can use to enhance support through myriad social services, making people dependant on them. But as long as they retain military capabilities, the group will always hold the political process hostage, threatening to flank it militarily when they deem it necessary.

When insurgents take part in the political process but constantly flank it with military means, and when the insurgency is an embedded part of the society, thanks to a persuasive story, then the insurgency itself has *political legitimacy*. And counterinsurgents have to come to terms with a painful reality.

This reality requires the counterinsurgents to outflank the insurgent flank militarily, but do so smartly—outflanking the insurgents politically at the same time by offering the people realistic incentives to cooperate with the counterinsurgents. At best, that cooperation can be turned into support by offering a coherent alternative and providing services on the ground that will make the sob story redundant: that is, by outflanking the insurgents on both sides, militarily and politically.

335

To outflank the insurgents on both sides is to bring people center stage; people remain the problem and the ultimate prize in the battle. When people don't buy into the sob story, it loses its meaning. The incongruity between the sob story and the reality on the ground is made obvious when people's real concerns are addressed. The true nature of its proponents becomes evident: Men with guns who try to reduce others into a figment of their own imagination. The true believers will not go away, of course, and they will inevitably require a heartfelt greeting. But when the sob story no longer resonates with people, not much will ever need to be said—a tall order. Difficult, but never impossible.

Another Long Beginning: The Jaish sl-Mahdi Neighborhood

So, one brisk morning, soldiers walked into the JAM neighborhood, equipped with a little experience, a satchel of old tricks, a clownish grin, and wide open eyes—keeping in mind that someone will probably try to take a random shot. A new neighborhood presents a very steep learning curve.

Walking into a new neighborhood in a counterinsurgency, the nature of the neighborhood gradually sinks into the skin; in no time it begins to feel like the burrowing of a thousand insects. The neighborhood, with its smells, dust, heat, and raucous din is like any other, with children, women, and men from all walks of life.

There are the rich, the affluent, and the professionals, who hide their wealth along with their stylishly dressed children, their English-speaking women and daughters. (In time, some of the daughters will call soldiers on their cell phones and chat on email.) They keep their BMWs covered in tarps in the garage. For fear of being kidnapped for ransom, they drive a beat-up Hyundai instead. Going to work means the death-defying sport of hopping from checkpoint to checkpoint, saying a prayer as they get close. It makes no difference whether the checkpoint is American, Iraqi Army, Iraqi Police, or insurgents, Iraqi friends used to tell us. No matter who runs it, there are nervous men with guns, never a comforting feeling to a civilian.

Then there are the people merely struggling to maintain a house. And there are the utterly destitute. The destitute in the neighborhood live a step above the filth while the internally displaced people generally live literally amid the garbage as their kids sift through it for sustenance. Every little open space is filled with these completely nonexistent people, the scattered, internally displaced people one can see everywhere in Iraq if one keeps eyes and ears open. Their ubiquity is what makes it so easy for everyone to ignore them.

Then there is the best kind, the shady cats in town, but not everyone sees them or wants to deal with them. They straddle all the worlds, the good, the bad, and the ugly. They wave at the soldiers, and soldiers drank much tea with them (and, at times, cups of alcohol); it is essential. They have such a good finger on the subversive reality in the neighborhood while walking a fine line of ambiguity. Shady cats can always outsmart any eagle scout, choirboy, or genius because it is their neighborhood and they know their stuff. It is always worthwhile to figure them out over time, adjudicating among them to find the least evil. For soldiers and leaders on the ground they can be very useful.

❖ Walking away

One phrase that we heard from nearly everyone in the neighborhood captured its essence. A wonderful family that eventually became dear friends put it best. The husband, Hussein, a former successful bureaucrat, was now the go-to guy for a series of local aid agencies, business contractors, and (much later) Iraqi contractors, working for the Americans. His wife, Huda, was a medical professional. They have two beautiful daughters Raeesa'h (age fourteen) and Najwa (age twenty-four). Then there was the toddler Muhammad—soldiers called him Mo—and the smartly dressed but sullen-looking son, Ali.

The first time we met them, the older daughter maintained her steady comportment of modesty, though her eyes could not hide her curiosity. The fourteen-year-old daughter was grinning from ear to ear, gesturing at the soldiers, while the adolescent son was simply hostile. Toddler Mo acted like he was face to face with a bunch of circus monkeys, and soldiers were quick to reciprocate.

337

Ali had that familiar, understandable look of apprehension. He did not want soldiers to get even a glimpse of his sisters. The hostility emanating from his every gesture made one wonder: Was it arrogance or fear he was trying to capture with his shit talking? He is either scared or he genuinely hates us. More often than not, it is the scared men who speak loudest, with the most braggadocio, because there is always a tiny little hamster spinning inside the heart. And even though soldiers are too tired for hamsters, they have no choice, so they give Ali his few minutes so he can feel like a man. The sisters were standing by their mom.

The father quickly brought everyone back to reality: "Of course, JAM controls this area," he said in crystal-clear English, as his wife nodded vigorously. "But JAM protects us from other groups, please don't come to our house again because we don't want any trouble. Please, sir, please, we don't want any trouble, please leave."

Soldiers are way too tired and jaded by now. The impulse is to say, "Goddamn, I'm tired of this shit," but it is the first time the family had seen this bunch of soldiers. Soldiers cannot say a word but just stand there, unwelcome, in their beautiful courtyard; it's a different place but the same old story.

Of course, the soldiers could say the hell with it, walk into the house and plant themselves on the couch, because they've got the guns. Or, they can take their hosts at their word, give them the moment and walk away; see where it might lead. After all, this is just a scouting patrol, trying to get a feel for the neighborhood, and soldiers will be around for a while. (As it turned out, they stayed so long that some joked about getting a real estate agent in the neighborhood.)

It was a very wise decision to walk away. Walking away in a counterinsurgency sometimes can be turned into a hearty welcome on another day.

No, the family was not lying—nearly every other family that soldiers talked to in the neighborhood came up with similar statements:

> Yes, JAM controls the area; NO, we don't know anything. This area is safe, all the trouble is in other areas; oh, no that is

not my area. Yes, JAM control the area; no they come from other areas. Please, *please* leave, we don't want any trouble. Please leave, we don't want you here, please.

It's a bad way to start. There is no welcome, you can't expect one. Soldiers don't have a choice in the matter—they can't just say "fuck it" and get on the next airplane—so they better figure it out and find a laugh.

❖ Martyrdom billboards: Marketing the sob story

The bustling normalcy is an illusion. JAM has control of the neighborhood, both overtly and subversively. JAM militants are anonymous yet their presence is always felt. Throughout the entire neighborhood, every intersection displays JAM martyrs and spiritual leaders, announcing JAM's overt control. People are complicit with them, while the supporters are in the open because it's a political party.

No one argues about whether the old Sadrist ayatollahs would actually support JAM's current course of military action: Their support is implicitly stated in every billboard and people take it for granted. Every picture tries to tell the same story. Ayatollah Baqir al-Sadr on the top left corner, Sadiq al-Sadr on the top right, Imam Hussein at the very top, and then rows of JAM fighters who died fighting the Americans. Muqtada al-Sadr follows at the very bottom in his grief-stricken glamor shot: looking down, face covered with both hands, he is mourning the martyrs. An irony—why would you ask them to be martyrs and then mourn them?

Not everyone overlooks the irony. Some Iraqis thrive on irony, breathe it; it was an Iraqi Shia who pointed this out to a soldier as he was giving the soldiers tactical advice. He had family members killed by JAM boys, and he was ready to burn every JAM poster in town. The martyrdom billboard became a running joke among some soldiers: One of the best ways for soldiers to keep count and figure out whether they have been doing their jobs right was when new faces—ones they knew well—kept popping up by the side of the road on the martyr posters.

But it is irrelevant whether the old Sadrist ayatollahs would agree with the current JAM program, with its anti-American, anti-Jew, anti-Iraqi, and nearly anti-everything invective. Because the attempt is to subsume everything into the sob story, demonstrating that the long-persecuted Shia are still persecuted. That's the point of the billboards.

It is no accident that all the leaders shown on the posters are people who ended up in a bad way, including the recent JAM guys killed by soldiers. The fact that Shia are in power and in control is deliberately hidden, and people are forced to believe otherwise.

The problem is that JAM control does not stop at reifying its story in the minds of men and women. They use it as part of the program, as a means to get control of neighborhoods while they continue to flank the political process militarily. JAM is smart, it's their people, their neighborhood, and they are fighting to stay.

Coming to Terms with the Neighborhood

JAM is a well-oiled, cunning machine that is also a legitimate political party—part of the government that they oppose. Their own people are the pawns in their own sob story. On the one hand, they do help their own people with myriad social services and try to address their immediate concerns. On the other hand, they maintain control on the ground subversively, keeping people in line with their implicit threat of violence, intimidation, and, when all else fails, dead bodies to get people to toe the line. The totality of control sinks in each day with every step down the neighborhood and its alleyways.

Given the American presence, the clerics in the mosques do not chant death to America. But they have come of age hearing "No, No, to America, No, No, to Zionism, and No, No, to the devil," chanted by Ayatollah Sadiq al-Sadr during the sanctions decade. They have been firmly schooled in the Sadrist brand of religious populism. These days the JAM clerics need not elaborate *anti-what-exactly*—it is understood who the clerics detest, who people are supposed to detest, and the mosque undeniably perpetuates the sob story. It is logical. There is no better way. The preachers can subsume the immediate reality into broader cosmic themes.

340

The real grievances of the Shia people are way too real on the ground: sectarian killings, militias from "the other neighborhoods." The list of immediate concerns is long: water, electricity, garbage, medicine, schools, children, jobs, and safety. The clerics, like any preacher, express empathy: "I feel your pain; I am living it too." Some of them may, but others decidedly did not. Some clerics that soldiers came to know (becoming a decided nuisance to them) lived very comfortably indeed. But never mind that—the sermons resonate very well. A good Sadrist mosque is like an octopus, its many tentacles reaching to every corner of the Sadrist-controlled neighborhood.

Public services collapsed and receded into oblivion during the sanctions decade, so mosques and religious organizations filled the space left behind, assisting people with basic necessities that would have been provided by the government. One should not overestimate the strength of the local mosques: the religious organizations cannot supplant the public services provided by the government. Even while receding from the public space, the government always kept paying the schoolteachers and doctors (for example)—although the purchasing power of their salaries kept declining as the economy collapsed. The mosque-based organizations (which are community organizations) complemented the meager resources that came from the government. JAM clerics could help out the schools and clinics, maybe even get JAM guys to clear the garbage.

Then, after the Americans rolled in and held the elections, the Sadrists and JAM hit the jackpot. Immediately after the elections in 2005, the Sadrists smartly plugged into the gravy train, getting some of the key Cabinet ministries, especially those that are best for their own program: health, social affairs, and transportation. Soldiers understood that the fact that they are part of the gravy train was the most difficult part of fighting JAM.

JAM, as part of the government, received an unending amount of resources. Not just the resources that go to help the people but also the advantages that come from having ownership of government institutions. Every ministry comes with an opportunity to fill positions

341

with loyalists: to control the health ministry was to have a stranglehold on the entire health sector, to have control of transportation is to corner all its resources. The Sadrists could become local heroes by giving people medical care, by providing it under the Sadrist banner—literally, under the photos of Sadrist ayatollahs and not the government flag. Every hospital and clinic was forced to display a picture of Muqtada (if not of Sadrist ayatollahs), and doctors who resisted would be swiftly put to an end. And in Shia strongholds, when Sadrists got hold of the health sector, it was easy to create the image of neighborhood heroes.

One rarely hears anyone mention that the Sadrists turned away Sunnis, that Sadrist Hospital security guards killed many Sunnis, that doctors were ordered to abide by that edict, and those who opposed were intimidated or killed outright. To hear these stories one simply has to sit down with the doctors or any medical professional.

But the advantage of the gravy train does not stop there. It also provides an opportunity and a great boon for a political-military organization. Every Iraqi ministry, including social services, comes with its own security organization. The health ministry has its own security establishment, staffed with armed men that guard myriad warehouses, hospitals, and clinics. And the same is true of the transportation ministry: The guys guarding the railway station are railway security. The problem is that some of the men who are security guards by day become militiamen at night. The same men kill, intimidate, and extort, and at times enforce the modesty of women and even engage in rape. The impact of the gravy train was pervasive; it could be seen and felt if one simply walked around with eyes and ears open.

The resources went to strengthening JAM social programs on the ground. While the Sadrists incessantly denounce the government, blame it, blame the Americans, call them occupiers, and ask them to leave, they spend government money for public services *under the Sadrist banner* as if saying, "Look, we are doing this for you." That is a genius way to keep the program alive, supported by the very process they denounce. And it had the compounded effect that JAM could dictate to nearly every government institution and institutional representation in the neighborhood (whether Sadrist-controlled or not).

There are many honest police officers who take pride in their profession. But many have JAM sympathies or even active militia members. Some who tried to do their jobs, going against the wishes of the JAM militia, were killed by their own colleagues for it. At the height of Sadrist control it was nearly impossible to join the local police without pledging loyalty to the Sadrists.

One police officer and his brother complained to the soldiers, asking them to kill one of the JAM gangsters who killed their younger brother because they, as police officers, cannot do anything about it. They stipulated their terms: We will tell you all the information, but no one can know we told you, and you must kill him, otherwise they will kill us.

Many Iraqi families and Iraqi police officers told soldiers (in private, at night, in their own homes) how the JAM-affiliated police officers engage in extortion, murder, and rape. Even more commonly, they use police authority as a cover to kill Sunnis, evict them from their houses, and bestow those houses upon their loyalists. One Shia man, whose (former) next-door neighbor was Sunni, lamented that they have been neighbors all their lives and that is far more important to him than sectarian identity.

Thus the security organizations on the ground—trained, equipped, and paid by Americans—were the same men who would fight the soldiers at night. Going into sticky neighborhoods with the precise objective of capturing high value individuals, every team leader and every leader on the ground instilled in their soldiers one guiding principle:

"Look man, it's the IA and IP that we will be fighting tonight, and they wear the same body armor we give them. When you shoot, take well-aimed head shots, always, well-aimed head shots."

❖ **The English teacher**

The English teacher, talking on the rooftop, was unequivocal: "It is the Iraqi Police that set up the explosion the other day, down the street.

343

I think it killed some Americans, and my brother saw it." It was a self-evident truth that soldiers understood from the first few weeks, having been at the receiving end. But her story is important and offers the potential for a future tactical reality. She added, "My brother called the police when he saw them fix it, but two hours later, JAM and police came to the house and beat him up."

Her crisp English was remarkable. So were the circumstances of the meeting. It was during a time sensitive target acquisition mission, smack in the middle of a Sadrist stronghold, in a lull between firefights. A sniper team was on the roof providing cover so that others on the ground could maneuver. The members of the household are also in a corner on the roof: the English teacher, her brother, her parents, and a couple of cousins are lying on the floor out of harm's way, as the sniper team leader had requested. The English teacher was sprawled on the ground next to one sniper, speaking non-stop, wearing a big grin on her face. It was a running joke that she had a soft spot for this lanky American sniper with a cheekful of chewing tobacco and a sleepy southern drawl. She always had this excited big old grin on her face at the sight of him and got animated with each new thread of conversation. "If we can't tell the police," she asked, "what *can* we do?"

The lanky soldier asked one of his friends to keep an eye on things below. He moved down, turning on his back and then sideways to face the English teacher who had crawled next to him. Her brother, lying next to her, added his two cents from time to time. He indeed had the scars on his face to show that someone had recently pummeled him. The whole family was pissed off, no one likes to get punched in the face. They wanted to talk to someone, and the English teacher was the messenger. Nevertheless, she had a big smile on her face talking to the sniper. He replied in his trademark drawl, "Weeeell, sweetie, I don't know who you *been* talking to, but you *should* be talking to *us*." She nods vigorously. It is the funniest and most heart-warming sight because in spite of all the rat-tat noises in the background she still had a grin on her face. Then he said, "Well, we know where you live, sweetheart, we will come by at night some time and you can tell us what you know."

"Yes, yes, please come."

He grunted acknowledgement (he communicates mainly through grunts and slow drawls) and turned his lanky body again, peering over the roof and snuggling closer to his weapon system, scanning the sector, looking for slithering rattlesnakes.

❖ The buck sergeant

Not everyone in the army and the police is a crook, as some Iraqi soldiers pointed out, and some were even willing to take lot of risks. Local Iraqi army garrisons are supposed to protect the neighborhoods. But who will protect the soldiers in the garrison from the insurgents that control the neighborhood?

The young buck sergeant in the Iraqi Army spoke candidly with a bunch of buck sergeants and staff sergeants in the U.S. Army about his job. His English was nearly impeccable, and his military knowledge far surpassed that of his peers or even superiors.

"This shit, I hate it!"

American soldiers had a ready response, leaning on the concrete and smoking cigarettes: "Yeah, no shit, we hate it too," and everyone shared a laugh. But the Iraqi sergeant had specific concerns. He had really wanted to be in the army, go to the military academy, become an officer, and be a commander one day. But by now, he was simply using the army pay to finish technical school and then get out of the army.

His love for the military comes from his family in Mosul: his father, grandfather, and many uncles were all former military officers. He has an intimate knowledge of Iraqi military history from listening to his relatives reminisce about the glory days. As a man from a proud military lineage, he resents being a Sunni stuck in a Shia neighborhood, surrounded by non-professional military men with a sectarian agenda. His friend, a fellow Sunni (from Kirkuk), also felt rather displaced in an ocean of Shia soldiers in the middle of a Shia neighborhood.[80]

---

[80] This pertains only to new Iraqi Army units, not Kurdish peshmerga units, which remain very cohesive and effective.

His tenuous situation became obvious: He would be talking, smoking, and laughing, but when certain members of his unit came near—those with Sadrist affiliations—the laughing and joking would stop in mid-sentence. He would switch the topic, or a soldier would, it was very necessary. His information and its tactical validity proved immensely valuable over time.

Yes, there was a field-grade Iraqi officer in charge of the scattered garrison, but though well-intentioned, he was effectively neutered from above and below. Underneath him are a number of politically appointed lieutenants, with no effective military training, who have the loyalty of the militia members within the army garrisons. Politically appointed Sadrist officers from the neighborhood come and go and do whatever they want with impunity, making sure the army stays out of the way when the militia is up to no good.

The buck sergeant was clearly frustrated. "Until you kill these guys and get rid of the militias, we cannot do anything, and the officers cannot do anything."

❖ The complacent slumber

Over time, another sinister reality became apparent with regard to the garrisons. Situated in a neighborhood controlled by Sadrist militias, the garrisons remain safe only because of a tacit agreement, a modus vivendi that works out for both sides. The militias get to go about their business with impunity, while the Iraqi soldiers remain out of harm's way. Neither side rocks the boat—they leave that to the Americans. It is that simple.

Iraqi Army soldiers, no matter how motivated they may be, do not (yet) have the luxury American soldiers take for granted. American soldiers can commit to a fight and stay committed and follow through as if nothing else mattered because at the point of decision they know that higher officers always come through with the big guns when necessary. That is the rule, not the exception. Later on they may give a tongue lashing to soldiers for taking unwarranted risks, but they always—always—come through for their soldiers in a fight and that's the norm. Of that we are certain.

Iraqi soldiers, at present, if they choose to fight JAM, cannot stay in the fight because they are never certain who will be on their side. JAM is very smart in the way they approach those Iraqi Army soldiers and officers who think for themselves. They will not fight IA in the streets: There are almost no random skirmishes. JAM wait until soldiers go home and then they get them. No JAM group (that soldiers have seen) has the capability to overpower an Iraqi Army garrison; instead, they go after individual soldiers when they are most vulnerable. That implicit threat, which is very real, works to create an understanding on the ground. The Iraqi buck sergeant and his friend put it simply. "We know which vehicles JAM uses, which ones to search and which ones we should not, because they tell us. They drive with RPGs, RPKs, AK-47s, and everything. Tell me, what I am going to do with one AK-47 and three magazines?" He wiggled his old Soviet-style hand grenade: "Oh yes, and one grenade."

Then he told the story of one of his friends. His friend was apparently not privy, on one particular day, to an important bit of information. He was not supposed to search the JAM car at the checkpoint, but he assumed it was a civilian vehicle and searched it. When he opened the trunk, a man—presumably a hostage—jumped out and started running and screaming, creating a ruckus at the checkpoint in front of a lot of people. Though his friend apologized to the militias, profusely and sincerely, two days later as he was walking to the bakery to get some bread he was shot in the head point blank in broad daylight. A simple message was succinctly sent: "We control this area, if you toe the line, you will be safe and if you don't, you will wind up dead."

There are somewhat humorous stories as well. The Iraqi field officers were having a big-time meeting with some very high-ranking American military officers to discuss JAM activity. Flanking the Iraqi field officers were the politically appointed lieutenants—militia members who would quickly send the word to their own authorities, who were thus able to listen in on the whole thing. The Iraqi officers, of course, know the reality of the situation and are unable to do anything about militia members in their own midst. They sat there hiding the reality with a sheepish grin, utterly fearful. Meanwhile, the American officers lectured them on what is expected of them, right in front of the very militia members that they are supposed to fight—without ever recognizing the parallel realities that existed in that room.

The Iraqi soldiers from Mosul and Kirkuk, though happy to talk with soldiers, said matter-of-factly, "Please don't talk to us in the street if you see us, JAM is everywhere, they are watching us."

It is not literally true that JAM members are everywhere. But in the ocean of people that walk in the streets are JAM sympathizers, and some of these sympathizers, including many members of the Iraqi Police and Army, also function as forward observers, calling JAM insurgents on their cell phones. Soldiers promised the Iraqi friends, "Yeah, no worries, just call us on the cell if there is anything." Cell phones, yes, soldiers have to learn from insurgents, it is critically important.

❖ Cell phones: There is no static

Uncle Sam will not provide or pay for local Iraqi cell phones. Most don't see their importance, but most soldiers are willing to dish out the cash to buy cell phones just to call home. And some soldiers had cell phones specifically to speak to Iraqis in the neighborhood. One had three; another had an all-time record of six local cell phones from various Iraqi cell phone networks. Slowly the idea spread.

Living in a neighborhood and getting control of it is different from chasing nut-jobs. Walking in the neighborhood is a start, and then staying in touch with the people one meets becomes critical. If there is some way for the people to be in touch with the soldiers (and vice versa), the result is a constant stream of information that helps illuminate the neighborhood, and its intricacies.

Most Iraqis will speak to American soldiers, but many preferred to speak to soldiers without the presence of interpreters. It is the strangest realization. Some Iraqis, worrying about life and death, are more comfortable with American soldiers than with the masked Iraqi interpreter. A masked interpreter is like a loudspeaker that screams, "Yes,

I work for the Americans, but I am scared for my life because they cannot protect me and my family when I leave them."

Those who seemed most suspicious were often the ones who came through with tactically valuable information and even took risks (beyond the risk of speaking in the presence of an interpreter). So soldiers who could learned a little Arabic, equipped with local cell phones, could begin to have a pretty good pulse on the neighborhood. The logic is simple.

Being in the neighborhood, soldiers have to at times learn from the enemy's tactics: Get some Iraqis to act as forward observers as insurgents do. They can keep an eye on things, even take photos on the cell phone. The expensive cell phones make a pretty dent in the pay check, but it is well worth it. Just give a reliable Iraqi—a man or woman—a good cell phone and a direct number to reach the soldier.

Not some random phone number where twenty million Iraqis call and speak to some random yahoo who gets easily excited hearing the claim, "Oh, mister, I know where there is a missile factory" or a car bomb factory or the IED factory. Someone in a cubicle always takes the report very seriously, as they should. But it always elicited lot of laughter on the ground. Because when they send the information down, the information gets embellished, but the details soldiers on the ground require at times get lost in the excitement, so soldiers on the ground go on a wild goose chase, but it is necessary and part of the job. There is nothing better than to get a call, walking home to the tent to commiserate at sunrise at three in the morning, to go look for a missile factory. "Ah shit, missing weapons of mass destruction, baby," and onward soldiers go with a heartwarming curse for motivation.

The Iraqi buck sergeant knew a couple of the soldiers and had their cell phones and email addresses. He would call or send emails when he went to the technical school. But on one simple condition: That the soldiers would not reveal to their higher American officers, or even any other American colleagues, his identity, existence, or whereabouts—anything at all. It was not because he was afraid of Americans, in fact he trusted them, but he was so afraid

349

the information would get out and he would quickly end up like his friend at the hands of some of the Iraqi soldiers.

One almost felt pity because here is an Iraqi soldier, frightened out of his mind not just of the enemy but of his own colleagues that he is supposed to trust with his life in a tight corner. At the same time, he loved being a soldier, took pride in it, and had the best intentions in his heart. But he is willing to help the soldiers on a very personal basis and that is good enough for now.

JAM Organization On The Ground

The local JAM insurgency presents a maddeningly coherent whole. It includes, of course, elected political leaders who have the support of the people and are untouchable, by the book. Other JAM functionaries, with nominal military titles, happen to be part-time clerics; they are also untouchable, by the book.

And there are also the side-kicks—the middle men, who are nei-ther legal nor illegal; they can navigate all realms without ever being directly implicated in violence. They include local elected politicians (District Advisory Council or Neighborhood Advisory Council mem-bers), who are not part of the insurgency but find themselves col-luding with it, whatever their political sympathies may be. They are also bureaucrats, businessmen, local clerics. They are the political and organizational gophers, doing their bit—and their bits adds up—while they always remain innocent.

In a neighborhood controlled by a political-military organization such as JAM, there are apparently no saints on the ground. Everyone is linked to it in some form or fashion. But not everyone in this politi-cal-military organization is a legitimate target soldiers need to chase, even if they are not completely innocent. Life on the ground exists in a gray area.

Walking that fine line of ambiguity is the gophers' shrewd strength. As soldiers saw it, their actions play the most critical role in perpetuat-ing insurgent control on the ground: Some of them provide social ser-vices, address people's immediate grievances, or preach the sob story;

others, the law and order authorities, collude with JAM combatants or look sideways at violations. One blatant example is simply taken for granted. The guy who controls the food—cooking oil, maize and all the subsidies—and hands them out to families with food ration cards does so under Muqtada's poster, wearing JAM memorabilia, praising JAM, and is a JAM appointee. If you happen to be looking at him with a sniper's scope, wondering whether to find a delicate but forbidden symmetry between the eyes, you see people kiss the guy's hand as they take their food and walk away. Yes, it's the Godfather. The families don't care whether he is JAM, American, or Martian, as long as they get food rations—and in this neck of the woods, the food comes from JAM. The totality of control, the limited choices of people, and how it is reinforced from below is a unique (and a pain in the ass) tactical reality.

But the critical muscle of the insurgency is provided by the combatant cells on the ground. The combatant cell is beautifully situated in the nexus where politics, social services, people, and sob stories come together.

❖ Mint tea in the courtyard: The JAM combatant cells and C2

One of the charms of being grunts is that, in every conceivable moment, there is always an element of humor. Soldiers have lots of laughs as they gear up to go into a sticky neighborhood with the objective of capturing another "high value individual" (HVI) in a TST.

The official operations order lays out everything in detail. The HVI is a "Brigade Commander"; the insurgents with him consist of "Battalion Commanders" and many "Lieutenants." The objective is not only to catch the HVIs but also to "disrupt and destroy" the "Command and Control (C2) structure," to disrupt the insurgent "network," "disrupt processes" and so on. It is all relevant because it explains the mission in relation to its wider impact.

But soldiers in the assault element (the guys who will blow the door and walk into the house and do the shooting) have a different set of questions and concerns. It's great that the targets are highly valued, but their command position is irrelevant. Whether it is a king, queen, or billionaire, he is just another rattlesnake that needs to be captured.

So soldiers' questions and concerns are more immediate. What is the nature of the fight tonight? Are the guys going to have to fight their way in *and* fight their way out? Is it a kill capture mission? How many rattlesnakes will be crawling around the neighborhood? What is the nature of the neighborhood, the garbage mounds, the cinder-block houses—are they stacked on top of each other? The spacing in between the alleys: Can rattlesnakes bring their vehicles in through the alleys? How many soldiers are going, do the soldiers have all the eyes and ears they could get from above and below, with all the high tech wizardry that could make or break the fight? How much time do soldiers have at the objective, and if the rattlesnakes decide to crawl out and sprint in a star cluster, do they need to be chased down or put an end to? *And what about the civilian presence in the neighborhood?* The time and the place matters.

With each breath, all these details sink into the bones. The senior enlisted non-commissioned officer who will personally lead the assault gets to the essence of it all, answering questions in his trade-mark style:

"Hey, listen up man, hey, shut up, and listen. You know this neighborhood; we're gonna fight our way in, and fight our way right back out.

"Yeah, we're going after a bunch of guys sitting around drinking their goddamn tea in the courtyard, they will either be shooting or running and we gotta stop 'em doing both.

"You know how this shit is done, this ain't rocket science, we know what we do, and this is what we know how to do best. Listen, when the rounds start pinging, it will be the Iraqi Army and Iraqi Police that will do the shooting wearing our fucking body armor, you know the deal. Well-aimed head shots man, *well-aimed head shots.*

"HEY, Squad Leaders and Team Leaders, make sure your guys' lasers are all bore-lighted (the IR lasers are up to snuff), radios, NODs, batteries, the usual; I want an up when the guys are ready. We don't have much time." Then, pointing his finger with a smile, "Hey, no fucking around tonight, you know how this shit is done. Listen man, when we go in, we will own this motherfucker tonight." Then he laughed his usual cackle, walking away.

When everyone does his job right, both higher and soldiers, things come together and soldiers on the ground own the moment and that's the ultimate simple charm of soldiering. A perfect combat mission is perfect and beautiful, it is the job. Soldiers on the ground are only as good as the leaders they work for, and leaders are only as good as the soldiers that work for them. When the two are a congruent whole, the life of soldiering is in perfect harmony. It is felt it in the bones with each step, and soldiers only have to capture the charms without wavering.

Charms are fine, but the guys in the courtyard drinking their tea are far more important. Each time soldiers capture an HVI, he is handed over to the authorities and sent higher for further questioning. Soldiers recognize that higher realities are varied and numerous. Nevertheless, there won't be any effective follow-on missions if his actionable intelligence gets stalled in official channels, hogged by our own middlemen. Quick follow-on missions become possible only if soldiers could cut out the middlemen and act immediately on the neighborhood gossip served up by the HVI. Insurgents swim safely in their own neighborhood: At the first whiff of danger, they flap their tails and disappear in order to fight another day. In follow-on missions, time is truly of the essence!

To overcome this minor difficulty at times, soldiers could (hypothetically speaking) delay handing the captured insurgent leaders into the netherworld of the detention center to the perfect people who conduct the questioning. Hypothetically speaking, delaying the handover not only can provide immediately actionable intelligence but also a valuable educational experience—to learn from the enemy the best way to fight this fight.

Sitting on the ground together is always charming, sharing cigarettes, eating, and commiserating about the creamsicle cookie from an army MRE, catching up on the neighborhood gossip. Insurgents are unencumbered by any procedural straightjackets: Insurgent organizations are not in the habit of holding their combatants accountable for their actions.

Soldiers, of course, must abide by procedures because they are men with guns who have to make life and death decisions and must be held responsible and accountable. Taking responsibility for one's actions and those of one's subordinates is the one tenet of military leadership that is never taken for granted and never forgiven, at least for military leaders on the ground. With rigid procedures, military leaders are required to strike a delicate balance between good ideas and good procedures. Because not every idea is good, the good idea fairy that comes fluttering around sometimes needs to be swiftly neutered to save smart soldiers from their own smart ideas. Some good ideas on the ground could be like pissing in one's own pants, momentarily warm and then comes the "oh shit" moment. "Oh shit" moments can be deadly, and it is thanks to some leaders on the ground, who swiftly and astutely neutered some soldiers' good idea fairy, that some soldiers are still living.

Insurgents don't have procedures; they are free to innovate. Innovation does not guarantee tactical success, but innovation without procedures—no accountability and responsibility—would undoubtedly make it a hell of a lot easier to fight. Insurgents have the ability to tactically innovate at every turn. Sit around, drink tea, smoke cigarettes, and figure out the best way to shoot some Americans or their own people, without regard to higher or below.

Insurgent combatants can react quickly to the situation on the ground. As part of the local society, they keep current on the neighborhood gossip. They learn from the adversary without regard to procedures, without accountability or responsibility. The foreign adversary is slow to learn and evolve, encumbered by the procedures inherent to an army. The need to navigate the terrain—and its people—as a foreign intervention force presents a double disadvantage.

The insurgent organization, while hierarchical, in essence remains a bunch of guys with combatant commanders on the ground retaining an incredible amount of autonomy of action. Autonomy of action on the part of insurgent commanders allows for the *independence* of the insurgent cell—a bunch of guys drinking tea in a courtyard. Cell leaders act autonomously on tactical matters without communicating with or compromising other cells. The vehement denials of insurgent footsoldiers regarding others in the same neighborhood are sometimes true, they really do *not* know them. And the middlemen, businessmen, and political leaders who facilitate and provide resources also remain anonymous.

Simplicity seems to go a long way in maintaining the subversive advantage of guys drinking mint tea in the courtyard. All coordination is done by the simplest of means: word of mouth, couriers, cell phones. And yes, the Internet, as one guy highlighted—"Oh! Ya'hoooo." At that point, the soldier conducting tactical questioning, smoking the cigarettes, actually asked him, "Yahoo, why yahoo? Use Gmail chat, that is much better, have you used Gmail chat?" The humor was lost on him; he was not familiar with Gmail. Shit, it seems Google has lot of work to do in Iraq.

Autonomy of action means that the guy who runs the missions and the guys who do the shooting can decide on the most propitious time based on their own reconnaissance: the word they get from the street vendors, kids, and police officers. Insurgents make their decisions based on the anticipated reaction of counterinsurgents. The vast majority of the JAM insurgents do not want to die fighting but very much want to live to fight another day. So they pay attention to coalition response tactics and response time. They study the different units since the nature of the response depends on the nature of the coalition unit: armor, cavalry, infantry, logistics, or civilian convoys. Each responds differently, contingent not only on the rules of engagement but also on their training and maneuverability. For an armored unit, there will always be just a few possible avenues of approach, giving a tactical advantage to the insurgent combatants.

Insurgents (like most smart Iraqis) are acutely aware—from historical memory, word of mouth, or their own experience—how to navigate around the various units. JAM fighters pay attention to details.

355

They recognize the distinctive vehicles and the soldiers' insignia; they even have the names and photos of unit leaders. Their forward observers—kids, street vendors, and lurkers—video the units' movements using cell phones. It is educational to be looking at this footage in their cell phones as soldiers share some tea with the guys they captured. Soldiers are treated to an explanation of the standard operating procedures of the American unit in an adjacent neighborhood, together with their patrol rotations—from a JAM combatant leader!

But there is always an opportunity, an opening in every moment, and exploiting that opening is critical. Insurgents, unencumbered by procedural straitjackets, are nevertheless very much encumbered by limited resources. Size matters, and insurgents are aware of this disadvantage. They put more emphasis on technique and breathless extra effort. The guys in the courtyard decide their engagement, contingent on the resources they have. Bigger may not always be better, smarter is sometimes better. An enemy that puts emphasis on the quality of engagement through innovation is unpredictable and therefore formidable.

The objective of JAM combatant cells is to harass, to keep at it while making it consistent with their sob story, *so they never win outright militarily.*

Of course, as soldiers, taking slow deliberate steps, there is nothing more heartwarming than to walk into the courtyard when least expected. Their hands hold the tea; the RPKs and AK 47s are lying on the ground. Their mouths are stuffed with sweet Basbousa and soldiers hear something intimately familiar that makes the heart warm and blood cold: "Oh, mister, please, mister."

❖ Fighting a sob story: JAM, Americans, and the Shia people in the middle of the battle space

The simple question keeps recurring: "Why can't we take that guy down?"

"No."

"What about this guy?"

"No, that is not possible."

And a new reality dawns on soldiers as they look up in frustration and the soul fills with rage.

But the higher commissioned officers, who manage the fight against JAM, have a far more difficult job. They have to carry the burden of decision, adjudicate who and why, and answer the phone that keeps ringing while managing the fight on the ground. Oh, and in addition, go on charm offensives with a smile: Try to do reconstruction!

Yet, for enlisted men it would be blasphemous to commend a commissioned officer, in defiance of a long and proud enlisted tradition. For enlisted men to stop giving commissioned officers a hard time at every opportunity would be to forgo one of the inalienable rights of enlisted humanity. But credit has to go where it is due because officers set the limits and command how much charm soldiers on the ground could capture.

The soldiers on the ground should always keep trying to push the logic a little further because there are no gains without taking risks in this peculiar fight. But commissioned officers and senior enlisted men—the best of them—don't have that luxury. There is always some responsibility to worry about. And in a rare moment of respite, there is always a psychedelic-looking PowerPoint that someone higher wants them to finish! "Oh yeah, just so you know, the deadline is eighteen hundred; we need it in three hours."

The obligatory charm offensive on the ground is what truly tests the senior leaders' sanity. Granted, it is filled with happy moments for soldiers, as there is nothing like having a good laugh at the expense of senior officers, commissioned or non-commissioned. A commander (or his right-hand senior enlisted man) leads an urban battle all night and gets nearly blown up by RPG fire. He's OK with that. But the next day, coming out of a gathering of local Iraqi politicians, he seems about to have a brain aneurism, a near panic attack. He has to attend, he has no choice in the matter. He can only wish for a different kind of fight.

357

Of course, a bunch of soldiers noting his misery walk up with a cackle as he emerges from a group of big-wigs. It is one of those moments.

"Hey, sir, looks like you need to snort some Xanax, with Jack for a chaser, what's up."

"You know, sir, it might calm the soul."

He just shakes his head, grinding his teeth. Then he mumbles, "I have a better idea. Give me your Frag (hand grenade)," and starts laughing. But he could not finish his sentence, as the prominent men who were making his life miserable—some of them undeniably allied with JAM militants—now come up to him, thanking and shaking hands.

So the soldier asks in a whisper, "So uh, sir, tell me, should I frag *you,* or these guys who want to kiss you?"

Now he has the look—Just be quiet, you are pushing the logic, and I am hurting here, I'll come after you later! He just might, but the moment is too priceless: to forgo the moment is to be blasphemous, and enlisted soldiers are never blasphemous.

"SIR, you are like Snow White and the Seven Perverts, SIR, how many balls did you massage in there?"

The officer turns to the soldier in utter disbelief, and the soldier takes a few quick steps away to avoid a muscular response. The officer takes a deep breath, there will be no punching people in the face, just a big line of hands to shake and balls to massage, all with a big grin. And the soldiers are laughing in the background, thanking themselves that they are not commissioned officers. Yes, the best of our officers rarely gets a break; they get it from all sides.

He shakes hands with all the local bigwigs, wearing a pained smile. Some of the supporters and minions of the very man shaking his hand are the same guys who tried to blow him and his soldiers into pieces the night before. But that is now forgotten, this is a different reality, the warmhearted charm offensive.

The Nature of the Fight and Getting Around

The top Jaish al-Mahdi military and political leaders who run the show are students of Ayatollah Sadiq al-Sadr. They seem to genuinely believe all the anti-American, anti-Jewish, anti-Western, and anti-everything rhetoric, infused with unending volleys of absurd claims. They make no equivocation about their goals. They want power, control, to create a virtuous society—and if they cannot seduce people into the sob-story then they will instill it with guns. The firm believers don't lie, and they are genuine about their belief, self-righteous in its pursuit, but they are very—very—shady and crooked in its execution.

Most people on the ground may not buy into everything in the sob story, given the more immediate concerns, but many take these prominent nut-jobs seriously. Men, women, and children literally go and kiss their hands, the hands of clerics who are simultaneously political leaders and military leaders, clerics with money, resources and guns. Wait, aren't these guys gangsters with a good sob story?

Americans, waging a counterinsurgency as a foreign intervention force, portrayed as an occupying force, are stuck in the middle of a family struggle. It requires discriminating assiduously and diligently between the enemy and the innocent. For our higher leaders it requires adjudicating among the contending sides, identifying the worst among a whole lot of crooks, and relentlessly pursue the military leaders on the ground while safeguarding the innocent.

There is no denying—it requires soldiers on the ground to perform with the utmost restraint. The idea is not to walk around kicking in doors and blowing up buildings, but to do so only when necessary. Soldiers too are required to discriminate between targets: Retain the ability to turn silhouettes into people and people into silhouettes.

Once in a while, by sheer strategic coincidence, soldiers may get one of the diehard nut-job political-military leaders in the crosshairs—but they are unable to follow the heartfelt impulse (unless one is willing to take a risk and trust the guys standing side-by-side).

There are serious second- and third-order political effects to consider, including the ramifications it may have on the ground in local opinion.

It is actually easier to fight a powerful enemy because force alone can overpower them. An enemy with limited power who fights astutely requires soldiers and leaders on the ground to be even more astute.

"We will have more buildings in this neighborhood when we leave than when we came in." It was not a cliché by any means, as maddening as it sounded when soldiers first heard it. It is a strange reality for commanders who are taught and trained to fight an adversary in the field of battle: *buildings*! AYFS?

A grunt added with a chuckle, "Yeah, we are in a new fucking business, it's called the fucking construction business."

A full-spectrum counterinsurgency operation means that officers, leaders, and soldiers on the ground are on a slow moving train. Changes on the ground come slowly with the steady accretion of marginal gains over time. It's a long ride, and everyone is on it, taking slow deliberate steps in the neighborhood and listening to stories of people. Eating food in people's homes and in every possible restaurant is good counterinsurgent strategy, whenever soldiers are not crawling on garbage mounds or rooftops, chasing high value targets in TST missions or assisting stability operations or charm offensives. It provides far more than good food.

❖ The strong against the weak: The tactical reality of fighting JAM

It is actually easier to fight a powerful enemy than a weak enemy because force alone can overpower them. Facing an enemy with limited power who fights astutely requires soldiers and leaders on the ground to be even more astute. The weak are never weak if they are willing to take risks and learn from their mistakes. The strong are never strong if they are smug in their strength, not smart, and unwilling to take risks.

The objective of JAM fighters is not to defeat the Americans militarily because they cannot; they recognize the tactical reality. Their objective is simply to create enough harassment to keep the sob story alive. Maintain the pretense of resistance—because if the sob story falls short, they will be seen as just like everybody else in the government. Their existence loses its meaning.

With each and every direct fire engagement there are a few certainties that soldiers come to terms with and internalize into the system.

JAM fighters will engage American soldiers running through the alleys. But if the soldiers stay and fight on foot, then JAM fighters inevitably drop their weapons, go home, and wait to fight another day.[81]

If soldiers go into the neighborhood with full force, JAM will fight for a bit, get a great ass whipping, and then go home and declare victory. JAM will always talk high and mighty from the loudspeakers: They will defeat the soldiers and American blood will be running down the gutter. But nothing on the ground matches the braggadocio coming out of the muezzin. It is important not to underestimate the enemy; however, some JAM fighters will certainly put up a fight. But the moment they see the soldiers in full force, most of them quickly hang their weapons, grab a cigarette, and sit there waving, "Welcome, mister, welcome."

This is tactically sound. JAM members look like anyone else, and soldiers will shoot only if it's a fighter with a weapon, so—if they choose not to fight, they will live another day. If they live another day, they keep their firepower intact; they can control the population and keep them in line. That is ultimately far more important than shooting at some American grunts that have lost their way. It is their neighborhood, and they are fighting to stay. And that makes the whole enterprise a different one, as soldiers used to mention to one another: If you fight smart, you don't have to fight hard.

---

[81] Once they drop their weapons to run away, they are no longer enemy combatants (as they wear no uniform).

❖ The shady fight

JAM objectives on the ground—as for any astute insurgents—are not to defeat American soldiers in military engagements, but to define the battle space by choosing the nature of the engagement.

JAM by its very nature is firmly embedded in the society and is uniquely positioned for this. JAM insurgents, like any good insurgents, retain no front and no flanks; all they have is depth. That is their greatest tactical strength. While they are numerically, technically, and tactically inferior, they have compensating *depth*—that is, the subversive capability that comes from being embedded in the society. They have ubiquity and autonomy. Insurgents could be nowhere and everywhere; they have the ability to choose when and where the engagement takes place.

Each time insurgents initiate the engagement, they have defined the battle space and soldiers are now fighting on their terms. The asymmetry of power is thus drastically minimized. Yes, given their technological and tactical superiority, soldiers always prevail, but it is erroneous (and counterproductive) to say that this moment of victory is taking the fight to the enemy. It is not. Looking from the side of insurgents, it is the insurgents that have brought the fight to the soldiers and they have defined the battle space, and even claim victory.

If soldiers put their faith in fighting on foot, as opposed to inside a fortified metal tube, they will see this reality first hand. They can see it transpire from the insurgents' vantage point: Literally, they are watching it go down as *insurgents behind insurgents.*

Some soldiers went almost anywhere to ambush insurgents on their own terrain, at times even catching them in the act. It meant going into the mud, shit holes and even sewage-infested garbage dumps, far from the main roads in the middle of the night. Above all, it requires taking risks—not so much physical risks, but the willingness to make judgment calls and not hesitate at the point of decision.

❖ The convoy

Soldiers are waist deep in a garbage mound in the middle of a cold night, smack in the middle of a JAM stronghold, and they see an

American convoy coming. Most American convoys are not in the habit of wearing night vision. They believe in the delusion that if you fix enough high-powered halogen lamps and swing them around, you might actually notice the IEDs by the side of the road and the insurgents in hiding. A counterproductive notion and sitting and looking at it from the vantage point of insurgents, the sight is heartbreaking.

The lead vehicle in an American convoy is like a doublewide trailer covered top to bottom with Christmas lights, rolling down the street. It is always humorous watching it from some hole, but the sight also sinks the heart. One sees the illumination a mile away, as if advertising to the insurgents, "Get ready, nut-jobs, we are on the way."

Maybe insurgents are indeed waiting in ambush—but the soldiers hiding in their shit-hole actually feel scared of our *own side*. Because if the guy who swings the lights gets a glimpse of the soldiers in hiding, there is a good chance he would light them up with his big guns. It is best to duck, crawl further down and wait, mumbling profanities for motivation.

Having caught many insurgents in the act in the dead of night, soldiers appreciate the intricacy of a JAM ambush. As the convoys appear in the distance, if JAM has decided on an ambush that night, there will be some Iraqi Police vehicles buzzing around like a bunch of honeybees on a single bright yellow flower.

JAM-affiliated Iraqi police provide security for the insurgents, guard the IEDs nonchalantly, and warn of the approaching convoy. At the moment of ambush the police swiftly drive away, leaving their buddies on the ground to do the simple work: flick a switch and boom it goes.

After the boom, the soldiers emerge from their hole, taking a circuitous route so they don't get shot at by some excited soldiers sitting on a gun. They find a bunch of American troops—National Guardsmen, Army reservists, or soldiers tasked with convoy duty (i.e., "drive around until you get blown the hell up" duty)—trapped in their burning or blown-up vehicle.

Other soldiers on convoy duty keep the rest of the convoy moving, while the damaged vehicle is surrounded by couple of HUMMVs. Soldiers that emerged from the hole assist the soldiers in the convoy with the medical evacuation of dead, dying, and wounded American soldiers.

Iraqi police vehicles are now buzzing around the scene with their lights flashing. Of course, they profess ignorance of the attack, and soldiers, technically, cannot do anything because IP is part of the government; they are the law and order. The Iraqi Army post down the street looks quiet, with the Iraqi Army soldiers in their usual comportment: "No, we have no idea, no, mister, sorry." Of course, soldiers cannot do anything to them either; they are part of the government, wearing the body armor that we provide them, and as they see it, it is not their fight. The fight is between Americans and JAM, and as long as the Iraqi Army stays out of it, they can keep sleeping on the mattresses saying sorry. Not everyone in the police and army is militia, but those who are run the show in the neighborhood because they have top-cover to get away with it and keep the others under control. A nice modicum of understanding exists between all sides, and soldiers on the ground are smack in the middle.

For soldiers hiding in the garbage dump, there is a difficult point of decision. Seeing the Iraqi Police cars, they expect an ambush. But if they shoot the IP and there's no ambush and no IED, it is murder: Soldiers may end up on national TV in a jumpsuit and manacles. If they don't shoot, and the U.S. convoy gets ambushed, soldiers sitting in the hole have to live with the fact they could have prevented it. Soldiers need to be both innovative and astute in the decisions they make.

The Perfect Trap

But insurgents are also predictable. Fighting an enemy who possesses an overwhelming amount of firepower, they are not deterred. Again and again, they invite soldiers to walk into a decided trap. They invite them to use their overwhelming firepower in situations where, if soldiers shoot, a whole lot of civilians stand to die.

JAM clearly understands the limits of overwhelming force. They know intimately that Americans are circumscribed by strict rules of engagement that prevent its use, unless it is absolutely necessary. Insurgents understand that if Americans actually resort to using their overwhelming force—say, bringing down a building with everyone inside—it inevitably ends up killing or injuring civilians in the neighborhood and it goes to reify the insurgent control on the ground and the broader sob story. The people in the neighborhood are pawns and puppets in the drama. The more deaths of the innocent at the hands of Americans, and the more destruction they can bring on their own people, it perpetuates the sob story as long as they can point the blame at the American soldiers. Insurgent tactics on the ground are always predictable on this count.

When people become an integral part of the battle space, the way one employs combat power must alter drastically. The mortar and sniper attacks and even ambushes of American soldiers are deliberately planned and executed, often in densely populated areas. Soldiers and leaders on the ground (and leaders higher) try to err on the side of soldiers taking more risks, keeping the idea of civilian safety paramount. That is the singular genius of our counterinsurgency strategy, as painful as it for grunts on the ground.

In a long-lasting direct fire engagement, some Apache crews made sure a number of armed insurgents lived a lifetime in a second. The Apaches were then very quickly formally disengaged: They must not use their 30mm cannons against the men assisting the wounded insurgents because the insurgents helping the wounded are no longer armed!

The insurgents watch the Apache video clips on the Internet, and they learn from them. They learn to throw their weapons in the gutter when they run to their wounded buddies, and as they are no longer technically armed, the rules of engagement have changed accordingly. Of course, it is the dead of night in a known enemy stronghold, following a long-lasting direct fire engagement. No civilian would run into the middle of a firefight to help the insurgents. But they are no longer armed and, therefore, they instantly become civilians and illegitimate targets.[82] Restrained use of force thus has lasting second- and third-order effects in a counterinsurgency centered on a population.

Soldiers and leaders on the ground in a counterinsurgency need to be astute in determining what information to send higher, so as to not make higher the prisoners of information. When the reality on the ground is incongruent with the higher reality, controlling the information helps to control the situation on the ground better, gives you tactical autonomy on the ground. Once committed, it is imperative to stay committed. Should the soldiers call off the birds (keeping in mind that Apaches have cameras) and finish what was started?

---

[82] This, of course, is one function of a uniform—to create a consistent identity of combatants. And it is another reason why combatants captured out of uniform forfeit POW status under the Geneva Conventions.

17

FIGHTING JAM: POLITICS, STRATEGY, TACTICS

> The movement started with a sound as soft as silk, then
> exploded into the rumble of thunder. That night, at the
> Café of the Emirs. . .
>
> —*Arabian Nights and Days*

J AM fighters callously use civilians as shields and not just for tactical purposes. It also has a wider impact. They do so as a means to pierce the complacent idea of deterrence that goes along with overwhelming force. In spite of vast asymmetries of power, deterrence turns out to be based on a false assumption when fighting an enemy that uses the innocent as part of the military engagement.

Empty Drum: Deterrence in COIN

Deterrence is based on the assumption of *fear* and *responsibility*—the assumption that the enemy is fearful of losing and feels responsible about inflicting harm to their own side.

But if the enemy has little or nothing to lose and is holding their own people hostage with guns in hand, there is little to fear and no sense of responsibility. Piercing the complacent assumptions of deterrence becomes an end in itself for insurgents.

So, soldiers find themselves in difficult traps set by JAM fighters taking refuge among civilians. A column of Strykers rolling down the main avenue of approach is so powerful that no tank company in the world would engage them. If the insurgents felt responsible for their own people's safety, they would blanch at the thought of unleashing that fire power. In fact, the insurgents, armed with RPGs, improvised explosives, and AK-47s, manage to flank them constantly as they move down the street, becoming a possibly lethal nuisance. They know they have impunity: There are buildings stacked along the route like cinder blocks. The Americans will sacrifice the advantage of deterrence to avoid endangering a densely populated neighborhood—and thus playing into the hands of ideologues, strengthening their sob story by inflicting damage on civilians.

In truth, any civilian who wakes up to a half-destroyed house or with family members killed will only remember the rumble of the American tank and its lethal boom, never noticing the insurgents that kept flanking them down the street. *It is one hell of a trap.*

❖ Lost in the labyrinth again

Some soldiers were once again wandering through labyrinthine alleyways of a densely populated Shia neighborhood in the middle of the night. Walking through this neighborhood became standard procedure, though not always with permission. Soldiers might take the wrong turn, as they sometimes should, in order to explore the labyrinth.

A column of tanks was rolling down the street, bristling with firepower. One soldier joked, "Watch, just watch, there will be *one* burst of fire—and everyone will stop." He mimicked the inevitable distress call: "Yeah, roger, we are in contact, one MAM (military age male) with AK; we are standing by with our big guns, please advise what we should do."

And that's just how it worked out, though there's no knowing about the actual distress call. The tank column stopped. You see the turrets move up, down, sideways, and slowly trundle down again. The soldiers on foot, following a couple of blocks behind the insurgents, have to empathize with the colleagues stuck in a tank. To be shot at, *and unable to respond*, is the most counter-intuitive challenge a soldier can face. Not every day is so funny.

The tankers were restrained by the consideration that a single man with an AK did not justify firing a 105mm explosive. A cold beer for the tankers because soldiers on foot were also hoping with all sincerity that the tankers would not shoot: "If that guy shoots, we will be toast." Everyone shakes their heads and starts laughing, mumbling profanities, hiding in an alley, stuck in a situation they had walked themselves into. "Jesus, oh mother fucking Christ, man, we will be in fucking pieces."

Those were a long few seconds.

Another night in the winding alleyways, another wrong turn, another one-sided firefight. Insurgents keep flanking these trundling hunks of metal with moving turrets that stay quiet. It takes a better sort of soldier to have all that fire power and not use it, and some soldiers are alive because of their restraint: A paranoid bunch would have leveled the whole place, including the soldiers on foot.

But the soldiers on foot have to cross the alley and turn into the street—and you knew that sooner or later it would come to this. They are now looking straight at the turret, aimed directly at them. In the night vision, the guy on the turret will see only a distant glimmer of armed silhouettes and will have difficulty adjudicating between friends and enemies. The only word that comes to mind is "Oh SHIT."

One could feel the heart sink. The leader pushes the guys back into the alley with a holler, "Get the fuck back," and just as they move into the alley the M242 Bushmaster 25mm cannons go off in bursts of three. Dum-dum-dum and another burst, dum-dum-dum. Soldiers hear the explosions straight down the street, but far off: Only a couple landed nearby, making the ears ring momentarily. "Damn that was close!"—but luckily they were only 25mm cannons, thank the tankers, someone was thinking straight. Anything bigger would have meant lots of phone calls.

Just then comes another burst of insurgent automatic fire. One of the leaders on the ground clenches his left fist and yells the way only he could yell, a trademark yell that is as legendary as the man himself because it comes from the depth of his being: "Goddamn this stupid shit, fuuuuuck." He calls one of his friends in a nearby alley and gives a warning, informs him where he and his colleagues will be and decides as one should decide.

Insurgents, for all their innovation are also predictable, soldiers learn. Insurgents will keep flanking the armored vehicles along the main avenue of approach, always running from one house to the other and hiding next to them. The armored column has to keep to the main street, so insurgents move from one city block to the other, staying next to cinderblock houses so the tankers cannot shoot. The tank guns are literally too big and too powerful. If insurgents get to a good vantage point they may fire off couple of RPGs (though more often than not they will miss). If they have some IEDs set up further down, this is the time for them. They will not miss. Walking an armored column into the IEDs is also an insurgent trademark. It is easy because the main roads are few—block a couple of roads, keep flanking, they will not get shot at, roll the tankers straight into the trap.

Being insurgents behind insurgents, soldiers see this clearly. So now the soldiers run a couple of blocks deeper, hang a deep left, and run through the alleys, far from the tanks and their moving turrets but parallel to them. They move into the same alley that insurgents are firing from, but a block or two farther ahead. The insurgents are now relocating as the vehicles come down the main road: half a dozen of them bebop down the street with their gear, completely confident and casual in their walk. They are about to settle in somewhere so as to flank again. Yes, they had the flank—but soldiers were also flanking them, and the insurgents walked into bristling bursts of automatic weapons fire.

The next block over, in the main street, the vehicles have now stopped, their turrets moving about like blind giants. They hear the gunfire, lots of it, but it is not directed at them, and they cannot see what's going on behind the cinderblock houses.

By this time, soldiers hope, someone would have informed the tankers (by way of higher) of the presence of soldiers on foot in their vicinity. But it is best *not to assume*: Assumptions in combat remain the mother of all fuck-ups. That's straight from the holy books of warfare—at least, everyone on the ground believes it religiously. So it's wisest to run deep into the alleyways, back into the labyrinth, and then cut across, it's the safest bet, no one wants to be at the receiving end of 25mm cannon fire.

But just then, another little twist rides into the riddle.

❖ To Serve and Protect: Police on the scene

Is it an opportunity or a liability? A brand new blue and white Iraqi Police land cruiser rolls up with six Iraqi police officers, blue and red lights lighting up the night, to the place where the insurgents are lying lifeless. The police vehicle gives them legal authority, they are the law and order, the flashing red lights scream their immunity: don't shoot, we are the police.

But the fact is that insurgents kept flanking because they kept getting cover from the police, as well as constant phone calls informing them of the movement of the convoy in the main avenue of approach. Insurgents do not need Apache helicopters for top cover when they have top cover on the ground from the police.

It is yet another point of decision in this counterinsurgency. Should the soldiers follow the letter, the rulebook, and walk away, and let the militia collect their friends under the cover of police immunity? They are the law and order; we have armed and trained them "to serve and protect."

Or should the soldiers follow their professional impulse? After all, it is a known enemy strongpoint. The police arrive immediately, as always, because they know exactly where to find them, having assisted their friends to flank the American armored column.

What if the soldiers decided to light up the six police officers, throw a Thermite incendiary grenade to make the land cruiser turn into a burning hunk of metal, slowly lighting up the entire block in bright yellow flames that would sparkle the eyes and slowly warm the heart? The real question is this: At this specific point in time, do these police officers constitute a target on the ground that fulfills everyone's moral, political, and legalistic requirements?

Soldiers eventually cut through and run down, straight into the labyrinth and back out to the other side, taking heavy deliberate steps, hiding their concerns in their rightful place with their usual laughs and cackles. They run back passed the main avenue of approach just as the last of the American armored vehicles are slowly beginning to move.

In the armored column, the soldiers had no idea that some other soldiers were now sitting behind a mound of garbage just next to them, replacing the tobacco in their cheeks for inspiration, waiting for them to move out. The sight through the NODs seems poignant. Every soldier takes risks—but to have all that fire power and not be able to use it, having decided against using it, while sitting inside a barely maneuverable heavy chunk of metal, that is perhaps the worst situation as soldiers.

The tankers try to adjudicate between the enemy and the innocent as best as they can, though it does not always work in textbook fashion. It is war, people die. But this is certainly a harder, more disciplined way to fight, when the battle is centered on a population.

Desperate Love Story

Insurgents using civilians as a shield happens so often, and so deliberately, it drives soldiers on the ground nearly insane.

Three insurgents, who were firing rapid bursts only moments ago, are now sprinting at top speed with weapons in hand. They were too quick for soldiers to get a clean shot, running right next to a corner store with people huddling inside looking out, and they quickly disappear around the corner into the alley. It is amazing how fast some of these guys could run, with their long waving jalabiyas flapping around them.

The alley is dark and quiet, with a few green infrared illuminations oozing out of cracks in the cinder block houses. Soldiers have a good guess about which house the insurgents ran into, but no one has the authority to call in an air strike in this densely populated neighborhood just because three people who were trying to kill the soldiers moments ago might be hiding somewhere. It would be disproportionate since the soldiers' lives are not in danger. As far as the soldiers are concerned, it is not even an option: Higher will never authorize it.

So, some soldiers are running full speed, headlong through the door and into the hallway and on to the living room, swiftly clearing the house. No weapons are inside. It feels retarded to run toward the enemy's strongpoint as if nothing else mattered, but following through at times is critical.

In the living room are two women, two kids, and five men standing wide-eyed, everyone deathly silent. Soldiers knew instinctively that they had arrived on the heels of insurgents, and three of the five men must be the insurgents—but how can you know? Everyone looks the same: fearful, even jittery. No one is sweating, everyone is huddled together; everyone is panting, with eyes fixed on the soldiers standing in front of them. One woman was holding to the two kids for dear life, shivering and shaking in a way that only mothers do.

A soldier just shook his head and yelled, almost to himself, "Goddamn man, goddamn this shit!"

Of course, there are no insurgents in the house, it is all one family. But the children and the mother, and some of the men, have those apprehensive eyes soldiers have seen before. The same eyes people have when they walk passed a dead guy by the side of the road, taking quick steps, desperately trying to mask the deeply felt fear. It is fear of the *insurgents*, not the soldiers. The insurgents have again inserted their battle into people's lives.

"OK, this shit will not be pretty. PUC them [tie their hands with plastic zip ties], everyone, every fucking one of them, men, women, and children."

Life is never fair, especially in a war, and life sometimes is very unpleasant.

Obviously it starts with the men, everyone obeys and complies, but as it gets to the women, some men start to object and then all of them, and as it got to the children, all the men and women are now begging, and in that begging was truly a scream.

There is no time to isolate the family in separate rooms and conduct extensive tactical questioning. Quick decisions have to be made, the night has only begun, and soldiers will be crawling around in this snake farm for a long while. Three of the guys could be insurgent rattlesnakes. Who it could be is felt instinctively, from watching the men's behavior in just those few minutes. But that cannot be enough, there has to be certitude, and only one person could give that answer. The one in this room who is the most fearful *and* the most fearless.

The mother of the children is trying to hold her children in a painful posture with her zip-tied hands. Her hands are tied at the wrist, and the children are next to her. All she wants to do is to hold onto them but she cannot. The leader on the ground simply said, "Hey, keep an eye on the guys," and he got hold of the two kids by their collars—a boy about six and a girl about seven—and started moving them to the adjacent room, where he kicked the door in (the room was already cleared) and threw the children inside vigorously, while keeping his eyes on the men and women.

A couple of the men at first, then all of them started begging. One woman just stood petrified, frozen in place, and the mother was simply frantic. She wanted to scream but in her deeply felt anguish she could not. With a contorted expression on her face, screaming black eyes and hair that looked like static electricity shot through her, she tried to follow the soldier and the kids.

Having put the kids in the room, the soldier grabbed the mother, his left hand on her neck while the right grabbed the zip ties on her wrists, and took her to the room with the kids, and closed the door while the men made pleading noises outside.

"SHUT THE FUCK UP!"

The soldier made the wide-eyed, moaning and terrified children sit on the bed. He grabbed a blanket, throwing it over their heads. The children are so scared that the blanket covering them keeps shaking in a steady rhythm. The soldier grabbed both hands of the mother, pulled her toward him and took out his 9mm and pointed it toward the shaking blanket, always looking at her pained face.

The soldier needed only one answer from the mother to know whether the instinctive and logical deduction was correct. Are the three men in the living room the three men that need to be sent higher? So there is only one question and it is short and to the point, in his slow voice.

"It is the three men in the corner, yes?"

She nodded vigorously, "Yes, yes," and even louder, "Yes, yes!"

The soldier moved his face very close to her face as he pushed the 9MM toward the blanket and cocked it, as a round dropped to the ground, and asked again while the mother's wide screaming eyes see only the shivering blanket. "Are you sure, the three men in the corner?"

Her *Yes* was unequivocal, so pained and anguished it hung there in the room for a while.

The soldier put his 9mm back in his holster and pulled out his knife simultaneously as he pulled off the shaking blanket and cut the plastic zip ties off the delicate hands of the two children. But the children sit still, as if nothing has changed, staring straight at their mother. The soldier did not exist in their minds and all they wanted was to be close to their mother. The soldier then took the mother's hands and cut her zip-tied wrists free.

In a second, she flew to her two children, hands flailing, and grabbed them by their chests, her arms around the kids. She held them so tight, with all the force she could muster, it was almost as if the kids might not be able to breathe: The two kids might end up choking because her grip was so strong. As soon as she got hold of her children, she let out a deep sigh, a deep cry, and fell to the ground sobbing, holding the children even closer and so tight as if it's the last time she would ever get to do it in her life. The scared children, whose world seemed to have stopped for a while, too terrified to make a noise, come instantly back to life. They start crying, shaking and shivering as their clothes were fast getting wet. The soft sobs of children have never sounded more haunting. The children will always remember that night, they will carry this night with them all their lives and to the grave, it is what it is. Life is certainly never fair, it is always better for some than for others.

The soldier opened the door and walked to the living room, and now he could feel all the devils inside him crackling and cackling. He looked at the standing men and it was as if the enemy and the innocent have been apparent all along.

He cut free the hands of the woman, standing like a lifeless silhouette, a petrified mannequin of fear. Even now she is still speechless and motionless. Every voice, every gesture only made her flinch, not move or speak: The total terror of the innocent, some soldiers have seen it too often. Then he cut loose the two innocent men. He gestured to all of them to move to the other room. They ran, almost flew—except the lone mannequin, the woman. She may be the wife of one of the men, or the mother's sister; she is still standing motionless with her wide eyes.

"Goddamn woman, just get out of the fucking way."

She is still standing there.

The soldier moves close to her and gestured toward the room where everyone else has fled to, but she is still motionless and speechless. Only her wide eyes and fluttering eyelids show she is not a mannequin but a living breathing woman, whose name the soldier does not know. One of the men has realized that she is still standing in the middle of the living room, and he is peering in, fearful to enter, just standing there staring and pleading.

The soldier shakes his head, "Oh man." Through clenched teeth: "what the fuck, this stupid shit!" There is so little time for this nonsense, but life is rarely the way one wants it in a counterinsurgency.

The soldier snaps his fingers and tells the two soldiers with him to keep an eye on the three rattlesnakes, who are standing with wide pleading eyes.

The soldier moves closer to her. Slowly and deliberately he gestures again, asking her to move to the room. She stands speechless and motionless, still utterly terrified. There is no telling how terrified people will react. Sometimes people completely freak out, which is dangerous for everyone. So he grabs her right wrist with his right hand and, with his left hand on her back, turns her toward the other room. One could see her flinch, her body going into spasms. His left hand could feel every single muscle in her back twitching. The fingers he held in his right hand were shaking hard. He walked her to the room, asked the man to take her inside and closed the door behind her. That room was now a family huddle, filled with gasps, sobs and involuntary shrieks of the innocent, still uncertain whether they will live or not.

It is understandable, outside you can hear explosions, countless rounds flying around.

Now the soldier closed the door to the room and turned around to stare at the three rattlesnakes still standing in the living room, his teeth grinding and hands clenched—fighting all the devils that crawled under his skin, devils that jeered at him, cackling and laughing. The three rattlesnakes were a strange sight, standing still. Their desperate eyes stared passed the soldier and into a distant empty space. The soldier walked to the one in the corner, grabbed his delicate neck with his left hand and stared at his eyes, and shoved him onto the wall with all his strength as his clenched right fist was shaking. He cocked his head sideways and grunted loud, shaking his head, and threw him across the floor with a solid swift kick across his chest as the rattlesnake dropped to the ground.

Then he pulled him up, "Get up mother fucker," and grabbed his neck with the left, shoved him to the wall and followed up with one full bear-knuckled punch and let him drop to the ground, his face now covered in blood. And now the soldier was about to follow the worst of his human impulses and land a square kick, but found he could not move. Two of his friends, one of them twice his size, were holding onto the back of his belt. The big one simply said, in his unperturbed voice, "What happened, I thought you were a goddamn vegetarian?"

The soldier swung around, with his cackling devils stuck in his bloodshot eyes and his shaking right fist, and stood staring at his colleague holding his belt. Saving colleagues and even superiors from themselves can be difficult, but that's why one always needs good men side by side.

He suddenly smiled as if he had just been offered a drink and replied in his normal voice, "Yeah, I am a goddamn vegetarian," and they all start laughing.

"Let's take them to the street; we need to find their weapons."

The look of the rattlesnakes was different now. There were no equivocations, only full agreement and the usual phrase one hears when they realize that their gig is up: "Please, mister, please, mister."

Of course, they are now looking for mercy, never mind that they tried to kill the same soldiers only moments before. Or that they just put an entire innocent family in danger with callous disregard. They simply could because they have the guns and because it's a very poor family, like many others in this neighborhood. The front door to the house was flimsy and the lock was so fragile, with one good push it opened and they ran inside.

The rattlesnakes had missed that little detail in their frantic moment. If you kick in a door, the lock is broken, the door is partly open—and those details are apparent even in the green haze of night vision, when the infrared glow from the house just oozes out. Paying attention to detail is why soldiers get paid the big bucks, $250 a month of hazardous duty pay (while their better civilian counterparts make more than that each day for living in Washington DC). So soldiers walk in and follow through. Following through at the point of decision at times is critical; it can mean everything on the ground.

Grabbing all three of the rattlesnakes by the neck and taking them downstairs, one encounters the ever reliable ayatollahs, Baqir al-Sadr and Sadiq al-Sadr, looking down from the wall. One wants to ask them, would you approve of this course of action? And would you approve of these AK-wielding virtue-enforcers seeking refuge amid children? Alas, these two ayatollahs lived a lifetime in a second a long time ago; Ayatollah Sistani, too, has the same unperturbed cosmic gaze from the wall.

Slowly moving outside, soldiers found near the gutter the weapons the rattlesnakes had thrown away in their mad dash. "Mister, please, please," that repentant voice again, nearly everyone becomes a poignant pathetic figure when he comes to terms with the immediate reality, as if a light bulb went on in the brain. The radio crackled and a voice from higher came through the static, "Hey, did you have any luck in the house?"

Soldiers face another paradox, the same one again and again on the ground in a counterinsurgency, if their primary job is to chase nut-jobs.

Should the soldiers take the three men with their weapons, write a novel-length report, and throw them in detention, only to see them released after a while? If they are released (and sooner or later it is bound to happen), they *know* who ratted them out: the mother who told the truth because she desperately loves her children. And they will kill her to get even, as so many nut-jobs have done.

The radio again: "This is six, did you have any luck over?"

So the soldiers wonder, should they answer with a short and simple radio call, "Negative six, it's a dry hole, we are moving to house number nine in the GRG, how copy over."

"That's a good copy, go ahead move to nine on the GRG, over."

Got it boss, we are at the door, two minutes Turkish, two minutes.

The same question: Are these three men, who tried to kill the soldiers, who nearly got an innocent family killed, legitimate targets on the ground that fulfill everyone's legal, moral, and political sensibilities?

The Sweet Nexus: Politics and Violence

Behind an insurgency is a political organization, including leaders who have political immunity. The counterinsurgency leaders cannot simply throw them behind bars. There are laws to abide by and political realities to be taken into account.

Soldiers, of course, cannot think of inflicting harm on the political leaders, given that they are never armed and, therefore, will never constitute a direct threat. Moreover, the American approach requires very diligent battlefield intelligence-gathering and evidence in order to take an insurgent into custody. The system prevents many innocent Iraqis from being thrown in jail. If an innocent person has been arrested, after his release he can be paid a daily stipend for time spent in American custody. This is a nearly revolutionary change in approach from only three years earlier—but that bit of news has not made an impression outside Iraq, in the scramble for metaphors in the news.

At the same time, this puts enormous requirements on soldiers and leaders on the ground. It turns soldiers into police detectives. And it makes capturing insurgents a soul-crushing affair. Because the final battle with insurgents is fought in the process of trying to put them into custody at the detention center. If soldiers' intelligence and evidence does not meet the standards, procedures reign supreme. Even the best-known militants sometimes get away because of political intervention on our own side, especially if soldiers have captured combatant leaders. The higher the value of the individual combatant, the trickier it gets.

❖ The Golden Ladder: The political pardon

It was one of those nights. As soldiers took off their gear, one leader slowly laid his weapon carefully on the ground and then grabbed a chair by its back. Yelling his trademark shriek, "Goddamn this shit, if we have this shit-bag, then we need to go nail him, fuuuck." He picked up the chair and swung it down, smacking it on the ground full force and shattering it into a million tiny pieces.

The "shit-bag" in question was a very, very high value individual, so high that Prime Minister Maliki had to approve of this mission. Only then he of course, cancelled it at the last minute—or so the word came down from higher. This was a time (middle of spring 2007) when Prime Minister Maliki was still in bed with the Sadrists, and he owed his position partly to them.

Every politician has some crooked cronies they want to take care of; this is not something unique to Iraq or the Iraqi prime minister. But this JAM HVI was practically in the bag, and to let him go because of political meddling is simply maddening. But it is also the nature of fighting a political-military organization: Tactical decisions have far-reaching political ramifications. The hardest challenge of all may be the delicate decisions and compromises that our higher commissioned officers have to make. Soldiers are fully aware of these responsibilities and challenges of higher leaders, but they, of course, always retain their inalienable right to break a thing or two, punch the walls, scream and unleash profanities, for simple purposes of motivation.

But every high value individual, no matter how valuable, and every crook, no matter how close to politicians—everyone sooner or later goes home, visits family members in the neighborhood, friends, mistresses, even does grocery shopping. And some apparently forget about their delicate situation, possibly enamored of their own power. As some soldiers always used to say, "Every man takes a shower like everybody else, fucking naked, but some forget, and they just need to be reminded of it."

When is a matter of intelligence gathering: Perhaps a wronged man or woman or a family member wanting to avenge a death or just confounding some minor personal grievance with righteous vengeance. If the soldiers have done their work well, a bit of prodding, encouragement, or guidance will find the whereabouts using a cell phone. It is never easy, but never impossible.

381

Hypothetically speaking, if by sheer luck, or due to a simple strategic coincidence, a handful of soldiers should run into one of the very high value individuals in the street, should they call higher, knowing their choices are limited? Should they just take him to custody, knowing that he will swiftly be released anyway? Should the soldiers point at the golden ladder that they could make sure to appear to the slightly inebriated big-shot in the back seat—and to the very sober driver and the sidekick in the front passenger seat, who seem to recognize the bleak reality far better?

After all the hard and quiet work behind the scenes, is this, in fact, a target on the ground that fulfills all the moral, political, and legalistic impulses of everyone concerned?

❖ **The reality of JAM control: The sob story on the ground**

It is by combining their political and military strength with an over-arching narrative that JAM becomes formidable and harder to fight. They astutely, deliberately, and callously hold the people hostage to their sob story, seducing or forcing them to cooperate. That is a somber reality soldiers learned when JAM members overplayed their hand.

The advantage of being a political-military organization is that, in neighborhoods where JAM has control, it is total: Everyone toes the line. Some are complicit and some have no choice. But JAM also has a weakness. In the quiet whispers of people, the underlying sinister reality comes to light.

The many believers and leaders who perpetuate the idealized sob story may even be well-intentioned, but those intentions don't always translate well on the ground when men with guns try to instill it. Well-intentioned men with self-righteous convictions have far more capacity to inflict misery than imperfect men ever could.

Soldiers learn about this reality from Iraqis themselves, slowly. People on the receiving end are stuck in a self-serving riddle with armed men, with no options except to complain. But complaints of people can also be turned into tactical realities by good soldiers who listen and think, always the best way to out-smart the enemy.

382

Yes, a lot of people support JAM, but it is not so much JAM itself as the underlying Sadrist idea that attracts them. Most Shia people have grown up listening to the Sadrist story. They elected a lot of Sadrists into the parliament and are dependent on the services they now provide. JAM members and affiliates also control the black market activities, electricity distribution, the generators, the gasoline distribution racket, the extortion racket that shop owners are subjected to, and all the other shady realities of the neighborhood. Astute criminals quickly bought into the JAM franchise because they can get away with murder with impunity. The infiltrated Sadrists in the Iraqi Army and Iraqi Police have law and order on their side. People are smack in the middle, and it is a genius way to keep them in line and retain control. On the one hand, people are dependent on the services and seduced by the sob story. On the other hand, men with guns on the ground keep opponents and would-be opponents in line.

JAM, as part of the Sadrist movement, started off with the idea of "power to the people"—but as they got closer to the idea of *power*, the *people* seemed to be dropped from the program. If getting power requires silencing their critics and forcing people to be believers at gunpoint, they will do so, and the JAM foot soldiers always, always overplay their hand. In that moment is an opportunity for counterinsurgents.

As soldiers learned fighting the Salafist nut-jobs, sometimes the best way to take the fight to the insurgents is to be *insurgents behind insurgents*—fight them from the margins. Be subtle, be quiet, but be relentless and effective.

Anguished Whispers: Insurgents Behind Insurgents

The ability to *listen,* for soldiers, is far more useful in a counterinsurgency than the ability to speak—listen hard enough to hear the anguished whispers of the dead in the quiet stories of the living.

Soldiers walking into a neighborhood could just bebop down the road, hand out leaflets and make promises, proclaiming their noble intentions. But the primary job of frontline infantrymen is not to hand out leaflets, blankets, and food packets, though it is sometimes necessary. The primary job is to go after the worst of the nut-jobs. Professing noble intentions does not usually get soldiers closer to the objective of catching the nut-jobs; only listening and actions do.

Iraqis seem rather inured to the self-professed good faith of men with guns, having heard it all too often from ideologues and tyrants—and let us not forget the many foreign armies that have marched through region, often professing good will. In the end, listening more and talking less yields far more valuable tactical information, and may win some minds if not hearts. (There is never any telling which way the heart will go, as deployed soldiers learn all too clearly.)

Soldiers who had served in Salafist neighborhoods and listened to their stories quickly recognized the similarities in a JAM neighborhood. The difference was a matter of degree: Given the totality of JAM control, people told their stories in very hushed tones. The subversive nature of control was pervasive. People had internalized it, come to terms with it, and everyone played a part maintaining it. But not everyone wants to go along when nut-jobs overplay their hand and people get punched in the face, abused, raped, and killed. People are complicit only because they are fearful and have little choice.

But there was also the English teacher, who would call soldiers on their cell phones (and who was especially interested in the lanky soldier); and many university students, male and female, who would call or send SMS messages and emails to soldiers. The Iraqi buck sergeant and his friends would occasionally call or send an email from the technical school or send SMS messages from the swanky new cell phone that soldiers bought him. And there was the patriarch: Soldiers would call and he would answer in his gruff voice, "Ahhhlooo," and say immediately, "Oh, Hello, hello," when he recognized the soldier on the phone. The list kept growing, as did the number of phone contacts, with an unavoidable emphasis on professionals and the wealthy and educated girls—people who shared some points of reference with soldiers. They were people who privately detested the JAM but stayed quiet about it.

And then there are the dead. Death of the innocent and the not-so-innocent is never random, always deliberate. Tracing their footsteps, soldiers can hear the whispers of the dead in the stories of the living, learn who was responsible and how they are connected. The family members and loved ones speak of the anguish, the pain, the feeling of being utterly powerless with no sense of security, of being afraid and never quite sure why. The themes soon form a consistent pattern.

❖ Predictable Pricks: JAM overreaches itself

> I saw the lady of the house—I take refuge in God from
> the violence of beauty when it dominates. . .

—Arabian Nights and Days

Then there are the gangsters who pretend to be part of JAM. They hand over a portion of the loot to JAM as they intimidate, kill, and engage in extortion to maintain the monopoly on their protection racket. They have firm control. Men and women who collaborate with Americans, who assist in going after JAM, and anyone who signs a sworn statement to help put JAM members in jail (which American lawyer came up with that brilliant idea?)—their days are surely numbered, and they better start counting.

And there is the sectarian killing of Sunnis. The nationalistic unifying rhetoric of JAM claims that they are building bridges of love to the Sunnis, Iraqis are one people, a people of peace. Some American commentators always get excited, even take these unifying themes seriously and call them nationalistic. Soldiers doubt whether Iraqi Sunnis (or even the Shia) buy it at all. The ones we met did not; their sectarian agenda was transparently obvious—sectarian killings, cleansing neighborhoods of Sunni people, and giving their houses to JAM loyalists.

And we heard a consistent theme from women, especially girls from educated and affluent families in the neighborhood. What is it with some (not all) Muslim men who find it so important to enforce modesty and virtues on women the moment they get their hands on an AK-47? What makes them confound their manhood with an AK? Is it the knowledge that they have coercive authority and impunity that makes them confound lascivious impulses with religious mores?

Sunni radical Islamists and Shia radical Islamists have their own unique stories and histories. But they are as similar as Tweedledee and Tweedledum in their treatment of their own women—the forced anonymity, and the idea that they have a god-given right to enforce modesty of women in the streets. The difference is a matter of degree but such differences do matter. The Taliban in Afghanistan and Pakistan will blow up schools to prevent women from getting an education, even throw acid in young schoolgirls' faces; in Saudi Arabia, driving is banned for women, though education itself is not; the Salafists in Iraq resorted to tactics that bordered on sheer lunacy. But the Shia—including JAM—would allow women go to school and get educated while retaining the right to enforce modesty on the streets they control.

The tactical advantage for soldiers in JAM neighborhoods arose from this simple fact: When young idiots with guns can enforce virtue with impunity, they overplay their hand and become the worst of human beings. They grope, abuse, rape, and kill, knowing they can get away with it and even feeling righteous about it if it is sanctioned by some cleric. The cleric certainly would not condone the excesses, but that subtlety is lost on the zealous enforcers. If you talk to students at prominent Iraqi universities, they will provide numbers, names, and places of what has happened to whom, including names of the girls that resisted and were eventually raped and killed by JAM or other virtue enforcers. It only takes listening carefully—and knowing when to talk and how.

How can robbing women of choice (or worse) be a path to the highest form of female virtue? Soldiers talked to many headstrong Arab women, devout Muslims who take their virtue seriously. Enforcement is not, in the end, about virtue and modesty. It is about keeping women in a subordinate position.

In JAM-controlled neighborhoods, just as in Salafist enclaves, this remains an invisible reality women have to navigate. The level of JAM enforcement varies from neighborhood to neighborhood, depending on the level of overall control and the rabidity of the enforcers. But when there is virtue enforcement, self-righteous abuses become rampant. For soldiers with some experience, it only required a little tact and simple human decency to turn those stories into effective tactical realities.

Soldiers became dear friends with the Iraqi lady doctor who runs the maternity ward. She was five feet two inches, a miniature woman who looked like a pear on fire, and she called everybody militia, including the soldiers—the "American militia"—and she always laid it down as it was. She disliked and generally despised everyone with a gun and cared only for her nurses and medical colleagues. As long as she feels soldiers have some credibility on the ground, that soldiers recognize the greater risks she has to take, she will be willing to provide information about her patients and employees. She has access to their papers, copies of ID cards, addresses, family members. And she is pissed-off because injustice is injustice. She hates the JAM guys and especially the security guards that protect the hospital. As a proud (if non-practicing) Shia, she is angry also about Sunnis being refused treatment or even killed by the militia boys that run hospital security. She cannot do much about it. Like most doctors, she is fearful of being kidnapped, as a target for ransom. Other doctors have been kidnapped with the collusion of the militias and criminals that have infiltrated hospital security.

The resident physician in another little hospital hates the JAM with all his might, after being punched in the face by the hospital security, part of the local JAM militia. So he will gladly give the information—on the condition, of course, that soldiers never acknowledge his presence and do not come by his house unless they go to all the other houses too. Soldiers just have to recognize that everyone has to live. Soldiers have to be careful not to mistake people's personal riddles for tactical realities.

Soldiers also become friends with the people who run the local clinic (everyone who needs stitches goes to the local clinic), under the aegis of the Sadrist Ayatollahs who still decorate the wall. The

Sadrists—given their complex distribution system and people skimming off the top—in fact cannot provide some items as well as they should. Soldiers, however, might be able to acquire painkillers to supply to the nurses (men and women) who are always in need of such things.

They can always obtain some medicine through channels—write the novel, do the mountains of paperwork, and wait around scratching their balls for five months. But on the ground time is of the essence. They just have to buy some damn medicine wherever they can—or, maybe, recognize that there are loads of it going unused in the medic tent. If soldiers could just manage to get a lot of medicine (steal it from the medic tent, hypothetically speaking), and take it to the nurses in the clinic, they would practically *own* the damn clinic. But nothing is ever easy.

❖ Victims of violence on center stage

Real life is never like Hollywood movies, where victims and random civilians can become, overnight, relentless fighters for justice. In the movies, a victim might stare straight at the perpetrators and seek justice. The Iraqi victims of violence always felt shamed, utterly powerless, overwhelmed with fear, every body part flinching involuntarily at the slightest noise.

People who have endured so much don't turn into fighters or killers— no matter how badly they want vengeance and no matter how long they have been hiding their pain, feeling wild in their sorrow. In real life, most people are terrified at the mere thought of facing the perpetrators. That makes it difficult, though never impossible—take our word. Some soldiers did manage to get a lot of Iraqis to take risks and help out, having listened to too many anguished whispers for too long.

For a man, woman, girl, or boy who has been on the receiving end of violence, taking a risk with the assistance of soldiers involved a strange mixture of vengeance and justice, along with some fleeting sense of security and safety. It required building the trust that they will indeed be safe and secure with the soldiers. Being insurgents behind insurgents is sometimes strange and inexplicable.

Iraqis are close to their families in a way that most Americans found strange. What would make someone defy their families' wishes? The family is pleading with them not to do it, afraid for their safety; even so, some chose to walk with bunch of American soldiers at night. They don't know the real names of the soldiers, it is the middle of the night, they will walk in dark alleys infested with rattlesnakes, with no night vision and no weapons in hand, entrusting their lives so completely to these soldiers who have been constantly goofing around in their house. Is it for the sake of justice, vengeance, power, security, trust? Or just feeling there is nothing to lose—who the hell knows? Soldiers only know that they have to capture the moment and good things can be made to happen, swiftly but always with a sense of responsibility.

A man or a boy finds strength in a facemask, walking flanked by soldiers at night. A woman finds anonymity in the abaya that was their greatest strength.[83] The sweet irony was not lost on the soldiers, though the self-righteous virtue enforcers perhaps missed it: Wrapping oneself in an abaya makes the women anonymous just as the enforcers require—their individuality is stripped from them, no one knows one from the other, and they are just women reduced into a nut-job's imagination.

That anonymity is the greatest strength; it made the women who were willing to take a risk far more effective than most men. No one would know who they are, other than the soldiers next to them. In that anonymity, many women found strength, when flanked by soldiers they feel they can trust, to blow the anonymity of the JAM enforcers. The most difficult part of waging a counterinsurgency as a foreign intervention force is identifying the enemy that hides amid the innocent. The willingness of some people to take a risk becomes the greatest (even the only) advantage that soldiers have.

Of course, once their anonymity is blown, the JAM virtue police will be awakened from their complacent subversive slumber. They could

---

[83] Most Iraqi women wear the abaya (and girls wear the scarf) simply because they want to.

even (hypothetically speaking) be easily transposed into the monthly JAM martyrdom billboards, but that's a different decision with a different set of ramifications, moral, political, and legal.

The more soldiers walk, the more they learn where and how to look. The more they listen, the more whispers they keep hearing. It's a war, and everyone is stuck in a sob story, soldiers included.

❖ The professionals

In a conventional war, soldiers may never meet any grieving family members, but in a counterinsurgency, if soldiers act as insurgents behind insurgents and listen well enough, they will eventually be faced with the result of their own or their colleagues' actions. At times there is no escape, soldiers have to deal with it as they must, being professionals.

Soldiers walked into the house of a prominent Iraqi military official, no longer living. Soldiers found him and his friends, with tons of stuff that goes boom, preparing to ambush some American soldiers. The soldiers—playing insurgents behind insurgents—had set an ambush for him and his friends, trying to outflank the insurgent flank. On this day, the official got off an Iraqi police vehicle with all the good stuff and was about to set up a very good Improvised Explosive Device and get out fast, as he and his friends always did, leaving others to finish the job. But this time, some soldiers were willing to take a risk with the decisions they made.

Walking to the house afterward, the soldiers are met by his wife and her father. They come running up with anguished screams, pleading for help from the American soldiers. The family members have no idea that these same soldiers are the ones responsible for her husband's fate. They assume that the JAM insurgents killed him while rolling with the big boys.

That is to do counterinsurgency better, to fight subversively as insurgents behind insurgents.

So the soldier and his friends played along, trying to calm the wife, the father, and the other family members. They conveyed their deepest sympathies while drinking the soft drinks, listening to their stories, taking all the information they can gather: names, places, friends, all the documents and sensitive items that the family is giving the soldiers. They are begging the soldiers to go and find the perpetrators and bring them to justice, or please just kill them. The wife takes a deep anguished gasping breath, sitting beside family members.

Soldiers promise to catch the perpetrators. One guy is listening with the gravest face; his advanced combat helmet is on one of the toddler's heads, and he occasionally pats it with a smile while listening to the conversation and talking, always with his calm smile and ready grin. He was the genius behind the event. He sits and evokes his salt-of-the-earth pensive gravity, his somber face taking in all the pain of the family along with all the tactical valuable information that the family keeps pouring out.

That is the most important objective; what is done is done, and preparing for what comes next is far more important. Some of the official's friends are now running, and soldiers need to get them. Counterinsurgency is very much a war, but a little different. The sight of the toddlers and their wailing mother will always be heartbreaking. It pains the heart; everyone is human. But no soldier can ever forget the fundamental reality outside. It's a war, and the enemy is the enemy. People die, soldiers included; they take the next step and soldier on, and that is the job, someone has to do it.

❖ **Miriam's anguish**

But sometimes soldiers are momentarily left speechless. This came in an email from a dear Iraqi friend, a woman university student.

"Oh I am so sad, so angry, and I am soooo crying, *American soldiers killed my friend's family!*"

Civilians sometimes die in firefights, caught in the crossfire. War is war, but American soldiers are not in the business of killing families and innocent civilians deliberately.

But how could soldiers explain this to an Iraqi friend who is in mourning, who was honest enough to take the trouble to inform the soldiers of her heartfelt anguish. Logic is irrelevant when someone is in anguish and looking for someone to blame and hardly any common ground exists.

There is obviously more to her story, but after the initial accusation, Miriam's email trails off into increasingly incoherent rambling. Soldiers look at it, look at each other, and wonder, WTF!

What is the best course of action—text her, call, or maybe during the next patrol, take a quick detour and go to the house? Soldiers are acquainted with the family, a sister and brother and her parents. What the hell do you do? It is never easy to be accused as murderers. Soldiers decide, to hell with it, whether it's a cold welcome, perhaps a haranguing, they'll go knock on the door anyway.

There was a melancholy but sincere welcome. There was certainly a haranguing and a lot of anguish in the sad story. The moment they named the place, the soldiers recognized the neighborhood, with its cinderblock houses packed to the gills. Based on the timing, they knew it was a bomb from a helicopter. Soldiers could have finished the story, but they let the family do it. What soldiers gathered from it was perhaps different from what was on the family's mind. All they know is that Americans killed Miriam's friend's family. Soldiers hear something very different.

A long firefight had taken place, soldiers knew, as part of a larger mission. Insurgents were shooting from the rooftop of the adjacent house and possibly the house next door, and some American soldiers were stuck in an alley. The air strikes were aimed at the insurgents, as the soldiers on the ground had requested, just as the soldiers sitting and listening had often done. The air strikes annihilated the insurgents, and soldiers walked away. But the family friends were next door, stuck in the house that was hit with the missile; the mother and father died. Miriam's friend, a fellow university student, survived, as did her siblings. They are now without parents.

The family is aware of the insurgent presence, of course, because they live in a JAM-controlled neighborhood. They have listened to

JAM fighting these same soldiers now sitting in their living room, though they do not know it. At the end of the day, the details are irrelevant: Their daughter's friend's family was killed by Americans, and this they say to the soldiers. It is gratifying, in a strange way, that they feel comfortable enough with the soldiers to be able to say it. Nevertheless, something needs to be done.

The soldiers are puzzled. The family speaks of the incident with such intimacy, as if it happened next door. They have seen it on TV; it was all over Iraqi TV and even on the Internet. Miriam herself sent the link to some soldier's email. All they know is that the friend's parents are gone, Americans are responsible, and Miriam is crying for her friend. The older brother wears a nonchalant look, almost as if saying "whatever," but her parents are clearly anguished. Soldiers cannot say whether it is for Miriam's personal grief or because they were close to the family.

The soldiers felt very hot in the living room, despite the air conditioner that was hissing, and the generator felt louder than usual.

A soldier asked permission from the father to smoke a cigarette, "yes, yes, that's fine"; words and apologies, while necessary, are not going to quite cut it, though they are better than nothing. A strange sense of responsibility creeps in with each drag of the cigarette, the death of the innocent, however abstract, carries a different sentiment. Soldiers suggested that perhaps they could speak to their bosses and try to get some money to help out the family, if it is needed. But they insisted, as Iraqis often do, that the family is OK at the moment, other family members are helping the children. They promised to call the soldiers if it is ever necessary.

Soldiers know that there is always a way to wiggle something out, and, in fact, it begins to be the way Americans fight. Solders pay back if they break the doors, pay for locks that are broken, even pay blood money for people accidentally killed. Innocent Iraqis who are accidentally detained actually get a stipend for time spent at detention centers. Though it is not always an easy idea for soldiers on the ground to grasp, the system undoubtedly has great benefits.

It was very necessary for soldiers to make that personal commitment and promise, and not just for reasons of kindness. This is a family that soldiers are friends with, a rather special family. They know nearly everything and everybody in the neighborhood, they are wealthy, their daughters and sons talk to the soldiers on email, text, and phone sharing innocuous stories. This is a family that always helped the soldiers see the neighborhood clearly.

Soldiers don't always look forward to stepping out of an air-conditioned house, especially a house that always offers good food and good stories in the middle of the day. But walking out of the house on that day, even the hundred-degree heat felt a little brisk in comparison. But because of that visit, the family kept serving the soldiers wonderful stories for many more months.

❖ **"Sources of intelligence" and people**

There is perhaps one singular lesson soldiers learned that always held true, every time: Treat the many people with respect, and treat the people who help you with the utmost respect.

Almost nobody wants to be "an informant"—or, as soldiers call them, "a source"—even the ones who help and take risks. The best of them don't want to be sources, even though everything they do fits the billing. They want to retain a sense of secrecy, a sense of trust because that is the only thing that makes them feel safe; it may be a matter of life and death. The people who help out would rather deal with the soldiers they are familiar and comfortable with and not be identified as "sources."

If soldiers meet someone who is willing to help, it is important to maintain awareness of the many real concerns they may have, especially the women and girls. It is a good idea not to give in to the temptation to let every Tom, Dick, and Harry bebop down the road, demanding information from people, because now he or she is an established "source." Soldiers come and go, people have to live, and American soldiers may be utterly incapable of helping families who get in trouble because they helped the soldiers. Soldiers cannot even help their own interpreters, so the average people who help are shit out of luck.

So It Is Again, Insurgents Behind Insurgents

The essence of the American counterinsurgency strategy lies in putting *people* front and center: secure and assist them, get their complicity and support. This is also its most maddening aspect for soldiers on the ground. It requires soldiers to use force with ultimate restraint—*never* all or nothing—and you better start walking the neighborhood. But it has a definite advantage on the ground if soldiers can capture it. People in the neighborhood are not afraid of the soldiers because they know that they will not be intentionally harmed.

Over time, having walked for too long, listened *far* too long, and talked very little, this approach seeps into the skin and becomes second nature. Yes, the nut-jobs control the neighborhood, but they always overplay their hand. Astute soldiers can then provide people an opportunity, a choice that is also a risk, to help the soldiers go after the nut-jobs. Depending on how well soldiers do their work, many people do step up. Some even take the initiative and offer to take risks with the soldiers. It is always a point of decision. Soldiers then have to check the veracity of the claims, take a risk, and follow through. If soldiers can manage to instill credibility on the ground, putting people center stage, good things come to pass.

Then there is the drawback that puts soldiers between a rock and a hard place. How do soldiers and leaders respond to the political, moral, and legalistic concerns of the good people in order to go after the nut-jobs?

❖ Ayatollahs in abayas

Soldiers fought their way in to reach an urban safe house where the insurgents hid most of their war loot. The safe house was ostensibly a mosque. A mosque is a mosque to good people only if they deem it so. The nut-jobs will always throw a shit fit if soldiers go to a mosque, *unless* we actually catch them in the act inside the mosque. But half the neighborhood is aware of the operation—after all, they provided the information—so where is the element of surprise? Soldiers and leaders on the ground will have to make judgment calls.

395

Now the Apaches are hovering, automatic weapons are firing every-where, there are multiple explosions, and scores of severed rattle-snakes scattered on the ground. The soldiers are taking slow deliberate steps in night vision, fighting their way to the insurgent safe house.

Behind this lethal drama was a tiny figure that made it possible, taking risks that most people would not have taken.

Aminah, who said "the answer is No" to the nut-jobs in the neighbor-hood. Aminah, an Iraqi woman, a mother of three. Aminah, who sim-ply volunteered to help. She had approached a young leader, one of the soldiers who had credibility on the ground and offered her help. On numerous occasions, she walked with soldiers through the neigh-borhood at night. Rounds might be pinging off near her feet but she would walk on, surrounded by a bunch of grunts from every corner of the U.S. Aminah, wrapped in her abaya, walking in her usual strut, will always remain one of the enduring images of fighting JAM—just as Insaf's walk through the orchard, holding on to the rack-system of a soldier in the middle of the night, will be an emblematic memory of fighting the Sunni insurgents. These two women will always remain in the hearts of soldiers, two incredibly remarkable people with a differ-ent sort of heart—precisely because they were women, the weakest on the ground, forced to be anonymous.[84]

Walking Aminah back to her house in the middle of the night (as with other men and women), soldiers had a bewildering moment. There were always Sadrist ayatollahs hanging on their walls, and one wants to ask the pictures, what you make of all this? Aminah, like many others who helped soldiers, really worshiped these men, looked to them for inspiration. But the nut-jobs who rule the streets also invoke the good name of the old ayatollahs. What is happening on the ground is different from what the ayatollahs might imagine.

---

[84] In fact, as noted above, there were more men that helped out, but women always had a special place in the heart—and the determined ones had an advantage, in the abaya, that men did not have.

18

ODE TO PROCEDURE: SAFETY, SECURITY, AND RANK

It did seem to me, in my early army days, that too many of the older officers, when they came to command posts, made it a study to think what orders they could publish to annoy their subordinates and render them uncomfortable. I noticed, however, a few years later, when the Mexican War broke out, that most of this class of officers discovered they were possessed of disabilities, which entirely incapacitated them for active field service. They had the moral courage to proclaim it, too. They were right; but they did not always give their disease the right name.

—General Ulysses S. Grant

Being insurgents behind insurgents has its drawbacks: It can get the occasional high-ranking diligent gopher highly animated. The majority of our leaders are smart and reasonable officers who recognize the need to make tradeoffs to keep fighting better—but there is always an exception to the rule. When that happens, it is never funny.

Empire Strikes Back: The Majestic Base

On that day, unfortunately, the grunts looked very wrong. It was early morning, sunrise, and soldiers were just dragging themselves back to their sleeping quarters inside the majestic base. Majestic army bases have some dangerous creatures that soldiers on the ground have to be constantly aware of: the army of uniformed gophers whose job is to enforce uniform standards and military courtesies—what you wear and how you salute. And on this day, the soldiers were shit out of luck.

Soldiers were walking to the sleeping area, completely disheveled, having not shaved in about four days, having not slept properly for far longer. It was as bad as it was ever going to get, at seven in the morning as the sun was coming up, returning from back-to-back missions four days straight. Some were wearing t-shirts because they had contributed their shirts to the cause, cutting them into pieces to create an urban scarecrow of a soldier in order to attract the neighborhood snipers. Some soldiers had their sleeves rolled all the way up to escape the heat; no one had nametapes or unit insignia; some were wearing shoes that were not army issue. Worst of all, no one was wearing the proper Army-issue body armor. Instead, they wore armor they had bought themselves that was lighter, more comfortable, and more mobile (though not as safe as the army issue).[85] And one soldier was on a cell phone while another had one phone to his ear and another in his hand, sending a text message!

The soldiers had become too comfortable, and when you get too comfortable, you let your guard down and walk into an ambush.

❖ The animated gopher

A luxurious four-wheel-drive vehicle came to a screeching halt, and everyone's heart sank.

"Fuuck."

Out came a very high-ranking man, whose achievements and service will always remain legendary. The man is not just a rank, he is a symbol of better men from earlier and representative of better men who will fill his shoes one day. Soldiers will always have respect and loyalty to the rank irrespective of who holds it.

---

[85] This substitute body armor is now authorized for some units.

He walked toward the soldiers, his steaming mug of coffee in hand. He has had some of these soldiers in the crosshairs for a while; this was his day, and the coffee steam coming out of his mug in the early morning looked so voluptuous. His purposeful walk, with the barrel chest and the eyes bulging out from his skull, was perhaps meant to look intimidating and impressive.

Soldiers knew only one certainty, this will be very bad, and everyone looks at each other as if at a best friend's funeral because they knew without a doubt they were wrong. Except those two soldiers on their cell phones. They were out of it, completely clueless, like two monkeys swinging on a tree and about to get raped by an ape. They were the first to get it. Bam. Another concussion.

Fire spewed forth, complete long flames that looked as if they could turn everything in their path to ash. The smoke rings that billowed from his ears made shapes of dancing fairies, jeering at the soldiers.

The two soldiers turned from their phones to the noise and the hot flames in bewilderment, their mouths agape in total surprise; there is no defense, the Man is absolutely right. Soldiers should not be walking and talking on the cell phones, and what is with the cell phones anyway? "Oh shit." He stomps the ground promising to get rid of them once and for all from *all of Iraq*! Difficult, though never impossible, but unhelpful given that cell phones remain one of the greatest advantages Iraqis have after the invasion.

But very true, soldiers should not have cell phones and should not be walking and talking; it is the standard. If he knew that the soldiers were on the phone with some local Iraqis there is no telling what else he would come up with, being that he is so close to heaven. So the soldiers quickly bid adieu and meekly put the phones in the side pocket. They were hoping the Man would not give into the confiscating impulse: There are so many other things wrong with the picture, soldiers were hoping he would concentrate on something else. Which he promptly did. He was just getting warmed up. So the soldiers getting raped by an ape took a deep breath and got ready for it. Now the man looks like he may get a brain aneurysm. Lord knows, it is his job, and there were many things wrong, and soldiers were so completely and unequivocally on the wrong side of the equation by the field manual and big army standard. Soldiers have no logical defense, they can only listen, and he is a man who is used to being listened to and not spoken to.

The uniforms are all jacked up, not worn properly, the body armor, who authorized this, and those shoes, who authorized it? "Why don't you have the unit patch, are you fucking scared to wear it?"

❖ Operational security

The soldiers are usually careful not to get busted. As soon as they get through the gates of a majestic army base, they all try their best to look pretty so as to avoid unpleasantness with the uniform mafia. But everyone slips when they are tired. So it is on this day, and it would be the last time—this never happened again, soldiers learned fast and did better.

The soldiers wore no nametapes or unit insignia and had jacked-up uniforms for a very distinct reason. Iraqi insurgents are smart, and they have seen pictures and videos of soldiers in cell phones. Sometimes unit insignia and nametapes are very important: For the warm-hearted charm offensives and when commanders play the role of the Snow White and the Seven Perverts, it is critical. But walking the streets at night, maybe taking the wrong turn and ending up in other neighborhoods, it is important not to wear the nametapes and unit insignia. Why should soldiers let Iraqis know who the hell soldiers are and where they come from? The Internet is already bad enough in this war! It is a simple question of operational security. But there is no way of explaining it to him, just shut up and listen.

Then there is the body armor!

Soldiers are as wrong as the day is long. There is no explaining because how could one explain—as so many soldiers always discussed—that safety is not, and should not be the operational concept in combat; *security* should be.

❖ Safety and security

When good people with best intentions try to turn the idea of safety into an operational concept in combat, they turn foot soldiers on the ground into medieval knights. Or, as the soldiers used to call the ones who abide strictly by procedures, Robo-Cops. It makes them look like they belong in a futuristic museum. Of course, it is not the look that counts, and soldiers know where they stand in the looks department. Enlisted soldiers come in two extremes. They are either good-looking sons of bitches or ugly fucking bastards, and this was an ugly lot. The looks are not the issue but fighting is: they believed that was their job and not looking pretty.

A good procedural soldier who wears all the army procedural body armor, the neck piece, butterfly flaps to cover the shoulders, the side plates, and a crotch protector that keeps flapping around—that guy will lose his mind if not his nuts. Then there is the Kevlar that holds in the heat, turning the chest into a two-hundred-degree oven where displaced Iraqis could perhaps bake their flatbread. A simple question, has anyone walked more than sixty kilometers over a four-day period across fields and orchards in August in Iraq wearing this ridiculous outfit?

Some soldiers would bet their manhood that not a single person who wears all the procedural body armor ever walks that much. And the men who walked—you can take our word on this—never wore all that nonsense. Worse, forget about the walking, how could a soldier hold his weapon at the high-ready position over the butterfly flaps, or sprint three hundred meters in a firefight to chase nut-jobs in this ridiculous outfit?

But such practical concerns are utterly irrelevant because it apparently looks very pretty, a mythical relic that belongs in the Smithsonian. People watching soldiers on TV may feel safe, but that sure as hell is not the way foot soldiers feel on the ground. We speak for a whole lot of grunts who put their faith in their feet: It is not safety, but security that matters in combat.

A foot soldier's sense of security comes not from covering himself in a medieval outfit that makes rounds ping off the body armor but from his ability to maneuver effectively in a fight. Safety and security are different concepts and have different ramifications on the ground. Safety—covered head-to-toe in bigger, heavier, and more expensive gear—is not always better. A whole lot of soldiers learned this quickly on the ground, and some spent their own money for body armor that is lighter, less protective, less expensive and with no Kevlar pieces. It allowed them to maneuver much more effectively and walk far longer, and even run—imagine that!—and that means *security*. Because the job includes serving in a firefight and putting oneself in a risky situation, security means having the ability to maneuver. But soldiers cannot explain that either, they must only listen.

This mythical beast does not make the decisions, he only implements them, and he is very good at it for he does so without a mind of his own. There is no defense against procedures. Logic and common sense do not hold up against procedures, procedures reign supreme.

It is critical to outsmart *some* procedures; they are there to be improved upon, especially in a counterinsurgency when constant learning is critical in order to stay in the fight and do better. But there is no escaping the procedures, soldiers just have to take a risk and say the hell with it because it is combat.

❖ The hell with it

There are moments when there is no escape from the army's uniform enforcers—even outside the wire, even in combat. Some animated gophers were determined to enforce uniform standards *in action*, which is, of course, necessary—or is it?

Two soldiers were taking a break. One wore his sniper ghilly suit bottom with all his camouflage, plus a T-shirt and a light plate carrier that he himself had bought, and no combat helmet. It is the middle of the day and the helmet is clipped to his back. He is standing with his sniper rifle slung across his shoulder, a legendary combat leader and nut case that soldiers loved. The guy next to him was a phenomenal combat leader and a legendary nut, just as crazy, and he wore no body armor whatsoever—he only had his rack system and everything that goes boom. They were taking a break, pulling security of sorts.

A convoy of American military vehicles came trundling along and stopped next to them. The up-armored window slowly opened and they could see flames coming out of it.

"Hey soldier, who are you with?"

The soldier was notorious for his smart-ass comments and always quick on his feet. But he was always too honest for his own good and one day his honesty might be his downfall. He just could not resist the moment.

"Uh, we are part of the best, you may have heard of them—it is called the United States Army!"

His friend next to him gives him a look that could be interpreted as, "Are you fucking serious? I can't believe you just said that to this worthless gopher!"

Their eyes share a laugh.

The man inside the armored vehicle was in no way pleased, one heard him slam the up-armored window, and he got out huffing and puffing and there was more fire. "Where is your commanding officer?"

The soldier put his hand in his pocket, pulled out a can of dip and put a dip in his mouth, deliberately taking his time before answering this fire-breathing dragon. Then he flicked the fingers to get the tobacco out and put his hands in his pockets to irk him even more, then motioned over his shoulder, "Oh, he is back there in that big house across the courtyard."

"I am going to talk to your commanding officer right now. I am going to drive over there."

Now the soldier, making things far worse, exploded. "NO MAN, you can't fucking drive, what the fuck, it's the damn *courtyard*, we're *staying* in that damn house!"

And the soldier added with all sincerity, "Look, we flew in here five days ago, killed everybody that was doing the shooting and the rest probably ran away, there is nobody around to do any shooting—why don't you *walk*?"

The man looked at him, breathed some more fire and started stomping toward the makeshift command post, surrounded by his minions. As they started walking one of his subordinates stepped out and walked to the two soldiers, looking them up and down.

"So, is this how you always roll?"

And he answered honestly, "No man, not always, it depends on the mission, we do what we have to to get the job done."

The subordinate laughed, "Damn, must be fucking nice, well done, Son, just keep doing what you are doing," and he ran toward the stomping gopher, already passed the courtyard. Yes, sometimes, there is no escape other than to hold the ground and hope higher will take care of the soldiers on the ground as the best of them always do.

But on this day, standing at seven in the morning, salivating at the steaming cup of voluptuous coffee he was holding, soldiers were facing the wrath. This man had no soft spot for the shoes soldiers were wearing.

❖ The one thing foot soldiers love: Their feet

Foot soldiers have very simple needs and pursue very simple pleasures. But one thing that they love, and love to hate, and try to take care of will always remain their ugly feet. Because that is the one thing they have to trust, other than the guys standing side by side and their immediate leaders.

The choice will always remain whether to wear shoes made by the lowest bidder or buy some very comfortable but very expensive shoes, maybe $200–300, and take care of one's own feet. (By now, these same shoes are, in fact, authorized gear.) An army that takes care of its foot soldiers can always be identified from the physical training uniform and the shoes.

Soldiers met and shared lot of love with some wonderful Australian and British female soldiers from the coalition of the willing. They did have great PT uniforms, boots, cold weather undergarments, and a lot of nice little things, whether or not they liked them. A smaller armed force can provide the little important things to their foot soldiers. But we are big, perhaps the biggest in the world: our Air Force has the best and biggest planes, our Navy has the best and the biggest ships, and somewhere out there, we also have the best high tech wizardry. So the cheap shoes and terrible PT uniforms for grunts can be forgiven. What the soldiers did (having said the hell with it) was buy their own shoes and wear them on missions, even though it goes against all procedures. It certainly helps them maneuver better, and that is the primary job function.

Usually, the moment they get back into a majestic army base, soldiers will change back to the army-issue boots made by the lowest bidder, so as to abide by rigid procedures. It is important to keep the uniform mafia from getting all riled up.

❖ The fuck face

Some soldiers walked into the MWR (Moral Welfare and Recreation) building in a majestic army base to send an email home. The soldiers had just returned from five days in a shit hole, still in their same uniforms, and no one is in a good mood. They sat down, quietly sent their emails, and were about to walk away when they got into the crosshairs of a high-ranking uniform mafia member in his crisp clean suit, reeking enviably of Axe deodorant. The soldiers' leader mumbles, "Man, I am too tired for this stupid shit, let's get out of here." And they simply walked away because, yes, their uniforms were all jacked up and they did not want any trouble.

The high-ranking minion would never understand why their uniforms are all jacked up because, by his job classification, "combat" means playing "Tour of Duty" on Xbox. But the gesture of walking away quietly was translated as either fear or insubordination, and he did something he should never have done, despite his rank.

He screamed out loud in the MWR computer center, "Don't you walk away from me. I'm talking to you! Hey, you! Look at me!" And then he crossed the line and did something unforgivable: He grabbed the soldier's hand and tried to turn him around. And that's when all hell broke loose.

All you heard was the soldier's low rumbling reaction: "Oh hell, motherfucking NO!"

The soldier turned, grabbed the uniform mafia man by the chest, and threw him into the wall, smacking his head squarely on the cinderblock wall. In the next second, the soldier's 9mm Beretta was out and at the ready.

"If you try to touch me one more time, one more fucking time, I'm going to fucking kill you right here you worthless pogue-ass motherfucker," he spat.

"Sitting here looking so motherfucking pretty—what are you looking at me for? Come on and say something, say one word motherfucker, just one. I just put two of my soldiers onto a bird *in fucking pieces*." This was not made up, he really did. It was a house-borne IED and he himself survived by only a second. "You think I give a shit, say one more fucking word, just one more fucking word, and I swear I won't even shoot you, you ain't worth it." He holstered the pistol. "I'll break your fucking head."

Thinking about it some more he changed his mind. "No, you know what? I'm not gonna break your head, I'll just slice your fucking throat and make you croak like a fucking goat." And he grabbed a keyboard from one of the computers and slung it full force at the wall. Everyone in the room was showered with shattered keys. The place went deadly silent.

Shaking with rage, he turned to the rest of the room. "Is there anybody else here who has any more fucking problems with my fucking uniform? Or any of my guys? Come on say it motherfucker, I want to fucking hear it, say it!" He threw another keyboard into the wall. The gopher was by now transformed into a cowering shit pile, crouching on the ground by the wall, covering his head. The place was stone silent.

"Say it."

No one said a word. Then he quietly walked to the highest ranking man there and took off his enlisted rank, handing it to him and saying, "Sir, that was conduct unbecoming of a soldier. I am wrong, and I know it. I am sure there will be UCMJ action, let me give you my standard name line." And he wrote down his name, unit, and social security number. Then he added as he was leaving, "But if any motherfucker tries to touch me again, I will do everything I said."

But nothing is ever that simple. Now the manager of the MWR gig—an ex-military man, getting fat in the process—felt the need to pipe up: "You will all be banned from MWR, soldier!"

"Are you fucking serious?" Did you just call me 'soldier'?

It is a very strange reality. Despite being ex-military, and even sometimes old friends, the private contractors are never the same goddamn thing! But some forget, and when they do and try to act it out, someone inevitably puts them in their place, if only to vent some rage and frustration.

Looking at this pathetic excuse of a man evoked a tidal wave of rage and revulsion. The worst possible human impulses crisscrossed the mind, hands shaking with distilled hatred. It is perhaps only by a miracle that soldiers managed to save them from themselves.

"Oh you worthless motherfucker"—and two soldiers grabbed the manager. He was swiftly airborne, planted against a wall, trying to regain his balance, while the first soldier yelled in his face. "Do you think I come here to shake my ass on hip-hop night like you do, fuck face? *Say something* fuck face, I will end you."

It is very quiet again. Everyone thought the soldiers had completely lost their minds. They came close, but not quite.

The soldiers' leader looked around and said simply, "Goddamn man, this place is just not good for my soul." The other soldiers burst into laughter and walked out, shaking their heads: "I am so tired of this stupid fucking shit."

Though it was undoubtedly and unequivocally wrong, there are some moments that feel perfect because they are so wrong.

There will always be unequivocal respect and loyalty to the rank, because it represents something more than the man wearing it. And because a military rank is earned, and the best of them have earned it with blood and sweat and that will always deserve respect. But it never—ever—means fear of the man wearing it.

When little men, especially those who play too much Xbox and sit pretty, confound rank with manhood or respect with fear, it is important to point it out and put them in their place when they cross the line, no matter how non-procedural and wrong it may be and despite the possibility of facing the full wrath of the Uniform Code of Military Justice.

It was the beginning of an avalanche of cosmic proportions. Now the immediate leadership had to scramble to save one of the most fearless leaders they have, along with some other leaders who together have killed more insurgents than damn near anybody. Now they have to try to save them from the wrath of the uniform mafia—and from their own "conduct unbecoming" impulsive behavior. But there were no apologies or regrets, only a lot of laughter—and making sure the soldiers were quickly back on a bird chasing insurgents on a new mission, where, it seems, they will be safest while in Iraq.

Talking to the Man

Facing the fire-breathing dragon in the majestic base on this day, looking at his steaming coffee mug, there was no humor because he is the man, and he goes for the touchdown in a big ball of fire.

"When I look at soldiers, I expect a goddamn standard. Looking at ya'll, all fucking jacked up—you are not that standard, you are a fucking disgrace to the army, what the fuck is this?"

He is absolutely right, there is no defense, every soldier standing listening to him looked like a disgrace, though the soldiers did not feel disgraced and had a far more serious concern. Some good people that soldiers love to death will end up in trouble.

Because this is a moment that will trickle down the chain of command, and at each step, the ringing in the ears for those who listen will be louder and more painful. Some very good people who fight side by side with the soldiers will bear most of the burden for this incident. Because they will protect the soldiers and bear the burden, as they always do repeatedly, and that is the worst part. No soldier wants to let the good people down as it breaks the heart, the only thing that makes soldiers bow their heads low in shame and hunch their shoulders. Getting in trouble is part of the job—but it has to be for something worthwhile, something good enough, or to have a good laugh. Not for something so fucking stupid.

❖ Let's get it on

One soldier, who held no soft spot in his heart for this man, decided on impulse to explicate the situation, which was a bad idea. The military is the military, it can never be a democracy. Even so, dealing with the majority of good people in the army, logic and reason has its place. But there are others who put the rank and procedures first; logic, reason, and common sense become subservient. This man, as respected and legendary as he is, is one of those exceptions. The soldier was not going to get anywhere by explaining, and one could see his long lanky hands shaking, so another soldier grabbed the back of his belt and mumbled, "Hey, calm down, don't go there." There is no defense, they were as wrong as the day is long, and everyone knew it was coming.

The Man bellowed, "LISTEN, ALL I EXPECT, IS TO DO WHAT YOU ARE FUCKING TOLD AND SQUEEZE THE GODDAMN TRIGGER! NOW SHUT THE FUCK UP, I DON'T WANT TO HEAR A GODDAMN THING. DO YOU FUCKING UNDERSTAND?"

Then he continued to threaten to bring down every conceivable mythical wrath on the soldiers and he stomped away, hollering that he will be watching, promising that this is just the beginning.

He was an exception in the army, not the rule—not representative in any form or fashion of the vast majority of our military leadership. The animated ape embodied the hard-charging spirit of procedural caricature.

And then, most memorably, he promised to destroy their army careers: *"I AM GOING TO FUCKING DESTROY EVERY FUCKING ONE OF YOU."*

Now that's interesting, that's not procedure, that's a *threat*—and a threat is always heartwarming. "Destroy us?" That is a *challenge*, and this will be a good fight.

❖ The stultified minds

Most of the men and women in the army, as they get older, also get wiser and better—like Yesterday's Wine, as some soldiers joked. There is far more sharing of ideas and honest debate inside the military than you might expect, ranging from literature to politics, from philosophy to warfare—and, of course, how best to appreciate the perfect female human form.

But there is also the group that never gets wiser over time; they can't help it, their brains seem to get stultified and oppressed. The moment they stop walking the ground with the rest and move on to the bigger and better things, they lose a bit more reason, logic, and common sense with every breath. This mythical ape was one of them, an entertaining exception to the rule. Soldiers respected his rank: He has earned it and it will always be bigger than himself, a symbol that represents better men from the past. But it is tragic that he holds a rank that means so much more than he is willing to understand. Fortunately, there will always be someone higher who follows reason and common sense and will step up and offset such procedural caricatures, making our army perfect—the only solace for soldiers.

Having threatened the soldiers with destruction, the man got into his luxury vehicle and blasted off quickly, engaging the Improbability Drive in a cloud of dust to hitchhike from Galaxy to Galaxy, bringing down his mythical wrath on unsuspecting soldiers just to feel alive and validate his own existence. Everyone watched the fast-receding cloud of dust, shaking their heads, and soldiers knew that they now had some serious work to do because they screwed up.

Soldiers are supposed to feel safe in this majestic army base. But they do not feel safe any longer, they feel stultified and oppressed in what now feels like a majestic concrete monkey farm. They feel like they just got raped by a silverback gorilla. The best way for soldiers to feel free and alive is to be outside the wire, walking the streets and alleys. Yes, the intermittent random Iraqi nut-jobs trying to harm them will only be an inconvenience, and at least in those moments soldiers will feel a little life inside them.

Now they took slow deliberate steps, each heavier than the last, to their sleeping quarters. Everyone that saw them coming knew that something was up. For people who sleep, eat, and fight next to each other, a lot of things were understood just by looking.

"Shit, boss-man, you would not believe what just happened!"

It is never a good phrase, and it can make any military leader's heart momentarily sink. They exhale deep breaths and get those eyes of disbelief, "What the hell did you guys do?" he asked with that pained, caring looking with that pained caring look distinctive to military leaders with too many soldiers to take care of.

The best of the leaders gather and exhale a deep heartfelt breath with that intense purposeful stare that only the best of our military leaders have. "Fuck—tell me exactly what just happened. I can't fucking help you if I don't know the whole story."

The Few Good Men

> There is among the mass of individuals who carry the rifles in war, a great amount of ingenuity and initiative. If men can naturally and without restraint talk to their officers, the products of their resourcefulness become available to all. Moreover, out of the habit grows mutual confidence, a feeling of partnership that is the essence of *espirit de corps*. An army fearful of its officers is never as good as one that trusts and confides in its leaders.
>
> —General Dwight D. Eisenhower

411

Part of military leadership is much like babysitting, a pain in the rear and a constant sense of responsibility, and the best of them handle it all with a smile and a curse. Leaders—commissioned and non-commissioned—have to command the fight, but they are also required to be many other things, free of charge.

Marriage counselor, for example. Threatening an estranged wife, who has now found comfort with a neighbor, is not a brilliant idea. Everyone needs to have his or her physical and emotional needs met, and neighbor Jody (as any deployed soldier knows) is right there to meet the need—and aims to please.

Threatening her over the phone while in Iraq is definitely not appropriate. But it is downright retarded[86] when she has the power of attorney and access to his bank account, so now the leader has to talk some sense. Thankfully he is deployed, and some common sense could be imbued in him. But the best make a note in the leader book: "This is a guy I need to keep my eyes on if he makes it back."

And financial advisor. They have to try to prevent some brilliantly idiotic plans, like spending all the savings on a luxury vehicle. Why would a twenty-four-year-old enlisted man, making a pittance of a salary, want to spend all his earnings on a Range Rover and be owned by it? Well, because he wants one!

If you call him a retard, he will definitely buy it anyway—over the Internet—but if you don't call him a retard, you are lying to him. How to convince him without calling him retarded? In the end, he gives up the Range Rover and buys a brand new Harley Davidson instead. His leader is sitting on the makeshift cot, bobbing his head. Well, what do you say to a guy who just signed his life away for four more years and then spends the reenlistment incentive money on a Harley—at the Harley Stand on the majestic army base? Cheesecake is bad enough, Harley Stands? Are you fucking serious? Guess there is always a way

---

[86] As noted above, "retarded" is a term widely used in the military to either commend a soldier's successful daring or to criticize his or her poor judgment—in this case, the latter.

to screw Joe in some fashion because there are always some Joes that are easily screwed, it never fails, that's our Joe.

And then there is the all time favorite. Infantrymen must be a lonely bunch, the biggest suckers around. There is always a youngling! Getting married right before the deployment to a woman who has two kids from two previous military marriages, who is now dangling from the pole in a night club in an army town. And then to give her power of attorney, no matter how madly one is in love, is not very smart. She may be well intentioned and in love, maybe not, her situation may even be heartbreaking, but taking care of one's own soldier is the most important.

"OK, listen man, fine, if you get married a week before the deployment, but are you *sure* you want to give her access to your bank account, you have known her for what, three, four weeks?" Give her unconditional power of attorney, for the love of god?

"Oh—but I thought—because she is my wife!"

"Look, listen, OK, I am sorry, yes, you love her, maybe, maybe not, I don't fucking know! But listen and listen good because this is not my first fucking rodeo, understood? When you deploy, it could be me, or it could be you, someone is going to die, and if you just get blown up to pieces, tell me, do you want some crack whore you knew for two weeks, who gave you a blow job, to have your life insurance money, or your mama and papa and family who took care of you all your life? Tell me. Tell me!"

He is quiet.

"Listen, man, look, it is your decision. It's your life and your goddamn money, you can do whatever you want with it, I am just telling you because you're my soldier and it's my job, believe me, in about two months, you will be singing a different tune, and I have to take care of you again, I am about to go on my fourth deployment, so think about it."

So he is looking, standing, thinking, like a man who has come across more than he expected, and he slowly changes his mind to a more sensible course of action. So the enlisted leader calls one of his subordinates. "Look man, I want you to go and square away your Joe. Take him to Legal, change his power of attorney to a conditional one, so this crack whore does not own this guy's life, but she is his wife now, and she has to have something."

The lover boy who has had too many blow jobs than his age could handle is standing there with a sheepish grin, nodding.

"Then take him to Finance and help him set up an allotment, so she gets a steady allotment but does not get all his deployment money." And then, "You take him to Brigade S1 shop and help him change his SGLV—life insurance—and DD93 because he has already changed it to this woman's name, all of it, 100 percent! Help him change it so it is distributed evenly, now that he has got some good sense."

"Oh, by the way, did you ever do a last will?"

"Uh no, I did not."

"Don't you think you need to do a will in the event you get killed?"

"Uh—." He has the blank stare as the world has landed heavily on his shoulders. The responsibility of what it means to be a frontline soldier seems to have hit him in the head with a big mallet, and it's good. It has to happen sooner or later.

"OK, do me a favor, talk to your mama and papa and figure out what exactly you want with your will. Get it done while you are at Legal, understood?"

"Roger."

Then the leader added with all sincerity, "Look, listen man, all I am asking you is to be a little wise, be responsible man, just be fucking responsible for god's sake, what the fuck, is it that fucking difficult, just be a little smart, OK, do it for me, do it for the guys?"

"ROGER."

The leader is shaking his head. Much more was in his face and eyes than words could capture. After lover boy leaves his office he calls in the kid's immediate supervisor, the team leader; he is actually the one at fault.

"How did you ignore this shit, it is your responsibility; he is your fucking soldier, do you fucking understand?"

"Roger."

"Don't tell me roger. If you want to be a leader, you better get your act straight, start being a little responsible about your guys, you fuck up one more time, I swear to you, I will crush your skull, you will be the sorriest mother fucker around, understood?"

"Understood, Sergeant, it will not happen again."

Every soldier needs a skull crushing sometime, leadership means a sense of responsibility and if it is not instilled, he is worthless. No one is ever perfect: Get it crushed, put it back in place and learn a thing or two, and do better, that's how it goes.

But the senior leader makes another entry in the green leader book. The lover boy will be cleaning weapons and making coffee before he starts missions, just to keep an eye on him!

No matter how many times they do it, every time it has the element of surprise. One week before a deployment, babysitting is just one part of the job. Generally the best of the leaders spend their time being twenty-four hours on call, trying to save soldiers from themselves. It is far more difficult than combat. One of the best enlisted leaders of all time, who has lost all his hair worrying about soldiers, use to say, "I will tell you man, the best time in the army is one month before the deployment and one week after the deployment." The best of them have the concerned eyes, the shaking head. They always look either pissed off or serenely calm because putting out constant fires is part of life and there is no end to them. Seeing them at work trying to take care of their guys generates enormous respect.

415

Knowing all this as well as we do, we hate to bring misery to the best of them while deployed. That is to let them down, and nothing—nothing—breaks the heart more than to let good men down.

❖ Buster Keaton is still around

By now, everyone wants to hear what transpired. A crowd gathers—including leaders, commissioned and noncommissioned. One soldier did a complete reenactment of the moment for the benefit of the jeering, laughing, and cheering crowd; he was dead on, right down to the walk to the luxury vehicle and engaging the Improbability Drive.

Everyone is laughing but amid the laughter, the higher-ranking ones have the look of a burden: They are about to hear it, and it will be loud. Soldiers apologize to them, "We promise we will not get busted," though it is heartbreaking. They accept the apology. One soldier points his finger at a high-ranking young officer that they fight side by side with and mimics the man: "Hey, sir, I expect you to do what you are told and squeeze the goddamn trigger alright!"

The officer turns, with the gravest face he can muster, and he puts out his barrel chest, wags the finger, and says, "Of course, it is critical you squeeze that goddamn trigger—do it haaard, you reeetaaard"—and then buckles in laughter, shaking his head, "Duude, this is great, I am going to hear this one for a long time."

Soldiers were back in business because at the end of the day, what matters in a counterinsurgency on the ground is not necessarily looking pretty. Standards are there for a reason, but soldiers need not be defined by them always. There has to be a delicate balance. On the ground, it is getting results, and for the guys who fight side by side, what matters is who has one's back.

But the man threatened to destroy every single fucking one of the soldiers that are a disgrace to procedure. The threat has to be taken seriously, very seriously, because he will be watching.

❖ Home of the ape: Gourmet coffee

Soldiers now need to get the ape, but how to do it in style and have a good laugh while doing it? It is a simple question of integrity. He made the threat to destroy the soldiers and someone needs to call his bluff. No one doubts that some soldiers need a good skull crushing, it is necessary, and this is the military, not a seminary. But it never ever means one fears the man because no sentient human being should ever have to fear another human being.

He has a great strength and it is captured in his rank and it is no joke, and soldiers will always be nothing in his shadow. But he also has a great weakness. He assumes everyone is an idiot and fears his power and authority. He is complacent in his mind and comfortable because everyone that surrounds him actually fears him—and he is dependent on them for everything, including how to make his coffee, print out the emails, even reset his own "secret" password. That will be the greatest advantage to soldiers.

He will watch the soldiers and soldiers will have to watch him. That is easy because he is big, easily noticed, and far too dependent on too many people that he has made utterly miserable. The miserable ones find solace, try to calm their souls and find inspiration commiserating at sunrise—along with the soldiers who are a disgrace.

In his absence (he was always traveling), soldiers paid a visit to his work and sleeping quarters, just to get to know him in a more intimate setting. It was a humbling experience. His many achievements, the many risks he has taken in his life, his continued selfless service will always mean respect because he has unquestioningly earned it. He is an honorable man who has risked his life far more than most.

Unfortunately, as soldiers learned, he will always be consistent in his thinking. Consistency in thinking translates into predictability in action, and insurgents can always outsmart consistency in a counterinsurgency.

The room, his office, looks majestic, the many accoutrements evoke power and authority from every nook and cranny: It is a room meant to intimidate. Another soldier was holding a bag of coffee and sniffing it while sitting on the oversized leather chair behind the majestic desk. He was reading through his military records, and he simply summed up the moment.

"You know, man, this guy, he has earned the right. Look at all this shit, look at everything he has done, goddamn!"

Indeed, his military accomplishments were awe-inspiring and humbling as the group gathered around the table and quietly and slowly perused them. With each line, each sentence, nothing more needed to be said, respect to the man, the rank, and his accomplishments without question—but that still does not mean fear him.

They will have to keep thinking.

The good men (and a few women) who work for him keep the soldiers apprised of his itinerary, his movements, his meetings. But they also did something far more valuable. They promptly gave the soldiers copies of his early morning reading materials, and even some of his emails that he reads with a steaming cup of coffee in hand. Because behind every animated gopher are a bunch of "dumb" and "worthless" enlisted men with access to everything who are made miserable by the mythical ape. There is no better way to be apprised of the battle space, to see the bigger picture, than to see what the people higher up the totem pole see, especially one who is looking to crush some skulls. And to see it, soldiers only have to help the many men and women who hate their lives by commiserating at sunrise in hiding. But they have to be careful and keep thinking.

Then the soldier sniffing the coffee begins messing around with his coffee maker, his many bags of coffee, and his many glamorous cups. Everyone is laughing hysterically at what he was doing. "Yeah, well, I am fucking taking this bag of coffee, this is some gourmet shit, and he's got plenty of it."

That is the kind of quick-thinking soldier, one wants to have side by side in a counterinsurgency.

Walking back amid the many concrete barriers inside the majestic army base, soldiers had an idea—a very good idea about hallucinations.

"Hey, man, let's drink some Arak with that that coffee; it will probably taste good!"

Good Arak is always so delicious.

19

ARAK-INDUCED HALLUCINATION IN MIDAQ ALLEY

How often have you killed the deviant for his
deviation—so why is it you spare sinners scandal?

—Arabian Nights and Days

A rak—good Arak, like El-Massaya or Fakra that comes from Lebanon—will always be the nectar of the gods for some good Iraqi people, but the local Iraqi Arak that comes in plastic packets would also serve the purpose without making anyone go blind. Having acquired the taste, it tastes good in everything—water, tea, coffee—and like all good things it can inspire the soul. Drinking enough good Arak gives the perfect hallucinations.

Hallucinations and Subversion

Hallucinations were sometimes all these soldiers had. Whether hiding and commiserating at dawn or feeling stultified and oppressed in a majestic monkey farm, Arak-induced hallucinations would help the imagination—the best form of subversion.

Soldiers were fortunate to be centrally located next to a JAM stronghold, in an affluent neighborhood where every Shia bigwig has houses and family.[87] Every family has stories to tell, and soldiers loved to listen to people's stories.

Soldiers are in hiding, commiserating again, while looking at a bunch of papers and a laptop with figures, photos, and random facts about the neighborhood. Sitting around inside the concrete blast wall bunker, holding a few bottles of good Arak, they look at each other with quiet stern grins.

It is very hot in the middle of the year in Iraq, even at three in the morning. Even the occasional breeze seems to sap the energy, soldiers just cannot let that happen and everyone has the same look. It was understood.

"Yeah, the hell with it, let's just do it, we have to try it, what do we have to lose? Nothing." A soldier grabs the Arak bottle and another grabs the second.

With the Arak bottles open, the heavenly anise aroma permeated the concrete mortar bunker, enlivening the place. Soldiers felt alive inside the blast walls. It works its magic slowly and soldiers feel the charm in their veins. The anise seed and licorice aroma permeates the air, the distinctive taste coating the throats, and inspiration is flowing through the veins as the minds of soldiers go into overdrive—their imaginations and hallucinations fast becoming the best form of subversion.

> Three fingers whiskey pleasures the drinkers
> And moving does more than the same thing for me,
> Willie, he tells me that doers and thinkers
> Say moving is the closest thing to being free.[88]

Having rosined their reggins, laid back their wages, they are dead set on riding in the big rodeo—the lanky wandering gypsy prodding, with his soft voice and mischievous smile: "Hey, gypsy, let's go."

---

[87] The most prominent players are connected to the Sadr, Hakim, Ha'aeri, and Yaquibi families.
[88] Waylon Jennings, "Willie the Wandering Gypsy."

Arak-Induced Hallucinations: Unraveling the Tapestry of Insurgent Control in Midaq Alley

"Oh please, sir, JAM controls everything, please leave; we don't want any trouble," said Hussein, the former bureaucrat; his wife, Huda, the medical professional, nodded vigorously. It was one of their first meetings with the soldiers, an eternity ago.

Soldiers granted their wish, apologized for the unsolicited intrusion and walked away looking like Sponge Bob with their ready stupid grins. Later on, the whole family will share their insights with the soldiers, while Mo, the toddler that stole every soldier's heart, crawled all over them. Yes, indeed, soldiers now know intimately what they meant, and they would always be grateful to many people in the neighborhood for their education of soldiers. Time has passed and soldiers have aged and the neighborhood has become a permanent part of their skin.

Jaish al-Mahdi—JAM—remains a formidable military and political creature. No matter how well soldiers keep going after them militarily, destroying combatant cells, those military achievements can quickly be offset by failures elsewhere because JAM retains control of the people. Jam has political power, legitimacy, and the economic resources to make control manifest on the ground. As long as they have that, they can offset the military setbacks politically.

But soldiers also realized, having been insurgents behind insurgents, that insurgent control in this neighborhood is actually a very delicate tapestry, held together by myriad individuals. Their combined efforts create the sense of control people feel crawling on their skin in the neighborhood. "Oh, mister, please, JAM is everywhere," people always said. But no, they are not everywhere; they are just very good at maintaining that illusion.

Combatants always overreach, and sometime or another they will be found. But the many middlemen and politicos can get away with impunity, maintaining the tapestry of control in the neighborhood as long as they remain untouchable. It's the middlemen and politicos that become the backbone of the insurgency, bankrolling the combatants.

As long as soldiers grant the middlemen immunity, they can get away with murder. That is the shrewd genius of a political-military organization with political legitimacy and international recognition. They are untouchable in the neighborhood because we have handed it to them. There may be many ways to unravel the delicate tapestry, but the way soldiers imagined (in their Arak-induced hallucinations) was to do it from the margins, be subversive and effective and relentless. The Iraqi people remain center stage, unharmed and going about their business, while soldiers traverse the night.

Soldiers cannot worry about big things, they can only do what they can. Many JAM bigwigs pass through the neighborhood, and at the end of the day it is the soldiers who are willing to walk the streets at night and nobody else. Soldiers can only commiserate with a nightcap at dawn, imagine, and engage in Arak-induced hallucinations, staying out of sight and out of mind . . . thinking about Midaq Alley.

❖ The delicate tapestry in hallucinations

It is a very delicate and intricate tapestry that JAM has woven in controlling Midaq Alley. The Iraqi Police, with its many militia members, remain complicit, allowing the combatants to get away or even providing top cover on the ground. The Iraqi Army stays out of the fight. In both the local police station and the local military garrison, amid the multitude of good men, there is a handful of mid-ranking members who wield more power than their official rank confers because of their JAM political affiliation.

The railway security men in Midaq Alley hang out at the railway station all day doing nothing but drinking tea; they also include a few such people. The same with hospital security—some of the worst, with their blue shirts and their AK-47s. It makes sense: JAM controls the health ministry and transportation ministry. But not everyone is militia, most of them want the jobs just to feed their families. A handful of believers actually run the show, and the people, especially the people who work for them, are very afraid of that handful.

Soldiers have encountered one very high-ranking hospital and health ministry administrator, with connections in the highest levels of the health ministry, who has no health-related training whatsoever. Now he is face down on the ground in his own bedroom with a soldier's boot on his neck. There was a Sancho Panza who tried to move, but he swiftly went airborne into a wall, and a few seconds later he is outside in his KIA vehicle, well under control. The soldiers in the room are smiling, recalling that they owe this beautiful moment to the angry physician and his cell phone. The H&H rattlesnake is trying to crawl on the ground with his pressed down paunch. He invokes higher authority, not just Iraqi but also American authorities. The soldier listens to him describe how terribly the soldiers will get in trouble because all his friends and authorities, including the Americans, will be after the soldiers. It is a very sweet and charming moment being insurgents behind insurgents.

❖ Shahrazad in Midaq Alley

> "Be careful, daughter, for thoughts assume concrete forms in palaces and give voice."
> "I sacrificed myself," she said sorrowfully, "in order to stem the torrent of blood."
> "God has His wisdom," he muttered.
> "And the Devil his supporters," she said in a fury.
>
> —*Arabian Nights and Days*

Authority and power have meaning only if others abide by it. This little man's power and authority rest on the assumption that everyone around him will always abide by it, click heels, and give him what he wants. Relying on his immunity, he is under the mistaken belief that soldiers, in their hallucinations, are also of this mindset. After so much hard work and taking risks, there is nothing more heartwarming than to catch a self-righteous prick that has blood on his hands. He needs to have his moment.

Yes, nothing would be more gratifying than to punch one of them in the face, somebody who has walked around swaggering for too long, feeling mighty in his position and assuming he will always be immune from harm. All it would take is one good heartfelt punch for the world to come crashing down. "How could you do this, you cannot do this, this is illegal!" But that need not ever be done, if soldiers hallucinate very, very carefully.

The man is insisting that it is illegal to catch him. The soldier grabs his chubby cheeks in his palms and looks at his eyes, resisting the worst of human impulses roiling inside him: "Oh really, illegal, eh?" Funny how a guy who bankrolls murder for a living feels righteous enough to invoke legality to save his own skin.

"Well, sir, tell me again, why is it illegal?"

His eyes look very intense, the cheeks wobbling frantically, the fat folds fluttering in fear and consternation. His power now is only in his imagination, and he will have to slowly come to terms with his precarious situation. It will take some time. No physical harm need be done in any form or fashion, for it is unnecessary and he is not worth it. So the soldiers try to give him some peace and solitude. They zip-tie his hands, duct-tape his mouth (hundred-mile-an-hour army-issue tape, made by the lowest bidder, is never sticky enough), put a facemask on him, and stuff him in the closet that smells like every other closet in an Iraqi house. It is important to let him have some time alone. Being alone, he will hopefully remember the many men and women who lived a lifetime in a second thanks to him. Each time he wobbles his head and knocks it on the locked door he will know what it feels like to be knocking on heaven's door; knock-knock.

Then the two soldiers in the room turn to the bed. Barging into bedrooms, looking for rattlesnakes when they least expect them, soldiers have run into awkward and humorous moments. It was not lost on the two soldiers that this is a huge bed, like no other, because it hurts the eyes. A soldier walks over and touches the top of it, "Are you serious, what the hell is this?" Delicately, he rubs his hand over it laughing, "Oooh very smooth." The huge bed is all bright yellow silk, a shiny florescent yellow; the pillows, the comforters, the sheets all have long ornate bright yellow frills. He turned to the other soldier with a cackle.

"So—check this man, so this is what an executive fuck chamber looks like, yellow silk and lots of it," he said and pats the bed. They are both laughing. The other soldier sits and bounces on it: "Oooh, very firm too."

The rattlesnake's wife is standing in the corner by the closet, wearing a shiny silk and polyester nightgown straight out of an American civil war movie. It seems the best way for a middle-aged man to have a mistress and not call her a mistress is to call her a wife. She is the third of his wives.

Her hands are tightly held together under her chin, long black hair all over the place. She wants to scream but nothing comes out. The soldier steps over to her and says quietly, "You know your husband is a murderer?"

She has a vague ambivalent look. The soldier waves his hand. Now he asks her about the stack of money that was in the closet. Obviously, she has no idea about the money, despite it being found in her closet. Of course, no one ever has any idea.

It was not lost on the two soldiers that she was remarkably pretty and looked terrified of her situation. She was certainly feeling older than her twenty-two years of age, surrounded by two gun-toting foreign soldiers in her bedroom in the middle of the night who have just shoved her fifty-year-old husband and master into a closet.

She may claim not to know, but soldiers know a thing or two about her husband, his money, and even about her, and they want to find out more about his friends. And that six-figure bundle of crisp clean U.S. dollars was in her closet. They are so clean, still in their brand new plastic casings, that one could perhaps trace the footsteps of the dollars all the way back to the Federal Reserve Bank by way of the health ministry of Iraq. She is insisting that it is money from the government, because her husband is a high-ranking member of the government, a member of the Sadrist party, and now she invokes higher authority.

"Of course," the soldier answers, "Ali is big, very big, that's why we are here." Ali has nothing do with the health ministry and everything to do with distributing cash to the minions and foot soldiers with the immunity his position provides. In soldiers' hallucinations, a guy who distributes the cash, who enables the combatant nut-jobs to do what they do, has as much American and Iraqi blood on his hands as combatants do. The real health ministry officials don't own a car, they take the mini-busses and go from clinic to clinic, and they point out to anybody that would listen their real grievances—the broken and missing equipment and never enough medicine. Where *does* that budget go to?

What Ali's beautiful mistress genuinely does not know is that in the trunk of his black Kia sedan are weapons and tools used for torture, the blood on them still warm if she cared to touch it. It is usually his friends who do the grunt work, not him, but that's a minor detail.

The beautiful mistress is agitated, even angry, justifiably since her master is now in the closet. A soldier grabbed her by the wrist, looked at her and said simply, "Shut up." He took her outside—pleading and begging, no doubt imagining the worst. She was surprised when they stopped at the KIA. He opened the trunk.

"Yes, it is real blood, go ahead grab it, touch the damn thing. *That* is what your husband does in the health ministry." The soldier grabbed a hairbrush-like tool that JAM uses and held it near her face, just a few inches away.

"Go ahead, you can comb your hair with it," and he gestured combing her hair as she stood bewildered and scared. Her eyes could not hide the bewilderment. Could someone be so naïve, so truly ignorant of her husband and master? Maybe, if one is locked up in the house. But it is also the best trick, and no one knows tricks better than a good looking woman with pink cheeks.

Clearly, the rattlesnake resting in the closet did not expect soldiers to be in his house that day. He does not have the KIA sedan parked in this carport every day, his minions handle the car. Comfortable in his position, he had forgotten how many people in the neighborhood live in sorrow because of him and his friends. Not every Iraqi in the neighborhood is afraid. Thanks to some of them, soldiers could hallucinate being insurgents behind insurgents.

The soldier again grabbed the mistress by her wrist and took her to the living room. "OK, now, be quiet, sit on that couch. One more word, just one more goddamn word and you and your husband will both go into that trunk."

She has no idea about her husband's business. She insists that he did not give her anything at the moment of his apprehension.

"OK, no problem."

A soldier brought her brother into the room. "This is your brother, yes?"

Yes, she nods her agreement and insists that he is just as ignorant as she is. The soldier went about six inches from her face and asked, "You are telling me that you don't know anything about your husband's business?"

"No."

"OK, no problem." The soldier quietly moved back, walked away and brought her brother and pulled down one of those big woven carpet things from the wall, a wall hanging, and wrapped it around her brother's head and face.

Looking at her again: "You don't know anything about your husband's business?"

"No." But now she has bewildered and scared eyes. The soldier nods. He asks two others to hold the brother and make him lie down on the ground. Then the soldier looks at the wife again. "No, you don't know anything about your husband's business?"

"No," but she is now pleading not to do any harm to her brother because he is as innocent as she is. They are both utterly ignorant, and she is insisting, pleading.

The soldier nods his acquiescence and grabs the breach tool—a pointless but scary-looking piece of equipment for opening a door. "No problem, tell me, you don't know anything about your husband's business?"

"No, No, No, No," and she is pleading, "please don't do any harm; we are both innocent."

He takes a good look at her face, and then aims the breach tool toward the head wrapped in the carpet with the body writhing about, and he looks like he is about to swing it. He looks at the wife again simply asking, "No?"

She is beginning to get hysterical. "Please, don't, he is my brother. We don't know anything. It is just Ali that is doing this business," and she has long, big tears running down her cheeks that have now turned completely red.

The soldier has one foot on her brother's back, very lightly and just for show. Because he is innocent and valuable, her brother is safe, but she does not know it and she is scared. So is the brother, trying to flap around like a fish out of water. Two soldiers are holding him down, and the soldier with his foot on the guy's back looks at her again, this time addressing her with a stern voice. "Your husband and his friends go around killing people and torturing them," and she is looking at him with a blank stare; she cannot deny it. She has seen the blood-soaked tools that he had in his misconceived sense of security left lying in the trunk. The soldier asks her, "Your husband's friends even killed your neighbor because he thought your neighbor was helping us—and you know nothing about his businesses?" He looked at her and simply said, "You are lying."

She is now crying. There is neither agreement nor disagreement, and she is just looking scared and hysterical.

He grunted a deliberate laugh, gruff and ominous.

"Lady, you are very pretty, very pretty, and your face will be covered in a lot of blood soon and you should cover it and do it now. DO YOU

FUCKING UNDERSTAND?" He yelled about three inches from her face in the most ominous voice he could muster, "Look at me!"

"We are first going to take care of your brother," and his index finger was almost touching her fair, pointy chin as he was yelling. Her eyes got wider as if they may explode out of her skull with gushing fountains of tears. "When we are done with your brother, it will be YOUR TURN and you will HATE YOUR LIFE." Then the soldier moved his face even closer to hers and screamed, "Look at this, watch this."

He grabs the shotgun that is used to breach doors and aims it at her brothers' head on the ground, still wrapped in the wall hanging. He is struggling to move, asking for mercy, begging for his life. He cocks the shotgun loudly and deliberately. A shotgun makes a very ominous noise when it is loaded, and one buckshot naturally drops to the ground with a noise that must have sounded to her like a deep thud: A shotgun, though silly as a weapon in the frontlines, has the ability to make a terrible noise. The buckshot bounces off the carpet and rolls by her feet.

The woman starts screaming and springs up from the couch, shrieking, wailing. She pulls the front of her silk and polyester nightgown, tearing it open, nearly exposing her breasts and reaches inside, pulling out two cell phones and a little notebook with a leather binding.

Nearly every insurgent, when soldiers surprise them at home, will stuff their most precious belongings down their wives' and daughters' chests, and this rattlesnake tied down in the closet in the next room is no different.

Now the soldier threw the shotgun at the soldier next to him, his best friend, and said with a smile, "Thank you, Dima, that's your name, right?" as if he had just walked in for a cup of coffee.

She collapsed back into her chair with a wild expression as if a million thoughts were crossing her mind at once.

The soldier then helped her brother up and freed his head and apologized to him. He looks scared, utterly terrified. Another soldier is asked to take him to the next room and give him some water and a cigarette to calm his nerves. Soldiers need to talk to him. He now needs to feel safe and comfortable so he can be coherent. The brother is just a student at the technical school, but what he knows of his brother-in-law is valuable to the soldiers.

The woman looks relieved, but she is crying. The word "crying" understates her anguish a million-fold, especially as her brother was taken to the next room and she is now sitting alone on the couch in her revealing night gown, alone with two soldiers—one of whom threatened her and nearly killed her brother—while her master is stuffed in the closet. His minion is curled up in the trunk of the KIA parked outside: He too needs some solitude before soldiers can talk to him so he can answer coherently. But Dima, the mistress, is far more important.

The soldier pulls a chair next to her and sits down, saying with all sincerity in a calm voice, "Please do not worry; we will not do any harm."

She is sitting with legs pressed together, fingers interlocked into a ball in front of her chest. Her hands shake, she is shaking, and her wide open honey-colored pleading eyes are locked on the soldier's.

So the soldier adds in the same voice, "We are very sorry, Dima, very sorry, we know you and your young brother are innocent. We will not take your brother or you, and please know that you and your family are safe."

Her eyes are still locked in with the soldiers and she is shaking; she looks as if she is worried her heart will stop beating at any moment. The slightest motion of the soldiers startles her, despite their now calm demeanor.

So he adds again, "I promise, no one, NO ONE, will harm you or your brother, OK, do you understand?"

She does not, as her brain is way too overwhelmed. She is sitting absolutely still, long black hair flowing down her back, hands still tightly clasped in a ball now covering her mouth, wearing her colorful polyester nightgown, and she looks as if she wants to curl into a fetal position.

The soldier stands up and walks to her bedroom, her eyes following him all the way to the room, and he disappears inside. After a few minutes he walks back to her, feeling the desperate wide eyes follow him still. Then the soldier spreads over her shoulders the black abaya that he found in the bedroom, draping it over her head and wrapping it completely around her. She quickly grabs it with her left hand and her eyes still have the same desperate gaze. The soldier kneels down on one knee next to her, and says again, looking at her eyes now peeking out of the abaya, "No soldier will harm you or your brother, trust me, you will always be safe."

Her eyes and face held a deep stare as if they were searching for the soldier's soul, and she had no words or nods, only the intermittent blinking of her long black eyelashes. If the blinking meant anything, it was not agreement or even understanding but simply hope. She just blinked her hope that she would not be harmed and would retain her dignity. After what she witnessed, and what she no doubt imagined, it is understandable but not useful because she needs to be normal, coherent, and comfortable. She has the answers to so many riddles.

So the soldier slowly gets off his knee and steps back, saying, "Trust me, you will be safe." He walks toward the room where her brother is being watched over by some other soldiers. He could feel her eyes following him everywhere. He stops at the door, laughs and talks to the soldiers and the brother, now smoking a nervous cigarette. He goes into the room and cuts the zip ties off so he can smoke freely and walks him to the door. His older sister is peeking toward the room and the soldier says with a smile, "Everyone is safe," and asks him to sit inside the room and keep smoking, no problem, have some Pepsi too if you want.

The soldier goes to Dima sitting on the red velvet couch. "Do you need some water, please drink some water." She is non-committal, still peeking at the soldier's eyes, but she has calmed down a lot. He gets a soldier to bring a glass of water from the fridge. Then he slowly takes a knee in front of her and offers the glass of water in the right hand. She is staring at the soldier's eyes, not moving.

The soldier, kneeling in front of her holding a glass of water with both hands, looking straight at her eyes says in his calm voice says, "We are sorry, but we promise, we mean no harm to you and your family; you will be safe, we promise." She nods now, her eyes still locked with his, and the soldier added, delicately offering the glass of water with both hands, "Please, please, drink some water, and you will feel much better, please."

Amazingly, she grabs the glass of water with both hands, closes her eyes, and drinks it down, as if she was parched the entire time. Then she opens her eyes, slowly brings the glass to her lap, and gives it back to the kneeling soldier, looking straight at him.

He grabbed the glass with his right hand, touching her left hand with his left, and said looking at her eyes, "Dima, right, that's your name, please, do not worry, you will be very safe with us, nothing, no soldier will harm you or your brother or anybody, I promise."

She nodded slowly, and uttered "yes" very quietly, and that was the first sign that she is coming back to life. Still kneeling, the soldier added, smiling slightly, "Please take deep breaths, you will feel better, OK," and she nodded. She is slowly coming back to being normal. If soldiers are to get any information from her she needs to be unafraid, comfortable, and coherent, so she can follow a little reason and logic and recount things in her memory, as soldiers know from experience.

He got up and took the glass, passed it onto another soldier and asked him to bring another glass of water. Then he peered into the other room where her brother is sitting, smoking a cigarette with some other soldiers keeping an eye on him, and he greets him, asks him whether he is OK: "Do you need anything, water, pepsi?" And a soldier also brought him a pepsi from the kitchen. It is so important to get them a little comfortable.

Now he is talking and laughing with the soldiers. Goofing around will give both of them some time to be comfortable and just be themselves, ignoring the surrounding always seems to put people a little at ease.

434

The soldier walks back to Dima, sitting on the couch, her eyes still following him. In fact, her eyes will always be following him, glued to his every move. He hands her the next glass of water and sits on the ground next to her feet, about six inches from her, leaning on the big chair next to the couch in this luxurious living room. Looking up at her, he says with a slight smile, "Please do not worry, trust me, no problem, no problem, I promise, everyone will be safe."

"Yes," she says, and her voice sounds shaky but a little steady. Her eyes shows that she doesn't believe it, but perhaps she wants to believe it, and that's making progress. Soldiers are finally getting somewhere in this rabbit hole.

Now another soldier, the wandering gypsy, waddles in smiling and sits down next to the other soldier on the ground. And the soldier closest to her feet looks up at her again, and says with a smile, "Well, you have to tell us a story."

She was looking from one to the other, first at his eyes, then the other's.

"Dima, I am sure you know lots of stories."

She was looking bewildered, with two guys sitting on the ground by her feet who are armed to the teeth and talking about stories with a smile. But she does not seem to be afraid, and that's the most important understanding. She needs to be normal to tell a good story. The same guy who threatened her and her brother about half an hour ago is now at her feet, asking her to tell stories.

"I am sure you know a lot of wonderful stories, like Shahrazad! I think I will have to call you Shahrazad, what do you think, did you read about Shahrazad in school, yes, maybe?"

She has wide brilliant honey-colored eyes sparkling and staring. "We read about Shahrazad all the time, the beautiful princess who knew so many stories."

The soldiers are quietly smiling; it is their inside joke. Because a whole lot of soldiers get addicted to different things, and reading was one of their addictions. They were sucked into everything related to these Middle Eastern authors they had never before heard of. One of the leaders kept spending so much money on books that his lovely wife threatened to give him a monthly allowance: "Listen here, you cannot send your entire paycheck to Amazon.com to buy books. I will give you 300 dollars a month," and yes, it quickly went for books or else to buy knickknacks for Iraqis. So, some of the best are books about Captain Sir Richard Francis Burton and his ultimately hilarious monstrosity, *The Book of One Thousand Nights and a Night* (popularly known as *A Thousand and One Nights*). It would rattle many cages given how politically incorrect it is; Sir Burton was nothing if not honest with his opinions. Besides, he was the ultimate wandering gypsy who had to keep moving to stay alive. No one soldiers knew had read the entire monstrosity, no matter how funny, but lots of them looked at the funny parts and they always liked Shahrazad.

Then it got better as some soldiers got addicted to Naguib Mahfouz in Iraq. How could one not get addicted to him? His fantastical fiction, *Arabian Nights and Days,* brought Shahrazad back into their lives, as some soldiers kept reading it again and again. Every Iraqi woman who would help the soldiers with stories would be quickly given a code name. But Shahrazad was always special, one who had the most tactically valuable information that can easily be turned into actionable intelligence and then into tactical realities.

Dima is looking down at the soldiers by her feet. One of them is now smoking a cigarette, after asking her permission, which she granted with a quizzical nod. The other has a kind of golf ball stuck in his lower lip (Copenhagen long cut). Her head is moving from side to side, perhaps puzzling out what to make of this. She is holding the glass of water in her lap with both hands with a death grip. The hot, humid night makes the glass sweat, and water covers her well-manicured fingers. Her eyes are watching every single move of the soldiers, but she is no longer peeking out of the abaya, which is now pulled back on her head and shoulders, revealing wide eyes and pink cheeks. The soldier by her feet asks the other one to bring some sort of napkin, and he brings a checkered piece of cloth from the kitchen to wrap the sweating glass of water.

Both soldiers sitting by her feet would look up, sometimes smiling, listening to her barely audible voice. But are they are smiling at the woman, who now looks uncomfortably comfortable sitting on the couch with soldiers at her feet, or at the myriad ayatollahs gazing down from the wall of the living room. Soldiers have been at this nonsense far too goddamn long, and in their Arak-induced hallucinations they can still feel the gaze from the wall, as they have nearly every day for the past several months.

The soldier by her feet very delicately reached for the holy grail. This is a Sadrist holy grail, and it pertained to this neighborhood and the adjacent neighborhoods. The little notebooks, his PDA that Shahrazad had kindly given the soldiers are the most important things in this household. Everything the soldier did revolved around how to could get Shahrazad to decipher these holy grails. After she finishes, soldiers can go get the brother, he will do more.

Ali, her master, will be the last. Because it's best to go to him not with questions, but with a definite point: There is no point in lying, the gig is up. Soldiers need him to clarify what they already know, and he will come to terms with it after being in the closet for a while. Then he can expand on the stories. He has to be the last, let him sit, tied down, in a distant dark corner in the closet coming to terms with his situation and not knowing what is happening on the other side of the house to his pretty mistress. That is the one thing he most wants to find out, but that is the one thing he will never find out. As long as he does not, he will always be ready for insightful battlefield tactical questioning. Let him wallow in his imagination all alone, no doubt imagining the worst of human beings, and that would be just fine. He is the hardest nut to crack but squirrels on a pine nut can always get it cracked.

The Holy grail is the opening to a rabbit hole—a long wonderful rabbit-hole matrix that would bring to life, from page to page, the JAM politicos, the many middlemen who believe they can remain immune and get away with their complicity in murder (of both Iraqis and Americans), the nominal health ministry officials with no health training, transportation ministry, social affairs, the security men, and combatants in police uniforms in these neighborhoods. She will bring to life everyone Ali is associated with in all the intricacies.

Shahrazad seems to be sitting comfortably, good progress, but her constant gaze at the soldier by her feet remained the same. After a while the soldier would want to ask her to quit staring. But she never did, the strangest thing, as if no one else in the room mattered. He could feel the gaze: Any way he turned, those two honey-colored eyes followed him around—whether anger, hate, fear, indifference, who the hell knows. It couldn't possibly be anything good.

Always looking down at the soldier by her feet, Dima indeed took the two soldiers on a guided tour through labyrinthine rabbit holes, bringing an intricate subversive reality to life with her now normal fair complexion and her calm ringing voice. The joke between the two soldiers was that perhaps Iraqi husbands—perhaps husbands nearly everywhere—need to give more credit to their wives, as Shahrazed was teaching them. She knew so much, perhaps more than she imagined she knew, and surely more than the soldiers imagined, with intimate knowledge of where he hides the Benjamin Franklins, not just in this house but also in others. How much she has learned simply by being an anonymous observer. Nearly everything she said checked out. Soldiers in their imagination find this moment wonderful, it is hard for foot soldiers to come up with Benjamin Franklins *and* solid stories—but in a careful hallucination, both are very necessary.

Shahrazad could certainly tell a story, keeping the soldiers by her feet absorbed and scribbling furiously. One soldier kept complimenting her as the other smiled genuinely, what a wonderful storyteller she was. Dima, sitting on the couch in Midaq Alley, could certainly give the mythical Shahrazad a run for her reputation.

Then the soldier asked permission to make some tea in her kitchen. She starts to get up, but they insist, "No, no, we will make it." But she refuses, no, she will make it. The soldiers insist again, "No, no, we will make it, could we?"

After all, this is not the first time soldiers have cooked in Iraqi kitchens; they have been around for a while. There have been moments, soldiers would get permission and pay the families and cook a great breakfast after a long night of soldiering. Trying to have an American-style breakfast with good scrambled eggs or omelets with fresh garden eggs in an Iraqi kitchen in the middle of nowhere was always a humorous sight. A squad or two of American soldiers, sometimes covered in a kind of soot, cooking in an Iraqi kitchen and the Iraqi kids running between, sometimes the men and women would be part of it, sometimes they help with the cooking. Sometimes they would join in on the crazy feast, laughing, joking, and with a little disbelief. Soldiers will finish a great breakfast and enjoy the simple pleasures of life, then clean it up—always clean up your goddamn mess—and get some sleep huddled on the floor wrapped in their blankets, insisting on paying for their hospitality, and then walk into a different part of the village for another night of soldiering.

Only this time, they are in a different house in their imagination. She will make the tea, she insists. "OK, thank you." Both soldiers follow her to her kitchen, and she makes the tea while continuing her stories.

It turned out that her brother was endowed with the same storytelling gift. He kept the soldiers enthralled, smoking cigarettes in the other room, with complete certainty that his sister was safe and sound and, amazingly enough, occasionally even smiling.

It was not lost on the soldiers that neither Shahrazad nor her brother ever asked about the fate of her husband. Every little detail can be important, particularly the incongruous ones that emerge through tactical questioning. It makes the story a bit richer, exposes the intricacies of JAM ideologues. Even her husband might croak a story or two with some effort, but he was the last one. He had to be outside, in the distance and anonymous.

Having listened to stories from Shahrazad and her brother in separate rooms, soldiers brought her brother to the living room. There was so much evident relief on their faces, it was wonderful. He sat next to his big sister, both feeling secure and comfortable, and that is most important when they are both cooperating. The little brother now becomes the big brother, and he is the one telling stories. But she will always remain the most important, with her knowledge.

They both speak, at times one correcting the other, and soldiers note the errors and corrections and keep coming back to them randomly. Soldiers are on a wonderful guided tour into a reality that they had already put together in pieces, and now they are filling the blanks and opening up new vistas. Battlefield tactical questioning is a rabbit hole with no end; at times, one just has to know when to end and leave an opening to go back. Strangely enough, soldiers will be in touch with both of them in their imagination for a long time—because Shahrazad knew a lot and, surprisingly, was always helpful with her stories.

In a counterinsurgency, even in imagination, it is always gratifying when efforts of soldiering pay off. Ali was too good, too connected, and too powerful, and as a mighty enabler with loads of cash who rolls with the high and mighty, he was always secure in his ways. He could travel, hang out, and visit family at his will, immune in his position. He knew everybody: police, army, JAM, the JAM politicians, and that is his strength. He rarely deemed it necessary to have an army of body-guards or militia men, usually just one or two grizzled men to make the point, walking around with his paunch: "I am who I am"—with the grizzly looking minion suckling on his power tit.

The middlemen, politicos, and enablers enjoy going everywhere with impunity; they surf the waves of ambiguity with ease, straddling all their worlds. This guy, alas, has now fallen off his surfboard and there are no lifeguards to pull him out, as soldiers had taken care of his lifeguards.

Soldiers feel heartfelt gratitude to the good physician at a hospital. Thanks to him, soldiers knew of Ali's other wives, knew enough to go after this guy in their imagination and come to this particular house with his third, most recent beautiful wife. Soldiers don't command massive resources, there is no need; paying attention to every little nook and cranny can be of value. Soldiers have been listening to vil-lage gossip for too long, walked the streets and been around the house numerous times, and they knew there is no end to a rabbit hole; they just have to keep listening.

Little details are important in soldiering. It was perhaps easier to try to get him at his first wife's house, with his three kids and a wife of twenty years. But would a wife of twenty years and the mother of his children have been as adept and willing to tell stories—whether she loved him or hated him? There is no telling.

Soldiers are getting ready to leave, thanking Shahrazad for her efforts, but they recognize her concerns and apprehensions. There is always an opportunity in everything, and how to capture it is the hardest part. They tell her that they will be taking the KIA vehicle (as it would be good to make it anonymous in their imagination), but there is the little detail of so many Benjamin Franklins. In the movies, people carry tons of the stuff so easily. But the stuff is heavy, cumbersome, and takes up a lot of space; when there is so much of it, something needs to be done. Soldiers decided on a way that may or may not work for the best.

In the bedroom, Shahrazad piled every single Benjamin on the ornate and shiny dresser, complete with a six-foot mirror and mind-numbing amounts of colorful shiny knickknacks. The soldiers tell her, "we will take a little of this, but we will leave the rest here with you. Can you take care of it. We trust you. We will come back some time later. You can feel free to use it, no problem."

Even half of it is a big stack, more than most Iraqis or Americans could imagine in a lifetime, and soldiers could put it to very good use in their imagination. It is not so much a question of whether she would look after the money or run with it: They are trying for another, more important possibility. While Shahrazad has been very helpful in her guided tour of the rabbit hole, deciphering her master's many lives and his friends, she could be of even more use. But would she do it?

In a day or two a lot of JAM guys, minions, middlemen, maybe even some police and politicos will be swarming all over Shahrazad's house, as she knows. As the favorite mistress (with very good lineage) of a very powerful man who has access to a whole lot of U.S. taxpayers' money, she is far older than her twenty-two years. She could rhyme a riddle like no other. If soldiers could get her to phone and tell them who came by her house, what questions they asked, and what their concerns were, it would be that much more useful in soldiers' imagination. One has to keep trying because it is important to learn who comes to the house and to learn their concerns.

"Dima, you need to be safe." She nodded her understanding. It is perhaps the one thing she has felt and known in her bones ever since soldiers got there.

"After we take your husband and his friend, we don't know what will happen, lot of JAM people will be coming to this house."

She is standing by her dresser in her bedroom with her hands folded in front of her, her eyes clearly showing her apprehensions. Behind her, on the big ornate and mind-numbingly complicated dresser, are the countless Benjamin Franklins that she obligingly stacked.

She knows that the moment soldiers leave, taking her master and the KIA (they would leave her the luxury vehicle for her own use, they told her), her life is about to change. Her heart must be beating as fast as it can. But she is not crying, not freaked out, very coherent and she hangs on every word that comes out of the mouths of the two soldiers talking to her.

"Dima, your husband is very powerful—you know that the moment we leave, a lot of people will come and try to talk to you and ask about the money too?" She nodded again, yes.

"We want you to be safe, do you understand?" and she nodded again. Soldiers asked her to take a seat, "Please, please."

"Look, Dima, no one will know what you told us, but many people will be afraid when they hear that Ali is gone. Don't tell anybody that you told us anything, no one will know."

She has the blank, wide stare that soldiers become familiar with in a counterinsurgency.

442

"The moment we leave, call your family, and ask them to come to your house and stay with you, *as many family as you can*, OK? It is very very important."

She has very big eyes still hanging on every word coming out of the soldier's mouth. For the two soldiers, she was undoubtedly a poignant and lonely figure. Well, life sucks, she is innocent, yes, and she has had no choice in the matter because Ali was her husband. She was his third wife and favorite mistress and he is the man who brings home the kebabs; she only cooked them. She knows her world will be different tomorrow when she wakes up and life, alas, is never fair. But still, it would be very useful if she could continue to help!

All the people that will cross her path in the next couple of weeks are important. But she also needs to live and be safe. There is no telling whether the JAM men that will come by her house will treat her with dignity and have respect for her life. Without Ali, her master, she could be reduced to nothing, and it is very important that she gets all the family members to her house as soon as she can. Because a lot of people will be coming looking for the money—and to find out what she has said.

"Dima, we have your phone number, and we will give you our phone numbers; you will always be safe with us. If anyone, *anyone* threatens you or tries to harm you, make sure you call us OK, we will take care of them. We want you to be safe."

Those eyes again.

"You have to be careful with the money. People will come looking for it. You have to say the soldiers took it, do you understand, you need to be safe?"

Then she looked deeply at the soldier standing in front of her, the one that she always kept staring at, and she asked, in her very soft voice, *shou-es-mak,* and then in her accented English: "What's your name?"

Soldiers in their hallucination were a little surprised, and thankful, that they never wore names or unit insignia in their jacked-up uniforms; it was so hot. They look carefully at Shahrazad sitting in that ridiculous bed, covered partially in her abaya, with her eyes moving from one soldier to the other—maybe pleading, quizzical, angered, or simply fatigued, nothing good could possibly be going on in her mind—and stopped at the same soldier she was always staring at.

Yes, soldiers genuinely cared about her life; she is innocent, but there is a job at hand, catch more men with American and Iraqi blood on their hands. The soldiers want to instill in her the sense that the only people that could answer her definitively about her master's fate are the soldiers, and that she will be safe with them.

The soldier answered her with a smile and tapped his friend on the shoulder saying, "Well, you can call him Mustapha Amer, and me, you can call me Amer Diyab."

For the first time she had something close to a genuine smile, perhaps surprised at his answer. The soldier added with a quizzical look, "Why, you don't think we are good, trust me, we are as good as both of them." She is still staring, almost with a laugh.

Then the soldier resumed his serious manner. "OK, OK, no problem. OK, you can call him Hani Shaker and me, I am Kazem al-Zaher—yes?"[89] This time, she genuinely laughed. She looked down at the ground and regained her serious comportment before looking up. "What is your name?"

She could not know what to make of these two soldiers, who started off threatening everyone and have now turned themselves progressively into clowns. But one thing will always be in her mind despite the unexpected laugh: The clowns had no soft spot for her master, and she does not know how he might end up at their hands. But she at least seems to have understood that she does not have to worry about her life and dignity with the soldiers. Soldiers have no doubt there are many wonderful stories she could tell in the coming weeks, if she would.

---

[89] All four are names of popular Arabic-language singers.

"OK, OK, no problem, Dima, oh, princess Shahrazad. This here is Willie Nelson and me, my name is Kris Kristofferson. Outside the door, that big guy, he is Waylon Jennings and our friend sitting in the room talking to your brother, that is Johnny Cash. The guy by the car, you can call him Bruce Springsteen." Not a single soldier in this house is worthy of the names of such good men. But they had to call themselves something, and what better than the names of people that keep them inspired in many a dark moment?

"You can call him Willie, and you can call me Kris." Her eyes moved from one to the other and there is no deciphering what in the world was going through her head, but it could not be anything good—let us not be ridiculous, her master was tied down in the closet, and now he is tied down inside a KIA about to be taken away.

"Dima, trust us, hide the money, do not tell anyone where you put it. Use it so you can help the family. If you want, you can keep all of it, OK?" She nodded, and the soldiers said, "Look, you can tell everyone—soldiers came and took the money and Ali and his friend." She nodded again, "Yes." She was staring at the soldier, she would have to process everything and do it well, that's the only way she could be safe.

The soldier moved closer to Shahrazad, still staring at him, sitting at the edge of her bed, hands folded on her lap. "Dima, please, you have to promise, please call your family and ask them to come to your house and do so soon. Ali's friends will not be able to help you, they will be scared, and they may try to harm you because they are scared."

She is staring at him and nodding. It was a very peculiar sight. He has his right hand delicately on the piston grip of his M4 Carbine hanging around his neck, along with hand grenades, flash bangs, GPS systems, and a whole lot more, and he is on his knee next to the bed, asking, "Please call your family, *before you call anybody else*, please, we want you to be safe."

She nodded looking down at him, and her honey-colored eyes were fixed on the soldier's eyes as so many terrible thoughts perhaps crossed her mind. "Dima, please will you call your family, we want you to be safe?"

Her eyes were glued to his. "Yes," she whispered, and she nodded and whispered her soft "Yes" again. The soldier asked her whether she remembers their names. Yes she does, and she pointed with a smile to one and the other, giving their names, and then asked, surprisingly, "Is it true?"

Soldiers laughed loud. "Of course, why you don't trust us, habibi? You should call us, you will know more about us." They laughed again, saying they must leave her, no doubt it broke her heart because her master was in the KIA and he was leaving too.

She had a very blank stare in her honey-colored eyes. The two soldiers took slow deliberate steps outside to the KIA. The KIA will ride them halfway home in their imagination.

It is a sad moment. Her life starting tomorrow will be different without her master, but life is never fair, if it were fair, soldiers would be out of a job. Dima is precariously safe, and it is, after all, a war, and she may have not asked for it, but she is in it. But there is a very serious practical concern.

Would she be willing to tell them about the people who would visit her? She could still be of value as a source of information. But the moment soldiers leave, she could pick up the phone and call her master's friends or her family or some JAM guys and say she wants to be an insurgent. She will decide depending on how she thinks and feels, and soldiers could do very little to influence what she might do, other than perhaps give her a call or two in their imaginations. Yes, life in a counterinsurgency is neither fair nor pretty, and getting after the worst of the nut-jobs while isolating the innocent will always remain the primary job for soldiers on the ground. As long as the biggest and the shrewdest of the nut-jobs are in control, the efforts of soldiers on the ground will never really matter: They can always offset their little losses with larger political gains. That is the genius of a political-military organization driven by a convincing sob story that has resonance on the ground.

In soldiers' imaginations, they called her soon to make sure she is well—and then she called to tell them about all the people who had crossed her path. Then soldiers stopped by to listen to more of her stories that were just as valuable.

Her stories were enchanting, illuminating the affluent world of JAM men, their wives and children, and her myriad of friends. It is a whole different rabbit hole, the secretive world of very powerful JAM families that Shahrazad traverses with ease as no American ever could. Alas, soldiers only have so much time being insurgents behind insurgents in their Arak-induced hallucinations, and they can only do what they can while out of sight and out of mind.

One day, after some time has passed, she called, as always, and asked whether soldiers will be around. She then asked the inevitable question that soldiers in their imagination knew she would want to know sooner or later: whether the stories she heard in the streets regarding the fate of her master and many of his friends had any semblance of truth. There is no one better situated to answer the question than the two soldiers standing in front of her once again. The soldier stood silent for a moment. His face looked pained because trying not to lie without actually telling the truth is far more difficult than either.

"Yes, we heard that too. We are very sorry, Dima," and he shrugged his shoulders.

She is hanging on the soldier's eyes as if trying to get a glimpse into his soul. Her own eyes refused to reveal an iota of her true sentiments. Then she said, calling him by his first name, still staring at his eyes, "Yes, I always thought so, I always knew this would happen."

He looked at her closely and asked, "Dima are you safe?" Yes, unequivocally safe. If she had any serious concerns about her the fate of her late husband she hid it incredibly well. Her house is now filled with her extended family, comforting and also a bit funny. Because soldiers would like to believe in their imagination that she followed soldiers' advice, a bunch of Americans who have been insurgents behind insurgents for too long who felt smart-ass enough to advise an Iraqi. Perhaps it was her own instinct. Either way, the place is swarming with family—and that increases her safety.

447

Because even if JAM guys want to go after her, they are aware that this is a very powerful man's beautiful mistress with good lineage. Yet they don't quite know what she said, what she knows, who she talks to. They certainly don't know that she inadvertently helps the soldiers because this is a hallucination, not reality. But even if JAM decides to kill her, it is not so easy to kill fourteen family members now packed into her house with all kinds of toddlers running around.

The soldier commented to Dima, "It is good you brought your family, that keeps you safe?" "Yes, it was a good idea."

Then she had a very unexpected but very practical question. She is planning to move south with her parents, back to her hometown, is it fine if she leaves town?

What a question! But it was strangely a relief, as helpful as she was. Though she understands that soldiers tried to keep her safe, the reality is that they cannot. What saved her was the simple fact that she had her entire extended family with good lineage guarding her from the day after her master was taken.

"Yes, please go, that's a great idea. You will be very safe with your family." But she wonders about all those Benjamins. "Take it all, no problem." Because Ali's friends and the many JAM minions that soldiers have been going after in their imaginations helped the soldiers more than they could dream in their wildest Arak-induced hallucinations.

"Everything?" and she has the most surprised look. "YES."

She can take it all, not a problem, because she has no idea how much she actually helped. She has the same surprised eyes again and a soldier simply said to her, "YES, please take it all, call if there is any trouble. So your family will take you home, they will help you. Yes?"

"Yes," she said in her familiar voice, her eyes hanging on the soldier's as always. He moved next to her with a wary smile, almost a deliberate grin. "Are you sure you will be safe?"

"Yes," she whispered, hanging on his eyes. Her family will bring her down to the family house in the south, and she will be as fine as she could be given her situation.

The soldier who did the most talking is sitting on a chair next to her, as she sits on the same couch where she sat that first day, on their first—unpleasant—meeting with her. Now he scoots off of the plush chair and takes a knee next to her. Soldiers by trade are used to taking knees, they feel safest and most ready to spring up at any moment. The soldier felt very relieved that she is leaving town. It was sad that she will be without a husband or master. But it's a war, and it is also life. She has run out of her value telling stories because soldiers now know everything and everybody that has ever crossed her path. She will be safe now, and soldiers are relieved that they will receive no distressed phone calls they would be unable to answer.

The soldier adds with a smile, "Well, Mustapha Amer and Amer Diyab will always miss you, Princess Shahrazad, please be safe, call us if you want."

Staring at the soldiers' eyes again, no one will ever know what crossed her mind in that strange moment, definitely nothing good. The soldier simply said, "Be safe"—perhaps for the millionth time since they first started listening to her stories. There is no handshake to bid adieu, only stare in her eyes, take a deep breath, and shake the head as soldiers step off from the house, again feeling the intolerable gaze of the ayatollahs from the wall. Shahrazad stands up from the plush red velvet couch, walks them to the door, and stares from the window as they recede into the night.

Soldiers are commiserating again at sunrise, staying out of sight and out of mind. Time to commiserate and indulge in Arak-induced hallucinations. They can make sure many good things happen on the ground, but only in their hallucinations, and ever so carefully, the last best form of subversion for enlisted humanity. Soldiers hypothesize that one day, when the Middle East runs out of oil, they could use Arak as a substitute.

20

HALLUCINATIONS AND BLIND ALLEYS

> "There, butchers
> are posted in passageways
> with bloody chopping blocks and cleavers:
> These are strange times, my dear."
>
> —"In This Blind Alley"[90]

Soldiers in their hallucinations see the man who distributes the food rations in the neighborhood (along with his minions) loudly singing the JAM tune. In spite of his kind face and deep set black eyes, soldiers had to resist many self-destructive impulses. All in good time, they mumble in their imagination.

Sugar Man[91]

He and his friends acquired this job by making the men who previously held the job run for their lives. They got the job and also their houses, which they distributed to loyalists. They are well situated at the nexus of politics, militants, food, and the people. As long as he and his friends control the food supply and its many distribution networks, he has control of the bottom rung of the neighborhood and the displaced people. He and his colleagues decide who gets food and who does not, and the criterion is never who genuinely needs the food. The

---

[90] A poem by the Iranian poet Ahmad Shamlu.
[91] "Sugar Man," by Jesus Rodriguez, "Cold Fact" (1969) and "Live Fact."

people will always kiss his hand under Muqtada's glamor shot on the wall—just as the same people want to thank and kiss soldiers when they give them food and sometimes money and medicine.

The Sugar Man is no joker. He plays a critical role in the tapestry of control on the ground. Soldiers yet again wonder in their hallucinations: Is the Sugar Man a valid target on the ground that fulfils everyone's legal, moral, and political sensibilities? After all, retaking control of the neighborhood is the mission at hand.

No Justice, No Honor

Soldiers are again commiserating in their imaginations, this time sitting at the good police officer's house, having snuck inside in the dark. They have been to his house numerous times, always at night and in hiding. They have been chatting with him about the general difficulties and the precarious existence of people in the neighborhood. Soldiers are good at complaining too; complaints have a strangely bonding effect. Misery loves company, but among the enlisted humanity in the military it is known as camaraderie. Stuck in the middle of some shit hole with limited choices, being out of sight and out of mind with only the imagination for solace, commiserating is a great way to build camaraderie.

Soldiers are desperately trying to feel the pain of the Iraqi Police officer whose brother got killed. "Sir, yes, we are sorry, very sorry about your brother," a soldier says to the police officer.

He grunts with what seemed like a twitch in his eyes.

"Sir, who takes care of his family now?"

He and another brother take care of the family now. But it is difficult, he has a number of kids, so does his brother and the brother who was killed, who ran a store and was relatively affluent.

"Does your brother's wife work?"

"No, she does not; it is very difficult here."

"Yes, we know, we are sorry, maybe we will try to help you out." He has a blank stare, as if saying, how in the hell could you help me?

452

"Tell me what happened, how did they kill your brother?"

He has that distant stare, hard to say whether it is sorrow or anger. Soldiers have heard anguished stories for a long time: The time span since the incident can be measured in the voice of the story, at least with some people. Over time, the passion of loss is reduced to almost a mechanical narrative.

A man and his friends walked to the store run by his brother (he tells the soldiers), and they shot him straight in the head, then the chest, and walked away from the store. He does not know the reason, only that there was some sort of a disagreement with JAM-affiliated extortionists.

Now the good police officer has the familiar comportment of many people who share the whispers of the dead, trying to control and hide the little emotion that is left, having walked with sorrow, consumed by vengeance for a long time and unable to do anything about it.

"And you cannot do anything about this?"

"No, he is JAM, and he has friends."

"But you are police?"

He shrugs the shoulders. Of course, soldiers already know it, but it's good to hear it from him: He recognizes that he is utterly powerless. He cannot even save himself or his brother. The soldier sums it up. "So there is no justice, no honor, and you have to now take care of his family." He shakes his head, then nods acknowledgement.

❖ What's what

"Tell me, sir, what if *we* catch him?"

He instantly looks up, eyes widen and puts his hands in the air, both palms facing the soldiers. "NO, you cannot, YOU SHOULD NOT! His friends will kill my family, and he has friends. He will not stay in jail, he will kill everybody."

The soldier nods his head in agreement and says, "Sir, don't worry about his friends, they are not a problem." Soldiers know that they all hang out and sleep in the same house, nearly every family in one courtyard. All it would take, in the soldiers' imagination, is to get some good guys on roofs who know how to hold their breath when greeting with their AKs in hand.

A soldier looks at him and asks with all sincerity, in his imagination, "Tell me, sir, what if we never send the guy to jail?"

He now sits still, nods his head in a steady rhythm from side to side, and whispers softly, "Yes, this is good."

So the soldier leans forward in the chair, feeling comfortable and asks him, "Tell me, sir, if we make sure that the man does not go to jail and his friends disappear, this is good for you—yes?"

Now he has an ominous foreboding, he is a smart man and knows that this could be a trap, so he is noncommittal, but listening intently. Soldiers in their imagination now ask the critical question as softly as possible, not to get him too riled up.

"Sir, listen, if something happens to him and his friends, and anyone knows that you told us anything about him, you know what will happen to your family, so you have to be quiet, do you understand?"

He has the look of a man who has just had his world crash down. The police officer is worried, for his family, himself, and his extended family. Soldiers try to reassure him, insisting that they are not about to do anything crazy because they always follow the law. But they point out, no one will know because soldiers will not tell any Iraqis or American soldiers about the good police officer.

"Have you told anybody that you have been talking to American soldiers?"

"NO!" Well, he has mentioned that soldiers had stopped by the house as they always do in that neighborhood, but he has said nothing about the growing acquaintance. So the soldiers reassure him, look, there is nothing for you to worry about, just keep doing what you are doing, forget about us, don't even think about us and no one will know. Just make sure your wife doesn't talk to her neighbors about us coming at night.

Soldiers tell him not to worry, "No worries, sir," but he has a very concerned and apprehensive look. So they reassure him, "Sir, do not worry, we will not tell anyone and nothing will happen to the guy, we promise. Listen, we want you to be safe." Around midnight they shook hands and stepped out from the side door into the neighborhood packed with cinderblock houses, one on top of the other.

❖ Who's who

It was another mild concussion, bewildering and unexpected, to learn that the guy who killed the good police officer's brother is actually the local guy who runs the pharmacy in the main street! In fact, he and his friends run one of the local extortion rackets, and they pay homage to JAM.

All the criminals in the neighborhood affiliate with JAM, from the petty shady cats who can find Arak and Johnny Walker Black for soldiers to affluent ones who live in the villas doing contracts for everybody—the government, the Americans, and JAM. Paying homage is necessary for them to stay in business and stay alive.

The black market gasoline distribution racket is also run in collusion with JAM. One of the guys deeply involved is a former army man, now sitting in his various shops in the main thoroughfare. He had his own private little lair where he always felt safest and enjoyed his comforts. In addition to the gasoline racket, he also plays middleman to the many combatant cells. He has blood on his hands, both American and Iraqi, everyone in the neighborhood says so, but it is hard to pin him down on a legalistic criteria and no one will sign a sworn statement. That is predictable. But soldiers, strangely enough, are always friends with him; he is that kind of man, who can play everyone like a violin telling stories.

Every one of these men who retain their position are dependent on many men who in turn do their bidding, who are in turn dependent on other people and their many connections. Their positions are secured by being in a circle inside many other circles; the best of them live safely inside an almost infinite number of concentric circles. All of them also have family visit them, have children and wives (sometimes multiple) have friends, go to functions and even drink.

But every one of them, figuratively speaking, takes a shower sometimes, feeling secure in their position. It's difficult and it takes time, but that's the moment to get them. Every powerful man eventually goes home, cuddles his wife and children and leaves his secure confines. Sooner or later they leave the intricate reality that makes it possible to project their power: When they go home and get naked in the shower, all that is left is the *idea* that they are powerful, not the reality of it. Every man who believes he wields power can be reduced to nothingness and made to come to terms with the new powerless reality with a heartfelt greeting. But soldiers cannot greet all the JAM men they would like. They can only imagine and hallucinate trying to alter the delicate tapestry of insurgent control in these small, interconnected neighborhoods.

In This Blind Alley[92]

> The man who knocks at your door in the noon of the night
> has come to kill the light
>
> Let's hide light in the larder.
>
> —"In This Blind Alley"

In their imaginations, they knew that the local police needed their cages rattled. Because they keep assisting in killing their own people as well as Americans, and they buzz around feeling utterly secure in the immunity that Americans grant them. Not everyone is guilty, it goes without saying, but the guilty ones can always take for granted the innocent police officers and the Americans. The tedious retinal scans, fingerprints, and investigations catch one or two; it is valid and necessary. But the complacency on the ground has to be shattered. There is an easier way to wake the police, both the innocent and the guilty, from their complacent slumber. Soldiers have to hallucinate well, and carefully.

The burst of AK tracer fire lit up the sky, coming from the supposedly "contained" neighborhood, actually run by insurgents. It was a

---

[92] A poem by the Iranian poet Ahmad Shamlu.

neighborhood where soldiers always wanted to go but were prevented by bureaucratic politics: Someone else supposedly "controls the area." For some soldiers and their higher officers it remained a running joke—there is no controlling a damn thing when men with guns roam the streets with impunity, in collusion with law and order that's on the side of the militia. Worse, no American soldier is walking the streets—only driving passed on the adjacent roads. Controlled, contained, let us not be ridiculous. Higher tried their best, but it is difficult to send soldiers in there because it is "someone else's area of control."

But that is the place to be because it is the ultimate snake farm. Well, soldiers need not give heartaches to higher, who already have enough things to worry about and too many battles to fight simultaneously. Soldiers developed a bad habit of losing their way and ending up in this neighborhood. And today, like other days, with each burst of fire the Iraqi Army soldiers in the lone guard post simply crawl deeper inside the sandbags. They feel it is not their fight. Well someone has to tell them that is a bunch of nonsense—but that must wait for later.

In their wildly hallucinating imaginations, a handful of soldiers say the hell with it and get into an Iraqi Police land cruiser and zip-tie the two officers and put them in the back of it, disarming and dismantling their weapons. Never before in Iraq have they felt as secure from all sides—both friendly and the insurgents. It is wonderfully comfortable, and soldiers feel absolutely safe in this toyota land cruiser, shit, immunity at last from law and order! Soldiers finally know intimately in their minds what the militiamen feel when they drive around in the land cruisers: safety. No one will shoot them, not the Americans, insurgents, Iraqi Army, or Iraqi Police—not as long as they are inside the Iraqi Police land cruiser with flashing lights. Damn, these insurgents and militias have it made, but soldiers have to hallucinate a happy ending for these pricks in this neighborhood.

They turn on the flashing lights and drive straight into that "contained" neighborhood, passing the concrete barriers, passing the deserted Iraqi Army checkpoint. They cut through to the alley where the AK tracer fire came from; they stop there and turn off the lights, just like the many Iraqi Police friends of insurgents. With the zip-tied and blindfolded police officers stowed in the back of the truck, the soldiers quickly hide in the alley, waiting for something predictable.

In a matter of minutes, soldiers see through night vision the distant figures of armed insurgents, waddling nonchalantly in their jogging outfits from the side street with their AKs and RPKs. A Hyundai sedan with its lights turned off follows them slowly as they approach the Iraqi Police vehicle, parked with its engine running. They are coming to meet their police friends. That's how the Iraqi Police always do it and soldiers, as insurgents behind insurgents, have learned a thing or two.

The rattlesnakes walking and driving come straight under the infrared floodlights that naked eyes cannot see, belonging to two of the best Squad Automatic Weapons Gunners in the unit—two soldiers who always recognized the need to hallucinate, always very carefully, always honoring their illustrious family traditions. They promptly emptied two nut-sacks worth of ammunition on burst (four-hundred 5.56 rounds in a matter of seconds). As they reloaded, one soldier put his faith in the M4, while the other put faith in his M203 grenade launcher that one so rarely gets to use, aiming towards the sedan. It is now stopped sideways, pushing the wall of a cinderblock house, and it will slowly be engulfed in yellow dancing flames. A soldier quickly sprints to it as others pull security to verify the situation of every single rattlesnake before running back.

They swiftly get back into the toyota land cruiser in their imaginations, feeling safe once again. Soldiers could smell the burnt CLP (Cleaner, Lubricant, and Protectant, the cleaning oil used on the weapons). Their SAW guns' short barrels glow in the brilliant green night vision. (SAW is a squad automatic weapon, a light machine gun.) The police officers in the back make muffled moans; it is not a good feeling to be shot at but not shoot back, even worse to be next to it and not know what the hell is happening. They will be safe, but not quite yet. Let them wallow in their imagination; it is good for the soul. Soldiers in their imagination have one stop to make, and it has to be quick, quiet, and deliberate: Just around the corner. This isn't New York; the neighborhoods are never that big.

They take a turn in the deserted street in their imagination, stopping at the affluent corner store run by the former army guy with wonderful stories. He is like an octopus, his many tentacles reaching numerous neighborhoods and alleyways. With any luck he will be there but maybe not. Either way, soldiers in their imagination must make a stop on this rare opportunity. There is no need to make any noise, only call him by name and say who is at the door. Even if he has armed friends inside, he will be quick to ask them to stay put and hide their weapons. It has happened often—soldiers will sit there smoking and talking while his buddies make peanut gallery comments, the same guys who shoot at night and are responsible for the murder of Iraqis and Americans. He and his friends, despite being militia, never want to pick fights with soldiers, only drink tea and share stories. They try to shoot and blow the soldiers into pieces only because they want to live and live very well. They are very pragmatic nut-jobs, the hardest to catch.

So a soldier calls his name. He would instantly recognize the voice through the opening between the two metal doors, where a green haze oozes out from the tiny light that illuminates the inside. Now they see the oozing infrared move, shatter, then get covered over. There are people inside, perhaps about four. The soldiers just want to buy some cigarettes and alcohol, as they always do. It's a risk, but some soldiers are willing to get into a good scrap with a heartfelt smile. Of course, two SAW guns are pointed at the inside from the windowsill—worst-case scenario, four-hundred links of 5.56 will fill the corner store.

Two soldiers amble in and greet him and his friends in their careful hallucinations and on behalf of all the lives in all the American convoys that he and his friends made to live a lifetime in a second, just down the street from where they hang out. Soldiers could feel the gaze of ayatollahs from the wall; they are ubiquitous. As soldiers step out, with a respectful nod to the ayatollahs, hopping over the rattlesnakes on the ground, one of them grabs the two bottles of alcohol that the man will sell the soldiers as he always did. He was just too comfortable in his position and in his subversive complacency. Complacency is the mother of all fuck-ups in a counterinsurgency.

459

Soldiers walk back to the Iraqi Police vehicle to feel secure in their imagination, the safest place they have found in all of Iraq. They can hear the crackling noises of small flames inside the store; in a moment it will be engulfed in flames with a big whoosh—Thermite. Soldiers had to be very imaginative to acquire it without a hand receipt, but soldiers are nothing if not imaginative. They can see the glow behind them in the rear view mirror of the vehicle.

Wait, the hallucinations cannot get the best of the soldiers, nothing is ever that easy. Soldiers are faced with the same question again and again in a puzzle of life and death: Do these guys who have murdered Americans and Iraqis present valid targets that would fulfill everyone's legal, moral, and political sensibilities?

Perfect people closer to heaven, who see the world with clarity, define the way soldiers fight on the ground. Yet there is a lot of life lived between heavenly clarity and the murky dirt soldiers traverse. Astute leaders on the ground have to come to terms with this paradox and transcend it to save their soldiers and themselves.

The next street over is deserted and dark, illuminated only by their own red and blue flashing lights, on the vehicle filled with soldiers in their hallucinations, far removed from reality. They drive through the main road, zipping past the Iraqi Army and Police post, being careful to flash them with intermittent high beams. That is what the police affiliates of the militiamen always do in their many crossings in and out of the contained neighborhood at night, when they are up to their usual militia business. So it is today, being insurgents behind insurgents in their hallucination.

Though it felt like an eternity in their imagination, soldiers were back out of the contained neighborhood and back in the non-contained neighborhood where they are supposed to be in a matter of ten minutes. Opening the back of the truck they find the two Iraqi police officers, maybe guilty or maybe innocent. They are scared out of all wits, and soldiers untie them and take the masks off and help them sit on the sidewalk with an apology.

Whatever they have heard runs through their minds wildly. Stuck in the back of their own vehicle, blindfolded and listening to gunfire and explosions, was obviously not very pleasant. Sitting on the sidewalk, feeling jittery, stomachs queasy, looking like they are about to have a panic attack despite being happy to be breathing real air, they look completely out of sorts. So a soldier gives them his pack of Gauloises and his lighter. He takes a knee next to them on the ground and pats them on the back, asking them to take deep breaths, "Yes, keep breathing, deep breaths," and he apologizes again. Their heads wobble. The soldier next to them speaks softly. "Listen, every time from now on, this is how we will drive around, do you understand?"

They have wide eyes, wide-open mouths, and wobbling heads, and can't seem to light a cigarette, having faced a bunch of soldiers in their wild imagination.

So he gets close, grabs the high-ranking guy by the collar and tells him, "Tell your friends, tell them what happened, and this is exactly how we will do, this will not be the last time, do you understand?"

He pulled him by the collar to make him stand up and stared at his contorted face, yelling, "Hey, do you fucking understand?"

"Yes, yes, mister, please." So the soldier adds, "We are very sorry; *Afwan, afwan jazeelan*—but you tell your friends." This time the guy nods his head vigorously, "Yes, yes."

The soldier and his friends help him sit down again and the soldier reaches into his light plate carrier and pulls out two stacks of Benjamin Franklins from his medic pouch and hands it to the two police officers. There is no need to burn bridges, only to build some—as many as they can—because this is, after all, a counterinsurgency. Soldiers in their imagination never counted how much each stack held, they only knew it was a lot. There is no need to count. The crisp clean U.S. dollars do not come from American authorities, that would mean more paperwork and balancing everything right down to the penny, and every missing dollar will come from a soldier's paycheck. Holding

461

foot soldiers and their leaders accountable for equipment and cash is critical; you break it, you own it; you lose it, you own it, and foot soldiers and their leaders are held accountable for every penny's worth of equipment in this war.

But this money is not from the U.S. taxpayers so no need to count. This money comes compliments of Ali's Sadrist-run Health Ministry of Iraq. Soldiers in their imagination need not bother higher when they can be insurgents behind insurgents, with Sadrist financing. Hell, as soldiers learned in their imagination that the Sadrists had such wonderful resources, soldiers found themselves being very, very generous.

The police officers have a look that all but guarantees they will remember and spread the word about this night. It is only a beginning, not an end. The complacent assumption of the Iraqi policemen with militia affiliations will continue to be shattered in this neighborhood. The immunity and sense of safety of JAM combatants will become tricky for them.

Though the two policemen do not know exactly what happened, as they were blindfolded and tied down in the back, they will try to recreate the night. As long as they spread the word, there will be many hamsters spinning in the minds of the innocent and the guilty. The innocent police will put pressure on the guilty police: They need to start thinking about what they are doing. The guilty, the insurgents and militias in the neighborhood, will always try to innovate, but if soldiers keep trying to imagine relentlessly from the margins at night, then the militias and their allies will have to risk shooting at the policemen and their vehicles, the same ones who give them immunity and top cover.

Soon enough, the militia in the Iraqi Police might have to think very hard in this neighborhood and the ones nearby. Because a different militia could be roaming the streets at night—the retarded part of the United States Army. Soldiers in their imagination would find the safety of the Iraqi Police vehicles at night very comforting and even addicting. Why be consistent in mind and take silly risks when they could be comfortable and have complete immunity from everyone riding with those blue and red flashing lights at night, buried in the leather seats of the new land cruisers that American tax-payers bought the militias? So reasoned the soldiers indulging in their Arak-induced hallucinations at sunrise, walking back to their assigned neighborhood, trying to be insurgents behind insurgents. Hallucinations: The last best form of subversion.

Siesta Time Is Over: Wake Up, Habibi

Soldiers in their imagination see the Iraqi Army soldiers in their complacent slumber, lounging about without a worry in the world because they are able to stay out of this fight. That basic understanding has to be rattled on the ground—difficult, but never impossible—if soldiers can only retain the capacity to hallucinate.

Strangely enough, the wake-up call is easy. It entails no lasting damage, no risk—just waking them up when they are comfortably snoozing. The sense of safety has to go; the Iraqi Army in this neighborhood has to pick a fight sometime.

A fighter can train to fight, punch a bag to kingdom come, but he will never be a fighter until he gets into a brawl and crawls his way out with his soul cleansed of all evil. Until that moment, a fighter is a mere apprentice and not a fighter. A soldier can train, fly, jump, and even do cheetah flips, but a soldier becomes complete only after he faces fire and learns how he reacts. An army can have all the weapons they want, but until they are blooded they are only good for the parade field.

Many foot soldiers and leaders on the ground consider the moment under the sun in the parade field the lowest point of their military career. It feels absolutely silly, like clowns in a French circus, and soldiers who don't care much for this tradition will try with all possible ingenuity to avoid being reduced to circus clowns. That hushed hissing noise emanating from the field appears to the inspired onlookers in the tent as a greeting of love and happiness—but it is actually the muffled volleys of unending profanities that soldiers unleash while having their moment under the sun. Thankfully, there are many wise and responsible men in the armed forces, and they take the firing pins out of the weapons in the parade field for a good reason.

Soldiers, thankfully, are not in Iraq to train for parade field maneuvers. They are there to help in the fight. This does not require them, even in their imagination, to pick fights with the Iraqi Army, only help them fight. And as any military leader knows, helping soldiers be better soldiers requires waking them up when they really want to sleep.

In a neighborhood infested with rattlesnakes, isn't it strange that Iraqi Army soldiers can sleep as soundly as babies in a crib? The Iraqi Army, representing the government, is actually supposed to take control of the neighborhood from rattlesnakes, but there seems to be a strange disconnect. No one is shooting at them; neither do they fire at anything. No one shoots at them because they are staying out of the fight, safe in their understanding with their current friends and future enemies: You don't shoot, we don't shoot.

Soldiers are commiserating at sunrise, hallucinating again, and in their imaginations they take a detour by the canal through the palm groves. And, in addition to their usual jacked up uniforms that make them a disgrace to the army, today some of them are carrying a handful of AK-47s. AKs in Iraq are a dime a dozen, and if all else fails, one can easily buy it from the Iraqi Army or Police. It is a little detail that is very relevant for this hallucination because the rat-tat burst of AK fire is as distinct as the color of the tracer rounds.

Soldiers in their imagination go passed the cinderblock houses to a half-completed vacant building with a good vantage point and cover. A bunch of them climb to the roof in the dark. They hide behind some concrete in this hallucination and put the AK over the roof, and aim at the general direction of the Iraqi Army checkpoint (as no actual harm should be done). Then they empty an entire magazine in one burst, with no return fire at all, and they climb down. The other soldiers, standing and pulling security, are now giggling like a bunch of little girls.

Then soldiers hear an Iraqi Army RPK machine gun fire off a few bursts. That is a long reaction time. Obviously, they were sleeping (as they usually do). In their slumber, they did not get their three

464

Ds right—Description, Distance, and Direction—and the burst of fire was way off. Then all is quiet, it's back to the mattresses, sit behind the concrete while their bosses get on the phone. Soldiers have a general idea from the word on the street: They are calling their buddies in the neighborhood, Ahmad, Muhammed, Ali, and Hussein, "Hey, what the hell, why are your boys shooting at us?" Then they will call the local police officers for clarification.

It is time for soldiers in their imaginations to cross the street, get to the vicinity of another checkpoint and continue imagining. The other checkpoint is the same, and the Iraqi Army soldiers at the checkpoint are good people. During the day, soldiers hang out, drink tea and goof around with them. No one wants to do them any harm. They are just harmless grunts that are taken for granted. They lack the singular luxury that U.S. grunts have: Most soldiers' leaders take care of the soldiers on the ground in good times and bad. When things go wrong, commissioned and noncommissioned officers always come to the soldiers' rescue, put themselves in the middle and save them from any fallout. But Iraqi Army soldiers do not have that singular luxury, not yet.

Soldiers only want to wake them to make them better soldiers. So they get next to a concrete barrier, get the AK and empty half a magazine at the concrete barricades surrounding the checkpoint. A good five minutes later, return fire goes into the air, and then it is quiet again. Someone will be on the phone again, screaming profanities.

There is one more checkpoint. It looks like concrete tubes stacked on top of the other in the middle of the major street. Parked next to it is an Iraqi HUMMV with a bunch of Iraqi soldiers sleeping in it. Inside the concrete tubes sleep a couple more soldiers. The same story, but this time, a soldier in the HUMMV returned fire with his RPK much more accurately. No one need worry because Iraqi Army, as of yet, is not in the habit of maneuvering when faced with fire, only returning fire and sitting tight. Three checkpoints in one hallucination, enough cages have been rattled. Tomorrow, some Iraqi Army and Police guys will be having some chats.

One of the best Squad Automatic Weapons Gunners is a guy who steps up to every hallucination with no complaints and a whole lot of enthusiasm and a long family tradition. He muses that these guys will step up only if we send some RPGs their way. It is a brilliant idea but it has its own risks. Because an RPG, when fired to a specific target, never, ever really hits the target but always misses it. But there is a real danger because it is so inaccurate. If the RPG is deliberately fired *away* from the target, there is a chance that it might hit the target that soldiers in their imagination do not want to hit! That is risky, even though it is true that nothing would wake them up from their complacent slumber more than a big flash followed by a boom. Any hallucination leader would have to carefully shoot down *that* good idea fairy—as entertaining as it might be.

There is no rhyme or reason to hurt the Iraqi Army grunts. Just ensure that the Iraqi soldiers are pissed off, as are their superiors who will make phone calls to the local police in the neighborhood, the politicians, and the few JAM guys on the ground, asking for explanations.

But JAM will insist that they have no explanation: "Oh, it could be some rogue elements." That is even better because it begins to unravel that delicate sense of security. JAM, like most insurgents on the ground, likes to maintain the illusion that they are a cohesive group and everyone walks to the same beat. The reality is that, although they more or less walk to the beat, combatants are not a disciplined group of soldiers. They include an amalgam of groups, ideologues, believers, random yahoos, criminals, and extortionists—and they do fight each other from time to time. They may have personal vendettas to avenge; hell, they might even start shooting at the Iraqi Army. Soldiers need to get the shady cats in the neighborhood to spread that rumor around, so the local JAM guys start looking at each other with suspicion. The delicate subversive reality would be unnerving: Someone is shooting, and it could be rogue elements in their own midst! At least in this neighborhood soldiers might give some JAM special groups a run for their money and create a reality that is far too close for comfort. And it would be sweet if JAM guys start fighting other JAM guys in the neighborhood. Rattle the cages and the tapestry will become ever more delicate.

Soldiers need to keep imagining with an AK in hand from time to time—carrying a few AKs is recommended, as it could be very useful at times—so they can keep giggling like schoolgirls. Keep aggravating the Iraqi Army, sooner or later they will pick a fight, and of all things they will fight the Iraqi Police, smack in the middle of a main road, and American commanders will have to be the mediators. Because when there is a fight between Iraqi Police and Iraqi Army, the Iraqi Army always prevails because they are better fighters.

Soldiers in their imaginations also need to make a stop at the local pharmacy—no, not to buy any illicit drugs, because soldiers are always law-abiding, and so are the good pharmacists in Iraq. Soldiers want to talk to the guy who owns the place. Soldiers know him a little now, they even bought his overpriced medicine (undoubtedly skimmed off the top from the hospital warehouse) to give to a local clinic. He has a good finger on the local extortion racket under the benevolent gaze of the Sadrist ayatollahs on the wall. Everyone needs some kind of blessing, and doubly so if one is up to no good.

The Thief and the Dogs[93]

> Once more he breathed the air of freedom. But there was stifling dust in the air, almost unbearable heat, and no one was waiting for him; nothing but his blue suit and gym shoes.
>
> —*The Thief and the Dogs*

Soldiers are once more commiserating, hallucinating. In their imagination they once again stop by the good Iraqi police officer's house. They go there surreptitiously (as they always did), at night, through deserted roads and vacant haunted dark alleys, places that evoked many thoughts and special memories. They sneak into the house and greet him, and convey their sympathies about the terrible fate that has befallen the pharmacist and his friends. They insist soldiers had nothing to do with it because they did not—it was just a hallucination. There are enough gangsters and shady cats in town who will do anything for Benjamin.

---

[93] *The Thief and the Dogs*, a short novel by Naguib Mahfouz.

But they tell him that they want him to be safe. If anyone, even in their slightest imagination, heard or saw that he had some American friends, some of his own police colleagues would most likely kill him. It was self-evident, and it only needs a subtle reminder. It is important because the soldiers want the good Iraqi police officer to help them with something.

They are sitting around again, talking, and a soldier leans forward in his chair and says to him, "Sir, tell me, we need your help, do you think you could help?" He may look unperturbed, but soldiers have been in Iraq for some time. Behind the eyebrows a hamster spins relentlessly, and soldiers follow through—because he, now, needs the soldiers more than soldiers need him. One word on the street of his assistance to soldiers, and he'll be history. And he knows it.

"Sir, we want you to help us get your boss, Mr. Ahmed, the police commander." A JAM-affiliated district police commander, with hands dripping with Iraqi and American blood, he walks around with impunity.

"WHAT??"

He stands up halfway from his chair, nearly falling off it. Now he looks like he is about to have a heart attack. Maybe he is just excited to hear it—not everyone is as afraid as we sometimes imagine.

The soldier raises his hands, palms toward the police officer, and quietly whispers, "Sir, calm down, calm down, we are just talking; it is not a problem."

The man's eyes widen, and he blurts out, "NO, NO, this is TROUBLE. He is so powerful, NO ONE CAN CATCH HIM."

"Yes, we know, that is exactly why we will get him."

"HE IS FERRY, FERRY POWERFUL!"

The soldier replies calmly, "Yes, we know, that's why we will get him."

468

Now there is complete silence, and the soldier lights and offers him a Gauloises cigarette, and it's so quiet they can hear the noise of the burning tobacco. His concerns are justified. Ahmed is not just any police commander, he is the dirtiest of them of all, so well plugged in he is nearly untouchable. So much blood—American, Sunni, Shia, even some Chaldeans—is on his hands. He rolls with the good, the bad, and the ugly. To get him and make him anonymous would rattle many cages.

The beauty of catching untouchables is that it only takes a handful to make everyone else start running for cover. The untouchables are never untouchable. The moment they think they are untouchable is the moment they start heading down. But Mr. Ahmed's power and control on the ground can never be underestimated. If anyone gets a whiff of an idea that such a conversation has passed through this poor guy's house in the middle of the night, he and his entire family, friends, even people who have loaned him money will disappear, appearing later by the side of the road, hogtied and baking under the hot sun. Yes, soldiers have walked the streets and listened far too long, and they know exactly what he means when he blurts out that he is powerful. That is why we want him.

He tries to end the conversation: "YOU CAN NEVER PUT HIM IN JAIL." In a series of rapidfire bursts he lists all the people he is friends with—but soldiers already know it. District Advisory Council members, all the JAM politicians, Iraqi Army commanders, even American colonels, all of them apparently drink tea occasionally with the highest-ranking JAM nut-jobs. Soldiers are neither impressed nor intimidated. Yeah, whatever, it makes no difference, he has American blood on his hands, and that's all there is to it. "Sir, we will get him, because he is a murderer, you know it, even you could not do anything about your brother because of Ahmed and his friends." The soldier points his finger, adding, "YES, you are right. We can never put him in jail."

The police officer nods, and the soldier adds casually, "Yes, because we will never put him in jail, he does not deserve to go to jail, he has killed too many Americans and too many Iraqis."

Now the good police officer sits up straight. Soldiers imagine offering him another cigarette, which he takes and lights off the one that is coming to an end.

The soldier keeps piling on details, one after the other. "You know, sir, in the next neighborhood JAM killed some Americans, some of our friends, and do you know that Ahmed and his friends helped JAM with the bombs?"

Yes, he has heard some of his friends in the police talk about it but he really does not know for sure.

"Do you know the big bomb that killed some Americans in a convoy a few months ago near the mosque; did you know Ahmed and his friends helped with that one too?"

Yes, he had heard some of his friends in the police talk about that one too. "Well, sir, then you know all about the Iraqis he and his friends killed too?" Yes, of course, he does, it is his neighborhood, and he has lived here all his life.

"You know, you know very well that Mr. Ahmed also knew your pharmacist friend, yes?" It is a fact: Ahmed, however remotely, is also connected to the personal tragedy of his family. It is important to remind him of it.

He exhales deeply and nods with a whisper, "Yes."

Walking the streets and listening to whispers of the dead in the stories of the living has great benefit in a counterinsurgency. Listening very carefully at times is everything.

So the soldier looks at him with a smile and adds, in his hallucinations, "Sir, no problem, we promise you will be safe, Ahmed will not go to jail, we are the ones who catch everybody, and guess what? We will decide who will and who will not go to jail" (hypothetically speaking, of course, because soldiers do not make that judgment, only perfect people closer to heaven do).

Now the poor police officer truly looks like he has the weight of the world on his shoulders, and soldiers know it; they have been in Iraq for too long. He is worried about himself, his wife, his children, and his extended family. He has no sanctuary to retire to. At least soldiers can go to a base, feeling safe amid their friends (and staying away from the dangerous dining facilities). But this guy has only one place he can call home, and that is in fact where he is most vulnerable. So he explains the obvious.

"Sir, if I help you, someone will kill me and my family." That is the opportunity in this imagination. The soldier adds with a grin, "Sir, no problem, we don't want you to do anything. Nothing at all."

Now the police officer looks a little bewildered.

"Sir, we know, if you try to help us, if you try to do anything, you will get killed and someone will kill your family. We understand, no problem, don't do anything, just keep doing your job, do what you do, OK? Don't even think about us."

He does not quite understand, certainly he looks a little more relieved but still a tad bewildered. The soldier added nonchalantly, "Sir, all we want you to do is to tell us if you hear anything, just call us and let us know, that's all, but don't do anything and don't even think about us OK? We want you and your family to be safe."

He nods his agreement, evidently relieved, who knows what may have gone through his wild imagination.

"Sir, don't worry, we will not call you. You call us if you hear anything OK?"

"Yes, no problem."

That's good, now soldiers are getting somewhere. So a soldier reaches into one of his medic pouches where he kept a few local Iraqi cell phones and gives him two phone numbers from two different cell phone networks and asks him to save the phone numbers.

As he is trying to punch the phone numbers, the soldier adds with a laugh, "Now, don't save it as 'The American.' I don't know, save it as Amer Diyab or Elissa, just don't say the damn American." The good police officer finally has a lighter moment and has a laugh, shaking his head, and the soldiers asked, "Why, don't you think we Americans like Elissa? Oh man, we love her!"

He agrees unequivocally, of course, he watches her sometimes on TV, and laughs at the soldiers. But this time it's a hearty laugh, perhaps as surprised to hear of Americans who appreciate Elissa's voice and her form. Nearly everybody watches her, including some JAM insurgents soldiers caught. Even they had heard her sing, seen her videos, and "yes," they agreed, she is beautiful. A soldier conducting tactical questioning could not resist the impulse and asked, "Do you watch those videos before you step out to enforce modesty and virtue and slap women?" Everyone was laughing, but the stressed-out JAM boys facing those good-hearted laughing soldiers missed the joke.

After he saved the phone numbers, the soldier asked him to call him, so as to save his number. But added, "Sir, don't worry, we will not give your number to anyone, and no one—no one—other than those of us in the house now, will ever know about you, not even Americans will know about you, we promise, trust me, we want you and your family to be safe."

"Yes, thank you."

"No, sir, don't thank us, thank *you*," and he reached into his medic pouch again and pulled out a wad of Benjamin Franklins—courtesy this time of the local JAM political office—and he handed it to the good man. It is a very nice setup, JAM is now financing the soldiers who are insurgents behind insurgents, why bother the U.S. taxpayers and worry about paperwork?

"Sir, please, please, take this, give it to your brother's family; we will try to help out more."

And he, of course, seemed genuinely pleased because Benjamin Franklin is an amazing man and has that incredible effect on people. Men, women, girls, boys, fat, skinny, plump, even the cognitively challenged have the same reaction to Benjamin Franklin. Ching-ching—the genius of counterinsurgency will always remain common sense on the ground and not rocket science. But until common sense is turned into procedures, it will always be challenging. But soldiers try to go for a touchdown on the fourth down. It is imperative.

"Sir, we need to leave soon and thank you for your help, but before we go we have one question. Sir, we have to leave, but tell me, do you know much about Mr. Ahmed?"

Well, just a little, like everybody else. The soldiers had some specific questions. How many wives does he have and resulting children? This means more houses and more places where he will be vulnerable. Soldiers know of only one and know where she lives, and about his children, family, and friends, but Mr. Ahmed is a busy man, he is always on the move. Does he have other wives? Does he drink, does he have a girlfriend, and is he looking for a new wife? What about his friends in this neighborhood that he visits often?

Every powerful man is always protected by a tapestry of power and control, people who click heels and march to his beat. To get the most powerful at their most vulnerable when they feel most powerful and take it for granted, it's best to know as much as one can, especially in a neighborhood that will always remain foreign no matter how long soldiers have kept walking.

Now the soldiers, in their imagination, have are two other questions. "So, Mr. Ahmed always travels with the same three people in his police vehicle, yes?"

The good man responds in the negative, actually it is four people. Two of them are somehow related to him and the other two are police that have worked with him for a long, long time, and they are all JAM.

Because even in soldiers' imagination, to have all of them in one truck and light it up would be difficult, a lot of noise, a lot of debris that cannot be cleaned up, and that is never too good given that they are, after all, police, the law and order, and he is used to hanging out with the best of them.

Soldiers are standing up to leave, and they have a request: "Sir, please turn off the lights outside so it's dark, also on the roof." Because soldiers would leave the house from the roof, crossing over to the next cinderblock house, and so on to the next block. Houses are so tightly packed that one can keep hopping without missing a beat.

After catching up on the neighborhood gossip, soldiers are at last shaking hands to go, and they have a last question about a little secret they discovered.

Every meeting of the Neighborhood Advisory Council (NAC) and District Advisory Council (DAC) is in reality a pair of meetings. The official one takes place in front of uniformed American soldiers and officers during the day. But there is another NAC/DAC meeting that takes place beforehand. Some of the more influential members get together in a prominent member's house to decide how to manipulate the agenda for the official meeting with the Americans. Decide who will get the contract—usually a JAM-affiliated contractor—and how they will approach (or gang up against) the American commander sitting at the meeting. Soldiers know this because they once crashed this party by a strategic coincidence, being insurgents behind insurgents and learning a thing or two in the process. Mr. Ahmed himself stops by these meetings from time to time—and that is the place to catch him. Because he is not afraid, because he is powerful and untouchable and complacent, he will always be easy to catch. All one has to do is wave, greet, and shake his hand. But finding him at the place is the hard part.

The last question: "Sir, you know every Wednesday, at Mr. Abbas's house, lot of important people get together, yes?"

Of course, he knows about it. He has driven some people to the house a couple of times.

474

"Do you know that sometimes, Mr. Ahmed goes there?"

Well, of course, it is Mr. Ahmed after all, a very high-ranking police-man, a powerful man. "He goes everywhere!"

"Can you call us if you ever hear from anyone that he might be going there?"

Yes, he would, but he cannot promise; Mr. Ahmed travels all the time.

Soldiers thank him but also remind him politely how he needs to be careful, especially after the fate of the pharmacist. Any word on the street that he is a friend of soldiers will put him next in line. He understands completely and he promises to call.

That's fine, sir, no problem, please, be safe, we want you to be safe. As the lights go off, only a tiny light for illumination remains. Soldiers are about to climb the stairs, and two soldiers go to the good man, shake his hand, and one takes his hand in both of his own, exhorting, "Sir, but please promise that you will be safe!"

Then the soldier added with a very serious voice (in this imagination), "Sir, you understand, these are powerful people, if you ever say any-thing to anybody, anybody, someone will try to kill you and your fam-ily." His "yes" was an entire novel of full agreement because he knows his situation better than almost anybody. The soldier added, holding his hands, "Be safe, and don't ever tell anything to anybody, even your wife. It's your family, and we want them to be safe."

Then he added with a grin, "Don't worry about Mr. Ahmed, we will worry about him—he is nothing."

"Yes, of course, no problem."

Soldiers took quick steps up the stairs and disappeared from the roof, turning into tiny distant silhouettes hopping from one roof to the other, trying to get to where they are supposed to be as fast as they could in this hallucination.

475

It is early morning again and time for a nightcap at dawn. The anise seed aroma of Arak hangs low inside the concrete barrier as soldiers are commiserating as their imagination begins to go into overdrive.

Nakeeb Ali-Baba and the Two Thieves

Soldiers know of an army captain—Nakeeb Ali-Baba as soldiers called him in their hallucinations—who is a JAM militia member and a politically appointed army commander. His sole assignment is to use the immunity the army uniform grants him to murder Americans and Iraqis—mainly Sunnis and some Shia big-wigs who might oppose JAM in the neighborhood. His fellow Iraqi soldiers fear him, including the major to whom he "reports."

There are also two Iraqi Army soldiers who are helping the American soldiers. They fear for their lives; they are taking a risk simply by using SMS or calling them on the cell phones that soldiers bought them. They don't do sworn statements. Even the major would not divulge the well-known secret that one of his captains is a murderer, even to the American officers who give him fuel for his patrols. If the major can pretend not to know the truth, why would two Iraqi grunts take the risk? Worse, if the guy gets picked up and released, the two soldiers will have to run for their lives.

Soldiers know from multiple sources (Iraqi Army, Police, and neighborhood) that this Nakeeb Ali-Baba is responsible for a recent attack that killed two American soldiers. They helped JAM ambush a convoy—only the latest crime in a long list. Nakeeb Ali-Baba and his two thieves set up the two armor-piercing IEDs, and one of their minions detonated it, instantly killing the American gunner in the convoy. He took the brunt of it to his head. It cut the driver of the HMMVW in half, the ball of copper slicing straight through him. Soldiers know this intimately, some of their buddies helped with the medical evacuation of the American National Guard soldiers in charge of the convoy. It may enrage the soul, but soldiers on the ground can never give in to rage and sentiment and get carried away: Keeping a cool head is better, it helps to capture the moment without losing a step or missing a beat.

Nakeeb Ali-Baba and his two thieves are legends in the Iraqi Army garrison and even in some parts of the neighborhood, and they enjoy their legendary status. To make them anonymous would send some ripples through the JAM militia. The legendary status gives them immunity because people fear them. But some people also hate them. Soldiers now have their pictures (via cell phone) and IDs on the vehicles they use—including one Iraqi Army vehicle, an old Soviet style truck with a covered back that allows him to keep whoever he kidnaps out of sight in the back.

Feeling safe in his uniform, immune from American authorities and Iraqis, he greets all the Americans—including commanding officers—with his ingratiating supplication. Soldiers are faced with a paradox. Just because soldiers know his true Ali-Baba character does not mean they should be excited. It is useful to see him unaware of the fact that soldiers know the truth, and to keep him unaware so he continues to treat the soldiers like idiots. It keeps him very comfortable and very secure.

But when an insurgent's subversive complacency is blown, then it is over: Soldiers need to get him swiftly because having lost his cover he will disappear in a second. Soldiers are a foreign intervention force, hamstrung by procedures, but they do not have the luxury of time. Everything at times moves in slow motion, and the same objective becomes a whole new mission, it becomes redundant. And it is an old army cliché, soldiers hate nothing more than to take the same objective twice.

A handful of soldiers in their hallucinations are greeting Ali-Baba and the two thieves at night, shaking hands, talking about families— and now they have a particular problem. Having greeted, disarmed and zip-tied them, a soldiers pulls out his iPod from his pouch for verification, checking the myriad pictures downloaded from cell phone memory cards of Iraqi friends and Iraqi Army soldiers.

Soldiers already know Ali-Baba, he is as clear as day, soldiers have known him and heard stories about him and looked at his picture for a while as he was driving around shaking hands with Americans. But of the other three, only two match perfectly, the same guys that always

477

roll with Ali Baba. But what about the other guy? They must find out. Soldiers throw the others into the back of their go-cart.

A soldier simply could not bear it any longer, listening to the profanities and threats coming out of Nakeeb Ali-Baba, zip-tied with the two thieves in the back of their multi-purpose Soviet-style vehicle. Yelling does not work for some soldiers, and Nakeeb Ali-Baba almost got punched in the face. Another soldier stepped in and said, "Hey, stop! Hold up, we need to talk to these two." Then he gets into the truck with Ali Baba, still high and mighty as he yanks him up by the throat then kneels on his chest and duct tapes his mouth. The muffled noises stopped quickly and the two soldiers could now only feel his gaze from two deep black eyes, screaming epithets. He is a persistent little fucker. The two minions who have always been privy to all of Al-Baba's escapades are sitting zip-tied, bewildered. That's more like it.

The soldier turns to them asking, "Good, yes?" and he repeats to himself, "Very good, yes." While Ali-Baba makes his muffled noises, his two adjutants are now looking at him with wide eyes, pondering how swiftly Ali-Baba has fallen from grace. Soldiers need to ask some quick questions to the two minions because they are privy to secrets, but they will not answer, definitely not in front of Mr. Ali-Baba. The soldier says to the two minions: Watch this.

He kneels on Ali Baba and puts two pieces of duct tape over his nose and mouth. He lights a cigarette very casually, as the two look on in disbelief. They flinch when one of the soldiers breaks the florescent light of a nearby corner store because it made the street much too bright for the work at hand.

Mr. Ali-Baba is slowly beginning to panic, and with increased panic he feels he is suffocating much faster than he is; his two minions become more and more agitated by the moment.

Soldiers inside the truck smoke a cigarette and stare at the two minions, disregarding Ali-Baba, who is struggling to survive right next to their feet inside the Iraqi Army truck. The soldier has one—and only one—question. One of his dear friends and old mentors was killed in an explosively formed projectile in an adjacent neighborhood; the details are irrelevant because he remembers them much too well. There are all kinds of high-level investigations, potential suspects and target packets being thrown around because the JAM world is sprawling and complicated. The target packets are right, it is a valid insurgent cell—but that overlooks the Iraqi Police and Iraqi Army people that made it possible for the minions to carry out the attack.

These guys in the truck were part of it and know all about it.

The two thieves are looking at their boss, now beginning to flap like a fish out of water in this Arak-induced hallucination. The two minions wordlessly look at the soldier in the truck, sitting on a seat right in front of them. He laughs at the sight of four pleading eyes: "What? I am still smoking," pointing to the cigarette that is only halfway down. It takes about five minutes for someone to suffocate at a minimum, and a cigarette takes about six minutes to burn all the way. And soldiers have learned from years of battlefield tactical questioning that laughs in a stressful situation are far more ominous than any physical harm.

He pulls Ali-Baba out of the truck and hands this flapping slimy fish to his friend, "Hey take care of him man."

He will take him to the alley. He takes the duct tape off so he can breathe and choke on clean air while feeling thankful that he can breathe again at all. The soldier gets back on the truck with a big smile asking, "OK, who is next?"

Crickets . . . crickets and big eyes.

He looks from one Iraqi soldier to the other with a smile, "OK, which one?" Crickets again. "*Yallah, Yallah, habibi,* why no volunteers?"

He points his finger, "You, come with me," and one hears the familiar, "Please, mister, please."

The soldier takes him out to a corner and asks questions he wanted answers to. The guy has some answers, others will have the rest. Then he goes to the truck again, looking at the other with a sly smile,

"Habibi, it is your turn," and he gets the expected reaction. The last guy is put in a different corner and everyone is properly isolated, each imagining the worst about the other, that is the point. Every single one of them is no doubt imagining the worst of human nightmares, having now fallen from grace.

They are cooperating except for Ali-Baba—he will, but not quite yet. There is so little time to ask all the questions, so they must be prioritized. Soldiers now know who were the enablers, who bankrolled the IED attack. Soldiers have learned that sometimes following the footsteps of Benjamin Franklins will lead one to strangely comfortable households overlooking rivers. They will have to be given a heartfelt greeting, on behalf of the friend, his wife, and his three children in soldiers' hallucinations, because everyone goes home sometime.

The rest of the guys responsible are near IED alley, and no one is supposed to go there, not without force. Well, soldiers wonder, what if they lose their way coming back from someplace: The places soldiers are not supposed to go in general become the single place that they must go. Hell, worst case scenario, soldiers can always call the big guns, there is no rhyme or reason to worry. Not a single American infantry squad ever needs to "break contact," no one here is that good. But they might have to walk, take the alleys and the worst roads that insurgents infest, assuming no American will ever walk them. That makes it that much easier in a strange sort of war.

But what about commo? Hmm, maybe they will have to place the vehicles high up someplace to maintain a good communications ladder in the event of an emergency; the radio checks have to be constant. Soldiers keep wondering, would it be possible? It is far from the "Area of Control" but no place is really that far, this ain't fucking New York, so soldiers keep thinking, imagining, and hallucinating.

After questioning, soldiers have now put Ali-Baba and his two famous thieves into the back of their own truck, they all seem a bit surprised and thankful: Hey, look, no one is actually dead. Soldiers in their hallucinations still have a problem.

Who in the hell is this other Iraqi soldier? Soldiers have to send an SMS message and make a phone call that they really don't want to. They get his personal information, and there is no choice. They send an SMS message to one of the Iraqi Army soldiers to verify this guy's identity and whether he is JAM or not. The answer was, no, he is an idiot but innocent.

"God-damn."

Things are always tricky despite the imagination in a counterinsurgency. Soldiers just have to point out to the innocent Iraqi soldier that he could end up inside with the rest of them. But if they let him go he also faces a huge risk: In his terrified state of mind he told them stories, and Ali-Baba and his thieves will certainly kill him, and soon. He has a choice he can make: Take the AK-47 the soldier just gave him, and if he wishes, close his eyes pointing it at the back of the truck. What would it be?

Why would people do what they do?

It's a choice, a terrible one. But he knows they are all JAM and have lot of blood in their hands. He can then run back to the garrison, straight to the major and tell them soldiers did it. The major just might keep him safe, and the word would spread that the JAM boys in the Iraqi Army now have no more immunity in the neighborhood, and he was in the wrong truck at the wrong time.

But no decision—in counterinsurgency as in life—is easy for soldiers on the ground. Soldiers are again faced with the elemental human paradox.

A king can conquer by hook or by crook and the music plays hail to the conquering hero, even though his decision ended the lives of hundreds or thousands or maybe hundreds of thousands. But soldiers have just caught Nakeeb Ali-Baba and his two legendary thieves, who they know with complete certainty and without a shred of doubt are responsible for the deaths of American soldiers and Iraqis. A king can conquer and get away with it, they always have and always will, it is the way it is. But if soldiers do any harm to Ali-Baba and friends, the soldiers will be in hiding in Mexico, if not in jail. Soldiers wonder in their hallucinations, men with guns on the ground are always held accountable for their actions by a very different standard than the men in power and it always will be the way it is. But to let him go is to let him get away and certainly to murder the people who he will suspect helped the soldiers. To hand him to legal is to write a masterpiece with little hope, and he will inevitably come out seeking vengeance. So the same question again: Is this a valid target that would fulfill the legal, political, and moralistic impulses on the ground?

Damned if you do and damned if you don't, sometimes soldiers with feet on the ground like to hallucinate about how perfect the world would be if it were as easy on the ground as it is usually pontificated by perfect people up in the heavens.

Soldiers can again feel the anise seed aroma inside the blast walls. This hallucination is about a trip they plan to make to meet a very powerful man who hangs with the high and the low, both Iraqi and American. Soldiers need to have a conversation with him precisely because they are not supposed to see or talk to him. Well, there is no official restraining order, but it's just not done because he is too good and too connected. He lives out of the way in an affluent part of town. He is a powerful District Advisory Council member, a very wealthy man, well plugged into everything and everybody. It is important for soldiers to introduce themselves and have a chat with him at night, preferably before he goes to the next DAC meeting.

He is on our side, but he easily traverses all the local worlds. That makes him best situated to pass the word, tell a story and send a message. Soldiers in their hallucinations need to send a message to JAM high-ranking men in this neighborhood, their middlemen, the politicos, and anyone else. This guy is the perfect man for the job.

But how to get him to do it—at the request of a bunch of soot-covered unkempt worthless grunts who are a disgrace on the ground? He is a powerful man who pays next to no attention to grunts; he does not have to, he talks to stars that shine in the neighborhood. Soldiers will need all their imaginative capacity on this one.

21

RESPECTED SIR IN HALLUCINATIONS: MR. AMER[94]

He opens his door with a quizzical look, wearing his jelabiya, and soldiers humbly ask if they could come inside for a minute because they need to talk to him. He opens the door with a blank stare and lets the soldiers in. Then he asks some very practical questions—who do you work for, which unit—because he has never seen these soldiers in this neighborhood. Soldiers are not wearing nametapes or unit insignia; they are in the pocket, ready to be pulled out the moment they return to the majestic moon base.

Soldiers laugh and say that they are in the neighborhood walking: "Oh, sir, you may not know us, but we have seen you everywhere." He settles into his throne while the three soldiers pull up some straight backed chairs after asking permission. "Of course, of course, please sit." He waves his hand, much like the patriarch soldiers know. Pleasantries are exchanged, and he begins to ask probing questions about the soldiers.

---

[94] *Respected Sir*, a short novel by Naguib Mahfouz.

"Respected Sir"

"Who are you?" he asks in that voice of authority, wobbling uncomfortably on his throne. Keep guessing, that's a good start.

His living room, with all the plush and baroque furniture, looks like any other very affluent Iraqi Shia house. It is so hard to avoid the benevolent gaze of the ayatollahs. A soldier points to Grand Ayatollah Sistani's picture and tells the Iraqi DAC member, "Sir, you know, I see him every day. I really want to have a cup of tea with Grand Ayatollah Sistani. I think I could learn a lot from him."

Their host looks puzzled for a minute and then laughs, "This is difficult," and everyone starts laughing.

Yes, apparently it is the cardinal rule of Grand Ayatollah Sistani that he does not talk to Americans, in fact he rarely talks to anyone, it seems. So the soldier asks, "Why doesn't he talk to Americans? I want to talk to him; I see him every day, every day"—and then he raises his index finger and wags it, Iraqi style, and adds solemnly, "Soon we will probably have dreams of talking to him; we see him every day!" Everyone is laughing. The soldier asks, "Sir, tell me, what do you think, who will succeed him as the grand ayatollah when he passes from the scene? Grand Ayatollah Najafi, Hakim? Which one do you think?" Another soldier asks, as there are four grand ayatollahs and one is the most powerful, "which one do you want to see succeed him?"

He has a seriously quizzical look. These are strange sort of questions coming from grunts. American soldiers are supposed to be blundering idiots and not interested in the succession of grand ayatollahs. But the soldiers look genuinely curious.

He attempts to explain the intricacy, the complicated succession process, still with the same quizzical look. A soldier asks him, "have you met any grand ayatollahs?" "No, he has not," he says, but the soldier thinks he is lying. Because one ayatollah—in fact many ayatollahs— pass through this neighborhood. Everyone has family to visit in this neighborhood. So the soldiers add, "Well, I thought you knew so-and-so?"

He did an Iraqi double take, "No." Then he clarified, "YES, I do know him, and also so-and-so, but No, no—they are ayatollahs, yes, but not grand ayatollahs, not objects of emulation by any means. They are just learned ayatollahs."

The soldier apologizes, well, sorry about that. "Sir, you are a powerful man, you know everybody—you need to meet some grand ayatollahs. Sir, I really want to meet one!"

With a look of curiosity and a laugh he said this was difficult.

Then the soldier said with a smile, "Sir, I really want to go to the Grand Mosque in Najaf, see it, walk through it, see what it's like; what do you think? Maybe we will go there and pretend to pray?"

He had a big gruff laugh, yes, this is a good idea, but soldiers will have to become Muslim first.

"Yes, Muslim, no problem. I will be anything if it gets the job done, but sir, I love Arak, how can I drink and be a Muslim?" And he imitates the Iraqi standard saying: "This—this—this is ferry ferry difficult," wagging his index finger. Everyone had a laugh.

"Arak? Oh you like Arak?"

"Of course, we all do! We love Arak. We drink some almost every day!" We like the stuff from Lebanon. It is expensive, but very good. It is hard to get, but we know a Jinn that will deliver for us. All the soldiers facing him nodded agreement with sparkling eyes, commenting on the intricate beauties of Arak. Now he has a laugh and has his hand raised, wagging a finger, and he gives the soldiers a spontaneous lecture on Arak, its varieties, the way it is made. And then a whole a lot of stories, not about Arak but about a different time.

He talks about the seventies and eighties and how good it used to be in Iraq, how alcohol used to flow freely, and he seems like a guy who had his fair share of drinks in his younger days. (Before he got his hand on the prayer beads, it seems, but that's now part of his image.) Maybe he has whiskey and Arak hidden someplace in this palatial house.

If he did, he sure was not sharing any. And now a soldier spontaneously asks, "Do you think Muqtada al-Sadr drinks Arak? He looks like he is drunk in every picture!"

The man cannot believe his ears. He has not heard such a contention before and he starts laughing, shrugging his shoulders. But no, he does not think so. So a soldier insists, no, no, just pay attention to the pictures—and he stands up from his chair, posing like Muqtada in his many glamor shots. "I think he does. He looks like he had too much," and he attempts the mean-faced Muqtada glamor shot. "I think he does, I think he likes Arak, the good Arak, not in plastic packets, only the best."

The DAC member is laughing. If he was offended, he did not show it. "Maybe, you never know." And that is true, one would never know with the self-righteous ones who believe they have figured it out.

Then the soldier laughs, "Sir, Muqtada really needs to have a drink; a lot of his trouble will go away if he just had a drink, man. These JAM boys in the streets, they just try to beat up the guys who sell Arak in plastic packets, and you know, we really liked those guys."

Everyone is laughing, and the DAC member adds with a smile, "Maybe he should have some Arak, good Arak!"

Soldiers were unanimous in agreement, "Yes, sir, thank you, thank you." But he was kind enough to point out that soldiers should watch out with the Arak in plastic packets. Yes, of course, soldiers agree. We are always careful. So a soldier points out, "Sir, we usually drink the best, and hey, yes, it might get us blind, but when we put these on"—pointing at the night vision attached to the ACH—"well, we are pretty blind anyway and Arak helps us see clearly."

He asks the soldiers, laughing, "Who are you, which unit do you work for?" and he mentions the commanders in the neighborhood and adjacent neighborhoods, and the commanders that oversee everything. "Do you work for any of them?" He truly knows everybody, and that is why he is the man for the job! Soldiers sit there staring at him with their ready grins telling him, "Oh, sir, do not worry about us, we are just bunch of *majnoun* [jackasses]." He has puzzled eyes.

The soldier asks him amid the laughter, "Mr. Amer, sir, we are sorry to bother you at this time of the night but we need your help, maybe you could help us."

He shifts slightly in his throne and looks a little agitated but there is no denying that he probably expected something like this the moment the soldiers walked into his house. Mr. Amer is no joke: The grunts are faced with a political eel of very good lineage, so slimy and slithery he could wiggle his way out of anything, that is his strength, and he is actually on soldiers' side, sort of. It is more accurate to say he is on his own side.

Now he is listening with non-committal eyes.

"Sir, we know you have lot of powerful friends, a lot of powerful JAM friends, politicians, clerics, and even insurgents in these neighbor-hoods. We know you have nothing to do with them, but you know them and we want you to take a message to them from us."

Now he really wants to know who the soldiers are and who they work for, he wants to know the commanders. This guy knows exactly how everything works. He can keep trying but that will not happen. It is utterly unnecessary in this hallucination.

Soldiers introduce themselves: Willie, Kris, Johnny—and the guys standing at the door looking everywhere, keeping an eye on things, they are Waylon and Bruce. He does not buy it, one sees it in the eyes, and soldiers also have a grin. It is hard to believe these clowns, and this man knows his stuff.

By now he is agitated and visibly annoyed. He wants none of this non-sense. He can directly deal with the powers that be, but he wants to know who the soldiers are. He claps his hands and rubs them, as if getting rid of imaginary flour stuck to his palms. "*Kallas!*" He does not know what this is about but he wants nothing to do with it. He is angry and it shows.

"Sir, please listen, that's all we ask."

"What is this?" He is pissed and wants the soldiers out of the house and he invokes higher authority, soldiers' own higher authorities, a long list of them—but those names are so close to heaven that soldiers need not worry. He is firing off names, assuming one of them would be the soldiers' own commander, like a nervous soldier shooting a 50-caliber machine gun at random without taking proper aim. A 50-caliber machine gun is great—every volley has the effect of warming the heart—but it might not be useful if not well deployed. It has the effect of giving away one's position instantaneously.

"Sir, please listen." But he is angry. He wants the soldiers to leave, and he threatens in his subtle way to call some people.

But his living room is so very bright, the fluorescent light was bright and flickering and after a while it got on soldiers' nerves. So a soldier stands up, walks to the light switch, turns it off and comes back, the large living room now illuminated by one ornate table lamp on top of a baroque, gaudy cabinet. The soldier walks back to his chair and looks at him and apologizes, "Sorry, the light was too bright, and it hurt my eyes."

"What is this, who are you, who do you work for?" And no, he does not want anything to do with this nonsense. So the soldier apologizes for their unmitigated insolence, begs him not to misconstrue anything because soldiers mean no harm. They know that Mr. Amer is on the soldiers' side.

A soldier looked at him and said, "Sir, you will listen; it will be good for you." His eyes are glistening with anger at this insolence and he is not listening.

The soldier takes a deep breath and reaches into his pouch in the rack system, pulling out his all-weather notebook, and begins to recite a list of names—Mr. Amer knows some of them. His dark black eyes are intense, his mustache is crisp and he is looking intensely at the soldier, his mouth half open.

488

"Sir, please, you need to listen to us," and he hands him the notebook so he can properly peruse it. Mr. Amer slowly returns the book, now with very long ears.

"Sir, you will always be safe with us. We are on your side and you know this." He nods his agreement or understanding.

"We know you have nothing to do with JAM, you just know a lot of them, most of the politicians and people that work for the government that are JAM, but we know you are innocent. You are a politician. You want to help the people." Another soldier listening in puts his fist in the air: "Yeah, power to the people, baby," and soldiers laugh at his smart-ass comment. Mr. Amer does not find any humor in this moment.

"Sir, in three days, you will attend the DAC meeting with a lot of powerful people, but first, on Saturday, you will get together at Mr. Abbas's house and discuss what to do at the DAC meeting. We know this, that's what you guys always do." His eyes could not hide his astonishment that soldiers are privy to something that is tantamount to a family secret—but it is not a secret, a lot of people in the neighborhood know this reality. Soldiers in their hallucinations just paid attention to some of the incongruities, and some good Iraqis pointed it out.

"Sir, when you meet your friends, could you pass them a message for us, so your friends can also pass on the message to others. That's all we ask of you, please, do you think you could do this for us?"

Soldiers have seen many different kinds of eyes in Iraq with all different colors, but his black eyes are fixed in their gaze. He seems to be listening with his eyes. That's very good.

"Yes, no problem, what is it?"

The soldiers finally lean back and straighten up while Mr. Amer seems buried in his plush throne, listening intensely.

"Sir, there are JAM boys who kill Americans and people in the neighborhood"—and he has a noncommittal look that suggests, well, you are stating the obvious. "But there are also JAM politicians—people

489

who work for the government, businessmen, and all kinds of powerful JAM people in this neighborhood, and you know lots of them."

"Yes," and he shrugs the shoulders: It is obviously his greatest strength.

"Sir, they do not fight, but they help the JAM boys fight and kill people, and for us, they are as guilty as everybody else, especially the worst and the most powerful of them, and you know lots of them."

He is again looking with his forehead and listening with his eyes.

"Tell them, for every American injured and killed, and every time JAM kills Iraqis in this neighborhood, they will also have to pay a price for paying the JAM boys. They keep them in business, do you understand? no more nonsense in this neighborhood."

"You tell your friends, and they can tell their friends, they have two choices. We don't care what JAM or whoever does in any other part of town, this is our neighborhood, we walk the streets. Either they stay and keep out of trouble, or they can pack their bags and move south. Do you understand?"

The strength of combatants is that they are comfortable in their anonymity. But powerful middlemen do not want anonymity. Their strength lies in being known, that gives them their immunity and power. They want more of it, they never want to move out of town and be a nobody in the boondocks. That is the greatest weakness that makes the middlemen who sustain an insurgency the soft under-belly. And without them, it is hard to keep breathing life into a polit-ical-military organization driven by a sob story because they play a critical role—they assist and bankroll the combatants.

Mr. Amer looks like someone who just heard an original idea, but he has a predictable response: "But this is illegal!"

"You are telling us this is illegal, but your JAM friends can get away with murdering Americans and Iraqis? Is that what you are telling me?"

Buried in his throne, Mr. Amer seems at a loss for words, his hamster wheels spinning like crazy, because he is a very smart and astute man.

"Sir, look at me, look at me, listen, everybody, every one of them goes home at night, and guess who walks the streets at night? We do!"

A soldier pulls out his all-weather notebook and shows him a list of names. He looks through it again, trying in his mind to put together any number of little stories he may have heard. Powerful men have antennas attuned to all the neighborhood gossip—*shaku maku*—and it is their neighborhood. They know it with an enviable subtlety and nuance. This is the moment and it is time to go for the touchdown.

The soldier pulls out his iPod from another pouch in its water-and-shock-proof case. "Look, Mr. Amer, let me show you something."

He pulls out the iPod; it is filled with tons of pilfered songs—yes, it is wrong, we know, please forgive us, one dollar for a song is a bit much for a grunt! But on this day, they had transferred some pictures of some friends of Mr. Amer. The iPod makes a slight clicking noise as he kept rotating his finger. Mr. Amer's eyes were glued to it, maybe he has not seen an iPod before, maybe he is just very curious. Then the soldier pulls his chair up to show him some of the pictures. Just a couple to make the point: "Oh that is Mr. Ali, your friend, remember from the Health Ministry, he was very powerful, a friend of yours, yes?" And this is so and so, and this—yes, you might want to pass the message. We don't care about other places, but this is our neighborhood, understood?

He is now looking at the soldiers very intently indeed.

The soldier promises him sincerely, "Sir, we are on your side, do not worry." He touches his hand with a tight grip, we are on your side. Maybe it's a funny moment: Being a powerful man, so high up on the totem pole, he has never had the gritty realities on the street brought home to him so intimately. Whatever it is, soldiers have only one certainty looking at his eyes. His little hamster inside is spinning, and soldiers have a good hold on the hamster cage and they will keep spinning it relentlessly.

The soldier tells Mr. Amer, "You tell them, leave town if they want to talk to their JAM boys, we don't care what they do or where they go, but not in this neighborhood. Ask all of them to take their families and leave town, you know exactly who."

Then the soldiers laugh, "No, they don't have to, it is up to them, stay here and help murder people, and we will do what we have to, or they can move south, yes?"

It is very unlikely that any of them will leave town, but that is really irrelevant, their cages will be sufficiently rattled. They will put a lot of stories together, trying to make sense of events, and Mr. Amer will certainly do his part to embellish the story, and they will be talking to the JAM boys. Soldiers' area of responsibility is limited, but there is no need to stop imagining.

Mr. Amer looks like a man who learned much in a short period. As befits his position, he wants to ask probing questions. Soldiers quietly smile without answering, shrugging their shoulders, and Mr. Amer gets buried in his plush throne once again. He promises that he will pass the word to his friends, but he does not know what they will do. Soldiers tell him, that is not a problem, that is not Mr. Amer's business, he only has to carry the message, what they do is their own business. "No worries, sir, no worries."

A soldier reaches across and grabs his right hand, telling him, "Sir, we are on your side, you are a good man, you will always be safe with us, do not ever worry!" He shakes the soldier's hand with his sweaty hand, and then shakes the hands of the others.

Soldiers leaning back on the chair tell him, "Sir, do you know what is funny? Do you know that some JAM boys—and even some of your friends—put a price tag on some soldiers' and some American commanders' heads? Did you know that?" And the soldiers laugh, pointing out that the American commanders and soldiers are very proud to have price tags on their head because that means they are doing a good job, and they laugh even more. Mr. Amer does not look puzzled, he agrees this is very possible.

"Oh, no, it is possible. We know it because some people told us about it. Did you know Mr. Ahmed? You knew him—the JAM-affiliated district police commander—he actually knew about it all along, a Jinn that we know actually brought us his cell phone and his PDA." Soldiers show Mr. Amer some of the photos in Mr. Ahmed's very personal cell phone that soldiers' received from a genie they had befriended. In his cell phone and PDA he had some photos of American commanders and soldiers that had price tags put on them by insurgents: It was wonderful to find definitive answers in soldiers' hallucinations.

Then the soldier leans toward Mr. Amer and tries to imitate the Iraqi accent again. "This is terrible, ferry terrible; Mr. Ahmed was too busy killing, and he had no time to mention this to any of his American friends! This is terrible, ferry terrible!"

Then there follows a little moment of quiet as soldiers sit there on their chairs chewing tobacco and Mr. Amer sits in his plush throne that looks larger than himself with eyes moving in all directions, gradually slowing down.

Soldiers now suggest that they should leave, and they thank him for agreeing to pass on the message and apologize profusely for breaking his peace and solitude at night. And they have an offer: "Sir, why don't you take our phone numbers and if you ever need anything, just call. But you cannot give the phone numbers to anybody else, do you understand?"

"Yes, this is a very good idea!" and he fumbles through a brown leather pouch and pulls out three cell phones. Like most prominent Iraqis, he has multiple cell phones from different carriers and probably multiple SIM cards with different numbers. Soldiers learned the trick from smart Iraqis. They have been doing the same thing. They have multiple phones and tons of SIM cards, none of the SIM cards belongs to them,

493

and it is absolutely great. Mr. Amer saves three phone numbers of soldiers, and he gives them his phone numbers. Finally, soldiers and Mr. Amer could have a first date if they ever needed one. It is irrelevant, given Mr. Amer's powerful position and soldiers' lowly existence, whether they go on a date. What matters is that they *could* if they wanted to, and that is miles and miles distant from when Mr. Amer first started invoking the high and mighty.

Soldiers apologize again, "Sir, we are sorry to bother you," but if he ever needed anything, he could always feel free to call. And soldiers promise him, as soon as they leave, he can forget all about them because they will never come by the house again, just call if there is anything we can do.

"Yes, no problem, thank you, thank you."

In soldiers' hallucinations, they really want to give in to the raging soul and say, "Listen, you cock-sucking worthless piece of shit, we know all about you, your family, and all your business, if you cross the line, we will make sure you start fucking running too." But it is very impolite and shows a conduct unbecoming of a frontline American soldier in a counterinsurgency to say something so tactless. Worse, it just might be very counterproductive. Soldiers, therefore, follow logic and take a different tack, precisely because they have done all their homework.

"Sir, can you call your brother, and ask him to turn off the neighborhood generators, all four of them," and they mention the generators he owns that keep the neighborhood lit at night and cool during the day. It is important to send Mr. Amer's brother a message, and also to make him understand that soldiers know a thing or two about the neighborhood—their own neighborhood, now.

This is too much for Mr. Amer, who is dressed in his jelabiya because he expected to have a good night's sleep, perhaps cuddling next to his kind-looking wife. But now he finds himself buried in his throne while his family is in another room being watched by Mr. Waylon at the door, who listens to the conversation and makes peanut gallery

494

comments the entire time. This seems like another concussion to him. He is about to say something but a soldier just waves his hand.

"Sir, just do it, this is not a problem, your brother does it for JAM boys, and he can do it for us. We want him to do us a favor." A pause. "Call him, and call him now, please."

Mr. Amer grabs one of the cell phones and simply hollers at it, and yes, it will be done shortly—and he never mentioned who asked for it, he simply asked him to do it soon, no doubt he will explain later over some tea. Mr. Amer is a very smart man; if soldiers had to, they could certainly do business with him and share a few dates together.

Soldiers thank him profusely and reach for the assault pack, giving him multiple stacks of Benjamin Franklins, recycled courtesy of the Sadrist political office. Benjamin is just incredible, he always has the expected effect on people's eyes, and he is the ultimate stud through and through and one hell of a charming man.

Soldiers tell Mr. Amer, "please give it to your brother, and this is for you." It is a breathtaking stack, even soldiers held their breath, he is a worthlessly powerful man now. Then the soldiers laugh, and one puts his finger on his lips, "Shhh," and asks Mr. Amer to forget that soldiers ever came by the house. "Forget us the moment we leave; we will never come to the house again!"

"Yes."

Soldiers have a lot of respect for Mr. Amer because he is smart, astute, and aware of his surroundings. His situational awareness is truly astounding. He is now way past asking questions or looking for logic behind the events. After about ten minutes of small talk, getting Mr. Amer comfortable and normal, bringing his hamster to a quiet halt, the neighborhood goes dark, including Mr. Amer's own house, and one could hear the ahhhh and oooh sounds of the family sitting in the spacious hookah room. They are obviously a little worried because this has not happened to them before. Soldiers pull out some green chemical lights—chemlights—break them, shake them, and put them on the table. They are getting ready to leave, shaking hands in the faint illumination of the green chemlights. Soldiers thank Mr. Amer again for his time, his kindness and agreeing to carry the message. They have no reason to doubt Mr. Amer.

Besides sending a good message, soldiers entertained another hope. Maybe when these good DAC members have their next meeting with the American commanders, in three or four days, the DAC members will have their feet firmly rooted on the ground. Maybe they will stop talking in riddles and start speaking coherently; they will certainly be a little perturbed and tired, so they might actually listen and try to make sense. The reality on the ground might become a little different. Soldiers have no way of knowing because that is done at a level far higher and soldiers stay the hell away from DAC meetings. It is not their business.

Soldiers only know a few things: Some of the DAC members' friends, who have been straddling all the worlds with immunity for so long, have already started running, and the rest of them better start running soon. Because soldiers who give into Arak-induced hallucinations find it difficult, if not impossible, to give immunity to astute murderers that bankroll killing while driving their nice Mercedes. Every single one of them goes home at night to cuddle, and at that point, their power is only in their imagination and most of them forget that reality. They can try to find immunity in their position bankrolling murder, but despite all their vanity, power, wealth, and connections, they will always be one heartbeat away from losing it all. In a counterinsurgency with the worst of them that feel high and mighty, it is sometimes very necessary to point out this reality. But it must be done in a very intimate setting so it slowly seeps in and settles in the heart. "Sir, you have a choice to make."

It was not a threat, only a simple promise—one that Mr. Amer now knew without a shred of doubt that the soldiers were dead set on keeping, in their hallucinations.

It is a different group of militiamen that walk the street at night, and let us see how far the little pricks want to go in this neighborhood. Mr. Amer will pass the message quickly, he will keep his word, and soldiers will keep their word in their hallucinations. As the word spreads, good things just might happen to bad people in a very good way.

Yes, it is a counterinsurgency and it is a different fight and the perfect people will always require the good officers to carry the DA Form 2823, the sworn statements. But it will also always be the responsibility of good enlisted leaders who fight the fight to make sure that the good officers never have to use the sworn statements.

Just before soldiers step out of the house, a soldier pulls out his cell phone and sends a text message to one of his friends who appreciates the hallucinations: "On the way back brother." His friend replies with a kind note as he always did, "Yeah, about time you retards—hurry the fuck up, I can't do this for too long." Everyone steps out into the dark side streets with a smile.

In their hallucinations soldiers always said, why use high-frequency radios when it could be so loud and filled with static. The radios are good for periodic radio checks so higher can keep accountability of soldiers. Radios are also critical when stuck in an alley to call the big guns or getting friends to give a hand. But cell phones work like a charm as long as they text—it is quiet and there is no static—though it has to be noted that the cell phone jamming technology of soldiers sometimes made it a pain. Soldiers in their hallucinations learned a thing or two from insurgents and tried to do one better because learning is the only way to effectively conduct counterinsurgency. To be out of sight, as the animated gophers taught the soldiers, is to be out of mind; to be out of earshot, as insurgents taught the soldiers, is to be utterly anonymous.

Yes, the army is in a new business called "liberation" and "reconstruction," but it will be essential to find a delicate balance—to fight and do it well, even while doing reconstruction.

In their hallucinations, soldiers will make one last stop at the house with the sweet tea and kenaffe. Soldiers always treated the women as decent human beings, though the soldiers disappointed them as men because they let the good man Benjamin Franklin do all the work for them. Now soldiers will ask a favor, in addition to the good stories they tell. Soldiers will ask the helpful women to spread ominous rumors that will reverberate inside the subversive world. The good women in this house hold the souls of the worst of men in their hands, and one could only hope that they spread the rumors in a very intimate setting. Who else could spread rumors and whisper convincingly to the worst of the men in the neighborhood better than a woman when she holds him in a warm illicit embrace.

Unfortunately, it is time to get off the hallucinations because it is nearly sunrise and people will start walking. It is time to get out of the concrete barriers and amble back into the tent as the Arak bottles have become empty. Being drunk, it is a funny realization. The neighborhood is filled with people like any other, and the large neighborhood shrinks in size the more one walks with eyes and ears open.

Back In Reality: The Last Patrol

Having walked the streets for so long, having become aged and fatigued, the last patrol always fills the heart with strange sentiments. One of the best senior non-commissioned officers—with six deployments—had a simple truth that always stuck in soldiers' minds. The best times of soldiers are one month before deployment and one week after deployment.

They dread the garrison, where diligent gophers reign supreme. It is the military, standards are important, especially in garrison. If foot soldiers had their way, they would, in no time, turn the place into a circus and the military standards would cease to exist. But every soldier is also aware that there will always be one guy that will screw it up for everybody, and the enlisted army standards will be defined in terms of the guy who screws it up for everybody—the lowest common denominator. So the mind dreads being subjected to the stultifying monotonous life of enlisted men in garrison. Yes there will be the fair share of fights to inspire the soul. But there is one charm, a different challenge, that makes every second of enlisted life worth it.

And that is the opportunity to make some men out of kids, make soldiers out of men, and make some fighters out of soldiers. So they will always be ready to walk through that door to the unknown, side by side, finding resolve and certitude in the heart and fortitude in the gut, so they are capable of walking into complete uncertainty ready with a greeting (raising their pain and risk thresholds to a level they did not know could be possible). To go through that door not knowing what is inside, it will always be some enlisted guys standing side by side. That will always be the singular pride and charm of being among the enlisted humanity that nothing else can ever capture.

But the thought of garrison aches the heart. Soldiers have not left Iraq, but they are already dreading the return home. A young officer who always enjoyed a good glass of jack in hiding with the soldiers, who always had their backs, who was always willing to take a risk with a cackle, once said, "Duude, yes, it is critical, let us do it, but we have to be careful"—he is now mumbling, "Complicated emotions brother, I am going to miss this place." It is the strangest sentiment, yes, as much as they hate to agree, they will strangely miss the place, the good, the bad and the ugly, the noises, sights, smells, and all the good people, yes they will miss them the most.

The last patrol is like any other, with the same level of sarcasm, grins, and jokes, but the heart feels a little heavy and melancholy. On the one hand they know so much more of the neighborhood than when they first came. On the other hand there is so much that they don't know and never will. Strangely, it feels as if they have not learned a damn thing. The feet feel heavy.

❖ Walking in circles

It was decided to pay a last visit. Soldiers cannot visit everyone, but the ones that mattered the most deserved an "adios," and there is one in particular. Soldiers figure, why the hell not, if we are still walking there is no reason to change now. A handful of soldiers are standing in Mr. Hussein's courtyard at dusk. It is still very hot, and even the breeze is humid and thick. Mr. Ahmed Hussein acknowledges them with a smile and welcomes them, "Please, come in, come in." His wife, Dr. Huda, is behind him. Soldiers have come so far since the first meeting on the first patrol, an eternity ago. Dr. Huda is ubiquitous. She comes out of the walls. She is everywhere and nowhere like a little pear on fire rolling around with a smile. No one can ever escape her sight. She seems to be a mother that keeps the family firmly in line, the enforcer.

Soldiers approach the front door through the courtyard and notice a green pipe with water trickling onto the grass. It's so hot and a soldier is sweating from walking so he grabs the plastic pipe, puts it over his head, face, and inside his plate carrier, and the water seeps through his clothes, feeling strangely comfortable. He holds it on his face and shakes his head like a bird taking a bath. Mrs. Hussein—Dr. Huda—comes out to the front step and yells at the soldier, "No, this is terrible, you should not do this!" The water is not safe, it is not suitable to drink, and she has the wagging finger, yelling at them. Soldiers are laughing because she will always be a good medical professional. She gives the soldiers a stern tongue lashing.

"You need to be careful, this is very dangerous, all kinds of germs are infested in the water, no one should ever drink this water unless it is boiled." The soldier laughs, "The water is cold; it feels good."

"NO," says the matriarch. Soldiers are invited in, and Dr. Huda rolls into the living room with a jug of ice cold water and some cups; boiled and chilled, it did taste very good. With the initial round of pleasantries, the rest of the family trickles into the living room: Ali, the stern brother; Najwa, the beautiful daughter who is studying in the university and wants to be a veterinarian; Raeesah, the twelve-year-old feisty girl; and Mo, the toddler, who always wanted to box with the soldiers. After all, it is a soldier who taught him all about boxing, right down to the footwork, one-one and two, boom.

Soldiers mention that they don't have much time; they just came by to bid *masallam* because they will be leaving Iraq in a few days.

"Oh," and everyone nods, and soldiers add, "well, we just wanted to come by and say thank you for all the help, the stories and food, the tea and the bakhlava. We will miss it!"

One soldier, who never could resist being a clown, is on his knees, his combat helmet on Mo's head, and Mo is boxing again. The soldier has his palms facing Mo, and Mo would punch the soldiers' palm with his tiny left hand twice and punch his chest with the right, and each time, the soldier would groan, "Ahhh, that is good, you are strong." And they would flex their hands as everyone sat there laughing.

Ali wants to take a picture of the little brother with the ACH. So the soldier takes off his M4 Carbine, takes the magazine out, clears the weapon, and now Mo is holding the M4, only a little shorter than he is, with an ACH on his head that is way too big and everyone is laughing.

Raeesah is now excited, she also wants a picture, so the soldiers now switch the M4 and the ACH, and she smiles her pretty smile.

A soldier suggests, "when you grow up, both of you need to join the army, the U.S. Army." Ahmed and Huda laugh at the suggestion. A soldier quips, "Oh, you are a recruiter now, trying to recruit Iraqis to the U.S. Army?" and they both start laughing. "Well, everyone keeps dying; we could use the bodies right?" and there is more laughter.

But it is Dr. Huda, with her eagle eyes not missing a thing, who asks, "Where is your friend? We have not seen him in a while."

"Oh, yeah, he died actually." She touches her heart with a her right hand, Ahmed is shaking his head, and Huda, the stern medical professional, said, with all sincerity, "Oh, I am so ferry, ferry sorry."

The soldier answers, "Well," with a shrug of his shoulders and a deliberate smile, "it is what it is, madam."

Then she said again, "This is terrible. I am so sorry," and she mentioned his name and added, "He was your good friend." She is such a perceptive matriarch.

Yes. He was a good friend—fearless of everything and everybody and never hesitant at the point of decision. Yet also fearlessly kind, with his enviable ability to grasp the nuances and subtleties in the battle space when others were wondering where to look. He had a knack that came from his salt of the earth soul to empathize with people and treat them with a level of respect and human decency that always disarmed children, women, and men. He felt free and full of life, wandering around like a gypsy in the streets doing his job. He was precisely the kind of leader needed for a counterinsurgency, and he loved every second of walking the streets, bouncing around like a rooster—though the majestic army bases always made him oppressed and stultified. No wonder he liked Sir Francis Burton, Sir T.E Lawrence and had read them all. Then again, he read everything, including books about the Roman legions, which was where he really wanted to be.

But he was always at his best when he would lay back his wages and whisper quietly with determined eyes and his mischievous smile, "Hey, OK, you ready? Let's go," and bounce away as if he was on a date. As he would always say, "It is important to be effective and relentless but do it in style." He was one of the men who always set the standard, always raised the bar a little higher, a leader who always led from the front, a prince among men. So, strangely enough, it was not shocking that Dr. Huda and Ahmed's family remember him by name. Yes, it undoubtedly put a smile on our faces that this good Iraqi family could remember him.

"Yes, madam, he was my dear friend."

Both Ahmed and Dr. Huda shake hands, conveying their sympathy and all the soldiers shake hands, "Yeah, well, thank you, thank you," and Ali and Najwa follow suit, "Yes, we are sorry."

Mo the boxing toddler and Raeesah are still in enamored army mode, and Najwa has returned to her standard grinning comportment. The kids are falling fast for the recruiting pitch as they try to peek into Night Optical Devices.

Soldiers point out that they need to leave, but they just wanted to give the kids some gifts they brought.

"Oh what? No, no, this is not necessary," they quickly say. Soldiers insist, "No, no, it is simple," and reach for the patrol pack, pulling out a bunch of MP3 players they had bought at the shopping mall, the

PX, in a majestic army base. One MP3 player for each of the children, Ali, Najwa, Raeesah, and Mo. Soldiers did not have enough time; they only managed to put music into one of them, and even that, an Iraqi interpreter did by transferring his Arabic songs into the MP3 player. Soldiers give that one to Raeesah. Parents insist that this is not necessary, but "thank you." Mr. Ahmed and Huda would never know, perhaps like so many others, how well they helped soldiers see the neighborhood clearly in their honest stories interspersed with tea and sweets.

Soldiers get ready to leave, shake hands, bid adieu. But even if it's the last time, despite being in front of the entire family, there is no rhyme or reason not to flirt with a beautiful woman one last time as she stands by with a smile. It is tricky but who cares? It is the last day and soldiers always need to have the last laugh.

Soldiers turn to Najwa. "You know, Najwa, we found someone that looks just like you. I think you know her too."

She has a puzzled look, with a smile as she always did, and asks, "Who is this; do I know this woman?"

"Of course, we know you do, we are sure you do, everybody does."

Now she is very intrigued but has a quizzical look. She has been engaging in many battles of wits with the soldiers, among her family. Najwa is a pretty, proud Arab Muslim girl like so many others soldiers have met in their travels. She seems to know instinctively how to walk delicately in circles without leaving you out, speak softly in riddles so the riddle always rhymes right, and time the riddles precisely with a lyrical voice. Yet she points out, subtly and elegantly, that it is a battle of wits and she is adamantly intent on winning it every time.

But not this day. Because soldiers are on the last patrol, they feel they can afford to take a little risk and be a bit brash.

"So Najwa, do you know who it is who looks like you? She even sounds like you." She has the squinty eyes that she always had when she was suspicious. The soldiers said, "Haiffe Wahbe, you know her, she looks like you and every time when we see her, we always think of you," and she wants to laugh but would not, the entire family is looking at her. It is tricky because Haiffa Wahbe is a beautiful Lebanese singer that everyone watches—but it is sometimes debated whether people listen to her because of her singing or because she is a beautiful and well-endowed women who knows her gifted endowments. Najwa has a grin and a smirk in her eyes, so the soldiers add, "Ahhh, there you go, keep smiling, Najwa, keep smiling," and then she laughed her usual laugh. Then the soldiers turned to Ali, her brother, who was standing by with a smile and said, "Ali, please take care of your sisters, you know there are lot of crazy people in this town, too many." Shaking his hand, they comment that they need to leave.

He agrees with a laugh, yes, too many crazy people. Soldiers step out saying, "Well, you have our email address, you should send us an email, Ali," and Ali promises to do it.

Najwa has another smirk because she already has some soldiers' email addresses and emails them intermittently, and she knows the remark was pointed at her. She has the same purposeful stubborn stare she has when she refuses to agree that she was outwitted by some grunts in front of her unknowing family, but now she smiles with a slight shake of her head. Yes, she will send emails.

Soldiers could also walk in circles and speak in riddles, even occasionally time the riddles right, yes, trying to charm a very pretty, modest and virtuous Muslim Iraqi girl because they have learned a thing or two from walking the streets. It is part of the new job description. Besides, it just might be a good idea to have some people they can visit in the event soldiers have to be back in Iraq.

A soldier adds, "Najwa, good luck in your exam at the university."

"Oh, thank you," she has the smirk again and then a smile because she was ranting and raving with the soldiers over email about her upcoming exams. Soldiers, always being soldiers, could never forget that she hated the virtue enforcers in her neighborhood. No one knows and detests AK-wielding virtue enforces more than the young university students, both male and female.

Mr. Ahmed, Dr. Huda, and Ali walk the soldiers passed the courtyard to the gate, and everyone shakes hands one last time as they part ways; soldiers disappear down the side streets to link up with the rest of the clowns. The end is near.

All good things come to an end. The simple charms in a counterinsurgency end the moment soldiers go through the gates of a majestic base, and this time, there is no escaping, only living with it. They will have to become acclimated to a new, different reality, learn new points of reference where diligent gophers rule so completely. If they come to terms with it quickly, they will make it through; those who do not will keep fighting it until they self-destruct. Because it is garrison and it is defined (it seems) in terms of Safety, Risk Mitigation, and "Army Strong."

❖ Army Strong?

One of the best of them always summed it up. The fluorescent yellow reflector safety belt that soldiers have to wear while running, no matter how annoying it is, and get yelled at for not wearing it by someone who has barely walked, that reflector belt captures the safety-obsessed "Army Strong." Army Strong, soldiers always wondered, it must be a civilian who has never put on a uniform that came up with the idea, and no one was man enough to simply ask what lot of foot soldiers kept asking their own superiors: "Sir, are you fucking serious, Army Strong? Why can't we just stick with what we know and stay with it—*This We'll Defend?*" The commanding officer had a good laugh and agreed, yes, someone is definitely retarded.

But those are minor concerns, and soldiers have work to do. They need to get rid of everything that they should not have—stuff on iPods and laptop computers and other documents, everything must go to the burn barrel. Soon, the uniform mafia will be doing the rounds, going through computers and iPods. Ironically, they will not look for material that would actually compromise operational security, which they actually should do. The uniform mafia comes around looking for contraband; they subject honest men who appreciate the perfect female human form to UCMJ action. They already busted one staff sergeant who had four combat deployments for the sin of appreciating the perfect female human form.

This was a guy who could walk into a neighborhood at night that was filled with tracer rounds, like fireworks on independence day, with a grin, a laugh, and a scream: "Hey, nice knowing all you mother fuckers, this is how it ends, baby. Catch you on the flip side my little bitches"—and he would start sprinting *toward* the tracer rounds with a hysterically laughing squad of soldiers behind him. But one high-ranking and incredibly diligent gopher caught him and there was no saving him. Besides, combat is over, one cannot save him now by sending him outside the wire to chase insurgents. Yes, this combat leader was punished for the ultimate sin of being an imperfect but honest man while hypocritical posers roam in the guise of men. It did not make soldiers angry, only completely and utterly disappointed.

❖ The last concussion

Back at the majestic base, the soldiers feel a strange gaze and start looking around desperately; are they missing something? They start looking at the walls for the benevolent gaze, but there are no pictures of ayatollahs hanging on the wall. Holy shit, it is our own virtue enforcers, enforcing morality with the law!

Perhaps it is unfortunate that the ayatollahs don't talk to the Americans. Perhaps they should talk to the ones who give in to the virtue temptation on our side and try to self-righteously instill impotent fantasies in the guise of virtue, turning imaginations of honest yet imperfect men into a punishable offense. Both groups might find common points of reference irrespective of creed if they start talking. This will be the last concussion. Oh, man, yes, soldiers have been insurgents behind insurgents and going down rabbit holes for far too long. It is definitely time to go home, drown the sorrows in a cold one, say fuck it, and get used to a new reality where no one other than the few good men in uniform will ever give a shit.

One Last Nightcap at Dawn

But it is time to commiserate one last time, hiding at sunrise. As the place grows dark and people fall asleep, some silhouettes are still walking outside with small backpacks. First they had to make some last phone calls to some of the good people who helped them: Soldiers will not be around, this is the last call, you can always send us an email, please be safe, dear friend.

Then cut a line to the burn barrel that has trickles for flames at this time of the night. Take the batteries off the cell phones and pour every other thing that needs to be disposed of into the burn barrel.

Then they throw some JP 8 gasoline and watch the memories dance away into nothingness in billowing yellow flames. So it is done and over with. The memories will always remain in their rightful resting place: In the minds of men.

There is one last stop before commiserating with friends. They stop by the interpreters. The best of them took exorbitant risks, and it takes something special to be willing to walk into a firefight without a weapon in hand. Some soldiers did not rely on interpreters because some Iraqis were only willing to help solders without interpreters. But the good guys needed to be seen, and they were teary-eyed, walking around shaking hands and hugging the soldiers that have been together for too long. One has his best friend's picture on the wall, a good man who is dead and gone in pieces, and he insisted on packing the soldier's belongings in the boxes with tearful eyes. That was his way of honoring his American friend.

Some soldiers strangely don't feel too bad leaving them. Yes, they are now on their own, life sucks, and soldiers cannot do everything. But they did what they could: Every single interpreter that worked with these soldiers managed to get their families out of Iraq to Syria, one to Jordan and one to Lebanon, after soldiers gave them exorbitant amounts of Benjamin Franklins that they had confiscated. Many American officers and soldiers did just that in many places. For some of them, the money was perhaps more than they would ever make in their lives, but no one—not a single one—ran away with it; they promptly came back to work with the soldiers. Yes, it may be illegal or defy procedures but who gives a shit because people near heaven not on the ground make the laws. Alas, there is a lot of life between heaven and earth and some laws at times needs to be broken because it is the right thing to do and there is never an excuse not to do it.

So most of the interpreters' families now have more than enough money courtesy of JAM, who were a wealthy bunch. Interpreters take a risk, it is their choice, and these soldiers always did what they could. Every single Benjamin they confiscated was put to good use and not a single soldier touched a single Benjamin for personal use because that would be theft, and soldiers and military leaders hate nothing more than thieves, liars, and weak-hearted men.

But soldiers did feel terribly for one interpreter who lost his girl-friend. She was the very pretty daughter of a former high-ranking Baathist intelligence official who is still in jail. She said she could not live with the stress of him putting his life in danger; she had nothing against the Americans, she insisted, and if she did, she hid it very well behind her pretty face and smile. He was thinking of quitting, and he has worked with Americans since 2003. Soldiers argued it had every-thing to do with her nerves and nothing to do with risking life and we have had to deal with the same problem. If she is going to stay, she will stay, if she will leave, she will leave. "Please man, do not quit right now, we need you brother—please!" they had begged.

Soldiers succeeded, he stayed, but his girlfriend went off to Jordan, married someone else and now lives in the affluent neighborhood of Shmeisani in Amman. He was heartbroken, and so were the soldiers, for him as well as for themselves, because she had wonderful affluent friends who emailed stories to soldiers. So now they offer him a part-ing gift, a few bottles of Johnny Walker brought by a magical genie from the thousand and one nights. "Drown the sorrows in a glass, say fuck it, and keep it together," "Stay in touch."

It is time to head to the usual place for one last time. Soldiers grab a bunch of one-liter water bottles and a twenty-pound bag of ice. They are lying about everywhere for soldiers to use. They take slow deliberate steps for the last time to the same place. So many decisions were taken or not taken, so many stories were repeated, and so many memories, secrets, imaginations, hallucinations were shared in this place. Soldiers empty the water bottles, cut them in half and fill it to the top with ice cubes.

It is an eclectic group of people—enlisted, some not enlisted, high and low—but all of them men who always helped soldiers. After countless periods of sustained combat, they know it is the end and all good things have to end sometime. They will not have this moment again, the experience and the same group of guys that have been together for so long, day and night, sober and drunk, in good times and bad. They were glad to be together side by side. Soon enough, everyone will scatter to the four winds and it is another elemental part of life. Time to put the memories in a lock box and throw the key chain around the neck and keep walking.

The place is quiet except for the distant noise of a Paladin firing 155mm rounds for fire missions, making the earth shake. They pour whiskey in the cups all the way to the top; it is a lot, but soldiers can feel prodigal today. They have a number of bottles left, and it is early, only around 0100. And they know with certainty that there will be no last-minute Time Sensitive Target Acquisition Missions tonight because combat for them is over. They feel they have earned the right for a drink despite it being against the laws of virtue enforcers on our own side. Well, an elemental part of soldiering will always remain breaking some laws sometimes—but only as long as it is done right.

One of the senior men did just that. After the last patrol he called all his men out yelling, "Every single fucking one of you, *outside*, grab a liter of water and get the fuck outside." Every soldier walked out, wondering, what the fuck? Are you serious? After all this shit? He rarely if ever yells and when he does, everyone listens, commissioned and non-commissioned alike.

He lined all his men outside and stared them down, glowering. Then he broke out laughing, and told everyone to empty their bottles and cut them in half. Then he provided them with—literally—gallons of alcohol that he had acquired, five deployments, too many alleyways, he knew how to find stuff by hook or by crook. It goes without saying he is one of the best senior enlisted noncommissioned officers the army has produced. He had few words, good work men, good work, but the good times are over, drink, and be responsible, be fucking responsible, understood?

Roger.

But the heart will always feel heavy because not everyone is around; it is what it is, and it is part of soldiering. They raise the glasses for the ones who are no longer around to share a drink, they unequivocally enjoyed this moment when they could. To them, "For a life well lived," and the second round, "Simple pleasures of life man," and then they take quiet sips, inhaling the alcohol, capturing the solitude of the moment. They can feel the quiet whisper of the dusty Iraqi breeze that they always found inexplicably inspiring when they walked the streets—no one knew why or how.

The conversation interspersed with alcohol slowly drifts to the topic of the moment. Given the slow movement of information between high and low, the multiple moving parts in the area, this was also the unofficial gathering place to plan on the best way to capture the simple charms walking the streets and the best way for a greeting. Besides, with so many gophers clicking heels, it was important to stay out of sight and this was their refuge, everyone needs one. On this day, the discussion was about the recent declaration of a cease-fire by Jaish al-Mahdi militia.

The soldiers have been battling them continuously for a long time, and they were in the streets the day of the ceasefire and some months afterwards. It was a moment that passed without any excitement among the soldiers, but they saw the difference in the streets through the stories of people. The people were less and less afraid. The combined efforts of the U.S. military and Iraqi forces may have forced JAM to declare a ceasefire, but no soldier felt it necessary to let up and feel prematurely optimistic. Things on the ground, soldiers and their leaders knew instinctively, could always change in a heartbeat. One senior non-commissioned officer said it best—a man that soldiers always respected for his achievements, honesty, and fearless leadership and who always posited reality as it is. "Hey, listen up, men, good news is good, get over it; bad news is great, you still have to deal with it."

❖ JAM declares a cease-fire

JAM has more or less stopped shooting—though they still shoot intermittently at the Americans. (Only they are called special groups, not JAM, and it is the greatest ruse. Wouldn't it be wonderful to have special groups that do our bidding, and we can distance ourselves and deny their existence?) The cease-fire was more about stopping the shooting and terrorizing of their own people.

Yes, the combined efforts of American and Iraqi militaries all over Iraq against JAM contributed to it, and much has been written on that. But there were also reasons intrinsic to JAM and their own constituency that led them to their decision.

JAM is a shrewd political-military creature driven by a sob story and they plan to stick around, do better, and keep growing, long after Americans leave Iraq. So much always depended on their central idea of power to the Shia people—an idea that slowly but surely got warped into an anti-American, anti-Jewish, anti-Western, and anti-everything sob story that many ideologues repeat today. Average Shia people in neighborhoods really do not give two shits about Americans, Jews, and cosmic dreams; most of them seem to want jobs, school for their kids, and a future where they don't have to navigate roadblocks wondering each time whether they will make it home alive.

But when JAM unleashed idiots with AK-47s, JAM slowly turned themselves into a reflection of their old ruthless masters. JAM tactics and treatment of their own people in the neighborhoods they controlled undoubtedly alienated a lot of people. Thankfully, people also had an alternative (though imperfect)—not the Americans, but the Government of Iraq, when it started paying salaries to people.

Immediately after the cease-fire, there were many amazing incidents in Shia neighborhoods rarely documented in the Western press. Men and women barged into JAM political offices, beat up JAM men and asked about loved ones they had killed. Some of the most vocal JAM clerics got the same reception. And even as the delicate tapestry of JAM control was unraveling at the seams, the gangsters, extortionists, and sociopaths continued to invoke JAM while doing their business, alienating people even further.

The cease-fire, as soldiers on the ground interpreted it, meant that the JAM guys who stayed in the neighborhoods simply oiled their weapons and hung them up to use another day. But it certainly neutered some of them: The complicity of the majority will be difficult to get without the AK-47s, and they just might have to rely more on the electoral process. Cease-fire for the people meant they had to navigate fewer and fewer absurdities; the virtue enforcers and gangsters had to get off the streets. And it meant that teachers, university professors, and lecturers could now teach without fearing for their lives, imagine that luxury!

❖ **The victory chronicles of the Magi**[95]

In a university, every student gets two attempts at the final exam, and some JAM boys, busy doing JAM stuff, managed to fail both tries. They requested another try, and the professors refused. They returned *with their guns* to demand a third try. The septuagenarian professor refused to grant this exception to policy. So the JAM boys resorted to an escalation of force—they locked up some hostages in a staff room: Their professor along with a few other professors and lecturers (including a friend of the soldiers, who later told them the story). They still refused!

The septuagenarian professor furiously asks them to shoot him. The others were genuinely scared, but somehow the moment was resolved without anyone dying and without making an exception to the policy. They were brave to face them down, especially the professor who led

---

[95] A novel by the Iranian author Hushang Golshiri.

from the front, and it was wonderful that soldiers had a friend there. She was still seething with rage telling the story months afterwards. Rage is good—because the professors know the names of the JAM students who threaten their lives. They have access to the university documents and maybe even keys to the registrar's office. They just might make copies and hand them over to the soldiers, making life perfect and counterinsurgency easier. After the cease-fire, such moments are few and far between.

❖ AK culture?

JAM may be weakened but they have one certainty: Americans come and go; they are there to stay. The cease-fire was a tactical decision. Whether it can be turned into a strategic advantage will depend on the astuteness of the ruling Shia coalition.

As long as JAM retains the military capabilities, it will always be able to flank the political system militarily. Each time, the Iraqi government (run by their Shia brethren) will be faced with a choice. They can either try to outflank JAM militarily and politically, which will be time-consuming and painful but in the long run effective. Or they can give into the impulse of scared men and rely on what soldiers called their AK-47 culture.

An AK-47 is a reliable weapon. It rarely malfunctions (given its piston mechanism), and it's cheap and easy to maintain—but it is only good on burst, shooting from the hip, not for well-aimed shots. The Iraqi government will have to avoid giving into the temptation to use overwhelming force against JAM, which would feel good momentarily. In a counterinsurgency, overwhelming force also means unnecessary civilian casualties and wanton destruction of civilian property. This inevitably strengthens the insurgents' hand: Violence always creates sorrow and misery and no one ever forgets the loss of loved ones.

The essential piece of American counterinsurgency strategy was to turn this elemental truth into an operational concept through selective use of force. If the Iraqi military resorts to overwhelming force, flattening everyone and everything in their wake, JAM will score points.

It will perfectly strengthen the sob story, and people will find common ground with JAM, making them stronger than before.

An M4 is arguably a less reliable weapon, given its gas-operated mechanism; it takes time, effort, and discipline to maintain it. But it will always stabilize better for well-aimed shots—and it will always mean target discrimination, so that only the ones that are necessary will end up living a lifetime in a second, while the civilians remain unharmed.

Politically, JAM ideologues who perpetuate the sob story will keep breathing fire, using the problems of the present as an excuse to seduce people into giving up the future. How will the JAM ideologues reinvent the sob story when the Americans leave—blame Canada perhaps? No, JAM will always pick on the ready bogeyman that never seems to get old in the Middle East.

But now that they take part in the political system, one can always hope that eventually the sob story will become irrelevant, and JAM will be just another political party pursuing power. They will cease to be ideologues, stop trying to create a perfect world of their imagination with guns in hand. But it requires more work by the ruling parties. Unless the government gets the complicity and support of the people by meeting their immediate needs, giving them some predictability and trust in the future, the JAM sob story will always have traction on the ground and resonance in the hearts of the Shia people.

The Sweet Wager

Muqtada al-Sadr, whose gaze soldiers have felt intimately, is apparently trying to get over his hangover in the holy city of Qom in Iran. He may complete his studies, elevate himself to ayatollah, and return to Iraq and ingratiate himself into the clerical establishment, carving out a place for himself as a political ayatollah in the Iraqi religious-political scene. At the moment, Muqtada, with all his fire and brimstone, in essence is just an outstanding clerical mediocrity who has the good fortune of a famous political-clerical lineage—a readily recognizable brand name—and shrewd advisors. He might try to become a "nonpolitical" cleric, claiming to be above politics but in reality being the most political of all, following in the footsteps of his forefathers, while the traditional Hawza continues to dabble in cosmic matters.

So Muqtada is studying in the holy city of Qom under an Iranian cleric; he is sponsored by one of his father-in-law's students (whose well-to-do relatives some soldiers visited). But since the holy city of Qom has the highest per capita ratio of women of the night in all of Iran, let us hope he gets seduced into being imperfect yet normal. That might be the best way to prevail on self-righteous men who believe in their own perfection, who want to reduce others into a figment of their own moralist imagination. Then again, it may turn out that his wife—the daughter of legendary Ayatollah Muhammed Baqir al-Sadr—holds his reins well and tight. This is a personal wager for some soldiers.

If he gets seduced and finds an Iranian mistress, he might also resort to what everyone else does: Make the pretty mistress a wife and bring her home. It is a running bet between some soldiers and some of their friends: If Muqtada is seduced by an Iranian, as our good friends are betting, the soldiers stand to lose. Yet, in everything is an opportunity, and some soldiers sincerely hope that they could perhaps capture the moment anyway. Only time will tell, and a lot depends on Muqtada's decision.

The Shia family saga will continue to evolve on the Iraqi national stage, and many Shia people in Iraq will keep feeling the gaze of ayatollahs for a long time.

❖ Last sunrise

It is very early and very late, the horizon past the concrete blast walls looks bright orange from the sun coming through the dust. The morning breeze is brisk and fresh. Soldiers know it is the perfect time to start another patrol—but not this day, today they can only feel nostalgic. Soon, soldiers will again feel the full wrath of the Iraqi sun, and it will hurt the heart and turn the eyes into a permanent squint. But today they will just dawdle in the tent: Curl inside the sleeping bag and put on the headphones with some of the last of the true American Highwaymen coming through.

515

A luxurious day of uninterrupted sleep that they have been craving for so damn long. It will be perfect, blissful, and serene.

Eventually, the last of the soldiers hiding out in the refuge inside the majestic base, who were determined to see it through and finish all the bottles, are no longer standing. They are all sitting inside a concrete bunker, finding shade from the diligent virtue enforces that will be making the rounds soon. With the last of the alcohol gone, recounting the stories, memories and much else, it was a high-ranking young officer that posited, totally and completely drunk: "Brother, I tell you, brother, a lot, a lot in the future will depend on how Iraqis perceive us, brother." Yes, in a counterinsurgency, the perception of the people just might mean everything.

PART VI

RETROSPECTIVE: A FEW SIMPLE SUGGESTIONS

Soldiers have a peculiar dual role while navigating on the ground in an insurgency. On the one hand, we are tasked with searching for and destroying the enemy. That will always be our primary job description; handing out blankets, candy packets, and trying to build bridges by professing our good intentions will always be secondary. On the other hand, we are required to win the support of the local neighborhood because positive outcomes in a counterinsurgency depend not solely on our actions but on how people react to what we do on the ground.

The perceptions of the people in the neighborhoods we walk through will always have extreme implications for the nature of the control we can attain in the area. Similarly, the wider perceptions of the Iraqi people will have ramifications on the broader mission.

As soldiers on the ground, winning at least some minds remains the most difficult part of the new job description. But it is not impossible, and some challenges can be overcome. In this area, soldiers can always use some help. We discuss honestly what we did and what we could not do.

22

KARNAK CAFÉ: PERCEPTION IN COUNTERINSURGENCY

> We had to arrange their minds in order to battle, just as
> carefully and as formally as other officers would arrange
> their bodies. And not only our own men's minds,
> though naturally they come first. *We must also arrange
> the minds of the enemy*, as far as we could reach them;
> then those other minds of the nations supporting us
> behind the firing line, since more than half the battle
> passed there in the back; then the minds of the enemy
> nation waiting the verdict; and of the neutrals looking
> on; circle beyond circle.
>
> —Lieutenant Colonel Thomas E. Lawrence

Is perception merely the reality most people believe, most of the time?

Soldiers' actions on the ground impact the way people make decisions—and their decisions in turn affect the way *soldiers* make decisions. Perceptions on the part of the local population have a profound impact on every step soldiers take in the neighborhood, and on the wider mission as well. The ultimate outcome—and the objective—in a counterinsurgency seems to lie somewhere at the confluence of *what soldiers do* and *how people react to it*.

519

Trying to alter people's perceptions will always be instrumental to achieving the objective. But that is the job of perfect people, men and women, in civilian outfits making the big bucks—not of soldiers tasked with distinguishing the enemy from the innocent and following through at the point of decision. But until the perfect people step up and out of their fortified bunkers and capture the simple charms in the street—as the best of the soldiers know how to do—trying to alter the perception of people becomes another unenviable job of soldiers on the ground.

Hearts, Minds, and Hollywood

The same question again: how and how best to achieve the objective?

Highwaymen walking down the street, wondering about people and perception, with no enemy in the vicinity to warm the heart. Instead, children, women, and men scurry about trying to live; the sight of them makes the heart sink. It is a war, after all—though it may seem like a circus in the abstract news streams you see in America. On the ground, there is the inevitable death, destruction, and suffering of the innocent. Soldiers hear it, see it, feel it, smell it, and one or two may have tasted it. The medic was trying to stop the arterial bleeding of an Iraqi man when the artery went into spasms and spewed blood all over his face. But he was a good medic, he just said, "shit," without even flinching, and kept doing what he was doing, stopped the bleeding with a tourniquet and a "hotclot." The man was stabilized with hextend (blood volumizer) and soldiers sent him off. There is no doubt he lived, but soldiers can only do what they can, and then move on.

Suffering of the innocent is inevitable in a war, though it is usually reduced to statistics and colorful charts, "collateral damage," when people pay any attention at all. But soldiers on the ground see families—children, women, and men, with faces, names, stories, and voices. Yes, the war has touched nearly every Iraqi family in some way. For reasons only the heart knows, the sight of suffering children, women, and men—in that order—left a bitter and at times enraged feeling in the soul.

It is undeniable: The greatest travesty is the suffering of Iraqi women as a result of this war and the callous disregard of perfect people for their suffering. Women in Iraq are twice victims. First, like all Iraqis, they suffer from violence. Second, they suffer abuse and neglect at the hands of some men, who like to believe they are above them. That makes a bad situation worse for many destitute Iraqi women. We met Iraqi women who have dedicated their lives to alleviating the suffering of the many women and children who live at the mercy of circumstances, some formidable and determined women who seemed larger than life: Hats off to them.

Altering the perception: It's twice as hard as soldiering. Walking down the street, the feet feel heavy, the heart sinks, and the soul begins to ache looking for a hiding place. And sometimes the soul finds a breath of inspiration instead.

❖ A Bridge Too Far?

Many, many Iraqi households were subjected to visits of soldiers. Many remained reluctant hosts, but many made us feel amazingly welcome. One amazing visit turned out surprisingly well—even though the soldiers entered from the roof instead of the door.

The soldiers were planning on greeting some insurgents in a couple of weeks, so they had to do some reconnaissance and surveillance work in a neighborhood of cinderblock houses packed together like sardines. The best way to get to the house that had the best vantage point was by jumping into it at night from the roof of the adjacent house.

So soldiers come down the stairs from the roof to encounter, as expected, a startled family. Soldiers are insisting, "No problem, no problem, no problem, everyone is safe"; they apologize for intruding. It is evidently family time in the living room. Actually, it is *movie time*, with multiple families sitting around. The soldiers ask them to keep watching, not to worry, and set about looking for the best possible greeting place for a later date, a Small Kill Team (SKT) ambush site.

Then a soldier peeks into the living room and does a double-take. "Are you serious?" The family is watching a movie, men, women, and children huddled together—and it is *Black Hawk Down*. Soldiers are cracking up, doubled up over with laughter, commenting on the movie.

521

The patriarch of the house asks the soldiers, "Good movie, yes?" Soldiers shrug their shoulders. "Well, it's OK, there are better ones though."

The patriarch turns to a charming young leader (yes, he is a charmer) and asks the most unexpected question any of the soldiers had heard in all their deployments: "Sir, mister, do you know Audie Murphy?"

"What?!!"

The patriarch repeated his question, "Audie Murphy, you know Audie Murphy?"

The leader answered in disbelief, "Yeah, Audie Murphy, of course I know Audie Murphy, but, wait, how do *you* know about him?"

"To Hell and *Back*, mister, To *Hell* and Back!"

The Iraqi not only knew about Audie Murphy, he was an avid fan. He knew the details of his life, the movies he was in—he mentioned movies not even the soldiers had seen. This Iraqi was well versed in nearly every American war epic.

He has also seen *A Bridge Too Far*. Nearly all the soldiers sitting looking at him had come of age—had become men—low crawling on Ardennes, as privates in H-Minus (a.k.a. the "Three-Kitty," as soldiers will always fondly remember 3 Panther, the outfit of General James Jumping Gavins). *A Bridge Too Far* was always close to the soldiers' heart; they had the DVD in Iraq and occasionally watched it. It is a story of better men who dared far more, and fared much worse, at a much tougher time. Every soldier since will always walk in their mighty shadow—trying to equal them but always being half the men they were. But not many Americans watch those epics, and here soldiers are staring at the dark eyes of an Iraqi patriarch movie buff, impressed as all hell, wondering: Is this real?

Yes, there is also hope. Despite the destruction, despite the many loudmouths that spew invective, despite the mistakes and the arrogance of Americans that cost Iraqis so much in life and suffering, the majority of Iraqis hold no deep-seated hatred of America or Americans, or even of these soldiers. Most Iraqis want to live, send their children to school, and dream of a future without worrying about rustling footsteps of either insurgents or soldiers.

❖ Winning minds, if not hearts[96]

Hearts are hard to win and easy to break, and there is no telling which way a heart will go in the end. But soldiers have a very peculiar job in a counterinsurgency. Soldiers are supposed to distinguish the enemy that hides among the innocent and follow through at the point of decision. Soldiers are also supposed to drive a definitive wedge between the insurgents and the population. But winning minds is hard, when people are stuck between a rock and a hard place.

The innocent are living life at the mercy of circumstances. Insurgents and counterinsurgents are locked in a lethal competition, and the people are caught in the middle of this awkward threesome. Their minds seem deadened with days and nights of worrying about life itself. Every day brings the same worries: "Will I make it home for dinner tonight? Will my family be there?" People see, hear, and feel coming events; they try to connect barely distinguishable and ever-changing dotted lines—images, events, times, places, stories of people. And soldiers walk in their midst keeping their eyes and ears open despite the catatonic state of mind; it's always a strange concussion.

As soldiers, fire team leaders, squad leaders and platoon leaders step off on a patrol, they are invariably forced to deal with issues that are generally considered "high politics"—but they do so on a very human level as a foreign intervention force on the ground trying to win over some minds, if not hearts. Every day, with each action, soldiers have to deal with the issues of state sovereignty as it applies at a very human level: That is, the credibility problem of the host nation government that relies on a foreign force for protection. And, above all, soldiers have to deal with the paradox of being soldiers of a superpower. It is

---

[96] This section reflects conversations between some buck-sergeants, staff sergeants, and a young captain in Iraq. The discussion (amid drinking in the early hours) revolved around one of the elemental challenges of walking the streets. See FM 3-24, perception of the host nation population: pp. 313–320 in the section, "A Guide for Action."

a blessing and a curse because people expect many things, but not all expectations can be met and one hates to disappoint.

The Great Excuse: The Issue of Sovereignty

The idea of sovereignty will always have validity in defining a country's place in relation to others and establishing its inherent right to conduct its own business without outside interference. But it is also a great excuse, one of the best ever invented. Sovereignty upholds the inalienable right of men in power to run their little fiefdoms and medieval kingdoms, trying to turn people into puppets and rob them of dignity.

Sovereignty at the human level seems to be about the simple, common-sense things that define our own place in relation to others: respect, human dignity, human decency, and the intrinsic value of human life. And these are precisely the values that soldiers instantaneously, deliberately strip away from the opponent when they follow through at the point of decision. A living breathing man, someone with a family, a name and a voice, in one instant becomes a mere silhouette. Violating personal sovereignty at its most elemental level is precisely the job of a frontline soldier; it is unavoidable at times. But what is *avoidable* in counterinsurgency—what is of primary importance, soldiers learned—is the unnecessary suffering of the innocent.

The genius of our counterinsurgency strategy as it pertains to soldiers on the ground is its simplicity. The three key tenets, as soldiers understood it, are these:

> *Proportional or judicious use of force*: Use only the force necessary; no need for a 50-caliber machine gun when an M4 will do.
> *Target discrimination*: Shoot only those who need to be shot. On this score, leaders on the ground decide—they bear the responsibility and risk.
> *Treat the innocent with respect, decency—human dignity*, and amazing things just might happen on the ground.

How fucking simple and how fucking brilliant! But it's also hard because soldiers are not saints and never will be.

To isolate the enemy is to drive a wedge between the insurgents and the population. But no one knows the enemy hiding amid the innocent better than—*ta-da!*—the innocent. Treating people with a little respect just might be the best way to get good stories that, in the heads of good soldiers, can quickly be translated into valuable tactical intelligence.

Sovereignty just adds an extra layer of complexity to the soup sandwich. Each encounter between an American soldier and a local Iraqi, that simple human interaction, is a defining moment. How it transpires—how the issue of personal sovereignty is handled—defines the way Iraqis view soldiers. That impression can be lasting, whether it's good, bad, or ugly.

Every instance when an American convoy (military or civilian) drives on the wrong side of the road—as they must at times for security—and Iraqis end up going off the road; each time an American soldier knocks on an Iraqi door and Iraqis have no choice but to open; every time a soldier breaches a door and walks through the house; and any time an American soldier frisks an Iraqi or points a weapon—these moments become unambiguous and long-remembered moments of breached personal sovereignty.

At that point, dealing with the second- and third-order effects of soldiering becomes a painful but necessary part of counterinsurgency. But there is always one man whose charm is legendary and who will always come through for soldiers in good times and bad: The honorable Benjamin Franklin.

LT's Finally Gotta Girlfriend!

It seems counterintuitive to be paying people back for destruction of property even when it's unavoidable, but now it is part of the job function. It is the way Americans fight: No wanton destruction of property. It has its charming moments.

Soldiers were on a patrol, cutting through a side street with their lieutenant, when a middle-aged woman came running up to him. She grabbed his hand—"Oh, you are my besta frienda, my besta frienda"—and insisted they come to her house for tea. Soldiers turn to the lieutanant, "Jesus, sir, what the hell have you been doing out here?" and they start to laugh. They all go to her house for tea. They learn that one of her children was injured during a firefight. American soldiers took care of him and paid money to the family. The kids, family members, everyone is there. The mother keeps coming back to the LT repeating the same thing, "My besta frienda, my besta frienda."

Soldiers were giddy with happiness. Nothing like a chance to give a good LT a hard time! Yes, LTs have it worst: If they are not good, their subordinates find genius ways to make them miserable. If he is good and has earned their respect, then soldiers go to even greater lengths to make him miserable. It is what it is, LTs make the big bucks to take all the grief from above and below and mumble in their sleep.

But this LT was a man, and soldiers enjoyed having him in the fight. The distinction is important. He was not a kid with baby fat and peach fuzz, running around like a wound-up doll, convinced that he was the first lieutenant ever to come out of the United States Military Academy. Good LTs are fast learners who rise to the occasion. With the worst of the LTs, enlisted leaders face a puzzle: By law he is in command, yet he acts like a know-it-all kid who refuses to learn, and what to do? If some man-to-man chats don't work, one tries to rein him in to keep him from going completely off the reservation. Good enlisted leaders and soldiers will give him the illusion that he is in control, though in reality, enlisted men control the reality in which he lives, and he runs around like a doll trying to please.

With a good LT, it is always a good fight. This was a good man who recognized the responsibility and challenge of leadership, and somehow he found that delicate balance between logic, the mission, and sentiment, taking care of his guys. Difficult warm-hearted cold decisions sometimes need to be made and one must be willing to take the risk and the responsibility—and he was ready for it. He came in as a man, not a kid, a simple distinction that at times means everything. It only meant one thing for soldiers: They now have to inflict twice the misery on the good man, that's how it goes.

526

"Well, sir, this is good, you finally got yourself a girlfriend. This might be good for you."

"Hey, check this out man, LT's finally got a girlfriend, the motherfucker has been going around us, shit, sir, this is good. We're impressed!"

The good LT sits there with his knowing laugh, as his deployment has just taken an ominous turn. He knows that soldiers will keep giving him grief about his Iraqi "girlfriend." "Oh, my besta frienda, besta frienda. . . . "

As soon as he walked into the tent, it was his platoon sergeant's turn. This was a good platoon sergeant—and that distinction is important because not every platoon sergeant is good and some have made it only by making the bus on time and now some young LT will have twice the usual job. But this LT was fortunate, as were the soldiers, to have the platoon daddy in the fight.

"Sir, is this true, you got yourself a little Iraqi lady friend in the neighborhood? Shit, sir, you take this hearts and minds shit to the next level, Shiiit LT, damn!"

The fact that this middle-aged Iraqi lady is not his girlfriend is utterly irrelevant. She will be now, and soldiers will visit the house and give a whole lot more grief to the LT. It is an elemental part of the job description.

❖ Getting punked, again

People know that American soldiers pay money for damages, and they can be adamant and incredibly demanding. A husband and wife walked straight at a group of soldiers and explained that during a mission some soldiers had destroyed their door and some chairs, and then left a note. The couple want their money.

OK, fair enough, where is the note?

"Here!" The woman did not hand it to the soldier; she pulled it out of nowhere and slapped it—smack—right on his chest.

The soldier resisted the initial visceral impulse one could see in his face and gave only a grunt. Then he took a good look at the little black-robed creature in front of him, flanked by the little man. About five feet, maybe ninety pounds at most, she looks as if she was present at the creation. She wears a haphazard abaya that has seen better days, covered in so much dust it looks brown instead of black. Her huge toes protrude from their plastic sandals. Her exposed hands appear to be skin, bones and a lot of veins; her dark brown face has a million crevices, like a terrain map with every imaginable terrain feature, and it is filled with green tattoos—a Bedouin custom. A pair of intensely dark, glittering eyes hide behind a permanent squint, staring at the soldier like a venomous lizard ready to pounce.

Soldiers guess she is a Marsh Arab like some others they have met in garbage dumps and displaced people's houses, where they have listened to many stories of destitute Marsh Arabs. The most destitute of them are still displaced, still scattered around Iraq since Saddam drained the marshes. Indeed, one of the quiet beneficiaries of the invasion is the Marsh Arab population for getting the water and their Marsh back. Some returned to the marshes after the invasion, most have moved on, and some have not and never will. The ones who are worst off wander around, living in huts along with other displaced people. She seems to be one of them.

The soldier smiled, grabbing the note. But she did not smile. She still stared with her permanent squint, and it was a strange impulse—damn!—to recruit her to be a fighter. Train and unleash her and she would undoubtedly be phenomenal: Those eyes, damn, what a woman. She is still staring.

Soldiers collect some money and give it to her, and she carefully goes through it, but her eyes never divulge a bit of sentiment. They are set in a permanent squint. She has seen so much in her time that bunch of colorful paper will not impress her.

"Good?" the soldier asks, and all that comes out is a sort of grunt, but she looks as if she was pleased. As soldiers step onward, and the wife and husband step off again, the soldier who talked to the woman on an impulse smiles and puts out his hand, as if to shake her hand. She stops, looks at the hand and looks at the soldier's face, whether in puzzlement or disgust, and then she grunts and turns around and keeps on walking.

His friends obviously will have a great day now: "Ouch, you just got punked, buddy."

Yes, he did, but he insists, "Hell, man, I tried."

Yes, it happens to everybody, and no, she will not be telling stories, she is certainly not in the mood. That's fine, there will always be others.

But war is war, counterinsurgency is counterinsurgency, and not every day is so pretty.

❖ Neither saints nor perfect

Another Time Sensitive Target Acquisition mission in a terrible neighborhood—a firefight. An Iraqi man emerges from a side street with a plastic bag in hand, and he is smack in the middle of a firefight with rounds pinging off. He recognizes his situation, freaks out, drops his bag and starts running—towards the soldiers: "No, mister, no, no, no, no, no, ahhh ohhhh." Soldiers can see him with their night vision, five lasers are pointed at him, his head and chest glisten with the deflected infrared lasers in the night vision. He looks like a contorted screaming freak, hands thrown every which way. Half the soldiers are watching their own sectors, the alleys, the roofs. The others have their weapons pointed at him. Everyone has one thought in their minds, "This guy is going to die." Five weapons, three M4's, and two automatic weapons. "This guy is a second away from being cut in half."

Yet no one is shooting, no one saw any reason, he drops his bag, he is not armed, OK, steady, any minute, but not quite yet. They are waiting, steady, but not yet. It's the thick of the night, he cannot see, and he starts running, zigzagging toward soldiers he cannot see, and screaming, "No, no, no"—and then he stumbles on a piece of concrete and falls, face first and full force. Now he is writhing and freaking out on the ground by the side of the road.

Two soldiers go and secure him, a boot on his back, a weapon on his head—because who knows what's in the bag.

"Hey, two of you go check the bag."

"Oh shit!"

"What! What's in it?"

"Oh man, he is just coming back from Subway. The dude has some fresh bread and sandwiches."

"Well, the wrong time to do a Subway run, ain't it buddy, that's a sandwich you will never forget."

Soldiers decide to throw him inside some house and tell him not to come outside until the sun comes up so he does not wind up dead. Here is a terrified man, fearing for his life begging for mercy, nothing soldiers say makes any sense to him. "No . . . no . . . mister . . . please, mister," he continues pleading for his life. They get him into a nearby house, knock on the door, and it's filled with men, women, and children huddled in a corner of the living room as they always do during firefights. They take him inside. He is still frantic, breathing heavily, a close to getting a panic attack, sweating uncontrollably. "Keep breathing."

"Hey, someone grab his bag, throw it in there with him, and tell the mother fucker to stay inside and not come out if he wants to live."

The family is watching with eyes of apprehension and fear. Soldiers ask them to keep an eye on him, give him some water, do not go outside; you will be dead. They agree, they say yes, nod their heads, and blink a million times with their long dark eyelashes as so many people do in those moments.

Soldiers step out of the house. One of them looks a bit odd in night vision, he seems like he is chomping on something. His team leader goes by him and asks, "Did you just grab a sandwich from his bag?"

Through a mouthful he can barely speak: "uhh uuhhh, no."

His team leader stares at him and laughs, "You are unbelievable, man."

He replies this time: "I am starving!"

His team leader asks, "Well, is it good?"

"Hell yeah, it's good."

"Well did you grab one for me?"

The soldier is always hungry; he was *always* hungry. He looks at his team leader: "Man, unbelievable, you are worthless, why do you want my sandwich," and laughs, reaching into his side pocket, and gives him the other half of the sandwich. It was good and tasted better in that night as the soldiers crawled through and got situated on a rooftop. The night has just begun. Soldiers will always be soldiers and never perfect people or saints. They have to do what is possible despite the difficulties.

Sucking On Lemons: The Credibility Problem

Violating personal sovereignty is the bottom rung of the sovereignty dilemma. But with every step into the street, soldiers in a counter-insurgency—as a foreign intervention force—deal with the issue of sovereignty in many forms, not just the personal level.

At moments of respite between missions, some soldiers and young officers began to read about all kinds of little-known insurgencies and counterinsurgency campaigns. Everyone's favorite was the Jebel Akdhar and Dhofar insurgency in Oman. It was even more wonderful to meet an old-time British soldier who had come of age as a British Para, schooled by the men who waged that campaign.

On this evening, an entire city block was filled with tracer fire, explosions and gunfire from all sides. Soldiers were waiting on a helipad for word from higher to get themselves into the fight. But given the politically sensitive nature of the neighborhood, nothing of import really happened. So they did what they always did, lay around and talk. And here was a British soldier with stories. The Dhofar campaign was arguably the best counterinsurgency in history; the subtle, quiet and effective way in which it was waged will always remain breathtaking. The fact that this campaign is rarely discussed—even today—is testament to its success.

A central insight, among other lessons to be learned from it, is the brilliant way the Brits handled the credibility problem inherent to upholding a local government. They put a government in place, installing the young Sultan Qaboos with an in-house palace coup d'état, and remained a foreign intervention force. They fought an insurgency, created and trained an army and assisted in building the state of Oman as we know it.

Of course, the Brits had many things on their side. It was the late sixties and early seventies. The world paid scant attention, if any, to the dusty corner in Oman called the Dhofar. They were fighting the Communists, who were supported from Yemen, which meant that the Brits and Sultan Qaboos had religion on their side. Not to mention that it was a near-medieval society, with traditional authority that the Brits and the Sultan could astutely exploit to their advantage. Yet the challenges were real: The Omanis almost lost and had it not been for the genius of the leadership it could have gone awry. Oman would have become a "People's Republic," with the Strait of Hormuz a waypoint for Soviet ships.

The times have changed, the sob stories have changed, the nature of the nut-jobs has changed, but some problems will always remain the same. A government upheld by an intervention force faces a credibility problem at the highest level: It is beholden to foreign interests, and no one wants to be a foreign stooge. The government needs the foreigners, yet they don't *want* to need them, given the negative perception. It is something like a love-hate relationship without the sex.

At the level of soldiers, it is neither a legal abstraction nor high politics, it is a simple commonsense problem. No one, no group of people with any sense of pride, history, and aspirations wants to be bossed around by armed foreigners—*no one*.

But part of the job of being soldiers of a foreign intervention force waging a counterinsurgency requires doing precisely that. Logic may argue that it is for the safety of people, but logic becomes subservient to sentiment when people are pissed off. The question on the ground is how to do the unpleasant without making the host nation government—and the people—feel as if they are sucking on sour lemons. The credibility problem on the ground, as soldiers understood it, was simple: wounded pride, dignity, and the self-respect of people.

Some Iraqis ask the Americans to do this and that, yet they also wish that they were gone; then they offer tea and ask: *Why can't you kill so-and-so?* Soldiers, alas, cannot simply follow their gut reaction, look at them and scream, WTF?! So they sit there thinking and laughing. Complicated emotions put the mind on a bender.

The foreigners' presence always highlights everything that the host nation population is not capable of achieving themselves, and for most human beings, it must be a hurtful reminder of what they can and cannot do. It is what it is. And the opponents will always rub this reality in everyone's face and point it out at every opportunity, as in the Salafist or JAM propaganda. Stripped of its cosmic religious jargon, the thesis of the JAM sob story is basically, "We are screwed no matter what we do"; it is an argument that is easily self-perpetuating.

How the credibility problem is resolved at higher levels—who knows? But on the ground it simply means treating the host nation population, and especially the men in authority, with a sense of humility and magnanimity. If not the reality of it, at least the pretense of it will go a long way and, in fact, is tactically valuable.

Soldiers cannot, and should not, go and yell at a corrupt militia-affiliated politician or police commander in front of his subordinates. They resist the heart-felt impulse, treat him with due respect as his corrupt rank deserves, even befriend him—and they can always have a very convincing one-on-one conversation *later*. Later, at night in his own house, out of sight of everyone, when he invites soldiers for a tea with a grin, comfortable in his power and authority. It is up to the soldiers and leaders on the ground to make sure his ears get long, eyes wide, and make sure he is dead set on telling a good story. At that point, soldiers only have to listen. It is what it is.

❖ Oh shit! We put a man on the moon: A modest recommendation

American soldiers, by virtue of being American, always engender unrealistic expectations. Whether you are liked or not, you are expected to be superhuman in your ability to deliver. After all, you put a man on the moon, didn't you? This is the paradox of being an

American soldier: In fact, few Americans have less access to material goods than a soldier in the field.[97]

Soldiers learned a simple rule. If they only make promises they can keep, and keep the promises they make, not a word ever needs to be said in public.

Because the word spreads. People talk, and the word they spread is the best there is, much better than any leaflet or broadcast. Credibility on the ground follows in soldiers' footsteps, and it helps open many doors. Sentiments, emotions, logic, propaganda, rhetoric—these may have their place in the catalog of elements that influence people's perceptions. With most people, however, nothing is more effective than delivering on promises, tactical and non-tactical, including some very simple promises.

In trying to deliver on real promises with lasting traction on the ground—that is, doing reconstruction—our soldiers are working under three big disadvantages. They are hampered by a job where fighting is the primary function; they are hampered by instinct and training that put primary emphasis on going after the enemy (as they should); they are hampered by the nature of the fight, where they have to fight for resources *on their own side.*

The Provincial Reconstruction Teams (PRTs) remain a Brigade Level asset, and that's great. But it would be very nice if soldiers could have some PRT guys at the company level who would be willing to walk with soldiers on a patrol and hang out with some squad leaders and LTs— the guys who do the most walking and have the most intimate knowledge of the neighborhood. Soldiers' knowledge is always limited to tactical matters, and they always think in tactical terms. A PRT member has different training and will always approach the problem differently.

❖ **The maestro and the printer**

One good officer, in a casual conversation with a school headmaster, promised him a printer (he already has a computer). But this is the U.S.

---

[97] FM 3-24: I-139, p. 44.

Army, and printers are a sensitive item. Someone has to sign a hand receipt and is held accountable for it: if he loses or breaks it, a statement of charges will follow, to come out of his paycheck. Otherwise, to get a printer allocated officially would require making the case to the commander, then to his higher; somewhere along the way a requisition has to be made, and waiting inevitably ensues, even if he is lucky enough to make the case right.

But time is of the essence. Time is everything on the ground. This is a moment when officers will just have to be officers and enlisted men will have to take charge.

"Sir, we get this shit, OK, you want a printer, we will get you a printer," they laugh. Cackling, they ask, "Sir, what kind do you want, a laser printer or an inkjet?"

The good officer shakes his head with a smile, "Oh brother, do I want to know this?"

"No, sir, you will not know and you do not need to know. We will get you your damn printer," and they disappear.

This is the U.S. Army in combat, so there is always some warehouse filled with all the essential items in some majestic base. Some virtue enforcers on our own side guard it as it sits collecting dust. Finding it is difficult but never impossible. Soldiers turn to one of their trusted colleagues, the Maestro, a man who knows how to get a thing or two when needed. An army veteran, he does what he wants and no one says peep. He is everywhere but nowhere, a permanent fixture; he rarely moves, he is always still, but he knows everything, especially about things he should not, that is his singular strength. That—and he has friends in very high places whose ghosts he safeguards. The ghosts will go to the grave with him, six consecutive deployments and he knows his stuff better than anybody else. In every majestic army base there are things that happen that should never happen, right under the nose of our own virtue enforcers. Some people are just good at keeping a firm finger on the subversive realities of life without effort, and the Maestro knew the pulse of everybody and

535

everything. He probably has enough ghosts in that closet to haunt a mid-sized city, but one would never know from his nonchalant manner.

"Boss man, we need a printer, what do you think?"

He cackles, grunts, and ignores the question nonchalantly as he always does when soldiers ask for something of importance. In everything is an opportunity for him. Soldiers have the utmost respect for him; he will always have their back. Besides, when soldiers were low-crawling privates, he was already a mentor of sorts, and many privates that followed his advice fared much better than they otherwise would have. "Boss man, we are flying to this place, do you have a hookup?" He would just laugh. It goes without saying he is an enlisted man, a very young but very senior noncommissioned officer.

"So, a printer eh?" He cackles, swiveling in his comfortable chair. By the way, how in the hell did he get the chair? Some questions you just never ask. He wants a nice chair, he will get a chair. It is that simple.

"Yes, Boss man, we need a printer."

He laughs, well, we only have these kinds of printers, and they are expensive, and the printer cartridges go for three hundred bucks apiece. And, he insists, someone has to sign a hand receipt.

It is understood. They all laugh in unison because no one is about to sign a hand receipt. He sends the soldiers in the right direction, as only he knows how, toward a nondescript warehouse, points out who to talk to, and yes, he will make a phone call, no problem. Yes, some Johnnie Walker Black Label would be fine, thank you. With so many virtue enforcers walking around, soldiers that have access to a steady supply of alcohol can always own half of any majestic army base—men, women, and even some virtue enforcers included, those that occasionally see the light. It is what it is.

Soldiers return with a printer, and this should not be miscon-strued as stealing government and taxpayer property, it is not. It is merely acquiring mission-essential items, and any executive offi-cer or noncommissioned officer who does not know how to acquire mission-essential items should promptly look for a different job. In fact, if soldiers and the best of our Executive Officers stop acquiring mission-essential items and rely on procedures, the big green machine will stop trundling and combat will stop instantaneously.

Headmaster was happy with his printer, and soldiers installed it. Then they did better. To ingratiate themselves with the English-speaking teachers—some of them young, female, and charming, of course, they brought in a boom box, a TV, and a DVD player for the staff room. And the printer in the headmaster's room has gone through a strange transformation. It has its own desk. It is in pristine condition, no doubt dusted daily. And it is covered in a light blue and rust silk cloth with tassels at the end; there is a vase next to it, complete with plastic flowers. Holy shit, the printer has ceased to be a printer and has been transformed into an ornament, maybe a shrine.

The headmaster is all smiles, his office seems complete. It now evokes his official stature, we see, from his reverential attitude to the printer. The printer is probably happy not collecting dust, and the headmaster now tells the soldiers wonderful stories. And having ingratiated themselves with the schoolteachers, now the soldiers have a good ten houses they can visit in the neighborhood to drink tea and listen to stories, even some friends they can call.

❖ Delivering on simple promises

But that is also the problem. Everything soldiers do is done with eyes and ears on future tactical possibilities. *A good PRT guy could do so much better* in listening to the many stories, recognizing people's needs, and most importantly, fighting to get resources at the brigade level without worrying about rank and virtue enforcers. It is not an LT's place to fight at brigade level. Enlisted men go to higher level Tactical Operations Centers only when they or their subordinates get in trouble to receive a dressing down. They may say the hell with it and just break in when they have to in order to acquire mission-essential items with the help of friends.

Recommendation: Please: embed Provincial Reconstruction Team representatives at the *company level*. Have them patrol with platoon and squad-size elements, hanging out with the platoon leaders, sergeants and squad leaders, and assisting soldiers with neighborhood assessment and support.

It would be nice to have some embedded PRT guys to walk the streets to recognize the needs and actually fight the fight on behalf of soldiers at higher level to get resources allocated more efficiently. Time, time, time is always of the essence on the ground. Time on the ground moves much faster than in heaven, yet heaven always has a stranglehold on what happens on the ground. More congruity could go a long way in assuaging the minds (if not hearts) of the host nation population.

While perfect people in heaven work on delivering a piece of the moon, if soldiers on the ground could make little promises and keep the little promises they make—with the help of PRT guys—that would help turn people's complicity into support. On this task, soldiers can certainly use all the help they can get.

At the end, the people need to support their own government and its institutions, not the foreign intervention force. Soldiers will get on a bird and be home, grab a cold one, drown the sorrows, and have a laugh. But the many good Iraqi people who invited soldiers into their lives, helped them distinguish the enemy from the innocent—who helped soldiers to be insurgents behind insurgents—*they* have to stay and keep on living. Millions of Iraqis have had their lives turned upside down. Soldiers always remember a lot of sad, thin lips, the eyes of the living without life, children without smiles, women that hide their sorrow and men that hide their anguish staring at the horizon.

The precarious situation of so many Iraqis also means that many nut-jobs will find Iraq a tantalizing pool of possible recruits. Apart from any ideological or religious reasons (and there are plenty of those), many men will shoot at anybody or anything, just for a glimpse of the good man Benjamin Franklin. The way the Iraqis fashion their future will always be of concern to us, it will always now be part of the long war. And it has obvious tactical implications on the ground. A population that looks favorably at us means that soldiers or police on the ground will find it easier to isolate the nutjobs that hide amid the innocent.

Is perception the reality people believe most of the time? We don't know. But we hope that a lot of perfect people will start making plans with a little magnanimity and humility, so as to win some minds if not hearts.

23

SUNDAY MORNING COMING DOWN: THE BEGINNING, AND THE END?

On the Sunday morning sidewalk,
Wishing, Lord, that I was stoned.
'Cos there's something in a Sunday,
That makes a body feel alone.
And there's nothin' short of dyin',
Half as lonesome as the sound
Of the sleepin' city sidewalks:
Sunday mornin' comin' down.

—Kris Kristofferson lyrics with Jonny Cash on vocals

Maybe counterinsurgencies come to an end in the same way soldiers deal with a Sunday morning come-down. A painful physical hangover and mental anguish, compounded with the harsh expectant pain of a dark Monday morning and the long week ahead.

The Beginning?

We marched into Iraq and successfully defeated the decrepit remnants of the Iraqi Army that decided to stay and fight. Yet we failed to secure the gains of our successful intervention when we failed to instill any control on the ground.[98] We defeated the remnants of Saddam's army and systematically dismantled the Baathist state, leaving no vestiges of the old structure of legitimate control that previously existed.[99] With that, the existing form of control on the ground vanished. It is irrelevant that a lot of people despised the Baathist state because a great many were still dependent on it for necessities as basic as food and cooking oil. The fact remained that many people were complicit in it, and the system of control through coercion, patronage and tribal arrangements was effective enough to have suzerainty over the contending groups. That's why the Baathist state (or any other state controlled by a jaw-jacking dictator for that matter) lasted as long as it did.

The failure to secure the gains of the intervention by instilling control meant that any semblance of formal control with traction on the ground disappeared. Instead, there was the Coalition Provisional Authority, upheld by the American Armed Forces, that claimed control of Iraq. They projected power and sought control.

When American officials appear on TV, make edicts that Iraqis are expected to abide by, when American airplanes thunder overhead, tanks roll down highways, and soldiers patrol the streets, these are all actions that project authority and power. And this simply means one thing: There is a new sheriff in town and you'd better get in line. Projections of authority and power, while necessary, have meaning only if they have traction on the ground. It is not what we do, but the way opponents and the larger population react to what we do, that gives validity and meaning to the idea. Projecting power is based on

---

[98] As an operational concept, we feel there is a distinction between a successful military intervention—beating the army of the country that one intervenes in—versus securing and consolidating the gains of the intervention by transitioning to successful control of the country. The latter is an aspect we have paid scant attention to in our interventions, a lesson we are coming to terms with slowly and painfully both in Iraq and in Afghanistan.

[99] We are not questioning or assessing the decision itself. If dismantling the Baathist state structure was the stated mission objective, then it is logically consistent to dismantle all remnants of it; how one prepares for the second- and third-order effects of one's decisions is a different question. We are merely positing the context so as to assess and make sense of the insurgency.

the assumption that one's opponents are also enamored of power, but fearful in their hearts. Or, as soldiers liked to call it, it was a simple bluff in a bar.

Anyone who has ever been in a street fight or talked shit in a bar knows that there is always some drunk that will call the bluff. At that point one has to be ready act, to follow through, to avoid looking like a fool: You've got to be ready to put up or shut up. Some Iraqis (including some who were the worst of the lot, but that is irrelevant) called our bluff. And that was the "Oh shit" moment.

Because for some incomprehensible reason there was no alternate, contingent or emergency plan, only the best of intentions and a blind belief in our own power. It is particularly ironic to enlisted grunts because every enlisted soldier receives a "Safety brief" every Friday before the weekend. So, before being released to their own devices to go out drinking or whatever, they are always instructed by their commanding officers and senior non-commissioned officers: "Men, listen up. Be responsible, have a good time, party hard, but always be responsible. If you roll out, make sure you roll deep, and always, always, ALWAYS have a plan. In fact, have four of them and you know what they are: Primary, Alternate, Contingent, and Emergency: PACE." And it is plastered all over the walls of company areas everywhere. Yet somebody in heaven, whoever it was, had not paid attention to the Friday evening safety brief before going on our drinking binge in Iraq.

When the worst of the Iraqis called the bluff, they found support from many of their countrymen, wrapped up in their passionate intensity and infused with an overwhelming amount of anti-American invective. But these normal, everyday Iraqi citizens who indulged in the initial enthusiasm of resistance found their dreams fast mislaid.

Without any sort of functioning institutions, without the complicity and the support of the innocent, with no suzerainty over the many groups and with the resistance of a large number of Iraqis, the projected U.S. power momentarily lost its meaning and Iraq burned. American soldiers sat on the big guns, waiting for orders that never came down, as the situation on the ground fast deteriorated before their eyes. Somewhere along the way the concept was lost. Magniloquence and self-exculpation, even with a self-righteous belief (no matter how deeply held), can never be a good substitute for prudent decisions that have traction on the ground.

On the ground, soldiers sitting on the big guns are hamstrung. Without guidance one is without a target; a soldier without a target, as Lawrence of Arabia said, owns only "the ground he sat on and what he could poke his rifle at." They are fast reduced to clowns that have lost their wit.[100] But a leader on the ground that has lost his wit is either dead or dying, or he has simply lost the initiative and is forced to play catch-up with the blood and sweat of others.

Why didn't U.S. soldiers act to change the situation, why did they sit around waiting for orders while the orders never came down? Why was there a fundamental failure in leadership in reacting to the fast-changing situation on the ground? These are militarily valid questions, integral to the issue of transitioning from a successful foreign intervention force to a force that is temporarily in control of a population and territory.

We failed to smoothly transition from a force of foreign intervention to one that is temporarily in control, having not paid attention to the Friday evening safety brief before binge-drinking all weekend. When we failed to secure the gains of the intervention in terms of control, we became prisoners of an evolving situation, losing momentum and initiative on the ground. But it is important to note: The failure to secure the gains of the successful intervention did not "create" the insurgencies in Iraq. Insurgencies are run deliberately; pissed-off people do not automatically become insurgents. The absence of power with traction on the ground—control—after the intervention undeniably created the perfect context for many groups with their own agendas to start fighting for control. Was this *The Beginning*?

---

[100] This is not an argument; we are only stating a simple fact: Talk to any number of soldiers and officers who marched into Iraq during OIF I (the initial invasion) and who sat around as Iraq burned, wondering, "What the hell?"

The absence of control meant that everyone had a fair chance to fight the Americans (already everyone's favorite bogeyman in this neighborhood)—but targets were quickly expanded to include the new Iraqi government and the innocent. The failure to get control gave the advantage to insurgents from all different sects, all ethnic groups, agendas, colors, and sob stories. They gained the momentum and initiative on the ground by creating pockets of control in neighborhoods, townships, even provinces. Iraq had an elected government, but the reality on the ground at the height of the many insurgencies was that it was tantamount to a nearly failed state with no semblance of stability, control or day-to-day predictability.

Thus, when the best and the brightest coterie of American intellectuals, professionals, and bureaucrats, along with some of their Iraqi counterparts, hightailed it out early, Iraq was truly a failed state—back to year zero, with no vestige of functioning institutions and no legitimate control on the ground. It was up to our American military commanders to play catch-up over a five-year period and continuing to today, partnering with Iraqis who were willing to assist in waging a counterinsurgency on behalf of the Iraqi government, elected by Iraqis with American assistance. They had to fight the insurgents to claim, regain, and instill some form of legitimate control on the ground. Over a five-year period, Iraq has gone from a nearly a failed state to a functional-dysfunctional state with some semblance of stability and control, albeit held together by some extremely delicate sinews.

The End?

The sinews—the complicity of the population and the tentative suzerainty over the many disparate groups—have created the delicate tapestry of control that allows for a new sense of stability in Iraq. But there are many nut-jobs always ready to rip apart this tapestry of stability.

The end game in Iraq will be defined in terms of how the many disparate Sunni groups become part of the political process, and the stake they will have within it. It will also depend on how the Kurdish land of imagination gets a sense of reality, and how the Shia people learn to deal with their own family problems without letting it spill out into the streets under the benevolent gaze of the ayatollahs. And it will be crucially defined by the instrumental role Americans play from the margins as Iraqis fashion their own future and we quietly aid them in managing the many conflicts. And if we have learned anything, it is that the end of a counterinsurgency will not be defined solely by the necessary death of the enemy (though that is always primary) but also by the way the people manage to fashion their own future.

But there is a lasting irony regarding the future of the mission. Soldiers absorbed it, slowly but surely, by spending time with Iraqis, but they only came to understand it while reminiscing over two shots of Calvados and a good cup of coffee one spring morning in a very different town, at a very different time.

Like many good Americans traveling in Europe, some soldiers went to the beaches of Normandy and stood, feeling humbled, at the graves of our predecessors who dared far more and fared much worse. This was quickly followed, in good American tradition, by bar crawling in the city of Caen for a number of days. Waking up one morning with a painful coming down, with a cup of coffee in hand and two shots of Calvados for inspiration (a sublime apple brandy that the good people of Normandy have perfected), one began to see an incongruity. Above the awnings and canopies of the many bars in the city of Caen, one sees American flags and flags of the other Allied countries along with a sign proclaiming, "We welcome our liberators." No one talks about it, there is no need, because it is understood.[101]

One never sees that in Iraq. Yes, there is a difference: The French were liberated from an occupier, and the Iraqis were released from the grips of their own tyrant that they could not rid themselves of and are now forced to live in a democracy. There is an irony in forcing people to be free at gunpoint.

---

[101] Though some soldiers had the good fortune of talking to quite a few people who lived through it as adolescents and listened to their stories.

Whatever the complicated reasoning behind the intervention (it is a matter for the heavens and not the ground), Iraqis were forced to be free, and are now forced to live in a democracy that they did not create, that was created for them. That leaves many Iraqis with what soldiers came to call "complicated emotions." The constant reminder of what they were unable to do on their own leaves them with a sense of robbed dignity and pride.

Democracy, an elemental human creation, will always be far from perfect. Indeed, the genius of it is the understanding that it is a decidedly an imperfect system, designed to govern citizens who are susceptible to all the human foibles. "If men were angels, no government would be necessary. If angels were to govern men, neither external nor internal controls on government would be necessary."[102] Therefore, it is a system with room for continual improvement, but one in which people can live without ever compromising (or fighting never to compromise) their elemental human dignities. For that singular reason, it will always be the most beautiful system humans have yet managed.

Having forced Iraqis to be beautiful (though some of them are certainly beautiful and wonderful), perhaps the future of our mission will be to assist Iraqis—from the margins and with a sense of respect and humility—in retaining the beauty as they fashion their future by helping them manage the simmering conflicts while maintaining the delicate tapestry of stability that holds the place together. But results will depend on decisions today that have lasting ramifications on future decisions.

Having spent Sunday "with no way to hold the head that didn't hurt," the thought of waking up at five in the morning makes the throbbing worse, depression crushing the soul. Yet, crawling out of bed, there are the soldiers, standing in the dark and saluting as the music plays and the flag goes up on another gloomy Monday morning. Taking the first step leading the guys, the head still aches; the first mile becomes a raging battle between the mind that screams stop and a heart that exhorts you to keep running. Passing the two-mile mark, the heart

---

[102] Federalist Papers 51, "Checks and Balances," op. cit.

has unequivocally won. And in the third mile—going up the hill, braving the sand and pines—the weakest guy is falling back, yes, we are only as fast as the weakest link, so everyone turns around to keep him motivated, get him up the hill, and the heart keeps screaming "keep at it," while the shins growl that this is madness, and the fourth mile now emerges as a battle against the vitriol of the hamstrings and a clouded mind that has long concurred.

But the fifth mile is strangely peaceful, the guys are running behind at a steady strut, with cackles and curses, feeling comfortably numb. And why stop at five miles just because everyone says it's the standard? Coming down from the landfill, cutting into the firebreaks, everyone has a smile knowing it is the last stretch, braving the pines and sand again, and it's eight miles on the dot. All the guys beat the standard again—without ever knowing how far or where they were going, they just kept at it. Even the weakest guy made it, though he was sucking, but he has that look of accomplishment. And looking at the guys, out of breath, cursing, yet feeling smug having made it, a cold one would be nice and well deserved but it's time to lay off the bottle (having relied on it for too long)—now it's time to grab an ice-cold water that will calm the heart. Sunday is now long forgotten, the early morning breeze that flutters the flag feels cool and soothes the soul, and the sun coming through the pines makes Monday look beautiful.

Though this counterinsurgency is far from over, maybe the end of counterinsurgencies should have a similar feeling. Perhaps they end the way soldiers make it through Monday morning, like a long run through the pines and sand with a heart that beats steady with every step and ending with a cool drink of water, swearing off the bottle until it's Friday night again. Who knows—maybe that is how this will end.

Epilogue:
More Scattered Crumbs

... and having made a promise with each other to record their impressions, experiences, and hallucinations, there was also an understanding. It is also a war; if any of us wound up dead, the first order of business was to get "positive control" of the journals, laptops, cameras, iPods, memory sticks, and passwords. Whoever stays alive will *finish what was started*.

It became a running joke: "Positive control man, positive control, always," and everyone would have a laugh. Because death, at times feeling it intimately on one's skin, is an elemental part of life in soldiering. They are very somber, yet strangely dignified moments where good reason often prevails over wild sentiments.

A soldier died in a firefight, saving the lives of two of his friends; he died fighting in a hail of bullets, shooting until his last breath. Half an hour after it quieted down, his friend came near his body, now lying on the ground and wrapped in a silk poncho liner waiting to be evacuated. His friend reached down into his side pocket and grabbed his can of dip, put a pinch of tobacco in his mouth and then put the can back in his dead friend's pocket. Taking a knee next to his friend's body, he looked at him closely, holding his hand for a few seconds. He will live the rest of his life knowing that he will owe every moment of it to this man on the ground. Then he stood up, took a few slow, deliberate steps with his head down, hiding his pain, and rode his sorrow, sprinting to link up with the rest of the team, continuing on a patrol with another follow-on mission in a theocratic enclave.

Another dear friend is in a body bag ready to be evacuated, the Black Hawk inbound to carry him on his last journey. His platoon sergeant grabbed him and put him on his shoulder. Others nearby wanted to give him a hand.

He took a knee, holding him on his left shoulder, his right hand gripping the hanging M4. He was fighting the tears but they are pouring down his sweat -and mud-covered cheeks, as he said, "Hey, he is my boy, my soldier. I am not putting him on the ground, this is how he is going to the bird, on my shoulder."

So he did leave Iraq on his platoon sergeant's shoulder, as others provided security. Putting his soldier on the bird, the sergeant bent down, grabbed his soldier's feet and kissed them, kissed the bottom of the body bag. That is the last time he will see him. He turned and walked back from the bird, barking: "Hey, grab the shit, make it quick, we have to move, hurry up, hurry up."

Another dear friend lay dying, living a lifetime in a second despite the best efforts of the best of medics. There is nothing better to do than to take a knee and stay with him. But he is in good hands, so his friend can only whisper softly, "Hey hang in there brother," and tell him that his family will be taken care of no matter what, holding his head and hand. Then step up and out, leaving him in good hands—because to follow sentiment is a luxury soldiers can ill afford. Someone with the worst intentions is always looking, searching for an opening. Logic prevails, tearing sentiment from it, leaving the best friend that lay dying so as to continue the job, the heart may ache intensely in those moments. It is what it is.

Another day, soldiers were drinking coffee they had brewed and splashed with some booze, still in their mud -and blood-covered clothes. The dirty ragged clothes seem a reflection of the fatigued mind. But they had positive control of everything they needed. Nothing needed to be said; everything was understood.

A lanky sniper came into the tent and dropped his gear, asking for a cup in his low growling drawl. "Damn, this is some good shit." He is a genius on a rooftop, one of the most dependable and loyal guys the soldiers could always count on, and now he had a blunt question. "So, y'all been working for a long time on this, you're still gonna finish this shit, right?"

The answer was unanimous: "Of course, man."

Yes, it's a war. People die, soldiers included. It will always be heart-breaking; the sadness goes to the bone, lodges inside and never leaves. But it also makes the bones strong. To mourn the best of them in pity-ing fashion is to let them down, insulting the memory of how they lived. They lived life with pride and dignity and without any regret. Soldiers always take the next step, trying to do better with each step they take: Because, in our world, the ultimate sin is letting good men down.

In that spirit, our only claim to credit in compiling these impressions is that we kept the simple promises we made to one another. We put together the many scattered crumbs: our words, those of our friends, including Iraqis—and the words written by our colleagues who are no longer with us.

Writing this book was a promise we made to one another, but it was also a lesson in what it means to be soldiers in our beloved United States Army. Some soldiers were in the hot seat: As enlisted soldiers in Iraq, they had cho-sen to express their opinion, *in print*, to point out the janus-faced nature of the enemies that we fight. (That decision was also the out-come of a wager among a bunch of soldiers, always trying to be crazy enough to avoid going completely insane.) Some civilians had called it a treasonous act, while others were offering them a free ride to Mexico. But a senior enlisted leader who fought side-by-side said, "Hey, men, in here with us, *don't worry about a goddamn thing.*"

Then a very senior commissioned officer called the soldiers into his office. He was a man with years of experience on the ground, whose judgment soldiers trusted without question at the point of deci-sion. First he cogently articulated his concerns. Then he said with a laugh, yet with all seriousness, and despite soldiers putting him in the hot seat, "Don't worry about a thing! Keep doing what you are doing. You are all my soldiers, and you are also thinking soldiers.

We need to fight, but we also need to out-think and outsmart this enemy. To think is also your duty as soldiers, that is the best way to fight this enemy.

"As for writing, keep writing, I know you are responsible soldiers— so be responsible—and keep writing, that is your duty as citizens. Remember, it is a right that we fight to keep."

We owe many, many debts that can never be repaid. To those we owe so much, we raise our glasses. The toast begins with the many military families and especially the family members of the friends that are no longer with us. Many of them read through the manuscript and gave us valuable insights.

Military families will always be the unacknowledged soldiers of any war, especially the Gold Star families. When their loved one leaves on a temporary sojourn, the world of family members stops until they return, although the world around them continues on inexorably.

They live two lives. One life consists of being part of the illusion of the world that surrounds them. The other, their own personal world, has ceased to turn until the loved one gets back. So they live, constantly apprehensive of the worst: a man in full dress uniform knocking on the door and carrying the worst imaginable news. They live in the understanding that it is the profession their loved one has chosen, and a life that they have chosen to support with pride and dignity.

For some, the worst nightmare does become the starkest of realities. On a bright morning, as the rest of the world continues on heedlessly, their own world comes crashing down. Slowly but surely they wrench up the fortitude to soldier on. They take the next step: They live. We will always owe everything to them for making it possible.

To the many friends and colleagues who are wounded, they may have limbs amputated but their spirits remain intact. Officers blinded in combat who now run triathlons with assistance; men and women who complete a five-mile run with prosthetic limbs; friends who remain paraplegic but still go to college. Another friend who was shot through the head and lived to defy all expectations and refused a medical dis- charge, fighting the bureaucracy to return to his unit and jump out of a C-17 Globemaster airplane with a hundred and fifty pounds of gear, his ACH covering a partially prosthetic skull. He would hit the ground in standard airborne fashion—feet, ass, head—then tap the prosthetic part of his skull and cackle, in the middle of the night in a drop zone, "Well, still not dead and not retarded, buddy, the old brain still in place." His friends quickly retorted, "Bullshit, man, your head was never in the right place, that's why we love you." And they continued on the training mission with a laugh.

When just living life and taking the next step becomes a fight, they continue to fight relentlessly because it is impossible to amputate their spirit, impossible to sap their resolve and fortitude. They will always be our inspiration, prodding us to try and do better with every step we take.

To all the friends in the army, from its many different branches, that crossed paths and worked with us: So many of their stories are intricately woven into this. They will always know which ones are theirs. We owe much to the countless friends that worked with us, who picked up the slack and drank obscene amounts of whiskey in our barracks rooms while offering their own unique insights. We owe them for all the reading material they gave us and for reading through this. To dear friends for keeping us inspired, prodding us on, as the best of the friends always do in good times and bad.

A very special mention is required for someone who was there from the beginning, a man who put his heart and soul into the fight, always ready to walk into any scrap with a smile, willing to indulge in a smiling imagination and hallucination of what could be. He was a consistent and instrumental intellectual force. Yes, he despised garrison (as most combat soldiers always do), but he enjoyed every bit of being part of the fight. Our dear friend and colleague, a man that never put on the pretty fake face required when standing around the flagpole. When his decisions and impulse sometimes got the best of him, he was always man enough to stand his ground and tell the truth. At the end of two consecutive tours he had learned Arabic well enough to find a basement bar in Iraq. He knew about Iraq, Iraqis, and the Middle East more than most others and would be chatting on the Internet with some of his Iraqi friends (yes, they all happened to be female university students). One could converse with him about the counterinsurgency in Oman, the tenuous political situation in Pakistan, the best Infantry Close Quarter Battle tactics on the ground or how to walk in through that door with the most appropriate greeting: "Peace, love, and happiness, baby." Yet you could also have a quiet meditative moment reading, *Notes from the Underground*, or discuss some of his favorite Middle Eastern authors.

One of the enduring memories will always be of him sitting in a C130-J aircraft, bouncing around in the air, waiting to jump, constricted in that damn parachute harness and all the requisite gear. He was sitting, laughing to himself, reading for the millionth time his favorite book by Mahfouz, *Adrift on the Nile*. At the green light, he put the little book in his side pocket and then proceeded to jump out of that perfectly good high-performance aircraft with a heartfelt curse, and land like a sack of bricks to continue mission. He will not be around to see the end of this project, though he was there at the beginning and throughout the writing of it. We will always miss him, his absence a palpable hole through our gut, especially those of us who walked side by side with him into many alleyways and houses with heartfelt greetings.

But it also meant something elementally simple: We had to put forth twice the effort to make him proud, to live up to his very large expectations. It is unforgivable to let a good man down.

None of it would have been possible, and our experience would mean nothing, without the many good Iraqis—the innumerable Iraqi children, women, and men to whom we owe so much for the education they gave us, the stories they shared, taking us down many a rabbit hole, and helping us be counterinsurgents and insurgents behind insurgents, and sharing a good honest laugh in the process. Some Iraqis defied our expectations by stepping up and taking extreme risks; those women and men would always remain an inspiration in many a dark moment. We only find heartfelt regret in the fact that we cannot relate all the stories, as valid, honest, and important as they all are.

We are also indebted to many learned Iraqis for introducing us to so many Middle Eastern authors. Were it not for our amazing Iraqi friends, we would never have been blessed with the insights of these artists. Incredibly brave men and women have had their skulls cracked, been jailed, stabbed, or even exiled, and yet they continue to write. It is a stunning indictment of the societies and governments who expelled them. Their lyricism and poignantly descriptive narration of the Middle East was indispensable to our understanding of that world. This book is an homage to these fiercely brave men and women who refused to cower to fundamentalist theological autocrats.

And we owe much to Miramar, our very dear friend. Chapter 3 was written in her honor and for her (and Part II, The Circling Song, is named after a story written by her favorite female, other than her own mother—another formidable woman). Who would be better situated to help some American soldiers navigate through the reality of Iraqi women than a feisty Iraqi girl with a penchant for subversion, and a passion for irking militia-affiliated virtue-enforcers? Miramar was instrumental in helping some of us see better, navigating the terrain of people—especially when it came to women. She was a guide, an adviser, and a teacher all rolled into one.

We raise our glasses to our many teachers, leaders, and mentors, who have done a remarkable job of corrupting our minds and instilling in us a fighting spirit. They know who they are and know that we would never want it in any other way.

Above all else, we owe everything—everything—to the best of the best that make up our beloved United States Army. The best of them live pride, resolve, and fortitude every day of their lives and bestow upon our army its true meaning and value. We will always walk in their mighty shadows, being half the men and women that they are. Some of us will always owe everything, including the borrowed lives that we live, to the best of them.

Three cheers to all of them, The Best. To the simple pleasures of life, boss: Let us have many of them.

"All The Way," ladies and gentlemen—grab a cold one—"Let's Go!"

18 April 2008

IN MEMORIAM

*For all those indomitable spirits for whom
there will never be a homecoming:
We will always be ghosts in their mighty shadows.*

ABOUT THE BOOK

Nightcap at Dawn was written collaboratively, through emails, by a group of American soldiers while serving in Iraq; they completed the manuscript immediately upon their return. Sgt. J. B. Walker was adopted as a collective pen name. The writers' aim was not only to capture their own experiences on the ground but also, more importantly, to consider some fundamental challenges in order to improve American counterinsurgency tactics and strategy.

The focus of this engrossing narrative is less on soldiers' actions than on their hard-won insights about the environment in which they operate: the cultural and social environment of Iraq, the bureaucratic and policy environment of the U.S. Armed Forces, and the trust and companionship and humor of their own squads. A sensitive, reflective, and often dramatic narrative carries the reader from alleys in Baghdad to the homes of long-suffering Iraqis, and from the soldiers' concrete bunkers to the "majestic" army base.

The soldier narrator's sharp wit skewers dysfunctional regulations while celebrating the formidable intelligence, resilience, and perseverance of some enlisted leaders. Along the way, the reader is asked to ponder the puzzles posed for a disciplined army engaged with an enemy that hides amid—and indeed, targets—a civilian population. Finally, the book invites controversy with its account of soldiers' "hallucination" of fighting a war as "insurgents behind insurgents."